DATE DUE

DE 14'98	7 07		
MY 20'99	6 07		
AP 25'00			
NY 24 00			
JA 29'01			
AP 3'02			
OC 13'02			
DE 9'02			
MY 30'03			
OC 3'03			
DE 5'03			
FE 11'04			

Saddam's Word

Studies in Middle Eastern History
Bernard Lewis, Itamar Rabinovich,
and Roger Savory
GENERAL EDITORS

THE TURBAN FOR THE CROWN
The Islamic Revolution in Iran
Said Amir Arjomand

THE PRESS IN THE ARAB MIDDLE EAST
A History
Ami Ayalon

IRAN'S FIRST REVOLUTION
*Shi'ism and the Constitutional
Revolution of 1905–1909*
Mangol Bayat

SADDAM'S WORD
Political Discourse in Iraq
Ofra Bengio

ISLAMIC REFORM
*Politics and Social Change in Late
Ottoman Syria*
David Dean Commins

KING HUSSEIN AND THE CHALLENGE
OF ARAB RADICALISM
Jordan, 1955–1967
Uriel Dann

NASSER'S "BLESSED MOVEMENT"
*Egypt's Free Officers and
the July Revolution*
Joel Gordon

THE YOUNG TURKS IN OPPOSITION
M. Şükrü Hanioğlu

THE FERTILE CRESCENT, 1800–1914
A Documentary Economic History
Edited by Charles Issawi

THE MAKING OF SAUDI ARABIA,
1916–1936
*From Chieftaincy to
Monarchical State*
Joseph Kostiner

EUNUCHS AND SACRED BOUNDARIES
IN ISLAMIC SOCIETY
Shaun Marmon

THE IMPERIAL HAREM
*Women and Sovereignty in the
Ottoman Empire*
Leslie Peirce

FROM ABDULLAH TO HUSSEIN
Jordan in Transition
Robert B. Satloff

OTHER VOLUMES
ARE IN PREPARATION

Saddam's Word

 Political Discourse in Iraq

OFRA BENGIO

New York   Oxford
Oxford University Press
1998

Oxford University Press

Oxford   New York
Athens   Auckland   Bangkok   Bogota   Bombay   Buenos Aires
Calcutta   Cape Town   Dar es Salaam   Delhi   Florence   Hong Kong
Istanbul   Karachi   Kuala Lumpur   Madras   Madrid   Melbourne
Mexico City   Nairobi   Paris   Singapore   Taipei   Tokyo   Toronto   Warsaw

and associated companies in
Berlin   Ibadan

Copyright © 1998 by Oxford University Press, Inc.

Published by Oxford University Press, Inc.
198 Madison Avenue, New York, New York 10016

Oxford is a registered trademark of Oxford University Press

Library of Congress Cataloging-in-Publication Data
Bengio, Ofra.
['Irak shel Tsadam. English]
Saddam's word : political discourse in Iraq / Ofra Bengio.
    p.   cm. — (Studies in Middle Eastern history)
Includes bibliographical references and index.
ISBN 0-19-511439-6
1. Iraq—Politics and government—1979–   2. Discourse analysis—
Political aspects—Iraq.   3. Government and the press—Iraq.
4. Mass media—Government policy—Iraq.   5. Hussein, Saddam, 1937–   .
I. Title.   II. Series: Studies in Middle Eastern history (New
York, N.Y.)
DS79.7.B4613   1998
320.9567'01'4—dc21   97-2308

9 8 7 6 5 4 3 2 1

Printed in the United States of America
on acid-free paper

In memory of
my mentor and friend

Uriel Dann

a humanist in the
true sense of the word

Preface

*T*he Gulf War has turned Saddam Husayn's Iraq into the centerpiece of world attention, yet it remains an enigma. My long years of study of this regime have convinced me that the best way to try to unravel this enigma is not through conventional narrative history but rather through an analysis of political discourse.

This unique approach enables me to present the Ba'th regime's world through its own eyes and voice, thus providing deeper insight into and greater understanding of its political culture, self-images, and guiding myths and, in particular, the making of Saddam Husayn's worldview. The book thus provides a new way to understand the Ba'th's motives, policies, and ultimately its survival for almost three decades in the most difficult circumstances ever experienced by an Arab regime or state.

Saddam's Word draws on a wide range of previously untapped Iraqi sources, notably party documents, pamphlets, newspapers, and books. Another important source is the Qur'an, to which the regime itself has made recourse, especially in its third decade in power. The method applied in the study is interdisciplinary, combining research into the meaning of language, political culture, myth-making, and symbolism while integrating them into the wider context of political and historical developments in Iraq.

The book deals with the five most important overlapping spheres of Iraqi public life: the Ba'th and revolution; the political system and its leader Saddam Husayn; nation-building and ethnic minorities; enemies and wars;

and history and Islam. Analyzing these themes through the prism of Iraq's political discourse, the book demonstrates how Saddam Husayn and his regime sought to manipulate language, tradition, and Islam in order to shape Iraqis' minds, mobilize them for his own political purposes, and portray a picture of virtual reality that was a far cry from the genuine one. Finally, the study shows how the regime itself became entrapped by its own totalitarian discourse, which did not allow feedback from the people.

Though a unique case, Ba'thi Iraq can nevertheless be taken as a case study for understanding other totalitarian regimes not only in the Middle East but also in the world at large. Moreover, in addition to expanding our knowledge of the modern Middle East, it demonstrates how the study of culture and semiotics can contribute to our understanding of politics and history.

It is a great pleasure to extend my heartfelt thanks to friends and colleagues who have contributed in many ways to this endeavor. My greatest debt goes to Ami Ayalon, whose expertise and friendship have been the best combination one can find in a guide through the labyrinth of language and political discourse. Asher Susser, the former head of the Moshe Dayan Center, and Martin Kramer, the present head of the center, have made the place my second home. The atmosphere of creativity with which they endowed the center encouraged me to complete the project despite all of the difficulties involved. My colleagues at the center have contributed in many ways through discussion and exchanges of ideas. I am especially indebted to Bruce Maddy-Weitzman, who has been so generous in extending moral and professional support. Joseph Kostiner read the manuscript and was kind enough to make suggestions for improving it. My friends Ester Levin and Shmuel Regolant enriched me with their creative ideas and thoughts on various subjects.

I wish to thank Lydia Gareh, who typed the manuscript, bringing with her not only technical experience but also deep knowledge of the subject matter. I am also greatly indebted to my assistant, Liat Kozma, who has been my right hand along the tortuous road of preparing the manuscript for press. Haim Gal, of the Moshe Dayan Documentation Center, was extremely helpful in locating the materials for the study. Paula Wald of Oxford University Press and the copyeditor Tim Mennel did an excellent job of preparing the manuscript for publication.

It is said of translators, "Traduttore traditore." If this is the rule, then Daniel Dishon is certainly an exception to it. I could not find a better and more faithful translator than he. Indeed, his deep knowledge of the history of the Middle East and his expertise as an editor contributed much to the final version. I am extremely grateful to him for the fine job he did.

My home has been all that a woman could desire when working on such an endeavor. My husband Shmuel and my sons Lavi and Adi have been my greatest source of inspiration and support. In fact, they are the principle reason and motivation for my writing this book.

My parents, Adina and Abraham Bassoul, did not live to see my job accomplished, but their spirit certainly guided me throughout. Natives of Aleppo, where they spent much of their lives, they were exposed to four different cultures: Jewish, Turkish, Arab, and French. In their own lives, they proved that cultures need not necessarily clash but can coexist in perfect harmony. It is this message that they have engraved in me since childhood, and to it I dedicate the book.

Tel Aviv, Israel   O. B.
May 1997

Contents

Saddam's Word

Introduction
Language and Politics

*I*n his novel *La nuit sacrée*, the Moroccan writer Tahar Ben Jelloun paints a surrealistic scene: In a desolate place away from the city, there stands a huge light-blue warehouse with many people arranged in a long and very orderly line in front of it. This unusual warehouse contains words of every conceivable kind, all neatly arranged in alphabetical order. It is called "the city's dictionary," and people come there to draw a weekly ration of words and expressions. Some are mute, some stutter, and some are the ordinary kind of blustering people. Some know their way around very well; others get lost and have to ask the guide to lead them to the words they want. The warehouse also has a section where other words have been thrown on the ground in large heaps that reach up to the ceiling.

Like those imaginary townspeople, this book attempts to draw from the immense store of words, terms, concepts, idioms, and ideas of one particular regime and to shape them into a prism through which to discern that regime's political culture and follow the political processes evolving in the society. The study has firm points of reference in time and space. It deals with the Ba'th regime in Iraq during about three decades of its existence since its inception in 1968 and with its use of the Arabic language in which it expressed itself. It is not the course of events that stands at the center of our endeavor; rather, it is the language, the expressions and verbal statements, that reflected events and at times shaped and nurtured them. This may seem puzzling, particularly in dealing with a regime like that of the Iraqi Ba'th, for which relentless activism is the breath of life. Despite this, and in some measure even because of it, a closer look at the language it employs can afford greater insight into deeper and more authentic layers that underlay the outward course of events and are charged with a heavy load of existential and historical sediments.

Focusing on certain verbal concepts and expressions and disregarding others is no arbitrary procedure; rather, it is helpful in eliciting from the enormous amount of current verbiage the key words that run like recurring motifs through the most significant expressions of the Ba'th regime. These key words and phrases are repeated over and over again like a spell until they seem to acquire a life of their own and come, in turn, to influence political action. It is not our aim to present an encyclopedia of Ba'th discourse but rather to highlight its most salient features. Before we delve into our subject matter, however, we should reflect on the nature of language in general and on the characteristics of the Arabic language in particular. As one scholar puts it, language draws a "magic circle" around one particular people, "a circle from which there is no escape save by stepping out of it into another."[1]

What then is the secret of words that makes them symbols of human speech?[2] Many major religions give speech an exalted place in their accounts of the creation, together with the creator himself, who either uses speech or puts it at the very origins of the created world.[3] In the theology of ancient Egypt, God is conceived as a spiritual entity who *thought* the world before using speech to create it. This primordial quality of words is one reason for their superior power. It explains the magic character of names and the rite of naming things and persons. In some societies and religions, a person who knows the names of things or people is believed to have power over them and to be able to protect them from evil. Ancient Egyptians believed in the magic of names; part of the ceremony of anointing kings consisted of transferring to them, in a precisely regulated manner, the various names of the god-king pharaoh. Each name conferred upon him one particular exalted quality or divine power. In the monotheistic religions, too, the name of God represents, as it were, the godhead itself and has acquired a power that inspires awe in the hearts of believers. The Christian liturgies make frequent use of expressions such as "in the name of God" or "in the name of the Lord," as if by merely enunciating the "right" name of God, humans gain divine protection.[4] In Judaism, "the name" has become a synonym for God. In Islam, *bism'illah* (in the name of Allah) has become a figure of everyday speech.

The name of a person, too, is more than just an appellation—it is an integral part of the person's individuality, a personal possession to be guarded jealously. The Eskimos, for example, think of humans as being made up of three parts: the body, the soul, and the name. This quality of the name as the alter ego is brought out in a maxim of Roman law that lays down that slaves have no "legal" names because giving them names would turn them into "legal" people. A similar belief in the magic power of names and their intrinsic link with their bearers' personalities under-lies the custom, common in many societies, of changing or adding to the name of a person facing adversity.[5]

We mention these practices in order to put into fuller context a Ba'th habit that became part and parcel of its political culture (and on which we shall dwell later on): the custom of giving names, sobriquets, or titles not only to persons but also to their deeds, special events, particular op-erations, et cetera, and then proceeding to build a cult around them.

The power of language as a social instrument that holds a group to-gether or marks it off from others needs only to be noted, not to be enlarged upon. Nor do we need to elaborate on the element of ambiguity inherent in every verbal statement. A veritable abyss may separate the listener's understanding from the speaker's intent, even when both belong to the same linguistic group. Ambiguity may occasionally be intended, such as in the language of agreements meant to satisfy two opposing sides. Furthermore, words change their meaning over time and must constantly be reexamined semantically in every new context.[6]

Ernst Cassirer distinguished between two properties of words: their semantic content and their magic quality. The former addresses itself to logic and intends to inform; the latter appeals to feelings and means to arouse emotion. He refers to early societies in which the sorcerer wielded words like weapons—magic words that he alone had mastered. In mod-ern times (his book was written during the Nazi period), he states, there has been a backsliding into the magical use of words at the expense of their semantic content. He saw this as a measure of the transvaluation of ethical values and transformation of human speech. He takes as an ex-ample words from the Nazi dictionary to illustrate that "what character-izes them is not so much their content and their objective meaning, as the emotional atmosphere which surrounds and envelops them."[7] Political propagandists were past masters in using the simplest of means—the word—to generate a whole gamut of overpowering emotions: hatred, anger, arrogance, contempt, mockery.

Another issue often dealt with by scholars is the interrelationship of myth and language, various interpretations of which have been suggested. Most agree that myths are an integral part of speech, poetry, and early histori-cal thought. Some have seen them as the "dark side" of language or as humanity's escape from the rational. Cassirer writes: "In desperate situa-tions man will always have recourse to desperate means—and our present-day political myths have been such desperate means."[8] Written during the period of totalitarian regimes in Europe, these words are still relevant today; the Ba'th regime in Iraq is a case in point. Its skill in using words and myths to promote its aims or find its way out of a crisis will become evident in the subsequent chapters.

Turning to the Arabic language itself, the first thing to note is that, from the beginning, its very origin had been thought of as a miracle. According to the Iraqi writer, poet, and critic Jabra Jabra, many Arab linguists agree that when Arabic first appeared in the world, it already possessed, through "divine inspiration," its full scope and force. The Arabic language is, to his mind, the essence of Arab culture such as it was a thousand years ago. Another Iraqi writer, Khalid Kishtainy, speaks of the miracle of Arabic. To the nomad, language was the only art form he or she could carry in his or her wanderings. Not being able to engage in arts (such as sculpture or painting) that required a settled life, nomads made language "a magic abstract world of words, in which langauge became the end and not the means." The linguistic genius of the Arabs made their language a storehouse of beauty shaped by the power, ring, rhythm, and inner associations of its words.[9] 'Abd al-Amir al-Ward, a Baghdad university professor who made untiring efforts to "purge" the influence of the spoken idiom (*'ammiyya*) from the literary language (*fusha*), likens classical Arabic to an "ocean" of treasures providing the answers to linguistic problems and offering material for verbal innovation "for a million years to come."[10]

Yet another Iraqi poet and writer, Karim 'Abd, speaks of the "fateful link" between Arabs and language and stresses the identity of language and culture—that is, the totality of "existing customs" and the "historical memory" that "turns into an Arab whoever lives within [the domain of] the Arabic language."[11]

Albert Hourani for his part speaks of Arabic as the "flawed mirror" in which Arabs perceive the world. Arabs love high-sounding and beautiful words for their own sake and place rhetoric and poetry higher than any other art form. He goes on to say that "through language and imagination again there enters an ethical system which exalts the heroic virtues: loyalty to friends, family and tribe; the sense of personal and family honor; hospitality; the magnanimity of the strong man who does not always insist on his rights."[12]

Like many peoples, Arabs consider their language vastly superior to others because of its beauty and its capacity to bind its speakers to it by bonds of magic. The vitality and strength of the language have remained evident over 1,300 years of upheavals. Foreign rulers, speaking foreign languages, came and went; but Arabic vanquished all their languages. Persians and Turks have absorbed much of the Arabic language into their own; by contrast, they have utterly failed to dislodge Arabic from its dominant position and have left "no more than a scratch" on its face. Others have noted the influence of Arabic on Urdu, Malay, and Swahili.[13] The Egyptian linguist Zahran al-Badrawi speaks of the great medieval "struggle for predominance" between Arabic and the Romance languages on the one hand, and Muslim languages such as Persian, Turkish, and Kurdish on the other. He sees the reason for the victory of Arabic in the faithfulness of Muslims to the Qur'an and its sacred language.[14] Furthermore, Arabic grammar was established as far back as the eighth century and has remained unchanged since. Jabra, too, dwells on the pivotal place of the Qur'an and how it combines sanctity with verbal beauty. The Qur'an has remained the model for correct Arabic; believers read it in the original, even if their native language is different. Jabra asserts that Arabic is logical like mathematics and rhythmic like music. He sums up by saying that the language has preserved the Arab nation through its darkest hours, has given it unity, and is the essence of the "Arab ethos."[15]

Another Arab scholar, Hisham Sharabi, has elaborated on the efficiency of Arabic as a powerful political instrument but notes that it loses much of its spell when translated into other languages. Translations, he goes on to say, can convey the meaning but fail to render the significance of allusions or psychological associations. He notes that Arab orators do not appeal to their audiences by means of direct, purposeful, and precise explanations but rather through repetition and an indirect approach. Their vocabulary is intended to elicit emotional responses rather than influence rational thought. Arabic is extremely well adapted to diplomacy because "behind the politeness and ceremony, intention is easily concealed and meaning only obliquely revealed." All this, he goes on, often makes Arabic imprecise and leaves room for misunderstandings. That, in turn, may be the reason why deliberations in the Arab world are often prolonged rather than decisive.[16]

Another characteristic of the use of Arabic in politics has been noted by a non-Arab scholar, who finds that statements that contain or imply a threat or proclaim an aim tend to assume a significance of their own, particularly if repeated over and over again. Their impact does not depend on whether they are carried out or not. There is therefore no "confusion between words and action, but rather a psychologically conditioned substitution of word for action."[17]

Whether we accept these opinions or reject them as anti-Arab, one thing is certain: In this age of mass media, Arab regimes—and none more so than the Ba'th regime in Iraq—have made conscious and intense efforts to impose on their polity certain sharply defined usages of political language. Theirs is a discourse of which a salient mark is the blurring of the line between rhetoric and action, between imagination and reality. It is a language that reveals little and conceals much, a language in which the word of the ruler is the word from on high.

Much has been written about the power of the modern media and about the tendency of media staff to turn themselves into part of the establishment.[18] If this is true of democracies of which the freedom of expression is an integral part, it is easy to imagine the degree of control over the spoken and the written word exercised by regimes such as that of the Ba'th. The Ba'th media serve as the most important source for this study precisely because they are a primary instrument in the hands of the rulers and because they themselves have become the "flawed mirror" through which the society of contemporary Iraq perceives reality. It is that which makes them so revealing.

How did the regime succeed in so totally subjecting the media, and what is the interrelationship between the political establishment and that of the media? In Iraq, as in other Arab countries, the press and other media have known only short spells of freedom.[19] Yet, both under the Iraqi monarchy and under the rule of Qasim that followed it, the press was not altogether "mobilized," and there was a fairly broad range of privately owned or party-affiliated newspapers. Together, they enjoyed a certain degree of freedom of expression. After the fall of Qasim in 1963, this freedom, limited though it had been, was gradually worn down. His immediate successor, 'Abd al-Salam 'Arif, decreed that publications critical of the regime were to be censored and that their publishers could have their licenses revoked. His brother, 'Abd al-Rahman, who succeeded him, nationalized the press in 1967. The electronic media, it must be remembered, had been under state control from the start.[20] But it was left to the Ba'th regime to achieve the media's total subjection.

At the beginning of 1969—within half a year of its advent to power—the regime issued a publications law that made the media the "fourth branch" (*al-sulta al-rabi'a*) of the government. Officially declared "independent," in actual fact they became mere branches of the central power.[21] The new law created a press monopoly for two dailies, *al-Thawra* and *al-Jumhuriyya*; later, a Kurdish paper, *al-Ta'akhi*, was added, but it appeared only for a short time. Later still, *al-'Iraq* and *al-Qadisiyya* were licensed, and, more recently, *Babil* has started to appear. To make sure that no outside interest might assert itself in the press or try to influence readers, commercial advertising was forbidden. Newspapers were thus also financially dependent on the government. Furthermore, the press served as an instrument of social and political mobility: those who excelled in carrying the regime's message to the public could expect to be rewarded.

A salient example is provided by the career of Tariq 'Aziz, who started out as editor of *al-Thawra* in the early years of the regime, rose to the highest ranks of the party hierarchy, and became information and later on foreign minister. Another example is that of Sa'd Qasim Hammudi, editor of *al-Jumhuriyya* in his early days and member of parliament and information minister later on. Latif Nusayyif al-Jasim, too, rose from being director-general of radio and television to the rank of minister. Another former director of radio and television, Muhammad Sa'id al-Sahhaf, is minister of foreign affairs. The same road can be traveled in the other direction: political personalities have been assigned posts in the media in the expectation that they will exercise firm authority there. In the early 1990s, for instance, Saddam Husayn's son 'Udayy was made the owner of *Babil* and later chairman of the association of journalists. Such measures not only ensure that the press is subordinate and "sterile" but also give those in charge direct access to Saddam Husayn. His speeches, his utterances, and his pictures are given disproportionate space in the newspaper columns and turn the press into his private property. By the same token, the press turns his personal political idiom into the common speech of many of the Iraqis who are exposed to it.

The pivotal importance attached to the conduct of propaganda is attested to by an article entitled, "On Propaganda and Mass Mobilization" (*Hawl al-di'aya wa-l-tahrik al-Jamahiri*), which was included in the 1977 party platform. It distinguished between the propaganda directed at Ba'th members and that meant to reach the public at large. Among the former, rational argument was capable of projecting uniform attitudes throughout the party; mass appeal, by contrast, needed other means, such as "very simple popular books, popular rallies, speeches with a mass audience, and the daily press." A major role was assigned to the theater, particularly in rural areas. Overall, mass mobilization was to arouse and organize the masses for active participation in government-initiated activities. The unnamed author warns of not treating the masses like a "flock of sheep" and asserts they must not be fed false or exaggerated news "as was done for decades by the Iraqi party press." To do so would create confusion and the masses would lose faith in the rulers. Mass mobilization was a matter of "science and art," and its two main conduits were the regime's slogans and the daily press. The latter's task was to "guide and mobilize" the masses, and it must therefore deal with issues that concern them directly. Its language must be "simple, attractive, and lively." There was no room for lengthy scientific or analytic articles, and all the means of modern journalism should be employed to win over the hearts of the masses.[22]

There is an obvious contradiction between the aim of "guiding" the readers' thoughts and that of providing correct and accurate information. In the contest between them, the first tendency triumphed. For most of the period reviewed here, with only a few exceptions, the Ba'th press was "engaged," one-dimensional, replete with verbiage, and boring. It also failed utterly to portray realities.[23] The artistic features that were supposed to attract the reader were also made subject to the commands of propagandistic intent. Cartoons—a medium taken over from Europe[24]—usually lacked humor, failed to even hint at domestic political criticism, and were for the most part meant to convey feelings of outrage against an external "enemy."[25] Poetry, too, was used as a political tool: Ba'th newspapers were full of political lyrics expressing adulation of Saddam Husayn, flattering his regime, and vilifying its enemies. This signifies a serious decline in the authentic Iraqi poetry that had long flourished under the comparatively tolerant periods of earlier regimes, recalling instead the poetical "command performances" of the nineteenth century and earlier.[26]

The overriding impression that the political idiom of the Ba'th gives us in newspapers, speeches, and writings is that of a language of slogans and clichés, of fixed "code words"—a language of totalitarianism that has been characterized as *écriture policière*. It is a "value-loaded" language in which every word is either "good" or "bad," an idiom in which words are not meant to reflect a given reality but rather to pass them through a filter of value significance. In the Ba'th jargon, for instance, and in the Marxist jargon before it, words such as "deviationist" and "deviationism" connote both a crime and its punishment. Roland Barthes holds that every regime has its own particular political language, and in each "intimidation" and "glorification" have a special place.[27] This is borne out by the Baʿth language, in which everything is divided starkly into black and white between what "glorifies" the ruler and what "threatens" domestic and foreign adversaries. In short, words become a smoke screen between the facts they purport to refer to and the impression they seek to create.

The Iraqi Baʿth regime came to power in 1968 and has so far lasted twenty-nine years; it has survived more sweeping upheavals—domestic and external—than befell any other modern Iraqi regime. The most salient were the fighting against the Iraqi Kurds in 1974–1975; the war with Iran from 1980 until 1988; the invasion of Kuwait and the Gulf War (1990/91), the worldwide economic and political embargo that came in its wake, and the subsequent Kurdish and Shiʿi uprisings. All these attest to the Baʿth regime's preference for the use of force. Obviously, there is some interaction between the constant extolling of strong-arm solutions and their actual implementation. Language may promote the use of force or else serve to make it appear legitimate after the event. Both approaches make it necessary to ignore failures of violent action, at least for a while, or to play them down.

Earlier Iraqi regimes may also have had their strong-arm predilections, but none acted them out the way the Baʿth have. To illustrate: Iraqi-Iranian hostility is as old as modern Iraq (and actually a legacy from Ottoman times), yet no earlier regime provoked Iran as openly as the Baʿth did. Or again: various pre-Baʿth Iraqi political figures spoke in favor of the annexation of Kuwait, but none dared do as they preached. Neither did any earlier Iraqi regime call into being, through its own action, a twenty-eight-member military alliance, including major powers, as Iraq did in 1990 and 1991, and then stand up to it for such a span of time. Similarly, no other regime had to fight off simultaneous uprisings on the part of the Kurds and the Shiʿis, who together make up a majority of the population. Yet the Baʿth survived. The very fact of the long survival in power of one and the same party makes the Iraqi Baʿth unique. A whole generation of young Iraqis has been educated solely in the tenets of Baʿth doctrine, exposed to its political language and political culture, and constrained to put them into practice. This long subjection to a single political idiom (all expressions of "deviant" thought having been suppressed) has created a monolithic polity that few have dared to defy.

Not only has a single party ruled Iraq for so long, but a single man has done so: Saddam Husayn, as strongman behind the scenes until 1979 and as sole leader since. He has left an incisive mark on Iraqi political thought and language, whether directly or not. Conscious of the power of words, he initiated the publication of the *Saddam Husayn Political Dictionary* (*Qamus Saddam Husayn al-Siyasi*), which contains some 500 entries of his favorite words and expressions and his "memorable quotes."[28] His speeches are not only printed verbatim in the press but have been collected in numerous special publications and distributed among party members, members of the armed forces, and the public at large. Journalists and political figures compete among themselves how best to imitate his personal style—a recognized means to gain favors or promotion. One journalist described Husayn as the "master of words" (*sayyid al-kalimat*), or as the "engineer of letters and words."[29] The way to enlist new party members, the party organ *al-Thawra al-ʿArabiyya* wrote, was to emulate Husayn's manner of speech and, like him, to appeal to the hearts of people of all walks of life by a simple style, the use of popular adages, and the faculty of striking the right note with every particular audience.[30] Perusing Husayn's hundreds of speeches, one is indeed struck by his frequent use of metaphors, popular proverbs, and figures of speech drawn from the vernacular. Often, his expressions are obscure, either intentionally or as the result of blurred thinking or possibly both. But when he wishes to convey a certain, well-defined message, his style can be clear and sharply honed.

Despite all the efforts of the Baʿth to impose a "total" language from above, the Arabic of Iraq still derives palpably from that country's special background and history. Beneath the outer shell of the language common to all speakers of Arabic, it is easy to discern how the country's nature and circumstances have shaped local speech. One of the characteristics of the Baʿthi language during the first decade of Baʿth rule, for instance, was the large-scale borrowing from the idiom of the Iraqi Communist Party. Regardless of the fact that the communists were then the chief rivals of the Baʿth, they continued for some time to be a subject of Baʿthi emulation. Another layer of local speech indicates the special problems posed by the presence of the large Kurdish and Shiʿi populations. Even though the regime has often enough tried to impose a news blackout on events surrounding the Kurds and Shiʿis, certain terms and expressions it uses reveal their presence under the official surface. Historical experience also influences the discourse. The word "yellow" for instance, ostensibly harmless, is used in contexts meant to evoke the memory of the thirteenth-century Mongol invasions—that is, the invasion by "yellow" people that led to the conquest and destruction of Baghdad. In current parlance, the term is used by the Baʿth to refer to the Iranians. This is a striking example of what linguists have called the "emotive," as distinct from the "symbolic" use of words—that is, speech that wishes "to express and excite feelings and attitudes" as distinct from speech that wishes to tell the listener something about the outside world.[31]

An analysis of Baʿth terminology, both from the point of view of "symbol" and of "emotion" (i.e., of both linguistic and political content), may afford us insights into Iraqi society, its concepts, and its past and present development. Semantic analysis may make it possible for us to follow the changes in the meaning of a word, layer after layer, as it were, much like the procedure of archaeology. Like every language, Arabic has changed over time.[32] A particularly dramatic change occurred as a result of cultural contacts with the West, beginning in the nineteenth century. Their political impact is well reflected in the development of Arabic. A further stage was reached in the present century, with the establishment of the modern Arab states and their "importing" of ideologies—mainly secular, sometimes leftist-revolutionary—from the West. That is as true of Iraq as of the other Arab countries.

Arabic was adapted to the needs of the era by various means: by borrowing foreign terms; by changing the connotations of certain Arabic words; and by neologisms. Despite the constant efforts of language purists, foreign terms made their way into Arabic. Some were "arabized," as it were; in other cases, old Islamic words were made to assume modern meanings different from their original connotations.[33] Ba'th parlance at times was inadvertently influenced by changes in the linguistic environment, and at others promoted them with clear political intent.

How did the Ba'th manipulate language? In picking a certain political term and repeating it endlessly, the party relied on the known power of a particular word, on its wealth of associations, its charge of historical memories, and its proven capacity of making listeners identify with it on an emotional level. At the same time, the Ba'th regime itself—being part and parcel of the political culture surrounding it—was conditioned by the connotations and associations of certain words. This study will focus on those Ba'thi terms that the party itself placed at the center of its idiom. They may remind us of what Blaise Pascal said of literary writing: "There are certain words which, suddenly and unexpectedly, make clear the sense of a whole book. Once we meet with these words we no longer can have any doubt about the character of the book."[34]

Our study deals with five spheres, overlapping in time and in scope; they center around five different aspects of the polity. Briefly, they may be named revolution; regime; state and nation; war; and religion. They are not sharply delineated (their differentiation is, after all, a methodological device); concepts and terms move from one sphere to another, and some speakers and writers use them indiscriminately, yet they provide a focus.

The first part deals with the time of the regime's rise to power: the revolution (*thawra*), as its spokespeople call it. The connotation of the term was soon broadened from signifying an event to indicating a lasting state of affairs: a badge of identity, logo, or flag, a permanent characteristic of the regime. The word had already had a long previous career. In the nineteenth century, it had the negative overtones of a rebellion against legitimate authority. Only the Arab revolutionary regimes of the 1950s gave it a positive ring. The Ba'th gave it an aura of magic. Repeating it countless times and linking it with everything that was noble, the party used it to elicit feelings of identification, loyalty, and respect. Alongside it appeared other terms with a similar meaning, such as *wathba* (outburst) or *intifada* (uprising). Together, they were ranged against "negative" words held in contempt such as "putsch" (*inqilab*), "reaction" (*ridda*), or "rebellion" (*tamarrud*). Such black-and-white usage stemmed from the desire to depict the regime as "good" and all others as "bad."

"Revolution" fits with other words referring to the Baʿthi party doctrine, taking as their point of departure the party's very name: "rebirth," "change," or "renewal." Just as the regime became identified with the concept of "revolution," so the party became identified with its maxims of "unity," "freedom," "socialism," "eternal mission," and others. Just as the term "revolution" became petrified and no longer carried its original connotation, so also the Baʿth catchwords became divorced from realities and turned into empty slogans.

The second part juxtaposes terms such as "democracy," "liberalism," and "parliamentarianism" with the concept of the leader. Perhaps surprisingly, the Baʿth party itself uses this juxtaposition to clearly extol the latter over the former. But it has had a long and difficult struggle with these terms. Democracy is indeed paid lip service, but liberalism is totally condemned. A parliamentary form of government has ostensibly been adopted, but parliament has been rendered impotent. The party's convolutions in this regard are motivated by the pursuit of two opposing ideals: on the one hand, democratic values were part and parcel of the "enlightened" world and the Baʿth endeavored to appear up to the mark, particularly as there were also domestic pressures to this effect; on the other hand, democratic ideals had not sprung from Iraqi soil but rather had been gleaned from the hated West. More than that, they conflicted with other elements of Baʿthi doctrine. Had Western democratic ideas prevailed in Iraq, they would have undermined the party's hegemony and the position of the one leader. The Baʿth, therefore, undertook a prolonged campaign to delegitimize democratic concepts; it took over terms that had become symbols of other societies and then emptied them of their original content. The forms became mere labels and were no longer dangerous.

The opposite road was traveled with regard to Saddam Husayn. The aim was to make him personally the very focus of identification, symbolism, and myth. For years, journalists, artists, politicians, and people from the rank and file were recruited to spin countless myths around him. The process of weaving myths around the leader is described by Cassirer. Modern politicians, he says, must combine the conflicting qualities of homo faber and of homo magus. They must become like the priests of a new, totally irrational religion. But when they go about spreading the new religion, they must plan ahead rationally, proceed methodically, and calculate their steps. Unlike the ancient myths, Cassirer goes on to say, modern political myths are artifacts produced by professionals. They are technological products, much like other kinds of weapons.[35] The final object is to turn leaders into something different altogether from flesh-and-blood images of ordinary human beings, to conceal their defects and weaknesses and attribute a degree of sanctity to them that deters, or better yet prevents, others from doing them damage.

The third part is a discussion of the sphere of state, homeland, and nation that encompasses the sensitive questions of identity and loyalty. A salient point that comes to the fore in this context is the question of who is entitled to take part in public political discourse. Here, too, language is a faithful reflection of the actual political circumstances of modern Iraq. The Sunni Arab minority dominates political discourse just as it dominates practical politics. In doing so, it tries to neutralize the two other large blocks in the Iraqi population—the Kurds and the Shiʿis—who together form the country's demographic majority, though politically they are its minority. When it touches on these questions, a hidden load of fear and tension can often be discerned underneath ostensibly self-confident words. Sunni Arabs think of themselves as the sole masters, entitled to determine Iraq's identity, character, and political framework. It is they who decree who are good and loyal Iraqis and who are unpatriotic "traitors." People are disqualified in various ways, all of which are given expression in the political idiom. One means is to avoid the mention of words disqualified groups use to speak of themselves. "Shiʿi" or "Kurdistan" are sometimes "nonwords." Such usage is meant to wipe out the identity of those groups and to melt them down in the crucible of "Iraqiness" in a way characteristic of Baʿthi thought. A more active way is to label groups as "communal" or "anti-Arab." These labels place them beyond the pale and rob them of their political weight.

In the rare cases in which Shiʿis who were openly identified as such took part in political discourse (more often than not from abroad), their note was apologetic. Their statements were frequently couched in the very terms the Baʿth had made current. Like in a mirror image, such spokespeople call the Baʿth "racist," but this and similar terms are clearly being used defensively. Kurdish participation is more frequent, in keeping with the Kurds' greater political salience compared with that of the Shiʿis. Their idiom mirrors their aspirations for national self-determination and the difficulties they grapple with along the road toward their aim. In sum, our presentation points to clear indications in the public idiom of the country's sharp internal social and political rifts and to expressions of fear and mutual suspicion. They show that no articulate Iraqi identity has evolved yet; part of the public seeks the road to national unity, others strive to move away.

The third part discusses the way adversaries are branded implicitly and indirectly; the fourth deals with expressions of open and explicit hostility. The Baʿth regime has known many external enemies, and the most intense hostility has usually been reserved for the "imperialist-Zionist-Iranian" triangle. All three components were considered excellent mass propaganda targets by the Baʿth. To maintain their image as a focus of evil and hatred, it was constantly necessary to create new stereotypes. The trinity was meant to demonstrate the constant plotting and collusion against Iraq, to deflect frustration and anger away from home toward external enemies, and to underpin the Baʿthi policy of violent action.

The emergence of the Ba'th party's doctrine of the use of force had its antecedents; it drew on ideas current in Iraq in the 1930s. It differs from its ideological predecessors by having moored language firmly to the doctrine. An ideology of force came to be applied by an apparatus of violence the like of which had never existed in Iraq or, for that matter, in the Middle East. The country, it may be said, became a captive both of the apparatus and of the language of violence. Together, they rendered Iraq incapable of searching for means other than the application of force to resolve its crises. Once engaged in actual hostilities, the regime had to develop additional organs to counteract the frustrations of prolonged warfare and keep tempers sufficiently incensed for people to want to continue the war. In order to do so, it drew on a multitude of words relating to traditional values, most particularly those involving feelings of honor. These were given first place among expressions thought capable of sending men into battle for values dearer to them than their own lives. The defense of honor justified death; *shahada* (a martyr's death) had its reward in the afterlife. The Ba'th took up that old Muslim belief and turned it into a veritable public ritual that was perceived as appropriate by believing Muslims. The ritual was to reaffirm again and again that to die for the nation and the country was a fitting sacrifice. The loss of life was thus laid at the door of Allah rather than of the Ba'th.

The fifth part leads into the inner recesses of history: religion and mythology. Their inclusion in the final part is not coincidental: it is indicative of the road the Ba'th regime itself has traveled, from its original secular ideology to its eventual return to the Islamic past and its values. In this return, we can find signs of a genuine search for deeper roots but also considerations of how best to extricate the regime from severe crises and grave dangers and how to manipulate language by evoking deeply felt religious sentiment for the purpose of political propaganda. Sunni Islam has always held that the study of history was of great importance in preparing man for the next world.[36] The Ba'th has taken this earlier tendency to its extreme and has made history an integral part of day-to-day political discourse. Saddam Husayn leads it in doing so. History is used to offer explanations and justifications for the present. More important, it is a means of giving today's regime the status of full legitimacy by marking it off from other regimes of recent history and by equating it with the glories of the distant past. Most of all, the Ba'th enlisted for its own purposes the vast power of ancient tales of heroism, using them to ignite the imagination of today's Iraqis and spur them on to emulate them.

Reviving the past means reviving Islam. Mainstream Arab historians hold that only with the advent of Islam does Arab history become significant. The Ba'th, which started out with a strongly secular doctrine, related to Islam as an instrument of power to be used to fend off those who— whether at home or abroad—were likely to employ religion against the regime. Only in a later phase did it begin to proclaim itself the champion of Islam, taking over all the trappings of Islamic discourse and at the same time suppressing all signs of genuine Islamic revival. In this respect, the Ba'th idiom has reversed its function: while on other issues it seeks to reinforce and underpin action, here it uses language as a brake; it puts up a smoke screen, provides an alibi for itself, and makes verbiage an alternative to action.

If such limitations govern the way current Islamic trends are being dealt with, the same does not apply to ancient Islamic or even pre-Islamic myths. On the contrary, these serve the regime as a kind of armor at times when its legitimacy seems to be questioned. At other times, they have been useful in carrying the masses forward into perilous adventures. The fact that supernatural myths are not subject to rational criticism has been exploited to the full. Myths are also useful in giving a deceptively rosy color to unpleasant realities and in deflecting public attention from them. In all this, the Ba'th regime proved to be not only in full control of all physical means of power but also a past master of verbal manipulation. It is this combination that has contributed greatly to the regime's longevity.

I

Revolution and Revival

A revolutionary movement with such qualities and characteristics may bend in the wind but will not break, because
its roots reach the very depth of the nation and it draws on
the nation's heritage and history and is inspired both from
heaven and earth.
  —*Al-Thawra al-'Arabiyya*, no. 11, November 1979

We must lead the party out of the rooms and halls . . . and
spread it over the face of the broad Arab earth and among
the toiling masses.
  —Michel 'Aflaq, *Nuqtat al-bidaya*

1

Revolution
Thesis and Antithesis

Revolutionism" lies at the center of modern Iraqi political life. Its salience is borne out not only by the number and frequency of revolutionary events but also by the multitude of forms they have assumed: popular or military rebellions against the British (1920, 1941); Kurdish or Shiʻi tribal uprisings against the central government (in the 1920s and 1930s, the former eventually growing into a national struggle); or full-fledged military coups. What is common to them all is the aim of overturning the existing order by the use of force. Underlying this historical affliction has been a combination of numerous factors: At its birth, Iraq was an artificial creation lacking historical continuity; its population has always been confessionally and ethnically heterogenous; political power has always resided with a Sunni-Arab minority that rules over a Shiʻi majority; traditional attitudes have been eroded by starkly conflicting modern ideologies; and, finally, there has emerged in recent decades a highly centralized form of government that set out to firmly suppress all centrifugal tendencies but ended up reinforcing them.[1]

Such a series of events must produce a string of expressions intended to describe and characterize them. The most important are *thawra* (revolution), *inqilab* (coup, putsch), *tamarrud* (rebellion), *haraka* (movement), *wathba* (outburst), *intifada* (uprising), *ʻisyan* (disobedience), *ridda* (reaction), and *fitna* (internecine war). None of these words were new, nor was their use confined to Iraq. Some were taken from the old Arab-Islamic vocabulary and simply applied to modern circumstances; others were the

19

result of the morphological or semantic development of old roots. The latter group contained words that emerged from the impact of foreign (Western) ideas. First among them was the idea of revolution.

The adoption of revolutionary thought in the twentieth century came in the wake of profound intellectual and ideological changes caused by the cultural clash with the West that began in the previous century. But it also had roots in changes that occurred within Arab society itself. Originally, the idea of revolutionary change was altogether foreign to Arab-Muslim society. A revolution proclaiming the concepts of liberty and equality and modeling new forms of government on them was in total conflict with the type of political thought current among Muslims, at least up to the end of the nineteenth century. Undermining legitimate authority was tantamount to anarchy and civil strife, either being worse than any kind of despotism. It took a full century for the new concepts to gain ground and for the word "revolution" to turn from a pejorative term to one encapsulating all that was good and positive.[2]

The catalyst for this, as for many other changes, was the clash between the Arab world and the West brought about by the institution of Great-Power mandates over many parts of the Middle East after the end of World War I. Violent outbursts occurred in Egypt (1919), Iraq (1920), and Syria (1925). They were termed "revolution" by those who launched them, although, viewed more soberly, they were rebellions against foreign rule. But the very use of the broader term gave a special aura both to the word and the concept. From the 1920s to the 1950s, the connotation of "revolution" gradually moved toward the sense it has in Western history. The many violent events of that period were changes of government through the use of force, rather than revolutions properly so called, although their initiators did call them that. It was only from 1950 onward that there were internal changes of a depth and scope that justified the use of the term. The second half of the present century is indeed the era of "revolutionary" regimes, with that of the Iraqi Baʻth occupying a central place among them.

Inqilab: Coup or Revolution?

Iraq's first military coup, carried out by General Bakr Sidqi in October 1936, was called *inqilab* by those who carried it out. At the time, the term indicated profound social, economic, and political change and had a positive ring to it. The word is a telling example of semantic change, moving from neutral or negative use in the nineteenth century to positive content in the first half of the twentieth and back to a negative sense in the second half. *Inqalaba* originally meant to stand a thing on its head. Classical Islamic texts speak of *al-inqilab ila Allah*, meaning to turn or to turn back to Allah, or else to pass from this world to the next.[3] By the nineteenth century, the word had acquired the meaning of political change, whether sudden or gradual. Egyptian writers of the period, for instance, sometimes called the French Revolution *al-inqilab al-faransawi* but would also describe a British government reshuffle as *inqilab al-wizara*. The Young Turks called their takeover in 1908 *inqilab* (the Arabic word having made its way into Turkish usage). By that time, the word had already come to mean "revolution."[4] This was now also the sense it carried in Arabic. In the 1930s, for instance, Sami Shawkat, a leading Iraqi ideologue with significant influence over his and subsequent generations, wrote favorably about the Young Turks and their (as he called it) spiritual and intellectual *inqilab*.[5]

Two months after Bakr Sidqi's coup, there appeared a booklet entitled "The *Inqilab* of 29 October." Its author, Yusuf Isma'il, a member of the Communist Party, went to great lengths in praising Sidqi's action, calling it "constitutional" and speaking of it as ushering in a "new era" in the history of Iraq. He left no doubt that he used the term *inqilab* as signifying an all-embracing change and depicted it as democratic, reformist, and progressive. Yet between the lines, we can discern a different approach that classifies it as a mere instance of the military using brute force. He writes: "Since the group of loyal [followers] and the angry masses were unable to oppose [the government] and to bring it down by opposition and elections, they had to remove the government by means of an *inqilab*, that is by bombs."[6]

Sidqi, who was in power for only nine months until he was assassinated in August 1937, set the fashion of military coups in Iraq and in other Arab countries as well. His death brought on another coup, which was also described as *inqilab* by those who carried it out and by their sympathizers. A book published soon after the second coup was entitled *Al-'Iraq bayn inqilabayn* (Iraq between two coups). However, its author, Muhammad 'Abd al-Fattah Abu al-Nasr al-Yafi, drew a line between the first *inqilab*, which he described as a terrible *fitna* (civil strife) and as a criminal and dictatorial act, and the second, with which he identified and which, he asserted, would propel Iraq along the road of patriotism, prosperity, and glory. It is worth noting that for him the word *thawra* still carried a negative load that made it tantamount to "rebellion." He writes, "People seeking strife were trying to drag the country into a general *thawra*, the outcome of which is known to Allah alone."[7]

The next Arab military coup occurred in March 1949 in Syria, under the leadership of Colonel Husni al-Za'im. Again, he and his followers used the term *inqilab* to describe their action, wishing to convey the impression of having carried out a constructive revolution. A commentator wrote that it differed from others in that it had avoided *fitna* and had not remained a mere *thawra*—here used to connote rebellion. Rather, it had sprung from a "revolutionary" freedom movement.[8] Like al-Yafi, al-Za'im distinguished between a positive and a negative (i.e., dictatorial) *inqilab*. The need to classify *inqilab* as either good or bad attests to the term's ambiguity and to a certain malaise on the part of its users. Their unease may well have applied both to the very idea of such an upheaval and the way it was carried out and to its results.

Nonetheless, the Ba'th party as well as others used the word in its "good" sense throughout and did not feel the need to qualify it. In its statutes of 1947, the party spoke of itself as "revolutionary" (*inqilabi*) and stated its belief that its major aims—national revival and the building of socialism—could only be achieved through struggle and *inqilab*.[9] Michel 'Aflaq (1910–1989), the foremost ideologue of the Syrian Ba'th, enlarged on the concept of revolution in his writings.[10] When speaking of an overall revolution in the positive sense of the word, he used, at least until the end of the 1950s, the term *inqilab*; the party's nature, he wrote, and its doctrine were *inqilabi*. He distinguished between *inqilab* and mere *islah* (reform); only a decisive, all-encompassing change could end Arab decline and decadence. Throughout their history, he held, Arabs knew only two states: either *inqilab* or *inhitat* (regression, decline). The advent of Islam had been a revolution, and in order to renew their links with the past, the Arabs must again choose the path of revolution. There were two camps in the modern Arab world, and that of *inqilab*, headed by the young generation, would prevail over the other. Only in 1958 did 'Aflaq stop using *inqilab* in favor of *thawra*, but he took pains to explain that the new expression stood in for the former.[11]

'Aflaq did not tell his readers why he had made that change in his terminology, though we may assume that he did so because of the Egyptian-Syrian merger of 1958, which established the United Arab Republic. The Ba'th had done a great deal to promote this merger but had also been the event's principal loser. The adoption of the term *thawra*, already current for long in Jamal 'Abd al-Nasir's Egypt, was an instructive indication of how much the party had, by its own action, placed itself in Nasir's shadow. This was true not only of the major domain of politics but also in the more marginal area of language. In actual fact, all over the Arab world, *inqilab* was being replaced by *thawra* as a result of Nasir's dominant position in Arab politics for some three decades. When 'Abd al-Karim Qasim seized power in Iraq in 1958, he, too, eventually called his takeover *thawra*, though he had initially clung to *inqilab*. The expression *inqilab thawri* was also sometimes used at first.[12] But the use of *inqilab* in a positive sense soon came to an end, and the word was employed only in the negative sense.

When the Ba'th party briefly came to power in Iraq in February 1963 through a military putsch, it might have been expected to describe its rise as an *inqilab*, in conformity with its mentor 'Aflaq's frequent usage. But *inqilab* had by then become a solely negative term, and the party had to fight off critics who pejoratively called its rise to power a "military *inqilab*."[13] The second and much longer period of Ba'th rule beginning on 17 July 1968 was also called *thawra*, and the party vigorously defended itself against its opponents' charge of having carried out an *inqilab*. "What was done on the blessed 17 July . . . was not just another military *inqilab* like so many earlier ones. . . . Rather, it was a great turning point in Iraq's history."[14] To mark itself off from earlier coups, it termed them all "mere" *inqilabat*. In the Ba'th historiography, all previous Iraqi putsches, with the exceptions of its own in 1963 and Qasim's (but not of Qasim's subsequent regime), are described as just that: putsches intended to satisfy the lust for power of their right-wing, reactionary, and opportunist perpetrators.[15]

The Ba'th claimed that there was a vast difference between its own revolution and all previous forcible takeovers. The party was, so its spokespeople asserted, a patriotic movement with a comprehensive ideology, enjoying broad mass support and capable of carrying on the fight until the revolution's aims were realized. The "putschists," by contrast, were single individuals with no other object than to personally benefit from holding office. The same was true, according to Saddam Husayn, of all other Arab military rulers.[16]

Attributing such a pejorative meaning to the word *inqilab* was also meant to discourage potential (or imaginary) conspirators against the Ba'th regime and to delegitimize them in advance. In January 1970, for example, such *inqilabiyyun* were branded as traitors of whom the Qur'an had said: "*Saya'lamu al-ladhin zalamu ayy munqalab yanqalibun*" (Those who do wrong shall surely know by what overturning they will be overturned).[17] The verse was turned into something of a slogan to be used against all those regarded as likely to harbor subversive thoughts. When Husayn was asked about rumors of an impending conspiracy (*mu'amara*) or coup (*inqilab*) against him, he answered that they were "a laughable fabrication"; anyone thinking along such lines, he went on, must first find out whether the army would support such an idea and whether the people would accept it, even for a brief span of time.[18] Husayn's adversaries—Kurds, Shi'is, and communists in whose eyes the Ba'th takeover was no more than a military putsch and a "black day" did call countless times on the army to carry out an *inqilab* against the party, even though they feared that it would involve a great deal of bloodshed.[19] But then Husayn decreed the death penalty for anyone other than Ba'th party members found to be politically active among the armed forces. Any party activity among servicemen, he said, was tantamount to "preparing a coup," always excepting the Ba'th party itself.[20]

Multifaceted *Intifada*

The fourteenth-century dictionary *Lisan al-'Arab*, composed by Muhammad bin al-Mukarram bin Manzur, explains the word *intifada* by quoting a *hadith* that reads: "Give me stones so that I should save [*astanfid*] my soul with them." It goes on to say that this meant that someone fleeing from pursuit should throw stones to keep his attackers at a distance. It is easy to see the semantic and practical continuity between the old interpretation and the use of the word to describe the *intifada* that broke

out on 9 December 1987 in the Palestinian areas occupied by Israel. It is
remarkable to note how the word preserved its essential meaning over six
centuries. *Intifada* has now come to mean a popular uprising in a just cause
and against an evil rule.

Though the word entered the international language of the media only
at the end of the 1980s, its use in Arabic had long been widespread. In a
booklet he wrote in 1950, 'Aflaq used the term to denote a popular awak-
ening and a revolt against the conditions that had so far retarded the
nation's development.[21] But that rather diffuse meaning gave way to a
clearly defined political significance with the outbreak of the unrest in Iraq
that became known as "the *intifada*," properly so called—the troubles
beginning on 23 October 1952 and lasting about a month in protest against
deteriorating social and economic conditions. The communists were a
leading element in the protest riots, which spread to most Iraqi towns.
The army was called in, and military emergency rule was proclaimed.[22]

After the overthrow of the Iraqi monarchy in 1958, the word *intifada*
became (though for a few days only) a synonym of *thawra*. It surfaced
again after the Ba'th coup of February 1963 in the text of "Communiqué
No. 1": "The people and the army have carried out this *intifada* in order
to continue along the glorious road of the revolution [*thawra*] of 14 July
[1958]."[23] But eventually, *intifada* did not turn into a synonym of *thawra*
in Ba'thi parlance (neither during the first nor the second period of the
party's rule), but it kept a place of honor for describing "popular" or
"spontaneous" action undertaken to correct deviations from the true revolutionary line. It was, for instance, used for two such disparate events as
'Abd al-Wahhab al-Shawwaf's revolt against Qasim in March 1959 and
Saddam Husayn's escape from prison on 4 September 1964.[24]

The most interesting use of *intifada* occurred at the time of the second
Ba'th coup in 1968. Its takeover was carried out in two phases: in the first,
on 17 July, the Ba'th cooperated with non-Ba'th army officers and then
shared power with them; in the second, on 30 July, the Ba'th rid itself of
those officers and established a Ba'th power monopoly. The second phase
was then termed a popular *intifada*, thus making the word a permanent
entry in the Ba'th political dictionary. It was this *intifada*, its executors
argued, that "purified" the July revolution, propelled Iraq along the road
to unity, freedom, and socialism (the three central Ba'thi slogans), and
laid the foundations for a "democratic, revolutionary" Iraq.[25] It is easy
to see why the Ba'th leadership chose this word: it was meant to describe
the second phase as a corrective action, more authentic and significant
than the first. Its use gave added praise and firmer legitimacy to a move
that others might have called a palace revolution or a court intrigue.

Since then, the term *intifada* has occupied a place of honor in Ba'th
parlance. It was applied retroactively to events that at the time they occurred were called by other names, like the anti-British uprising of 1920
or Rashid 'Ali al-Kaylani's 1941 *haraka* (movement).[26] Some events outside Iraq were also given the appellation *intifada* by the Ba'th, such as the

1976 "Land Day" of the Israeli Arabs, various demonstrations and clashes in the Israeli-occupied territories after 1974,[27] and the overthrow in Romania of Nicolae Ceausescu in 1989. Later, the Iraqi defense minister also applied the word to his country's invasion of Kuwait, saying that Iraq had taken action in response to a Kuwaiti *intifada* against the corrupt Sabah family, the ruling dynasty of Kuwait.[28]

The expression was, however, also employed by the Ba'th party's adversaries. The Shi'is, for instance, used it to describe their large-scale antigovernment riots of 1977.[29] The Kurds for their part so described their various uprisings against Baghdad, including the 1974–1975 war against the Ba'th[30] and their rebellions in the spring and summer of 1987, at the height of the Iraqi-Iranian war.[31] Though the Palestinian *intifada*, rather than any of the others, was adopted by the world media, this may attest less to its greater persistence than to the greater accessibility of the events in Gaza and the West Bank to journalists. One way or another, it is the only such term that made its way into the international language of news and news comment; *inqilab* or *thawra* did not. Moreover, it became associated solely with the Palestinians; the Kurdish and Shi'i rebellions after the 1991 Gulf War that were called *intifada* in Arabic were never so termed in other media.

Thawra: Highest on the Value Scale

From among the many terms associated with the idea of "revolutionism," the word *thawra* has gained pride of place in modern Iraq. More than that, in the political culture and language of the Ba'th, *thawra* came to denote a value concept of the highest order, of almost sacred significance. As elsewhere, it is used to describe profound and fundamental change throughout society, the economy, and politics. As such, it is "good" and "just." Unlike the resigned acceptance of existing conditions characteristic of earlier periods, the cry for action against conditions of degeneracy and decline became a value in itself.

In the Qur'an, the verb *athara* (from the same root) is used to denote plowing or turning over of a clod of earth (sura *al-Rum*, v. 30; *al-Baqara*, v. 71). *Lisan al-'Arab* explains *thara* as meaning "very angry" or "extremely furious." It also has the entry *thawra*, explained as "storm," "ferment," "war," or "civil strife." The dictionary mentions the role of the ox (*thawr*) in rousing the cows from their resting place and leading them to the water—a remark that clarifies the connection between *thawr* and *thawra*. In the modern sense, we do not find *thawra* before the nineteenth century, when it was first used with a neutral or negative note, later becoming positive. The transition is indicative of the change in the value system prevalent in Arab society.

In Iraq, as in other Arab countries, *thawra* came to mean two different things: an uprising against a foreign occupier or the violent overturn of a native regime held to be corrupt.[32] An example of the first was the 1920 "great Iraqi revolution" (*al-thawra al-'Iraqiyya al-kubra*) against the British, which failed to remove the mandatory regime but may have somewhat shortened its life. Iraqi nationalists, particularly Ba'thists, also called Rashid 'Ali al-Kaylani's "movement" of 1941 a revolution.[33] Examples of using the word in the second sense are Qasim's overthrow of the monarchy in 1958, the Ba'thi coup against Qasim in February 1963, and the Ba'th takeover of 1968. The fact that the Ba'th's revolution was only one in a series of revolutions had highly complex political and propagandistic implications: In what respect was the "final" revolution better than its predecessors? How to prevent similar revolutions in the future—whether originating at home or inspired from abroad—that would use the same argument of taking action to remove a regime grown corrupt? And how to settle the contradiction between needing to institutionalize Ba'th rule and giving the appearance of being in a state of permanent revolution?

It is beyond the scope of this study to describe the political and military steps taken to counteract such questions. Suffice it to say that, alongside a multitude of propagandistic tricks, political language was fully manipulated to make the questions seem pointless. The lack of enthusiasm that greeted the final Ba'th takeover on the part of a people who had had their fill of "revolutions" made it incumbent on the Ba'th to constantly hammer away at the theme that what it had done was "good" and constructive. Indeed, *thawra* ended up as a synonym for "good." Whereas Qasim's coup (for which there had been a great deal of popular enthusiasm) caused people to name baby girls *tha'ira* or *thawra* (the revolutionary, the rebellious),[34] the Ba'th named places and things *thawra* or *thawri* by decree. Saddam Husayn was termed a "revolutionary"; Iraq became the land of *thawra*. A neologism of sorts was invented: *'Iraq al-thawra* (Iraq of the revolution). Sometimes, the term was personified: the first Ba'th coup, for instance, was at times called *'arus al-thawrat* (the bride of revolutions), at other times *al-thawra al-mazluma* (the mistreated revolution) because of the short life of the ensuing Ba'th regime.[35] The country's internal security service (*al-mukhabarat*) was called the "eyes of the revolution," simultaneously using the Arabic *'ayn* in its two meanings of "eye" and "spy."[36] The eye was made the emblem of the service, and huge metal signs in the forms of an eye were affixed to the entrances of *mukhabarat* offices.[37]

Thawra was used from the start in the designation of the regime's highest legislative and executive authority, the Revolutionary Command Council (Majlis qiyadat al-thawra), and its highest court, the Revolutionary Court (Mahkamat al-thawra). It is ironic to notice that these bodies, so named to exemplify pristine revolutionary élan, have proved to be the longest-living institutions of Ba'th rule. These names, with their connotation of the merely temporary, may indicate something of a sense of impermanence and lack of self-confidence on the part of the leadership, but they are meant to convey that the party, being truly revolutionary, is everchanging and that a new revolution is therefore unnecessary.

The Ba'th felt itself to be in a permanently defensive position vis-à-vis other revolutions and therefore constantly compared itself with them and tried to delegitimize them. It was easy for the Ba'th to depict itself as the party that had continued and completed the events of 1920 and 1941—a motif evoked in connection with the war against Iran.[38] The Gulf War, too, was described in terms of a link completing the warlike patriotic and revolutionary actions of 1920 and 1941. In this way, earlier rebellions against foreign rule were used to demonstrate the "validity" of the Ba'th regime and give it an additional aura of patriotism and continuity. Earlier military coups, by contrast, had to be shown up as illegitimate. Bakr Sidqi's coup of 1936 therefore had to be described by the word *inqilab* and depicted as the employment of sheer violence. Qasim's regime was described in terms of a revolution subsequently deviating from its proper course, while the first Ba'th takeover was spoken of as a true and progressive revolution later beset by mistakes. 'Abd al-Salam 'Arif's regime that followed was, in the Ba'thi book, just one mistake after another.[39] With regard to the events of July 1968, the first phase (carried out in collaboration with non-Ba'this) was called a mere "revolutionary plan" or "project" (*mashru' thawra*); the real revolution only occurred when the Ba'th party rid itself of its erstwhile colleagues.

The Ba'th party endeavored to answer doubters who needed to be convinced that its takeover surpassed that of others and that the party had indeed earned the application of the word *thawra*. One of its chief arguments was that its revolution had been "white"—that is, bloodless—as well as popular. Unlike all previous events of a similar nature, the two phases of the July 1968 coup did indeed pass without bloodshed. The claim to popularity, however, is totally ungrounded in reality. It can in no way be compared with, for example, the 1979 Islamic revolution in Iran. Qasim's coup had elicited a great deal more enthusiasm than did that of the Ba'th. Perhaps in response, the Ba'th party still prefers to speak of its own revolution not so much as a single act but rather as a prolonged series of major changes. Saddam Husayn himself said: "Our revolution is of a new type: it is not a revolution of 'Communiqué No. 1' but of basic principles, of policy . . . and of strategic objectives."[40] A Ba'th document asserted that the party's aim was to carry out a "deep" revolution in all fields of human activity: education, economics, politics, and the armed forces.[41]

But the most vital thing that needed to be done was to indoctrinate the young generation. As the daily *al-Thawra* put it: "Revolution means young people because the revolution is renewal and movement, and therefore the young generation are a vital and active element in it."[42] The paper's view was clearly inspired by Saddam Husayn, who had formed firm ideas of the role of youth even before taking power. According to him, children and youths were, so to speak, "revolutionary projects" or "revolutionary tasks." With their longer life expectancy, they would be able to do more for the future of the revolution than older people. They were "the children of the revolution" (*abna' al-thawra*); it was to the revolution, rather than to their biological family, that they owed their highest loyalty. The child or youth must turn into the representative of the revolution within the circle of his or her family, and it was his or her task to teach them its principles. The child must become a source of "radiation" (*ish'a'*) in the midst of the family and must change them for the better, rather than allowing them to change him or her for the worse. Just as young people must act as the "nuclei" of the Iraqi revolution within their families, so the Iraqi revolution must be the "nucleus" of the Arab revolution, "which will reach the most remote points of the Arab world."[43]

In realizing its objectives, the Ba'th had to fend off the grave danger of a counterrevolution, a takeover bid by domestic or foreign-inspired groups pretending to be the "truer" revolutionaries. To invalidate such attempts before they were even undertaken, it coined the expression *thawri la thawri* (the revolutionary who is not revolutionary). *Al-Thawra* published a whole series of articles about this. False revolutionaries, it wrote, were candidates for treason against the true revolution. They were opportunists by nature and only out for benefits for themselves and their families. They endeavored to place themselves above the people, the party, and the revolution. But if faced with a genuinely revolutionary party, even the seizure of the broadcasting station and the transmission of the proverbial "Communiqué No. 1" would not avail them, because the party was everywhere.[44]

Some upheavals elsewhere in the Third World were called "half revolutions" (*nisf thawra*) because they had failed to go all the way. Leaders of other Arab countries claiming to have carried out revolutions came in for particularly scathing criticism. It had become so easy to usurp the title of revolutionary, a press comment noted, that there were "twice as many" such claimants than there were "sons of the [Arab] nation." Such pseudo-revolutionaries were disdainfully called "traders in revolutionary wares" or "shopkeepers of revolution." The Libyan leader Mu'ammar al-Qadhdhafi's claims to have achieved a revolution were on occasion dismissed as "specialization" in political murder.[45] Husayn invented a word to describe them: *al-thawrajiyya* (the revolutionaries by profession), using the Turkish suffix "-ji," which denotes professions and is sometimes so employed in colloquial Arabic. Such people, he said, were egotists by nature, their thought was shallow, and they were more dangerous to the Arab nation than the leaders of the political right.[46] Another pejorative phrase was "thief of the revolution," applied, for instance, to 'Abd al-Salam 'Arif, a collaborator with the Ba'th during its brief first tenure of power in 1963. When he carried out his own coup, he "stole" the revolution from the Ba'th. Iran's Ayatollah Khomeini, for his part, "stole" the "popular revolution" from the Iranians.[47]

It was indeed Khomeini who posed the greatest challenge of all to the Ba'th in Iraq by applying to it his doctrine of "exporting the revolution," just as Iraq itself had wanted to export its own revolution to other Arab countries. This made it necessary to take on Iran not only by means of warfare but also in the field of persuasion and propaganda. The press endeavored to ridicule Iran's attempts at carrying the Islamic revolution into Iraq: that was "the joke of the generation," for the Ba'th itself had much greater "seniority" than the Iranian revolution, and it had been the Ba'thi model that had caused the Iranians "to wake up, though only late in the day," and to follow the Iraqi example.[48] But unlike the Iraqi revolution, Iran's not only had failed to advance the country but also had thrown it back all the way to the dark ages preceding Islam (*jahiliyya*). Oddly enough, Iraqi Shi'is agreed with the spokespeople of the regime in singling out Iraq's revolutionary centrality. For instance, Muhammad Taqi al-Mudarrisi, an Iraqi Shi'i leader, declared that the holy cities in Iraq (holy to the Shi'a, that is) had been the centers from which Iranian revolutionary movements had started out; that was as true of the Constitutional Revolution of 1906 as of Khomeini's. But very much unlike the Ba'th, Mudarrisi saw the advent of the Islamic regime in Iran as the "mother of revolutions" (*umm al-thawrat*) and, in a mirror image of the Iraqi argument, asserted that Iraq should follow the Iranian model. He had to concede, however, that the expected Iraqi Islamic revolution was slow in coming.[49]

But harsh words about Khomeini's regime did not absolve the Ba'th from dealing with the issue of the precise nature of the link between revolution and Islam. Already, 'Aflaq had written that the advent of Islam had been a revolution and Muhammad the first Arab revolutionary. The 1982 party resolutions dealt at length with the issue of religion. They repeated, rather anachronistically, that "the party regards Islam as one of the most powerful revolutions recorded by human history; in the eyes of the party, Muhammad (God's prayer be upon him) was a great leader . . . and a great revolutionary."[50] The party also invested Husayn ('Ali's son and the prophet's grandson) with the title of revolutionary and termed the Arab armies that had carried out the conquests of early Islam "a revolutionary organization." (These themes will be more fully developed in chapters 13 and 14.)

Ridda: From Apostasy to Reaction

The indelibly traumatic event for the Ba'th party was its overthrow in 1963 after ruling for only nine months.[51] The shock was all the greater as it had come from within the regime's inner circle: it was 'Arif, who had held the post of president, who had brought it down. His coup was called *ridda*, today signifying reaction, treachery, deviation, or conspiracy but still loaded with its early historical meaning: apostasy from Islam, as happened among a number of tribes immediately after the death of Muhammad. They were returned to the fold by means of the "wars of the *ridda*" (632–634).

Why did the Ba'th—a self-declared secular party—choose this religiously charged term when it could have used modern language, such as *thawra mudadda* (counterrevolution) or *mu'amara* (conspiracy)? One possible explanation is that the Ba'th considered the term *ridda* better capable than its alternatives to reach and impress the public at large, as it was meaningful to Sunnis and Shi'is alike. But there may have been deeper reasons. For one thing, those who define themselves as secular Muslims remain susceptible to the weight of tradition, and there is a desire—conscious or unconscious—for a link with the Islamic past. In Arab-Muslim societies, the line dividing the present from the past is not firm and clear-cut, and the preference for a rather archaic term may attest to its somewhat blurred implications. For another, *ridda* conveys frustration and hope at the same time in a manner not found in the other possible terms. Just as, historically, it meant both apostasy and the return to the true faith, so for the Ba'th party it meant both the fall and the resolve to regain power. Moreover, the use of the word implied a useful reminder that apostasy was to be punished by death or, if committed by a people, by war.[52] Finally, by denigrating opponents by means of a word associated with disbelief, the Ba'th party itself assumed the role of a body of true believers.

Ridda and *murtaddun* (those who practice *ridda*) go back to the early days of the first Ba'th period and were used by President 'Arif himself. But at that time *ridda* was meant to point either to communists or to opponents of Pan-Arabism. Only after the fall of the Ba'th regime did it start to denote the chain of events that had brought the party down. It was then used very frequently in the Ba'thi media; the fall of the regime was often called "the *ridda* of Black November." Later, the entire period from 1963 until the return of the Ba'th in 1968 became known as "the time of the *ridda*" or the "regime of the *ridda*," sometimes expanded to read "the black, reactionary *ridda*." Ahmad Hasan al-Bakr, the first president of the second Ba'th regime, said that "the great [1968 Ba'th] revolution" had overthrown "the regime of the *ridda*."[53] The fact that in 1963 Bakr had been privy to the anti-Ba'th plot and that he became vice president of the regime that had replaced the party did not trouble him later on. He probably said what he did to clear himself from suspicion and reaffirm his loyalty.

At a later stage, Ba'thi writers tried to give the occurrences of 1963 a different coloration. *Al-Thawra al-'Arabiyya*, the internal party organ, wrote that the lessons of 1963 had later prevented the party from making similar mistakes again. For all the damage it had done, the *ridda* had—historically speaking—given the Ba'th the high level of political experience it demonstrated later on.[54]

The Ba'th party dealt with the *ridda* of 1963 for a long time after 1968, but after its return to power, it expanded the use of the term, applying it to every kind of opposition at home or hostility abroad, whether actual or imaginary. To illustrate: the party's original collaborators, relegated in the second phase of the July 1968 event, became known as *murtaddun*;

so did the "spies" hanged the following year. The Kurdish revolt was a *ridda*, and even the "Prague spring" of 1968 was a *ridda*. The Egyptian-Israeli Interim Agreement of 1975 was described as a move from "aggressiveness to *ridda*" (a rhyme in Arabic) and as an "apostasy" from true Arab nationalism. Most particularly, however, it was employed to denote the regime of the Syrian Ba'th. The Iraqi party spoke of the Syrian coup of February 1966 (which ousted 'Aflaq and his closest associates from the Syrian party) as the "February *ridda*."[55] Since then, the fall of the Ba'th regime in Iraq in 1963 and the Syrian putsch of 1966 were often referred to together as "the two *riddas*." As with the regimes of 'Abd al Salam 'Arif and 'Abd al-Rahman 'Arif in Iraq, so also in Syria the term was then extended to mean the entire duration of Hafiz al-Asad's regime, beginning in 1970. The use of the word *ridda* is more than a mere propaganda device; it is part of the overall struggle for legitimacy: which is the true Ba'th and which is the usurper? The eleventh congress of the Iraqi Ba'th stated that during the first years of the Iraqi Ba'th regime, "the *ridda* in Syria competed with the Iraqi Ba'th and weakened it."[56]

If *ridda* is applied, with great suspicion, to enemies abroad, its meaning and the underlying suspicion are sharper when domestic opponents are meant. Addressing the students at a preparatory school for party membership, Husayn warned his listeners that the roots of *ridda* are found within Iraq and even within the apparatus of the state and that *ridda* was capable of quickly destroying all that had been built up laboriously over many years. He dwelt on the fact that the *ridda* in Czechoslovakia had taken place two full decades after the establishment of communist rule there and said it is imperative for the Ba'th to learn from the experience of others. The party paper that printed Husayn's speech elaborated that *ridda* could have many reasons: weakness; failure to develop once the initial revolution had taken place; or "neglect of the most important bodies of the state, such as the armed forces." *Ridda*, it went on to say, was the "sickness of the revolution." This sickness could attack it by three methods, the worst of which was by armed action (as in the case of the Kurdish rebellion), though it had the advantage of making the forces of the *ridda* immediately detectable. The second was by means of an army putsch, and the third—and most complex—was the slow wearing down of the revolution from within. By this method, the forces of the *ridda* drill a hole, as it were, in the defensive fence of the revolution, and "this slowly becomes a gaping breech and finally an abyss into which the revolution falls." The best way to fend off this danger was to stop being on the defensive and take the offensive.[57]

As in a self-fulfilling prophecy, a "plot" occurred as soon as Husayn had officially finalized his takeover in 1979. Quite possibly, there was no actual plot but rather an application of the doctrine of preventive action. The plot, if there was one, cost the lives of twenty-one members from among the party's highest echelons. It was not termed a "conspiracy" but rather a *ridda* and was compared in great detail with the *ridda* of earliest

Islam. In a speech after the execution of the twenty-one, Husayn reminded his listeners that Muhammad, too, had been betrayed by some of his close associates (the *sahaba*). He referred to the "wars of the *ridda*" and went on to say that the history of Islam was replete with splits and rivalries, often enough led by those who had been leaders of the Islamic community. On another occasion, he justified the shedding of blood by saying, "Yes, indeed; whenever we discover someone [engaged in treason] we behead him without mercy and in public. This is what our forefathers did at the beginnings of [the era of] Islam. Khalid bin al-Walid beheaded thirty thousand people during the wars of the *ridda* because of his loyalty to his mission and his faithfulness to his belief."[58] This need to rely on examples of the heroic age of pristine Islam gradually turned into a characteristic of Husayn and his rhetoric. Not only did he borrow words from the distant past, but also he transposed modern occurrences into events comparable in all their details to the great turning points of past history.

The theme of *ridda* came to the fore again in connection with Syria's and Libya's cooperation with Iran during Iraq's war with that country. Asad and Qadhdhafi were compared to Musaylima, the false prophet who led his men against the Muslims in the "wars of the *ridda*" and was killed. "Can a nation win . . . while being led by types like Musaylima?"[59] Not only Asad and Qadhdhafi were called *murtaddun*, but also the rulers of postrevolutionary Iran. Somewhat illogically, they were also spoken of as belonging to the *jahiliyya*, the era preceding Islam. The language of the press came close to proclaiming Saddam Husayn a true prophet by contrasting him with leaders of the Musaylima kind: "Praise be to God! While you saw the *murtaddun* in Iran and their ignorance [*jahiliyya*], you have sent your prophet along the straight path and [set him] on the road of true justice for him to give light [to the nation] and guide it."[60]

2

Ba'th
The Word and the Party

The Ba'th: "Permanent Revolution and the Renewal of Youth"

Clause 6 of the Ba'th party's "Permanent Principles" reads: "The Ba'th is a revolutionary party. It believes that its principal aims in [the process of] realizing an Arab national renaissance and of building socialism will not be attained except by revolution and struggle."[1] Yet it is not "revolutionism" that marks off the Ba'th from earlier Arab movements; rather, it is its firmly ideological character and the existence of a program of action. No less important is its prolonged grip on power, which has been longer than that of any of its predecessors. The party has so far ruled for more than a third of modern Iraq's existence as an independent state. This would seem all the more remarkable considering that the Ba'th, its ideology, and its vocabulary are not homegrown Iraqi products. The Ba'th originated in Syria, and nearly all of its founders, ideologues, and actual leaders during its formative years were Syrians. No Iraqi was among them. The original Ba'th took shape in the 1940s, and only a decade later was it "exported" to Iraq. This explains why the original political language of the Ba'thi "branch" there was a foreign product. Only much later, after the party had been in power in Iraq for a length of time, did it develop authentic and unique, typically Iraqi elements of its own.

The name Ba'th (or to give its full name, Hizb al-Ba'th al-'Arabi al-Ishtiraki, the Arab Socialist Ba'th Party) was coined by a Syrian belonging to the 'Alawi community, Zaki al-Arsuzi, one of the three principal authors of Ba'thi doctrine. Arsuzi formed a circle of six like-minded men in Damascus in 1940 under the name al-Ba'th al-'Arabi. In 1943, the two other founding fathers, Michel 'Aflaq and Salah al-Din Bitar, adopted the same name for their group. Some of Arsuzi's followers joined them, but he himself did not. 'Aflaq and Bitar had earlier headed a group called the *ihya'* (revive) association.[2] However, as this word is neutral, they prob-ably decided to adopt the term ba'th with its deeper meaning. In early religious literature, the root *ba'th* is used to connote the sending of a prophet or the resurrection of the dead. The Last Judgment is sometimes called *yawm al-ba'th*.[3]

Arsuzi himself explained in one of his works why he used that particu-lar word. In doing so, he drew both on Arab tradition and on Western thought, with which he was familiar since he had graduated from the Sorbonne. He discerned two forms of "renewal" in European history: the Renaissance and the rise of nineteenth-century European nationalism. The former, he held, was an attempt at reviving Greek and Roman cul-ture; the latter a reawakening of an ancient ethnic, cultural, and linguis-tic heritage. Among the Arabs, too, Arsuzi argued, *ba'th* meant the return to the "springs of national [*qawmi*] life": the revival of the language and of the cultural genius of the Arabs.

Surprisingly, Arsuzi found the glory he wanted to revive in the pre-Islamic era of the *jahiliyya* (ignorance) rather than in early Islam. In his view, the *jahiliyya* was the source of the Arabic language and its litera-ture; it was an era in which poetry and heroism were held in highest esteem. He contrasted them unfavorably with the piety and asceticism of later ages. In Arsuzi's opinion, one of the most salient means to revive the glories of the past was the "return to the language." Language was "the most important expression of the Arab genius." Interestingly, Arsuzi him-self did not dwell on the religious overtones of the word *ba'th*—perhaps because his convictions were of the nationalist and secular kind—though it is hard to imagine that he was altogether unaware of them. His declared major aims were the revival of Arab culture (both renewed and adapted to modern conditions) and the establishment of a comprehensive Arab state (*dawla*) under whose banner all Arabs would unite.[4]

'Aflaq for his part spoke of the revival of the Arab spirit rather than of the language. The dire circumstances of the Arabs in modern times, he averred, had roots going back hundreds of years; they did not, as many others thought, result from the advent of imperialism. Such a long period of decline attested to "extremely deep" fault lines running through theArab nation. It was therefore most imperative to restore (*ba'th*) the Arab spirit and give back to the Arab nation its former positive and active outlook. This required carrying out a revolution powerful enough to deeply agi-tate the national spirit. The very concept of *Ba'th* was tantamount to revolution.[5]

It was only thirty years later, when the use of Islamic symbols and as-sociations was already frequent in Iraqi Ba'th parlance, that a party leader referred explicitly to the religious content of the party's name. The name *Ba'th*, Saddam Husayn explained, was not chosen incidentally; rather, it was meant to evoke its original Islamic connotations of revival. Hence, he said, "every believing Muslim is a Ba'thi, even if he does not belong to the party."[6] Husayn's "court writers" for their part elaborated on another old meaning of the word: the sending of a prophet. In a book on Husayn's scale of values, Zuhayr Sadiq Rida al-Khalidi wrote that the "sending" (*inbi'ath*) of a leader of Husayn's greatness was "not coincidental": "it stemmed from centuries of suffering, ever since the conquest of Baghdad by [the Mongol leader] Hulagu in 1258."[7] Similarly, the daily *al-Qadisiyya* wrote that the birth of Husayn was in itself a revival (*ba'th*) of "the spirit of Iraq and of the Arab nation."[8] Here, the personality cult was reinforced by recourse to providence.

"A Single Arab Nation"

The name *Ba'th* at once evokes the party's central slogans: "A single Arab nation with an eternal mission" and "Unity, freedom, socialism." The first slogan echoes several verses of the Qur'an where the words *umma wahida* (one nation) appear. Verse 209 of the sura *al-Baqara*, for instance, reads: "The people were one nation; then God sent forth the Prophets, good tidings to bear and warning." The whole party phrase, with its internal rhyme in Arabic, elicits a longing for completeness, a yearning for a messianic transformation. The glorious past of the Arabs is made the source and aim of emulation. Arsuzi wrote: "The Arabs conquered the world in order to civilize it and for that vision they sacrificed their lives. . . . They spread their rule from the Chinese Wall to the Atlantic Ocean and from the center of Europe to the center of Africa. . . . One caliph, one law, one official language."[9]

The word *umma* worked magic, not only with the first Ba'th ideologues but also with subsequent generations. Arsuzi surmised, probably correctly, that it had a common root with *umm* (mother). The *umma*, he says, relates to its members as a mother does to her child. The *umma* is the wellspring of all things: language, art, and everything to do with public life. The Arab nation renews itself like the phoenix (whose resurrection Arsuzi describes with the word *ba'th*). Foreigners may regard Arabs as a passing meteor, but in reality, he concludes, they are a steady beacon.[10]

In classical Arabic, *umma* had many meanings: a group of people, religion, time, as well as physical and moral qualities marking off one group of people from another.[11] In the political sense, it developed through various stages, beginning with its use to denote the community of Muslim believers, up to its modern meaning of the nation as the body politic.[12] In Iraq during the 1920s and up to the 1960s, *umma* was used to connote the Iraqi people (rather than the Arab nation as a whole) and was employed as an alternative to *sha'b*. In his famous memorandum of 1932,

King Faysal used the term *umma* several times when speaking of the Iraqi people.[13] The lower house of parliament was called *majlis al-umma* under the monarchy, again making *umma* refer only to the Iraqi people. But the word also carried the broader meaning of "the Arab nation."[14]

After the rise of the Ba'th to power, however, the word *umma* was reserved for the Arab nation as a whole and ceased to be employed in the narrower, Iraqi sense. Rather, the Iraqi people were now described as forming "part of the Arab *umma*" and as "the revolutionary base of the Arab *umma*." The first definition, admitting a possible contradiction in people's self-definition between being Arab and being Iraqi, was to become highly problematic (a point we shall return to later on). Unlike an Iraqi identity, an Arab one denies the separate character of the Kurds, who are ethnically and linguistically non-Arab. The second claim raised Iraq above the other components of the all-Arab mosaic and assigned it a leading role in the overall Arab revival. Addressing a gathering of military men in 1978, Husayn said that the Iraqi regime was resolved to make the country a firm base for the Arab nation as a whole and assume a leading role both within and outside Iraq.[15]

This sense of mission (*risala*) was clearly derived from the main tenets of Ba'thi doctrine, but it had historical roots as well and was also used to respond to immediate political requirements. *Risala* occurs once in the Qur'an, in the sura *al-A'raf*, verse 77: "I have delivered to you the message of my Lord." The qur'anic meaning is that of prophetic mission addressed to all mankind.[16] It is in this sense that 'Aflaq employs the term. The Ba'thi *risala*, he says, is both all-Arab and universal. In an essay written in 1946, 'Aflaq explains that the use of the term "eternal mission" signifies that the Arabs do not accept their present deplorable circumstances and do not renounce their claim to a place of honor among the nations. Therefore, their principal aim is the renewal of the nation. On another occasion, he speaks of the "new Arab mission" to all peoples, saying that it is the gift the Arabs make to mankind.[17] Though there is no direct evidence, we may assume that 'Aflaq was influenced by the French phrase *mission civilisatrice*, which was used to denote one of the major aims of the French mandate for Syria and Lebanon. The theme is taken up in a clause of the Ba'th statutes of 1947 that reads: "The Arab nation has an eternal mission. This mission becomes evident again and again in different forms at different times in history. It strives to renew human values, to expedite human progress, and to strengthen harmony and mutual assistance between nations."[18]

Following early Ba'th thinking, Iraq ascribed to itself an Arab as well as a universal mission. In Saddam Husayn's words: "A nation which has no national [*watani*], all-Arab and universal mission of its own, will not have a well-defined and dignified historical role to play." The Arabs, he went on, had attained great cultural achievements at a time when others were locked in darkness. Iraq's inter-Arab mission was threefold: to defend the Arab nation, to unite it, and to revive its past glories. Similarly, before the outbreak of the war against Iran in September 1980, he declared: "Anyone showing hostility toward Iraq or the Arab nation will find us in the vanguard of war against him."[19]

But it was during the war with Iran that this particular motif turned into the veritable cornerstone of Iraqi rhetoric. Iraq stood "like a mighty dam to defend the nation against an outburst of hatred from the east." If Iraq had been conquered, "the Arab nation would have fallen into the hands of Iran like a ripe fruit."[20] Soldiers who were decorated during the war received medals bearing the words "In defense of the [Arab] nation, its glory and might, against the Iranian enemy." Once Iraq had emerged victorious, the Arab nation "felt absolute confidence in itself."[21] Underlying the rhetoric is an Iraqi desire to seek a framework of "belonging" and find assurance in it in times of crisis.

Together with the sense of mission, there is a tendency to relate to Iraq as the symbol of, and the spearhead for, the return to past glories. On the eve of the invasion of Kuwait, for instance, Husayn spoke of the Arab nation's unique opportunity to regain, through the efforts of Baghdad, its former place of global centrality. "The opportunity we speak of is a historic opportunity; the Arab nation will either . . . move to regain its . . . universal task, or else it will remain in the state its enemies wish to see it in."[22] Iraq is capable of fulfilling this task, one newspaper explained, because it had the *rafidan* (the two rivers; an idiomatic expression customarily used to denote the Tigris and the Euphrates). In this context, the writer makes clear, the two are the Ba'th and Husayn. The Arab nation itself was "born through the birth of the Ba'th and the birth of Saddam Husayn, for through them it found what it desired and through them, or rather through him, it achieved greatness."[23]

The use of the term "mission" also elicited comparison with the original Islamic mission. The Arabs were the nation that Allah chose for a leading role. The Arabs, Husayn maintained, must act "in the light of the heavenly mission which [the angel] Gabriel passed on to Muhammad."[24] Iraq, it was stated, had proved up to the task. The heroism and fighting quality of the Iraqi army did not fall short of that required of an "army of the eternal mission," and Husayn "realized the meaning of the Islamic mission for the unity of the nation and the building of its noble human culture." Trying to combine the political and theological meanings of the word *ba'th*, Husayn said that the Ba'th party was in itself the "renewal of the nation's mission" (i.e., its original, Islamic mission). It was only during the Gulf War, he went on, after the struggle of the Ba'th party had already lasted fifty years, that the Iraqi army "rose to the level of the [Islamic] mission." And it was only then, he said, that the Arab nations fully recognized Iraq's role.[25]

The Threefold Way: Unity, Freedom, Socialism

After the motif of "mission," the second most important Ba'thi slogan was "Unity, freedom, socialism" (*Wahda, hurriyya, ishtirakiyya*). It is a short, easily remembered, emotionally appealing catchphrase encapsulating the party's principal aims. There is an echo here of other revolutions and their triple slogans: the French "*Liberté, égalité, fraternité*"; or the Bolshevik "Soil, bread, peace." The order in which the three are named does not necessary reflect their relative weight. "Freedom" and "socialism" were imported terms initially foreign to Arab society. "Unity" is not a term of long standing either; it does not occur once in the Qur'an.

The party's early ideologues differed in the importance they attributed to each of the three components. Arsuzi put freedom first.[26] ʿAflaq for his part wrote that all three were equally important but that unity had "priority and greater moral weight and the ranks of the Baʿth cannot ignore that fact."[27] Today it is evident that the party has indeed followed ʿAflaq. The reason may be ʿAflaq's greater influence on party doctrine; more probably, unity comes first because it elicits greater enthusiasm and has greater resonance among a greater number of Arabs. Obviously, it is easier to grasp than the other two.

Hurriyya is derived from an old Semitic root, *hurr*, meaning that a man was free rather than a slave; it appears in this sense in the Qur'an.[28] *Hurriyya* is not found in the fourteenth-century dictionary *Lisan al-ʿArab*. It seems to have been used for the first time in Napoleon's famous proclamation to the Egyptians of 1798, where it appears as an attribute of the French republic. At that time, it was still generally used to tell a free man from a slave, and its significance was legal rather than political.[29] In the nineteenth century, Arab thinkers under the influence of the West began discussing the concept of freedom. The Egyptian ideologue and politician Ahmad Lutfi al-Sayyid did much to give it currency in Arab society. In Iraq, the concept began to be used and discussed in the twentieth century. A periodical called *al-Hadith*, which started appearing in 1927, declared itself to be a "free" publication because "it is devoted to free thought."[30] General Bakr Sidqi and his associates spoke of expanding personal freedom in political and economic life. In the same breath, however, they declared that "all the rights" of their predecessors should be taken away because they would use them "to do away with freedom."[31] This ambiguity was characteristic of all the regimes of modern Iraq, and of none more so than the Baʿth.

In the twentieth century, *hurriyya* underwent another semantic change. In addition to "freedom," it now came to mean the liberation of Arab countries from Western domination (direct or indirect).[32] When the Baʿth party coined its slogans, it employed *hurriyya* in both senses simultaneously. As ʿAflaq put it: "Freedom from the outside, against the foreigner, the imperialist; and freedom inside, opposite oppressive rulers."[33] Some scholars hold that, to the Baʿth, *hurriyya* meant only independence from outside domination.[34] But one cannot overlook that Baʿth statutes lay down that the party "believes freedom of speech, freedom of association, and freedom of worship and art to be sacred; no government can impair them." In actual practice, however, freedom from imperialist overlordship was a great deal more important to the Ba'th than respect for individual rights. This comes through in an essay by 'Aflaq written in 1947. The West, he wrote, "accuses us of total or partial disrespect for human rights . . . and of lack of belief in the concept of liberty or in civil rights or in the people's right to equality and sovereignty and [claims] that we do not uphold the freedom of worship and opinion." He does not deny the charges; on the contrary, he goes on to say that Arab politicians and even intellectuals only pretend to accept such foreign principles and that they do so with the sole aim of warding off Western attacks on them.[35]

Quite in keeping with 'Aflaq's approach, the Iraqi Ba'th did not even feign respect for domestic liberty and had no inhibitions about denying it to its citizens.[36] For some two decades, *hurriyya* simply did not figure in the Ba'th political vocabulary in Iraq. One of the very few exceptions can be found in *al-Thawra al-'Arabiyya* in 1976. It wrote: "The *hurriyya* the party struggles for [signifies] the elimination of all kinds of exploitation and oppression which are being forced upon the Arab nation"; however, the Ba'th rejects "all falsified forms of freedom such as are current in bourgeois democracy." The party "has created a link between liberty and social justice, and between individual freedom and the liberation of the soil [of Palestine]."[37] By wrapping it in a thick layer of verbiage about the liberation of the nation and the soil, the paper emasculates the proper political and civil meaning of freedom. As will be shown in later chapters, in its actual governmental practice the Ba'th party has stifled every idea of liberalism, parliamentarianism, or democracy.

There was, however, a certain departure in this regard after the end of the war against Iran in 1988. The war's conclusion had unleashed social, economic, and political pressures that the regime thought wise to mitigate by means of its press. Already in 1980, Husayn had declared that journalists must write without "being afraid of whether the state is pleased or displeased with what they write." He encouraged them to "analyze global or Arab affairs with complete freedom." But it was only in 1989, after a public debate on pluralism, a new constitution, and freedom of expression, that the press hesitantly, and for a short time only, took up the issue of freedom, in particular freedom of expression. Some journalists dared to write that freedom was indivisible and that no part of it must be impaired; that the right to criticize social or political developments was inalienable; and that true freedom meant the right to protect citizens from the military, from professional politicians, and from "false" ideologues.[38]

Other journalists who understood the game better came out with harsh attacks on freedom. "There is no more than a hair's breadth between anarchy and liberty," one wrote. The same writer warned of the danger of freedom sliding over into anarchy, as it had done many times in Arab and world history, and concluded, "I am afraid of freedom, for the sake of my people and my country, and I do not seek freedom. . . . It is under the rule of law that each man knows his worth and his own rights, as well as those of others." Challenging this view, another journalist wrote that only backward peoples were afraid of freedom; not so the Iraqis, who were entitled to full democratic freedom.[39] Interestingly enough, nobody made the point that "freedom" was part of the Ba'th party's official slogans and that to ignore it meant to undermine the party's legitimacy. But then the entire episode was short-lived, and just as it had been started by a signal from the authorities, so it was called off by one.

The concept of socialism reached the Arab world at the turn of the century. It was first rendered as *ijtima'iyya*, then as *ishtirakiyya*, meaning participation or commonalty. One of the first to use it was Jamal al-Din al-Afghani, who spoke of *ishtirakiyya islamiyya* in articles written between 1892 and 1897. Some twenty years later, an Egyptian Copt, Musa Salama, wrote a booklet entitled *al-Ishtirakiyya*. But in his generation, socialism was still generally thought of as foreign and dangerous.[40] In the 1930s, however (somewhat ironically, under the influence of German national socialism and Italian fascism), socialist movements of sorts began springing up in the Arab world. One such radical, quasi-socialist grouping was al-Ahali in Iraq.[41]

But the most representative Arab body to call itself socialist was the Ba'th, and it was 'Aflaq who coined the expression "Arab socialism," a phrase calculated to neutralize the foreign flavor of the word "socialism" and also to mark it off from the Marxist and social democrat varieties. Arab socialism developed in no small measure as a response to the rise of communist parties in the Arab world. "Arab socialists" combated Marxism and objected in particular to the latter's rejection of nationalism. Indeed, if it is possible to point to a single crucial characteristic that distinguishes Arab socialism from the other kinds, it is its intrinsic link with the concept of nationalism.

Quite consistently, Ba'thi socialism is not an aim in its own right but is subject to national objectives and the cause of Arab unity. Another feature that distinguishes it from other forms of socialism is its foundation in Islamic moral philosophy. It stresses social justice as it was traditionally understood in Islamic societies and is reformist rather than revolutionary in its approach to economic and social change.[42] Yet it affirms that revolution is the only road leading to such change. The revolution issues from the "popular masses." Workers and peasants are its vanguard. Landowners and merchants will have no part in the revolution because they are "reactionary."

Apart from such rather crude generalizations, one cannot find a real theory of Arab socialism. Much of the writing on the subject is obscure. Generalizations abound, such as in Arsuzi's definition that socialism means "preparing all citizens to participate in the common destiny."[43] 'Aflaq endeavored to enhance the value of Arab socialism by lessening that of the Western varieties, which he described as "negative." In particular, he was critical of the communists who, he said, "tried to cure one sickness by means of another." Of Arab socialism, he said that he considered it a "doctrine [*din*] of life and a victory of life over death." It was most closely linked with nationalism; indeed, it was "the body for the soul which is Arab unity."[44]

The Ba'th statutes of 1947 made an attempt to grapple with the issue of implementing socialism. They called for a just division of wealth; for state ownership of public services, mines, major factories, and domestic and foreign trade; for workers' participation in plant management; and for limits on land ownership. Significantly, however, they also recognized the right to private property. On the other hand, they were silent on the question of land reform and did not mention nationalization, so it remained unclear how state ownership should be brought about. Trade unions or any other form of mass organization do not figure in the statutes.[45] In practical terms, little was done to introduce socialism in the Arab world until Egypt's Nasir borrowed Ba'thi doctrines, made them popular throughout the Arab world, and, in the early 1960s, based his political program on them.[46]

In Iraq, we find one of the first uses of *ishtirakiyya* in 1921 when a newspaper by the name of *Dijla* wrote that socialism had "become the most powerful concept."[47] It was soon given currency by groupings and parties such as al-Ahali, the National Democratic Party (al-Hizb al-watani al-dimuqrati), the Communist Party, and the Ba'th. By the time the Ba'th came to power, some socialist measures had already been taken—some under Qasim,[48] some during the first period of Ba'th rule, and some under the two 'Arif brothers. These earlier measures, together with the ideological commitment of the Ba'th, exerted strong pressures on the party to adopt a radical socialist policy. The Syrian Ba'th party, which accused the Iraqi party of "rightist deviations," added pressures of its own. Moreover, Iraqi communists were breathing down the neck of the Ba'th. The Ba'th sometimes adopted radical measures for the sole purpose of outdoing the communists. Indeed, the rivalry with the communists—whether overt or concealed, as between 1973 and 1978, when the communists entered into a "coalition" with the Ba'th—had a major effect on Ba'thi political language.

To define its overall aspirations with regard to socialism, the Iraqi Ba'th used the phrase "Building a new, socialist society." Only socialism was capable of rescuing the peoples of Asia, Africa, and Latin America. At the same time, with a broad hint in the direction of the communists, the Ba'th warned of imitating "socialist experiments" in "certain" other regions. In 1976, a Ba'th document declared explicitly: "The socialism of the liberated and united [Arab] fatherland is not a stage on the road to communism."[49]

The basic commitment of the Ba'th to socialism was reaffirmed in Iraq's provisional constitution of 1970, which defined the central objective of the Iraqi republic as "the establishment of a single, comprehensive Arab state and the realization of a socialist regime." The Iraqi Ba'th party congress of 1973 made the same point and went on to say that the party's aim must be to "strengthen the socialist sector, turn it into the best [field of the ecomomy], and make it dominant."[50] This was carried out by the application of a policy of etatism that made the state dominant in most economic fields. Foreign holdings in the oil industry, Iraq's major source of wealth, had already been nationalized by the government in 1972. Military industries were also owned and run by the state. Private business found itself relegated to the sidelines. Land reform continued much along the lines of earlier regimes, and the establishment of agricultural cooperatives and of collective farms was accelerated. The trade unions that were set up were controlled by the Ba'th.

All the above measures were taken in the first decade of Ba'th rule. Already, however, voices were raised in protest against socialist policies, at times in the context of anticommunism, at times in response to failures in their implementation. The reaction against socialist policies was led personally by Saddam Husayn, the very man who had instituted them in the first place. Thus, he said that Iraq would not abandon socialism but would apply it in its own way. A balance must be struck between the implementation of socialism on the one hand and popular consciousness on the other. Socialism must not be allowed to erase the permitted measures of creativity, initiative, and competition.[51]

Elaborating on 'Aflaq's obscure statements on socialism, Husayn said that socialism must be understood as meeting the requirements of people "in all their material aspects, and not solely as filling their bellies." In similarly ambivalent fashion, Husayn advocated state ownership of the means of production but dissociated himself from carrying that trend too far; if this was done, Iraq would end up as a "state of shops [*dawlat dakakin*]."[52] This kind of halfhearted criticism was made explicit in two speeches by Husayn in 1981, when he explained that the party was a living organism and must be capable of change and of adapting itself to circumstances. Socialism was not a rigid dogma, and if it proved a failure, a different approach must be sought. He himself, he went on to say, had noted, by means of his personal contacts with peasants, the lack of popularity of socialist measures among them. He had understood that they wished to leave the cooperatives. Hence, they should be allowed to do so, particularly because often enough "the achievements of the private sector far exceed those of the socialist sector."[53]

The most scathing criticism of Iraqi socialism was expressed the following year in the political report of the 1982 party congress (convened while the Iraqi-Iranian war was in progress, after an interval of some ten years since the preceding congress). Clearly inspired by Husayn, the report expressed grave disappointment with socialism and its application. It complained of the public sector's domination of industry, agriculture, trade, and public services, taking up Husayn's expression of a "state of shops." It referred with disapproval to the blurring of the line between the public and the private sector and to the stifling of the latter. Implicitly accusing what was obviously a more doctrinaire trend within the Ba'th, it spoke of those who had failed to properly understand the concept of socialism; it was, after all, not an unchangeable dogma. In conclusion, the report demanded limiting the public sector to big plants and allowing more room for private business in all fields of economic endeavor. In this way, Iraq would be better able to compete in the race between the capitalist and the socialist economies.[54]

The prolonged fighting and the many pressures of the wartime economy further eroded the ideology of socialism. In 1987, more of the socialist measures of the past were reversed. *Al-Thawra* argued that there was now a "new Ba'thi way" that called for "opening up" the private sector because it had proved more efficient than the state sector.[55] This was the signal for the Ba'th to initiate what it called "the administrative revolution," which was to turn the clock back and lead to massive privatization. Land reform was revoked; the Ministry of Agriculture and Land Reform became the plain Ministry of Agriculture. Apparently, there was some resistance to the "new way" within the party. Husayn found it necessary to warn of "fanatics" who considered that there was no possible alternative to socialism. On the contrary, he went on: rigid pursuit of socialist doctrines would make people tire of socialism. As previously, Husayn stressed that he had been impressed by personal contacts: during a tour of the marshlands in the south, farmers had asked him to "rescue" them from the cooperatives.[56]

There can be no doubt that the antisocialist turn was greatly influenced by the collapse of the communist parties in Eastern Europe. Most interesting, however, the ambivalence toward socialism continued to be part of the Iraqi political discourse. While Saddam Husayn and the Iraqi press were attacking socialism, the 1990 draft for a new Iraqi constitution reaffirmed that "the political regime of Iraq is based on democracy and socialism." It required candidates for the presidency to "believe in socialism and to possess the qualities of a socialist."[57] There is no room to assume that such ambiguities attest to the existence of two different trends within the party; rather, they point to the ideological convolutions characteristic of Husayn in his endeavors to preserve political myths while acting against them or emptying them of all content. Eventually, at the 1991 party congress, he came out with a formula that seemed to bring to an end the long meanderings of the Ba'thi concept of socialism: "Socialism is social justice inspired by the practice of the early Muslim-Arabs and adapted to each [subsequent] stage."[58]

"Arab *unity*—our most cherished goal—has been lingering for decades. We proclaim it and ache for it to be realized, but it is being shattered before our eyes like a phantom."[59] These are 'Aflaq's words, uttered in the late 1960s when pan-Arabism had already passed its peak. They sum up the experience of a whole Arab generation: a strong, almost obsessive yearning for unity, followed by a sense of frustration and impotence as soon as an attempt is made to turn it into practical politics. All the while, many continue to think of it as the cure-all for Arab woes.

Just as the theory of Arab unity is ambivalent, the word *wahda* itself is remarkable in that it can express "standing apart" and "unity" at one and the same time. Its early connotations were primarily loneliness and separateness. *Lisan al-ʿArab* has only these meanings; so does Edward Lane's nineteenth-century *Arabic English Lexicon*. The latter mentions the expression *layla al-wahda* (the night of loneliness), the first night after burial, in which the soul remains in the tomb before it goes to heaven.[60] Only in the early twentieth-century dictionary *Al-Munjid* is there a listing of the sense of "unity."

Another problematic aspect of the word is that it may be used in a somewhat abstract manner—for instance, when speaking of "like-minded men" or of "hearts being united"—but it may also mean "union" in the formal, constitutional, or legal sense. Arab ideologues and politicians were not always careful to distinguish between one use or the other; nor did they make clear whether the harmony of ideas and sentiment precedes formal union or the other way around. Formal union was also used loosely: its meaning might vary from "merger" (*wahda indimajiyya*) to "confederation" or "federation." Such usage makes it difficult for researchers to follow closely the emergence of ideas and the changes they go through later on.

The founding fathers of the Baʿth were neither the first nor the last to take up the issue of Arab unity, nor were they the most original of the many Arab thinkers whom it preoccupied. But they offered up their doctrine as if it contained the secret key to Arab unity and presented their party as the only grouping in the Arab world totally faithful to the idea of unity and alone capable of realizing it.[61] What was it that made this aim paramount? More than anything else, it was perceived as the way to achieve strength and power. In Arsuzi's words, "We Arabs are so numerous that this [alone] can raise us to the position of peoples who influence the fate of the world. All we have to do . . . is to achieve unity, and then we shall be as strong as the Soviet Union or the United States."[62] But such a *wahda*, as ʿAflaq said, must be more than just institutional; it must encompass "minds, thoughts, feelings, and traditions, so that Arab society will turn into a society of unity, homogeneity, solidarity, and harmony."[63]

This could only be achieved through struggle. Unity was not "something mechanical"; it would not simply emerge by its own accord. Circumstances might be unhelpful or even hostile. A kind of vicious circle existed: "If the Arab nation does not struggle for unity, there will be no unity in the struggle." Unity must be militant and armed; it must be on the offensive. The great majority of the people must bear arms to achieve it and to defend it once it comes about. Unity's greatest enemies are imperialism and Israel, who regard Arab unity as a grave danger to themselves. As soon as they sense any measure of success on the part of the seekers of unity, they will try to "send the Arabs to hell." Israel was set up for no other purpose than to obstruct unity. Taken all in all, the struggle for unity is the most difficult of the fights the Arabs have to engage in.[64]

In Iraq, Pan-Arabism was older than the writings of Arsuzi or ʿAflaq. Iraqis were among the first in the Arab world to formulate its doctrines.[65]

To give just one example: in the 1930s, Sami Shawkat preached a radical version of Arab unity. He held that "all the Arabs are deeply immersed in Arab nationalism [*qawmiyya*; i.e., all-Arab nationalism]." He went on: "Our past, our present, and our future cry out to us today: 'Unite!'" Education in all Arab countries must prepare young people for "Arabism." If this was done, a new, young, "homogeneous" generation would arise and pave the road to unity.[66]

In Iraq, the issue of Arab unity was more complex than in any other Arab country. Throughout its existence as an independent state, the country has been torn between two forms of national cohesion: *wahda wataniyya* (signifying unity within Iraq) and *wahda qawmiyya* (all-Arab unity). It was a tension that had greatly preoccupied Iraqi leaders before the advent of the Ba'th, but it became more pointed after that party's rise to power. This was so because, on the one hand, the Ba'th was firmly committed to its pan-Arab ideology, but on the other, it sought unity at home and attempted to overcome the country's grave religious and ethnic divisions. Ideally, the two forms of unity should have complemented each other. President Ahmad Hasan al-Bakr, for instance, said in a speech in 1972 that Iraq "must move quickly to realize [Iraqi] national unity [*wahda wataniyya*] because that was the way to place all-Arab unity on firm foundations."[67]

In actual fact, the two clashed sharply. The Kurds, as well as some of the Shi'is, objected to the very idea of Arab unity. Instead of each being a sizable segment of Iraqi society with significant domestic bargaining power, in a wider Arab body they would become small, insignificant, and powerless groupings. Therefore, whenever the issue of uniting Iraq with another Arab country arose, Kurds and to a lesser extent Shi'is came out against it. As in a mirror image, it was the numerical and political strength of the Kurds and Shi'is that made the ruling Sunni Arab minority feel insecure and isolated and pushed it into seeking a broader power base in unity schemes with other Sunni Arab countries. Throughout, the issue of domestic cohesion proved inseparable from that of Arab unity.

From the outset, the second Ba'th regime drew on three sources to make Pan-Arabism a tenet of the political theory and a principle of political practice: the pre-Ba'th Iraqi heritage; Ba'th ideology; and an ingredient added later by the regime—the expectation that *wahda* would provide the jumping-off point for the establishment of Iraqi hegemony in the Arab world. The more strongly such convictions were held, the more relentlessly they clashed with domestic and inter-Arab realities. In the 1970s, the Arab world had already had its fill of unity slogans and of the long series of failures in trying to implement them. For the Ba'th to keep speaking the worn-out language of yesterday meant widening the gulf between words and action. But even the Ba'th idiom began to show signs of exhaustion with the outmoded ideas and slogans. Though still in full bloom in the 1970s, by the 1980s they were overcome by fatigue, and the Ba'th party was looking for alternatives.

The provisional constitution of 1970 had declared the "establishment of a single Arab state" to be the "central aim" of the Iraqi republic.[68] In 1972, during the abortive attempts to bring about a union between Iraq, Syria, and Egypt, the Revolutionary Command Council reaffirmed that action for the sake of unity had been, was, and would continue to be a "cornerstone of [Ba'thi] doctrine and struggle." Echoing 'Aflaq, the council spoke of "militant unity [*wahda muqatila*]."[69] In 1975, the Council issued a decree granting Iraqi citizenship to every Arab who applied for it. Its purpose, the council explained, was "to put into place objective foundations for the unity of all the members of the Arab nation in all its parts." Also in 1975, Husayn asserted: "We are all unionists [*wahdawiyyun*]. [To us,] unity is a strategic concept and all our ideological, political, social, and economic attitudes stem from it." No "surrogate [*badil*])" was acceptable.[70] The eleventh Pan-Arab party congress (1977) proclaimed that the party was "the pioneer of unity" and was correctly called "the party of unity [*hizb al-wahda*]." In its final report, the congress claimed that "for the first time ... after the fall of the Abbasids [in 1258], there existed in the Arab homeland a truly national [*qawmi*; i.e., all-Arab] state."[71]

Iraq's actual attempts at unity—in 1972 with Syria and Egypt and in 1978 and 1979 with Syria alone—came to nothing. It is beyond the scope of this study to detail the reasons for those failures.[72] Suffice it to say that the failures (and in particular the second, more serious one) contributed to the erosion of *wahdawi* talk. Already during the negotiations, some ambiguity can be discerned in Husayn's various statements. At times, he spoke of unity with Syria as a merger of two states into a single new one; at other times, he warned that unity must not look like a "wedding party"; rather, it required a great deal of caution as well as ideological and political maturity.[73]

Soon after the breakdown of the Syrian-Iraqi talks, we find in the early 1980s a change in the terminology relating to unity in the press as well as in Husayn's utterances. True, the word *wahda* was still being used, but quite often it was replaced by other, less binding and less explicit expressions such as *tadamun* (solidarity), *takaful* (mutual responsibility), *ta'awun* (cooperation, mutual assistance), or *'alaqat akhawiyya* (fraternal relations). They attested to a sobering-up process in the wake of the failed unity schemes. This was as true of Iraq as it was of the Arab world at large. No less important, some Arab states had found alternatives of a looser sort that could not measure up to the union of states but possessed the advantage of being feasible. In 1981, for instance, the Gulf Cooperation Council was set up, implicitly acknowledging that being second best was better than nothing at all. Another factor influencing Iraqi parlance was the war with Iran, which necessitated cooperation with other Arab countries, particularly in the Gulf, on terms acceptable to them. In their eyes, Iraq's insistence on mergers had something threatening about it, and Baghdad felt the need to tone it down.

The first clear sign of a change in this direction came in February 1980, when Saddam Husayn (only some seven months after taking over the presidency) issued what he called "an all-Arab proclamation." Today, we can say with assurance that its wording was preparing the ground for the opening of war with Iran, which started the following September. The proclamation purported to offer a new basis for inter-Arab relations; it did not employ the word *wahda* in any of its eight points. Instead, it spoke of "solidarity among all the Arab states against any acts of hostility . . . on the part of a foreign [*ajnabi*; i.e., non-Arab] party acting to impair the territorial sovereignty of any Arab state or entering into actual warfare against it." Furthermore, it contained a clause prohibiting any Arab country from using force against another. (Ten years later, at the time of the invasion of Kuwait, this became a good example of Iraq's policy of saying one thing and doing another.) With regard to the economy, the proclamation stresses the principle of *takaful* (mutual responsibility), here used to convey that oil-rich Arab states should aid "other" fellow countries. (The word "poor" is studiously avoided.) This was necessary, the proclamation explained, so as to free them from dependence on aid from non-Arab countries since outside assistance was likely to erode their sovereignty.[74]

For the next decade—from the date of this proclamation until the invasion of Kuwait—Iraqi declarations offered an uneasy combination of reaffirming the principle of *wahda* and attempting to calm the fears of other Arab states, particularly in the Gulf. In September 1982, Husayn undertook to reaffirm the concept of *wahda*, while at the same time allaying the fears of those suspicious of it. He declared that "*wahda* could not come about except by maintaining the present frontiers between the [Arab] states." More than that, "unity must not do away with the unique local features or with local patriotism [*wataniyya*]."[75] A few years later, in 1986, he made his attitude even more explicit. "The Arabs today," he said, "are twenty-two states, twenty-two leaders or rulers, twenty-two different circumstances, twenty-two economic and social conditions, and twenty-two distinctive national [*watani*] situations." On another occasion, he likened the Arab world to a Bedouin encampment: a realistic approach prescribed not to destroy the individual tents but to erect one large tent over the many smaller ones.[76]

These principles were supposed to be given practical expression by the establishment, in February 1989, of the Arab Cooperation Council (Majlis al-ta'awun al-'Arabi), made up of Iraq, Egypt, Jordan, and Yemen. Its very name pointed to the abandonment of "unity" and its replacement by "cooperation." It proved short-lived, falling apart in 1990 after the Kuwait crisis. Iraq's ambivalence toward unity came to the fore more than once. Husayn, for instance, said: "Brotherhood [*ukhuwwa*] is always the most important step—[but] *wahda* remains the nation's aim." On another, earlier occasion, he stated that the series of failures did not matter; what mattered was that the Arabs kept trying to achieve union. "For us, unity is sacred."[77] The 1990 draft of a new constitution again proclaimed Iraq to be "part of the Arab homeland, acting for the realization of comprehensive Arab unity."[78]

Ambiguity came to a sudden end at the time of the invasion of Kuwait. The move into Kuwait was described as the "unification of Iraq" (*wahdat al-'Iraq*) and as a revolutionary victory for Arab unity. The press wrote of "Kuwait's honorable and noble return to its family and its relations." Iraq had become unified by including "Kuwaiti Iraq [*Kuwayt al-'Iraq*]." The merger became the cornerstone of that comprehensive Arab unity for which generations of Arabs and Muslims had yearned.[79] In Kuwait, Iraq had carried out what 'Aflaq and other Ba'th leaders had dreamed of. An imaginary line was thus drawn between 'Aflaq's words about unity being "militant" and "aggressive" to what Iraq had done on the ground. Perhaps the constant references to unity through the use of force had prepared the ground for violence and breached the borderline between the political idiom and political action.

Mention of Arab unity ended all at once after Iraq was driven out of Kuwait in March 1991. Current phraseology offered expressions such as "unity of the Iraqi people" or "the road to realize Iraq's happy dream."[80] But the circumstances of the Kuwaiti adventure brought in their wake the Kurdish and Shi'i rebellion that jeopardized Iraq's own unity. Iraq's removal from Kuwait and the subsequent economic embargo and regional and global ostracism demonstrated to Iraq the dark side of *wahda*— isolation, and not of the splendid kind.

3

Language and Action

The "Ba'thization" of Iraqi Society

When the Ba'th came to power in Iraq, it possessed a ready-made ideology that had come down to it from the party's founders. It could thus preoccupy itself with the practice of government rather than with doctrines, formulas, and terminology. Slogans did, inevitably, change over time, but these changes were no more than variations on constant themes. In practical politics, the Ba'th had three objectives: to establish its rule firmly; to give it an air of legitimacy; and to perpetuate it.

With the 1968 takeover in Iraq, tension between the Iraqi and the Syrian Ba'th parties mounted considerably, and each party's claims of legitimacy and authenticity were propounded in increasingly strident tones. Michel 'Aflaq, who had been relegated from the leadership of the Syrian party, was promptly appointed to the post of secretary-general of the all-Arab Ba'th leadership based in Iraq. (Both parties had an all-Arab leadership as well as "regional leaderships" in as many individual Arab countries as would allow them to operate. In Iraq, the all-Arab forum had only nominal functions; real power resided with the "regional" [qutri] party.) 'Aflaq's appointment gave a dimension of depth and authenticity to the Iraqi party and reinforced its ambitions to make itself the only representative of the true all-Arab Ba'th. Baghdad not only attacked the Syrian Ba'th but actually denied its very right to exist. As Ahmad Hasan al-Bakr put it in 1969: "There is a single Arab Ba'th [based in Iraq] · · · and I know of no other in the region."[1]

49

But the primary concern of the Ba'th was the domestic scene, where the principal aim was to make the party dominant in all sectors of society. The effort to make it spread out and to indoctrinate the largest possible proportion of the population was pursued in such a comprehensive and consistent manner that the party's rivals invented a neologism to describe it: *tab'ith*, meaning "Ba'thization": turning everyone into a Ba'thi and giving everything a Ba'thi coloration.[2] The campaign of *tab'ith* lasted for more than a decade. "Ba'thi" and "Iraqi" were supposed to become synonyms.[3] Later, Husayn would say that all Iraqis, whether officially members of the party or not, would defend it to the point of laying down their lives for the sake of its principles.[4]

"Ba'thization" proceeded at a forced pace under the names of *tawjih fikri* (mental guidance) and *tathqif ba'thi* (Ba'thi education). Alongside the overall indoctrination by means of the media and through Saddam Husayn's many speeches, there were special campaigns tailored to appeal to certain population sectors or organizations. A major effort was devoted to the "guidance" of the armed forces. Fadil Barrak, who wrote a book on the subject, said that the foremost task of the party members in the armed forces was to spread "revolutionary ideas" and to engage in indoctrination (*taw'iya*) for the sake of the party. In addition, they must take note of hostile activities and "immediately report to the party leadership every oppositionary move or step." One of the slogans used in the army was "A good soldier is a Ba'thi soldier."[5]

A Ba'th document published in 1979 gave a very detailed description of the "channels of guidance" used for the indoctrination of the civilian population. One method was to address special publications to certain sectors, for instance: *Sawt al-Fallah* (The voice of the farmer); *Wa'y, al-'Ummal* (The workers' consciousness); *Majallat al-Mar'a* (The woman's magazine); and *Sawt al-Talaba* (Voice of the students). Another method was actual fieldwork: visits to people's homes and the distribution of party booklets to them; opening libraries in coffeehouses and posting party publications on walls. Yet another approach for what Husayn termed "action for the overall change of the society" was to hold rallies and colloquiums. These would employ direct methods of persuasion or else work indirectly by means of the theater, poetry readings, exhibitions, or other social events.

Youth was a target of particular importance. Schools and universities became Ba'thi propaganda centers. Textbooks, particularly of history, geography, and education, were rewritten for party purposes. Even magazines for small children were filled with little stories, poems, and maxims carrying a party message. University teachers were mobilized to arrange for rallies and meetings with senior party functionaries. There were regular "cultural guidance periods" at which the party's attitudes on current affairs were expounded. Yet the Ba'th complained that too few members of the teaching staff devoted sufficient time to these activities or took them as seriously as they should.[6] In 1976, Husayn revealed that only party members were being admitted to the teachers' college.[7]

Struggle and Violence: End or Means?

It was 'Aflaq who laid down the theoretical basis for the practice of the second Ba'th regime. In his book *Nuqtat al-Bidaya*, he wrote: "The Ba'th is a historical movement [destined] to be active for centuries; it therefore sees in struggle [*nidal*] the fundamental basis of party [work] and the source of its ideas and revolutionary qualities." Struggle transcended the exercise of authority; it was "above and beyond" it. Elsewhere, he drew a distinction between struggle against "outside forces," including Zionism and imperialism, as well as the domestic struggle against corrupt rulers, and the inner struggle in the souls of the fighters themselves. Nothing could be more dangerous, he asserted, than for those in charge of carrying out the revolution to lose their revolutionary élan. If they themselves fell victim to stagnation, how could they keep up the momentum of "the struggle"? He contrasted the Ba'th with the communist movement, saying that the latter started from a doctrine, while the former started from "struggle" and only afterward developed its teachings. For the Iraqi Ba'th, struggle had truly become "a matter of life and death."[8] And, indeed, *nidal* became the "badge of identity" of the Iraqi Ba'th.

In classical Arabic, *nidal* means "boastfulness" as well as an "arrow-shooting contest." In the nineteenth century, it is found with the additional meaning of "defending one's faith." It was only in the twentieth century that leftist Arab writers gave it the broader meaning in which it subsequently entered the Ba'th dictionary.[9] The extent to which it became dominant in political speech and in everyday life is perhaps best illustrated by the fact that *munadil* has become the synonym of "party member," replacing paler terms such as *rafiq* (comrade) or "man of the party." The same word also became the constant sobriquet of Husayn. The 1982 party congress stated that on the day of the 1968 Ba'th coup, Husayn had been the "civilian fighter" (*al-munadil al-madani*) who "led the first tank in the assault on the presidential palace and ignited the spark of revolution."[10] The historical truth of this belated account need not concern us here; what matters is that Husayn felt it necessary to stress that, civilian though he was, he was just as capable of commanding a tank as any army officer. The verbal combination of "civilian fighter" was to make it seem irrelevant that Husayn had not served in the armed forces at any time. Moreover, its timing (at the height of the war with Iran) was intended to stress that Husayn and other party members had done as much for the war effort as the army itself. (The Ba'th distinguished between *muqatil* [combat soldier] and *munadil* in the sense explained here.) To give visual expression to equating the two, party members wore khaki throughout the war with Iran and again during the Gulf War.

According to Ba'th doctrine, the struggle must go on because the Arabs in general, and the Iraqis in particular, have "eternal" enemies. It distinguished between *nidal salbi* (negative struggle; i.e., against something) and *nidal ijabi* (positive struggle; i.e., for the sake of something). The former term was used to refer to the party's activities up to its advent to power, the second to its actions while in power. In both periods, however, the struggler is required to act in the "popular spirit," to display "revolutionary modesty," and to know how to keep a secret.

The party document that enlarged on these points approximately a decade after the coup stressed in particular that secretiveness was required not only during the stage of struggle for power. On the contrary, it was especially important during the period of Ba'thi rule."[11] Secretiveness has indeed remained a salient characteristic of the Ba'th regime throughout its rule. The internal party organ warned of the danger of ceasing the struggle after power had been achieved: "The torpor and arrogance which come over a *munadil* when he enters office" made him inclined to consider the conquest of power as the "conclusion of the struggle" and think that all that was left was to "reap its fruits." But the dangers of backsliding and of reaction were more severe for a party in office than for one still struggling for power. The way to fight these dangers, the document went on to say, was by deepening the commitment of the *munadil* (here in the technical sense of "party member") to the party's teachings; "improving his economic and social situation"; creating a "commitment to the social environment from which the Ba'th and its fighters have sprung"; and performing acts capable of "reminding the *munadil* of his fighting past, such as enrolling in the frontier guard, taking part in camps organized for collective undertakings, or working in rural or popular areas."[12]

This constant emphasis on perpetual struggle leads by necessity to the issue of using violence in its pursuit. The Ba'th regime justifies, even sanctifies, the use of force (as will be shown in Chapter 11), but its political language does distinguish between two kinds of violence: *irhab* and *'unf*. The former means "terror," "intimidation," and "threat." It is a comparatively modern word, not found in the *Lisan al-'Arab*. *'Unf* ("stubbornness," "violence," "cruelty"), by contrast, is already found in the *hadith* literature, connoting the opposite of "mercy." "God grants to mercy what He does not grant to cruelty ['*unf*]." *Lisan al-'Arab* adds that all good is found in mercy, all evil in cruelty. The Ba'th, interestingly enough, gave a ring of legitimacy to *'unf*, but not to *irhab*. We may surmise that this was done to project an image of toughness and of the ability to suppress actual or imaginary rivals but to avoid charges of using terror and intimidation.

'Unf as a positive term was stressed in particular during the years of consolidation beginning with the Ba'th takeover. Only later did it acquire negative overtones. But there was, from the early times of Ba'th rule, a division into "good" and "bad" violence. Only a few months after the

takeover, a daily paper expounded on the need for violence in certain situations when progress had to be made. But there was "necessary violence" (*'unf daruri*) and "unnecessary violence" (*'unf ghayr daruri*). It was necessary to tell "revolutionary violence" from mere terror; the latter could not be justified. Another newspaper tried to establish a difference between "revolutionary," "barbarous," and "reactionary" violence. History, it wrote, was one long struggle, conducted in cycles of violence and counterviolence. "Barbarous and reactionary" violence always launched a new cycle, and "revolutionary" violence, like the Ba'th's, came in response to it. When forty conspirators (actual or imaginary) were put to death in January 1970, *al-Thawra* spoke of the "justified," "legitimate," and "revolutionary" violence that was part and parcel of the revolution and was needed for it to remain on course and defend itself against its enemies. It must not be compared to the sort of violence employed by the police or the armed forces. Only the revolution itself was entitled to use force, "within the limits of legitimacy and humanity."[13]

The Ba'th regime differs from all its predecessors in Iraq not only in the sanctification of violence in its ideology and its idiom but also in having made it into a pivotal tool in running the country. It has built up security services that are among the best endowed and most skillful in the world and that have penetrated every sector of Iraqi society, including economic life. They have turned themselves into a vast apparatus of terror and violence.[14] An Iraqi opposition newspaper published in London pointed to violence as the central problem of Iraqi society as a whole (rather than of the Ba'th or of Saddam Husayn alone). Violence and admiration of force were imprinted deeply in the Iraqi character, it went on to say; an Iraqi had "something of a dictator about him," even if he did no more than run a shop. It concluded that only a comprehensive "social armistice" and the advent of democracy could break the cycle.[15] One can take issue with such a sweeping generalization regarding the Iraqi national character by a politically motivated source. Nonetheless, the depths of division within Iraqi society and repeated cycles of political violence during its modern history have heavily shaped Iraq's political culture and social mores.

II

From "Popular" to Totalitarian Democracy

> We want a society that will find its inspiration in our Arab
> and Muslim history. . . . In their [early] history, the Mus-
> lims were democratic in their debates among themselves, but
> when they dictated their terms to those conquered by them,
> and the latter refused, . . . then it was the sword that became
> democratic in the most radical manner, turning into the most
> violent sword.
> —Saddam Husayn, *al-Jumhuriyya*, 10 September 1976

When modern Iraq was put together from what used to be three Ottoman provinces, it possessed no tradition of self-government and had no
clear political model to emulate. The British mandate brought with it
an array of Western political terms and concepts (democracy, freedom
of expression, separation of powers) and tried to apply them in Iraq. But
they did not take hold there, and the rather shaky political bodies that
had been formed according to them were wiped out by the overthrow
of the monarchy in 1958. Their prompt collapse attested to their artificial growth in a foreign soil. Instead of being held up as models, they
became the hated trappings of foreign rule. Qasim, the first ruler after
1958, introduced clearly totalitarian elements into his manner of ruling, but the weakness of his regime prevented him from carrying them
to their logical conclusion.

The first Ba'th regime in 1963 tried to model its political practice and
its institutions on the communist paradigm. Communist terminology had
been introduced into Iraq by the local Communist Party starting in the
1930s. As already noted, the communists became the chief adversaries of
the Ba'th. Initially, nonetheless, the Ba'th took over much of their language, though at times with noticeable reluctance. The second Ba'th regime carried on where the first had left off. It called its regime a "popular
democracy" and used a multitude of other political terms derived from
the sages of the far left. These terms were foreign to Iraq and seemed
strange to the public at large. Their use diminished gradually, and they

were finally abandoned when Saddam Husayn took over the presidency in 1979. The regime he instituted came to show all the hallmarks of totalitarianism and centralism. At the center stood Husayn's personality cult, which purported to negate all possible alternatives to his one-man rule. Over time, elements of the Islamic political tradition were woven into this pattern.

4

The Intricacies
of "Democracy"

"The Dictatorship of Popular Democracy"

The first provisional constitution of the Ba'th regime, promulgated in 1968, stated that Iraq was a "popular democratic state [*dawla dimuqratiyya sha'biyya*] that derives its democratic foundations and its popular character from the Arab heritage and the spirit of Islam."[1] This hybrid of a sentence combines three concepts from three totally different, totally incompatible worlds. "Popular democracy" comes from the communist political idiom and, in slightly different shapes, has become the synonym of totalitarian regimes in various places. It is contradictory in itself, since "democracy" alone connotes popular rule and the addition of "popular" is meaningless. By contrast, "democratic foundations" are words derived from the Western political concepts of freedom and liberalism. Finally, the reference to "the spirit of Islam" stems from an altogether different value scale that—at least in part—is incompatible with the other two components. The strange combination attests not only to blurred thinking on the part of those who chose the language but also, and more important, to their inner tensions and conflicts in defining and expressing their political identity. The second provisional constitution of 1970 circumvented the difficulties by defining Iraq as a "popular democratic, sovereign republic," dropping the rest of the elements.[2]

Why did the Ba'th pick the word "popular" to go with "democratic," and what meaning has their combination assumed in the Iraqi context?

The Iraqi Ba'th drew its inspiration from two sources: from the Iraqi Communist Party, which predated the Ba'th by some fifteen years and which had long called for a "popular democracy,"[3] and from Damascus, where, in the course of far-reaching ideological changes occurring at the end of 1963, the Syrian Ba'th adopted the concept of "popular democracy" as a basic tenet. The adoption of the term by the Iraqi party at the start of its first period in power, in February 1963, attests to the influence of the communists.[4] This is true despite the bloody clashes with them during the early days of Ba'th rule, or rather because of them: the Ba'th needed to appear as radical as their rivals or more so. In 1968, however, we can attribute its use to the indirect influence of Damascus; it was needed in order to counter the accusations of the Syrian party that the Iraqi "branch" was guilty of "rightist deviation." The newly reinstated regime's angling for Soviet support also played a role; lip service to Soviet terminology was part of that endeavor.[5] Finally, the term also helped to resolve problems of political identity. A reference to "democracy" was, after all, de rigueur in the twentieth century. But combining it with "popular" allowed the Ba'th to make it appear different from the common variety, with its Western overtones. Also, the term could be said to allude to the party's (supposed) popularity.

In the party's book, "popular democracy" meant something broader, deeper, more stable, and healthier than Western democracy. It was led by revolutionary cadres truly representative of the people, but "it is not the democracy of the enemies of the revolution who represent nothing but their own egotistical and narrow interests." Democracy was not an end in itself but a means "to build a revolutionary political regime." "Popular democracy" differed from "bourgeois parliamentary democracy" in that it did not distinguish between the executive and the legislative power but rather strove "to combine the two powers and place them in the hand of the people as a perpetual trust." It was this aim that the daily *al-Thawra* (perhaps through a slip of the pen, perhaps intentionally) described as the "dictatorship of popular democracy" (*diktaturiyyat al-dimuqratiyya al-sha'biyya*).[6]

True to its negation of the separation of powers, the Ba'th endowed its Revolutionary Command Council with the full array of executive and legislative powers. Its members (varying in number from five to twenty-two) were coopted into it without the benefit of any electoral procedure. The cabinet had no independent functions and merely carried out the administrative work needed to implement the council's and the president's decisions. The "popular classes" so fulsomely praised by the regime had no say. Until 1980, there was no elected political body of any kind. When such a body was eventually created, it acted as a rubber stamp. The supposed "popular" character of the regime was expressed by the establishment of a group of bodies that became known collectively as "popular organizations" (*munazzamat sha'biyya*). They included trade unions, the farmers' association, and students' and women's organizations. In addition, popular councils (*majalis shaʿbiyya*) were set up. They were declared to be elected local councils, but in fact their members were party appointees and served as local party informers. The term "popular army" (*al-jaysh al-shaʿbi*) was used to refer to the party militia.

The use of the term "popular democracy" brought with it a string of expressions taken over from communist discourse, such as *taqaddumi* (progressive) or *al-kadihun* (the toilers).[7] During the first ten years or so of its existence, the regime defined itself as "progressive," frequently employing expressions such as "patriotic, progressive, antiimperialist, antireactionary rule," "progressive achievements," or "the progressive July [1968] revolution." The Baʿth also likened Iraq to other Arab regimes that it considered progressive (Egypt, Libya, Algeria). The alliance established in 1973 with the communists (after years of bitter rivalry) was called al-Jabha al-wataniyya wal-qawmiyya al-taqaddumiyya (The national and all-Arab progressive front).

Like the use of "popular democracy," the adoption of the term "progressive" was to improve the image of the Baʿth both in its competition with the communists within Iraq and in its relation with the Soviet Union. It took the regime a great deal of persuasion to obtain, in 1971, Soviet recognition of its progressive character, which, much to Baghdad's displeasure, the rival Baʿth in Syria had received much earlier.[8] But during the second half of the 1970s, the term became unfashionable in Iraq. A note of dissociation was first struck by Saddam Husayn in 1975 when he said: "We sometimes use incorrect terms to describe the revolution and say that the revolution of 17 July [1968] was progressive, and regard the quality of being progressive as a panacea. But the revolution is basically nationalist [*qawmi*] and socialist and by calling it progressive we diminish its real worth."[9]

Another term borrowed from communist parlance was *kadih*. The word appears once in the Qurʾan, in the sura *al-Inshiqaq* (v. 84), where it refers to laboring for the sake of Allah. Later, it came to mean a worker, particularly one doing physical work. The Arab left began using it to connote the oppressed proletariat; we find it in Iraq in the 1930s.[10] Like other leftists, the Baʿth used it as a collective term for industrial workers and farmers or for any individual salary earner. Formulas such as "the transfer of power from the bourgeois classes to the toiling masses" entered general usage. One of the names of the party itself was "the party of the toilers." A Baʿth document spoke of the violence used by bourgeois regimes "whenever the toiling masses assert themselves against them in revolutionary movements."[11]

Such attacks against the *burjwaziyya* were common in the first decade of Baʿthi rule.[12] Here, too, we can discern the influence of the Arab left, which, in turn, had borrowed most of its terminology from European socialists. The party declared that it was working "to free national [*watani*] culture from the influence and the mentality of the [pre-Baʿth] imperialist bourgeoisie." It also charged that the "national [*watani*] bourgeoisie" had caused "all the crises that had beset the nationalist revolution." (In other Arab countries that had gone through a revolution, it was customary to give the name "national bourgeoisie" to those quarters of the middle class who were ready to cooperate with the new rulers.) Husayn warned against letting antirevolutionary bourgeois attitudes assert themselves in the universities and called on the students to oppose them. "Popular democracy" was to be the "healthy alternative to bourgeois democracy."[13]

Despite its original use as a clarion call, the glamour of the term "popular democracy" gradually diminished and was replaced by terms such as "socialist democracy," "revolutionary democracy," "direct democracy," or "Ba'thi democracy" (a term used by Husayn himself). The most common word to stand in for it after the mid-1970s was "central [or centralized] democracy" (*dimuqratiyya markaziyya*). A Ba'th document of 1976 explained "centralized" as meaning that party members would "obey the party in all things"; "democracy" meant that they were entitled to state their personal opinions about the point at issue, but only after they had carried out the party's instructions. The two terms in the expression needed to be carefully balanced. Only their combination, the document went on, was capable of restraining arbitrariness and anarchy and of withstanding both "absolute democracy" and "bureaucratic dictatorship."[14]

During the second decade of Ba'th rule, "democracy" was commonly used without another word to qualify it. There may have been several reasons for this change. First and foremost, it probably signaled that the Ba'th no longer owed ideological lip service to anyone. The communists had been forced to go underground in 1978. Unity talks with Syria had failed in 1979, and the Iraqi Ba'th had emerged stronger than the Syrian party from the encounter and no longer needed to fear its criticism. The alliance with the Soviet Union had passed its peak, and rather than working to maintain it, Iraq was busy finding openings to the West. The change probably also reflects Husayn's personal preferences. As far as can be established, he had never spoken of "popular democracy" himself, presumably because of his aversion to the Iraqi communists and their school of thought. Furthermore, Husayn was, as always, greatly preoccupied with his image and wished to appear in the eyes of the Iraqis and of the world as an unqualified democrat, without quotation marks. The distance covered since the regime's early days became evident in the new draft constitution of 1990, which avoids the term "popular democracy" altogether and defines Iraq as "an independent, sovereign state whose form of government is that of a presidential republic." Elsewhere, it states that the regime is "based on democracy."[15]

The Sword of Democracy

In no area do we find as wide a gulf between word and action as in that of democracy, if we take the word in the sense accepted in the countries where it first emerged.[16] While totally denying all the elements commonly attributed to democracy, the Ba'th regime presented itself as the most democratic government Iraq had ever had and claimed for itself the status of a democracy truer than any found elsewhere. We have already noted that the party, like other totalitarian parties before it, sensed that the twentieth century demanded democratic credentials. But apart from that cynical gesture, there actually were political groups that attributed more genuine democratic attitudes to themselves or clamored for the democratization of the existing regime. In addition to the communists, the Kurds, too, expressed their criticism implicitly by calling their party the Kurdistan Democratic Party and explicitly by calling for "democracy for Iraq and autonomy for Kurdistan."[17] All these pressures produced, in response, the verbiage behind which the Ba'th regime concealed its actual loathing for democracy.

The best way to understand the Ba'th attitude toward democracy is to look at its attacks on Western democracies, as well as against those who demanded democracy in Iraq. In Michel 'Aflaq's later writings, his youthful ideas and their somewhat liberal coloring gave way to more expressly totalitarian thoughts. In his *Fi sabil al-Ba'th*, he attacked "Western democracy which gave rise to capitalism."[18] *Al-Thawra* wrote that "the assumption that democracy means freedom of speech [*hurriyyat kalamiyya*] seems ridiculous to Iraqis." Similarly, the assumption that "the freedom of forming parties [*hurriyyat al-ahzab*]" was the only correct interpretation of democracy was a "bourgeois assumption" that had succeeded in influencing Ba'th thinking. "The socialist revolution and the rule of the one socialist party [the Ba'th] have made nonsense of this unbalanced assumption. Can it be said that socialist countries are not democratic because of their being directed by a single party?"[19]

"Bourgeois" or "parliamentary" democracies were denigrated as "sham democracies" and described as contemptuous of the masses and "inflicting terror" on workers and peasants.[20] They were said to be sustained by "reactionary forces." Likewise, "liberal democracy" was in a permanently precarious state and always on the brink of fascism. A Ba'th document stated curtly that "Hitlerite fascism and British democracy belong to the same school of thought."[21] The words recall a statement by Salah al-Din al-Sabbagh, one of al-Kaylani's close associates at the time of the 1941 coup, who said that "the spirit of Islam and God's commands preserve us from the evils of Bolshevism, Nazism, and English democracy," all of which concealed "barbaric and materialistic ideals" hostile to the "superior ideals" of Arab nationalism.[22]

Again and again, the Ba'th regime attacked Western democracy but failed to argue the point rationally or to spell out clearly what its own approach to democracy was. Elections to the trade unions and the students' association (both no more than offshoots of the party apparatus) were presented as tantamount to parliamentary elections; agrarian reform was spoken of as an instrument to reinforce village democracy; the activities of the so-called popular surveillance (*al-raqaba al-sha'biyya*) that turned common people into informers (often on economic crimes) were also referred to as democratic procedures.[23] In the obscure manner typical of him, Husayn declared: "Our party has implemented democracy . . . drawing on noble and eternal sources and origins compatible with the conscience of the people."[24] Another party statement declared that, in developing countries, the armed forces have the role of "strengthening democratic rights." Commentators, as well as Husayn himself, found it easier to say what democracy was against than what it stood for. One writer saw the principal tasks of democracy as "settling accounts with the enemies of the people" and heading off "liberal values." Husayn proclaimed: "There is no freedom and no democracy and not even life for him who chooses a place other than inside the tent of revolution and its values." In implementing democracy, "we shall use the rifle against the enemies of the revolution."[25] When all is said and done, the word "democracy," despite the frequency of its use, remained empty of all content.

A sudden change, however, occurred in 1989, when a much more serious public debate was brought about by the combination of the changes then engulfing Eastern Europe and the domestic pressures following the end of the war against Iran. The regime seems to have decided that a public debate would allow people to voice their grievances without undermining its rule. The sign was given by Husayn, who became known as "the engineer of democracy" or the "shepherd of democracy" and whose utterances on democracy now filled the newspaper columns. Most frequently quoted were his statements "Democracy is the source of strength of the individual and of society" and "All democracy to the people, all liberty to the people, all rights to the people."[26]

The more daring journalists took these slogans seriously enough to sound notes not previously permitted. They quoted a *hadith* to give legitimacy to their views: *Ikhtilaf ummati rahma*—literally, "Differing opinions among my nation are a grace [of God]." It was used as proof that democracy had existed in early Islam, as well as for the justification of current demands. The Iraqi writer and critic Muhammad Mubarak wrote that it should be made the chief slogan of all those wishing to "build a genuine democracy."[27] Much more surprising was that a journalist quoted a sentence from a Jewish source, Hillel the Elder's well-known phrase, "If I am not for myself, who is for me, but if I am for my own self [only] what am I, and if not now, when?" The journalist did not say where the words came from but used them to encourage those struggling for freedom of expression.[28] Their use attests to the strength of the cultural and linguistic sediments left behind by the long history of the Jewish community in Iraq. (Hillel himself was born in Babylon in 75 B.C.)

Only a minute minority spoke out forcefully for democratization; most journalists continued to write as they had been accustomed. Those who did speak out, though conceding that democracy had numerous defects, still held it up as comparatively the best form of government and spoke of it as "vital for the progress of the people and for establishing law and justice in their midst." Democracy, they argued, was "indivisible." Free speech was one of its principal demands. A journalist writing under the pen name "Juhayna" accused his colleagues of acting as mere sounding boards for the official Iraqi news agency. They did not have enough courage to criticize or investigate, and so their work remained boring, unimaginative, and superficial. They did not deserve the name of journalist.[29]

Under the heading "How Sweet Is Democracy," another journalist wrote that "the barrier of fear" had been overcome, both for journalists and for the citizens at large. Others demanded the right to criticize government actions, adding that without free criticism there could be no democracy. Others again called for freedom of association and for pluralism "like in Western democracies." This was probably the first time that the words "Western democracies" were used in a laudatory rather than a pejorative sense. Demands in the fields of education and culture were also raised. Free elections—"the foundation stones of democracy and of modern life" —should also be held at the universities. Young people should be educated from an early age to respect "the values of democracy." Fresh minds should be admitted to the cultural and literary columns of the press, run by the same writers for thirty years.[30]

Alongside such explicit statements, there were indirect ways of making similar points, in the fashion used by all newspapers controlled by totalitarian regimes. There appeared, for instance, an allegorical tale about a corrupt family. The family's head was spoken of as "a leader whose justice was sharper than a sword." No names were mentioned, but the reader would assume as a matter of course that the family must be Saddam Husayn's. The fall of the Romanian dictator Ceausescu in December 1989 became the occasion of indirect attacks on Husayn. Parallels between Ceausescu's policy of nepotism, violence, and intimidation and that of Husayn were drawn without actually saying so. The total subjection of the Romanian press to government control was also mentioned with a cautionary note.[31] Again, the real target could not be mistaken by the Iraqi readers, accustomed as they were to reading between the lines.

As noted, this episode of free speech did not last for more than a few months and had no effect whatsoever on the practice of the Ba'th regime. Husayn himself soon reverted to his customary clichés about the uniqueness of Iraqi democracy and the dangers of the Western variety.[32] Some of his close associates brought back the term "popular democracy," letting it be understood that Ba'thi democracy was not of the liberal kind. Establishment journalists, more experienced in the ways of the regime than some of their rasher colleagues, were quick to toe the line. Western democracy, one of them wrote, was "not suited to Iraq's political, social, and economic conditions." Others, backed by the minister of culture and information, Latif Nusayyif al-Jasim, attacked their more daring colleagues for having turned themselves into Iraq's "greatest enemies." Jasim himself, reaffirming that "democracy is not anarchy," spoke mockingly of those writers who had risen like meteors and would fall as quickly.[33]

A similar, though less pronounced, episode occurred after the end of the Gulf War. This time, groups of Iraqi expatriate opposition figures joined the chorus through their newspapers published in London and elsewhere. It is doubtful whether these rather irregular publications were read in Iraq, where the mere possession of a copy could endanger a person's life. They attacked the regime's "antidemocratic" and "totalitarian" practices. One of them, *al-Tayyar al-Jadid*, reflecting the Shi'i point of view, had a satirical column written in the vernacular and entitled, "The Trouble Is—It's Funny." It derided anything described as "democratic" by the Ba'th. On one occasion, it wrote: "Ho Iraqis: the winds of democracy and the gases of liberty are blowing on you again. . . . A new sun has risen— it is square and has a green spot on it. Such is the democracy of Nebuchadnezzar the Second, the leader of the Arabs."[34]

By contrast, all the various expatriate opposition groupings presented themselves as capable of giving Iraq an alternative and more genuine form of government. The Ba'th regime for its part labeled as traitors all who were cooperating with their country's external enemies and had thus disqualified themselves. Husayn summed up the debate in his characteristic way when answering a French journalist who had asked him about Iraqi democracy: "What is important to us," he said, "is that our people is satisfied with us and is convinced that the leadership in charge is democratic."[35]

The Pejorative Triplet:
Libiraliyya, Barlamaniyya, Ta'addudiyya

"Democracy" was a word the Ba'th could pay lip service to; "liberalism" (*libiraliyya*) was not. The formal reason given by the party was that "liberal" was a concept of the bourgeoisie, while the party was antibourgeois on principle. But there were deeper reasons: the Ba'th was opposed to individual and collective liberties, to private enterprise, and to the separation of powers. It opposed anything that might limit the powers of the regime, whether a free press, free elections, any alternative power centers, or an independent judiciary. In its view, the individual was not an end in itself: it existed for the sake of the state. Liberalism was equated with disorder, not to say with anarchy. Unlike its blurred references to democracy, the party was forthright and consistent in its condemnation of liberalism.

If there was a contradiction between the assertion of democracy and the denial of liberalism, the Ba'th saw no need to resolve or explain it. It spoke of its predecessors, in particular Qasim and the 'Arif brothers, as dictators and of itself as having struggled all along against any manifestation of dictatorship. Husayn in particular was depicted as a valiant fighter against dictatorship.[36] At the same time, liberalism was equated with all that was bad in the Ba'th book: reaction, anarchy, rightism, imperialism, and the bourgeoisie. For example, a Ba'th document on the educational system the party had inherited from its predecessors had this to say about it: "The educational and information apparatuses were technically as well as ideologically backward; the prevalent trends were reaction, bureaucracy, rightism, and liberalism." It went on to say that, despite the changes introduced there, the universities were still places where "backward, liberal, and rightist trends" were at work. Such "reactionary, bourgeois, and liberal trends" must be excised from the curricula and from the "educational apparatus."[37]

In a more discursive manner, *al-Thawra* explained to its readers that in the past, when the bourgeoisie had a constructive role to play in the struggle against feudalism, "liberalism" had not been a negative concept. But soon enough, the bourgeois regimes became as regressive as those they had replaced and were no longer capable of granting the people real freedom and human dignity. Appeals for "total" freedom and human rights were nothing more than expressions of class interest the bourgeoisie used to defend the capitalist system and exploit workers and peasants.[38] The most dangerous thing about liberalism was that it was capable of undermining party discipline. In the words of the above Ba'th document: "Pride, egotism, arrogance, the rejection of criticism, organizational liberalism [here used as a synonym of anarchy], and idle chatter are the sworn enemies of healthy party life and of revolutionary qualities." Party members must be on guard against them and "fight all manifestations of organizational feebleness and liberalism."[39]

The danger of liberalism was that in a liberal democracy "the state lacks the power and the ability to act or take the initiative and . . . [merely] looks on from the sidelines while social strife goes on." The "enemies of the people" were always on the ready to exploit such weakness for a takeover bid.[40] The Ba'th had therefore rejected such liberal thinking right from the start as conflicting with the building of a revolutionary society and with the elimination of exploitation. Instead, the party insisted on "social justice and equal opportunities." Unlike an "unrestrained" capitalist regime, it saw its task as balancing the requirements of the individual and the needs of the revolution. Unlike liberalism, the Ba'th state was engaged in introducing social and economic change and technological development and in raising the inhabitants' educational and cultural level.[41]

Parliamentarism (*barlamaniyya*) was likewise a target of severe criticism. Parliament had been an institution introduced by "Western imperialism." Under the monarchy, there was an upper and a lower house, but both became mockeries of real parliaments, playthings of Baghdad politicians. Rather than encouraging broader political participation, they engendered frustration and caused disappointment.[42] Certainly, other Arab countries had similar experiences; the Ba'th itself formed its ideology under the influence of events in Syria. The original party statutes of 1947 had laid down that the future Arab state would have a "constitutional parliamentary" form of government. By 1963, however, this had been replaced by "popular democracy."[43]

Ironically enough, to counter pressures for greater liberalization and more democracy (mainly from the Kurds, but also from the communists), the party had recourse to Lenin's writings against parliamentarianism. Like Lenin, al-Thawra argued, the Ba'th thought that parliaments would endanger "the socialist revolution." Nonetheless, it did not reject the principle of political representation; on the contrary, "popular democracies" insisted on it more vigorously than Western ones.[44] The paper did not spell out how a representative system would work without a parliament.

The Ba'th also argued that parliamentarianism was in decline all over the world, its descent having been triggered by the Bolshevik revolution. Parliaments brought the bourgeoisie to power, strengthened it, and allowed it to oppress the people. This was a mockery of true democracy. Parliamentary debates were "a waste of time . . . and empty talk." In the Arab countries, parliaments had failed because Arab society was not really bourgeois; therefore, parliamentary institutions were no more than "sorry caricatures" and "unsuccessful imitations" of the West.[45]

Attacks on parliamentarianism ceased when Saddam Husayn became president in 1979. Wishing to create an enlightened image of himself, as well as to establish that he differed from his predecessors, he was quick to set up a quasi-parliament. The body he set up in 1980 differed in name and in substance from Iraq's past institutions and was certainly very different from parliaments in the West. It was called al-majlis al-watani (the national, or patriotic assembly), obviously an allusion to what Husayn wanted it to be and do. If its predecessors had nominal functions they did not exercise, the new body fully met the expectations placed on it.

The law setting up the assembly did not make it the sole legislative body; on the contrary, most legislative powers remained reserved for the Revolutionary Command Council. The assembly was not empowered to withhold its confidence from the cabinet, let alone the president; the council, by contrast, was entitled to dissolve the assembly at any time. Members had to take an oath of loyalty to the Ba'th, and there was no room for opposition representatives.[46] The assembly passed no important laws, nor did it debate vital issues. It confirmed without fail what the president or the Revolutionary Command Council asked it to affirm, beginning with the revocation, in 1980, of the existing Iraqi-Iranian border agreements (an act followed by the war) and up to sanctioning the invasion of Kuwait ten years later. The political report of the ninth party congress (1982) noted that "the party could have conducted parliamentary elections in the traditional fashion, . . . but it preferred another approach: the road of truth and justice."[47]

At the end of 1988, Husayn inserted a neologism into the Ba'th political lexicon, ta'addudiyya, a translation of "pluralism." No such word appears in the 1984 edition of the dictionary Mu'jam al-mustalahat al-'arabiyya. It may possibly have been used in the sense of "pluralism" earlier on in circles of writers or journalists, but it was Husayn's use of it in 1988 that gave it public currency. He spoke of it in the context of a new proposal to establish a broader base of representation (but not power sharing) by allowing the formation of parties. These would enjoy freedom of expression and perform the task of *ta'addudiyya* in society. He added that the party had recognized the need for pluralism years earlier but had refrained from saying so because the term had become fashionable in various places abroad and the Ba'th did not want to appear as "running with the herd or jumping on the bandwagon—certainly not!"[48]

In fact, that was precisely what he was doing: jumping on the bandwagon of glasnost that had started rolling in Soviet Russia; at least, he wished to appear to move with the times. The fate of Eastern European regimes, and above all the end of Ceausescu, had left its mark on him. It was the latter's fate he had in mind when he said that Iraq needed democratization and "openness" just as a person opens the windows "lest they shatter at the moment of an explosion."[49] But pluralism, let alone a multiparty system, was no more than lip service: the Ba'th insisted on, its role as the "leading party" (*al-hizb al-qa'id*) under all circumstances.[50]

Rather than encourage opposition groupings, talk of *ta'addudiyya* caused disquiet in the ranks of the Ba'th. This became clearly apparent in the public debate that followed Husayn's statement. *Al-'Iraq* wrote of the "shock" suffered by party members when they heard what Husayn had said. It derided "those good party people" who were so loyal to the Ba'th and to their country but who "put up barricades against Iraqi politicians no different from themselves to whom Saddam Husayn decided to grant freedom of political action." There were, after all, people with an ideology different from the party's who were nonetheless "good patriots." In another article, the paper reminded the Ba'th that "freedom" was after all the "centerpiece" of its "sacred" slogan ("unity, freedom, socialism"). A Ba'th daily dared give a factual description of what pluralism meant in a Western multiparty system.[51] A literary critic, Muhammad Mubarak, wrote of the positive interaction between political and cultural pluralism. Before and after World War II, he stated, such pluralism had existed in Iraq and there had been, at that time, important innovations in poetry and prose and in scholarly thought.[52]

As this debate about pluralism was going on, the Ba'th started using a word that had all but disappeared from public discourse for many years: "opposition" (*mu'arada*). In Ba'th thinking, there had been no room for an opposition, and to merely use the word might have been construed as meaning that such a thing existed and was permissible. During these years, any groups or individuals who were critical of the state, the party, or their various offshoots were classed as "hostile forces." Did the readmission of the word attest to a change in this attitude? First, the new opposition was required to be "honorable" and not of the kind who were ready to "gamble" with the fate of the state and the people. Neither would it "turn its weapons" against the existing leadership, which, after all, had the trust of the people. Next, it must be "patriotic" (*watani*) and participate in "the political and economic building of the state." It must neither criticize everything nor go along with the government in everything. A senior party functionary, Taha Yasin Ramadan, said in a similar fashion that the multiplication of parties did not necessarily mean "constant opposition." Elaborating on his statement, *al-Qadisiyya* wrote that it was a mistake to assume that an opposition party must necessarily be against the government, even when the latter is supported by the majority of the people.[53]

What, then, did the Ba'th mean when it spoke of "opposition"? Did it have to fear that it might lose its power monopoly? Its members could hardly have entertained such fears. There was no room for any kind of voluntary association in Husayn's regime. Only two years or so before this debate, in 1987, he had disbanded all trade unions, even though they were run by party functionaries, and had thus deprived workers of what little protection they might have had. If such bodies, tamed though they were, needed to be dissolved, no wonder that talk about political pluralism did not, in fact, lead to the establishment of new parties. No opposition newspapers were licensed, and no representatives of the Kurds, the Shi'is, or the communists were allowed to voice their opinions during the debate on pluralism. The issue was dealt with, as it were, entirely within the family.

The clearest indication of what was really intended was provided by the procedures applied during the 1989 elections for the national assembly. No opposition candidates were allowed to run; on the contrary, a yardstick even stricter than in the past was used to prevent the entry of opposition figures into the house, even if they were likely to act merely as individuals rather than in organized opposition groups. One condition to run for membership in the council was for candidates to have contributed to the war against Iran and to believe that it had resounded to the glory of Iraq. Since most opposition elements had been against the war, this alone was enough to disqualify them.[54]

Talk of pluralism stopped after the elections and was not revived until the outbreak of the Kurdish and Shi'i uprisings after the Gulf War. Again, it was Husayn who set the tone. "Pluralism and the participation of good citizens in political life," he said, would give "responsible freedom" to all Iraqis.[55] It would appear that Husayn was well aware of the power of words to serve as safety valves in times of crises and excelled in their use to that effect, his intentions to the contrary notwithstanding. There was, after all, nobody to compel him to account for the use he made of them.

5

An Irreplaceable Regime

*I*n an article marking the first anniversary of the Gulf War, *al-Qadisiyya* wrote: "We have Saddam Husayn and they have their democracy." It attacked the United States for acting according to the "law of the jungle" and for expecting "others" to do the same, as if they had no history of their own, no tradition of government, and no leaders capable of sacrifice for the honor of their country. Iraq was telling the United States, the article went on, that "we have rejected, are rejecting, and shall always reject" such values. "Let them enjoy their democracy . . . but we are content to have an Arab leader, a Muslim seeker of justice ['*adil*], Saddam Husayn, may God preserve him."[1] In other words: other places might have democracy as their form of government, but in Iraq, Husayn was a "form of government" in himself—he *was* the regime. The two systems were utterly opposed to each other; in preferring Husayn's one-man rule, Iraq was following the old Muslim tradition of a single honest, just ruler—the embodiment of good government.

To reinforce his one-man rule, Husayn drew on the models of Mesopotamian and Arab rulers of the distant past to whom he likened himself. True, he used the modern party apparatus (unparalleled in older Arab history) as a principal vehicle for his rule, but within the party he was autocratic. Indeed, the Arabic "*hizb*," though commonly translated as "party," is not fully synonymous with the latter. In classical Arabic, it was used in a neutral or a positive sense to denote a group, association, or circle of people, or negatively to describe divisiveness. Only when political parties

69

were formed in Arab countries around the turn of the twentieth century was the term applied consistently to them.[2] In Iraq, too, parties sprang up in the twentieth century, but they differed from the Western model in two respects: first, in their weakness compared with the armed forces (in the last account, the army shaped political events); second, in their inability to compete with each other except by using force. Under the Ba'th, even such vestiges of pluralism disappeared altogether. After the communist and the Kurdish parties had gone underground in the 1970s, Iraq turned into a single-party state. The cadres of this single party, the Ba'th, were at the sole disposal of the ruler.

The methods of state and party propagandists, even though they used all modern information techniques, were surprisingly similar to those of ancient times.[3] As in the past, poets, writers, men of religion, and professional propagandists now combined their efforts to glorify Husayn and to mock and vilify his adversaries. However exaggerated and magnified this personality cult became, there is no denying that it contained an element of historical authenticity and continuity. In Iraq, it may have evoked a note familiar from the past and may therefore have been easier to obey.

The Indispensable Leader

In early 1978, a historical novel entitled *The Long Days* was published in Iraq. Its author, 'Abd al-Amir Mu'alla, explained that his intention had been to describe the emergence of a leader (*qa'id*) "who has reached his position by virtue of his qualities, a leader who has struggled and opposed, has been expelled from his land and has suffered, but has not renounced his revolutionary principles." He called his hero Muhammad bin Husayn al-Saqr (the Falcon) and described how he had taken part in the unsuccessful attempt on Qasim's life on 7 October 1959 and had subsequently been forced to flee to Egypt. Even though the attempt had failed, al-Saqr had already shown his heroic qualities and his great love of Iraq; when he fled abroad, "half his heart" remained behind in Baghdad.[4] The practiced Iraqi reader would have had no trouble equating al-Saqr with Husayn.[5] However, at the time (about a year and a half before Husayn's final takeover), the author preferred to present a fictional figure, albeit one to which he attributed all the qualities and all the biographical details of the real man. He may have wanted to deepen the mystery surrounding Husayn, or he may have wished to prepare the ground for Husayn's emergence as the sole leader, or he may have feared to play up Husayn under his real name at a time when Ahmad Hasan al-Bakr was still president. Bakr might have exploited such a publication to block Husayn's way.

A few months after the novel was published, another writer, 'Abd al-Jabbar Muhsin, discussed the qualities needed in a leader in an article in *al-Thawra*. "The leader is a requirement of history [*ibn al-darura al-ta'rikhiyya*]," Muhsin wrote; "he sets historical events into motion."

(Muhsin may have been influenced by debates among European historians about the role of the individual in history and about the concept of "historical inevitability.")[6] The leadership that took over in July 1968, he goes on, received "the people's love even before it began to rule"—an allusion to Husayn taking second place until 1979. He then quoted the following verse from the Qur'an: "As for the scum, it vanishes as jetsam, and what profits men abides in the earth."[7] Whether he wanted this to be applied to Bakr on his way out and to Husayn on the way up is a moot point.

Saddam Husayn took an active part in preparing for the personality cult that he developed fully after his takeover. His relations with his "court writers" form an instructive chapter in the study of social mobility in Ba'thi Iraq, as well as in understanding how certain political phrases were turned into household words. Husayn started the debate on the issue of leadership back in 1975, well before his assumption of the presidency. He wrote that "the leader must, at one and the same time, be the son of society and its father." But being the "father of society" did not mean that he was a "backward tribal father" who acted as the "guardian" of his tribe. Rather, "his fatherhood is in the framework of democratic-revolutionary relations."[8] In another essay written about a year later, Husayn distinguished between "leader" (*qa'id*) and "ruler" (*hakim*). In order to lead, he stated, "you must give those you lead the feeling that you are just, even if circumstances require you to act with a heavy hand." If a person is not just, he may be a ruler but cannot be a leader.[9] A ruler could achieve power in many ways; a leader only through the people and by virtue of their "extraordinary affinity [with him] and their constant loyalty." If these conditions were fulfilled, then the advent of the leader was "*a historic birth*" (emphasis added) and not merely an "artificial" event.[10]

The purpose of such theorizing was to project an ideal image of a single leader, as opposed to "collective leadership" (*al-qiyada al-jama'iyya*). The latter had originally been adopted by the Ba'th as a basic point of its doctrine, and ostensibly the party remained committed to it. Here, however, we encounter a remarkable ambiguity. During the decade from the Ba'th takeover until the beginning of Husayn's presidency, the principle of collective leadership was extolled in public, at times by Husayn himself;[11] yet at the same time, the ideal of the single leader was fostered vigorously, with Husayn's unmistakable encouragement. This was plainly a matter of pure political pragmatism: as long as Bakr was president, Husayn and his associates were interested in upholding collective leadership in order to circumscribe Bakr's powers and enhance their own. At the same time, talk of a single leader was to ready people's minds for the moment when Husayn would set up his one-man rule. Until then, caution was indicated. Husayn therefore joined others in calling Bakr by the title of *qa'id*, and at times "father-leader" (*al-abb al-qa'id*).[12]

While preparing to replace Bakr, Husayn made ready to appropriate his titles, too. He preferred that of *qa'id* over its possible alternatives.

Qasim had borne the title of *za'im*, and so had Bakr during the first period of Ba'th rule. But any word associated with Qasim was best avoided. Moreover, in classical Arabic *za'im* could be used to denote a commander or leader but also a usurper. *Hakim*, though always used in a positive sense, with associations including wisdom, medical science, and justice, was disliked by Husayn, as was *hukuma* (government).[13] He explained that he preferred terms such as "leadership" or "command council."[14] Indeed, the word *hukuma* disappeared almost entirely from public parlance during his tenure, being replaced by *majlis al-wuzara'* (council of ministers).

Husayn apparently understood *hakim* to denote a rather narrow, technical function of leadership, while to him *qa'id* connoted innate qualities and a superior, almost metaphysical, station. This led him to call political rivals, most particularly Hafiz al-Asad, by the name of *hakim*. He called Asad a dictator and said that his only objective was to stay in power.[15] Another "Arab *hakim*" was Qadhdhafi. A journalist, using the always fashionable rhyming technique, wrote: "*Al-Qadhdhafi—wahl fi-l-ard wa-shawk fi-l-fayafi*" (Qadhdhafi—dirt on the earth and a thorn in the desert). Such people, one of the "court writers" declared later, did not act with honesty and justice. That was why their people punished them, just as the Iraqis had punished their earlier leaders.[16]

The title *qa'id* suited Husayn's taste particularly well because it meant both a military commander and a civilian leader. In the Middle Ages, the term had been used specifically to refer to the supreme commander of the armed forces.[17] This was important to Husayn not only because, taking both meanings together, the title indicated integrated total rule but also because it made his command over the armed forces seem legitimate. He had never served in the army, and the need to project the image of a genuine military leader turned into an obsession with him—in a trait no doubt connected with his violent and expansionist aspirations. Indeed, the use of the title *qa'id* began in 1975, about the time that he "promoted" himself to the rank of general (*fariq awwal*). (Later, when he became sole ruler, he took the rank of field-marshal [*muhib*].) This seems to have caused some dissatisfaction among senior officers who had risen to their present ranks through the laborious procedure of graded promotion. He answered them indirectly by saying that "according to our tradition, each of us, regardless of his status or rank in the armed forces, is a *qa'id* and serves the people in his particular capacity."[18]

Husayn's ideas were taken up dutifully by the writers at his disposal, who elaborated on them and gave them general currency, a labor often resulting in great benefits to themselves. After Husayn's final takeover, for instance, Mu'alla became director-general of the General Authority for the Cinema and the Theater. Using his new position, he had his novel made into a film as well as into a television series and, apart from their distribution in Iraq, had them marketed in other Arab countries. Needless to say, in the film version, the fictional name of the hero was abandoned and he was called Saddam Husayn. The role of the hero was played by Saddam's cousin and son-in-law, Saddam Kamil. Later, Mu'alla published two more parts of his novel. *Al-Jumhuriyya* noted that they were received enthusiastically by readers who were eager to learn more details of the life "of the historic leader [*al-qa'id al-ta'rikhi*], the hero Saddam Husayn . . . who realized the dreams of the Iraqis and the Arabs of what a real leader should be."[19] In 1980, Mu'alla was elected to the national assembly. 'Abd al-Jabbar Muhsin, by then also a member of the house, became director of the research center attached to the Revolutionary Command Council. In 1981, he was appointed deputy minister of culture and information. Later, he became the chief military spokesman and director of the department for political indoctrination in the Ministry of Defense.

Muhsin's conception of "the leader" seems to have made its way directly into the political report of the 1982 party congress. As a matter of fact, the language in the report makes it likely that he himself worded the relevant section. The congress was held in an atmosphere of crisis: Iraq had just been forced out of Iranian territory; Khomeini had challenged the Ba'th by making the end of hostilities conditional on the removal of Husayn from power; and the party itself had apparently become restive. One way to meet these challenges was to reinforce the myth of the indispensable leader. The report therefore devoted a very long chapter to the image and the tasks of Husayn. Nothing similar had been included in the report of the preceding congress, held in 1974 when Bakr was still president. The 1982 report spoke of Husayn as the man who had sustained and consolidated the party after its overthrow late in 1963; who had led it back to power in 1968; who, within the space of a few years, had given Iraq stability and prosperity; and who had commanded the army in a brilliant campaign against Iran—the most successful war ever fought by the Arabs. The campaign had been so extraordinary because there had been "full coordination between the political and the military leadership . . . both headed by the same leader."[20]

The report coined a new expression that later turned into a household phrase: *al-qa'id al-darura* (approximately, the leader by necessity). This combination had originally been used by Muhsin and became current despite its strange, grammatically incorrect form.[21] How, then, was it to be understood? The report explained that "in bitter, hard circumstances there appeared *al-qa'id al-darura*. . . . Saddam Husayn's leadership of the party and of the revolution had been a historical necessity right from the start and it was incumbent on every party struggler with a sense of honor to maintain it." Over time, his leadership became "a national necessity" (*darura wataniyya*).[22]

Darura can be understood in its customary sense, indicating historical inevitability—a sense suited to a determinist worldview. But there is a more meaningful way to interpret it, and it is that meaning that may have underlain the choice of the word. That meaning is connected with its use to denote the sources or roots of Islamic religious law. There had originally been four such roots: the Qur'an, the *sunna* (tradition), *al-qiyas* (analogy), and *ijma'* (consensus). But some later jurists recognized additional categories as applicable for rulings on points of religious law, among them *darura* and *haja* (compulsion, force of circumstances). Later still, the idea of *darura* was extended from legal to political use. The famous eleventh-century theologian Abu Hamid al-Ghazali, for instance, justified citizens subjecting themselves to tyranny on the principle of *darura*.[23] Religious law recognizes *al-daruriyyat al-khams*, the "five necessities" that must be upheld under all circumstances: religion, the soul, the intellect, the honor of the family, and the right to property. It may be assumed that the author or authors of the political report had these verbal association in mind when they chose the term. Overall, the word carried a clear message to Iraqis that perhaps also implied a refutation of Khomeini's demand to rid themselves of Husayn. Saddam Husayn, the message read, was leader by force of necessity, and his leadership was no more to be questioned than a good Muslim would question an authoritative ruling on a point of religious law.

It may be significant that one of the first newspapers to introduce the term *al-qa'id al-darura* was the organ of the armed forces, *al-Yarmuk*, which was apparently already under Mushin's control.[24] From then onward, the expression was used almost as a synonym of Saddam Husayn. There were, however, other attributes by which he became known: *qa'id al-nasr* (the victorious leader), *qa'id al-salam* (the leader of peace), and eventually, after the invasion of Kuwait, *qa'id al-umma* (leader of the nation, implying all-Arab leadership). He was described as the *sani'* (shaper) of history; the founder of modern Iraq; and "the man of the long days" (*al-ayyam al-tawila*)—the days of Arab glory.[25] In the pre-Islamic heroic poetry, *ayyam* meant the days of battle and tribal glory.

Another writer close to Husayn, Zuhayr Sadiq Rida al-Khalidi, asked rhetorically: What other leader could have "created a new Arab man," and who could have produced an invincible Iraq? Husayn was an "eternal" (*khalid*) leader whose influence would be felt long after his disappearance as an actual "historical leader."[26] Even the new national anthem contained an implicit reference to Husayn in a line calling on the leader "to make the horizon the limit of the revolution." Children, too, were mobilized for the personality cult. The poet Faruq al-Sallum wrote an operetta for the use of kindergartens entitled, "The Leader and the Future."[27]

Oath of Allegiance

The *bay'a* (ceremony of the oath of allegiance) performed for Husayn on 13 November 1982 was unprecedented in the long history of such ceremonies. Four million Iraqis in Baghdad and other large cities came out into the streets, waving portraits of Husayn and shouting in unison: "Yes,

yes, oh Saddam; this, this is the plebiscite!" No less remarkable was the "document of allegiance" (*wathiqat al-bay'a*) handed to Husayn shortly afterward. Allegedly written with the blood of members of the national assembly, it proclaimed: "With love we swear, with our soul we shall redeem, and with our blood we make this covenant with the president, the struggler Saddam Husayn. . . . Ba'thi Iraq shall live for ever and the flag . . . of the hero of all-Arab [*qawmi*] liberation, Saddam Husayn, shall fly forever."[28]

This was not only a manifestation of the personality cult customary under absolute rulers in modern times, but also a link with much older elements stemming from the ancient Arab and Muslim political culture. Traditionally, the *bay'a* was a covenant made between a ruler and the community of Muslim believers, and as such it was one of the main pillars of the Islamic polity. Muhammad was the first to receive a *bay'a*; the last were the Ottoman sultans.[29] The most ancient meaning of the word was that of concluding a deal by means of a handshake. After becoming a political term, it retained the connotation of a mutual obligation. The ruler would fulfill the traditional duties of a Muslim ruler; the subjects would obey him. *Bay'a* could mean one of two things: adherence to a doctrine and recognition of the preestablished authority of the person who teaches it (like the *bay'a* given to Muhammad) or allegiance to a political and military leader, particularly to a caliph. In the latter sense, it was first and foremost intended to indicate a voluntary act on the part of the public in its entirety, which then created a binding obligation. Under the Abbasids in particular, allegiance to the ruler assumed the dimensions of an obligation toward Allah, and transgressors risked sentence of death.[30] The oath remained valid for as long as the leader lived, but the leader was entitled to demand its periodic renewal (*tajdid al-bay'a*) in order to reaffirm subjects' loyalty. This was indeed done often under the Umayyids. The rulers' principal duty was to obey the religious commands; failure to do so was the only valid reason for abrogating the *bay'a*.

In the early days of modern Iraq, the term *bay'a* continued to be used, although rather more symbolically. It came to mean much the same as *istifta' 'amm* (a general referendum or plebiscite).[31] To illustrate: in his description of the *bay'a* given to the Amir Faysal when he became king in 1921, the well-known Iraqi historian 'Abd al-Razzaq al-Hasani narrated how the British high commissioner "decided to ask the people with regard to a *mubaya'a* [a synonym of *bay'a*] and told the provisional government to send delegations to the [various] towns to ask the people." The *bay'a* document spoke of the "unanimous election" of Faysal, but the condition attached to it was no longer that of fulfilling God's commandments but that of heading a "legal, democratic and independent government."[32] King Ghazi, who ascended the throne in 1933, no longer used the *bay'a* ceremony; he made do with a simple *tahlif* (taking an oath).

Why did Husayn choose to revive the ancient ceremony? As we have already noted, 1982 was a year of crisis, both in the war against Iran and with respect to mounting tensions at home, with some in the party in favor of Husayn stepping down. On 9 November, Husayn called on the Iraqi and Iranian people to hold a popular referendum (*istifta'*) to decide the popularity of Husayn and Khomeini. The leader who gathered more than two-thirds of the votes cast would be considered the valid head of his state. However, Husayn himself buried the idea within the short space of five days and hastened to declare that he was not like other "rulers" who did not know what their people thought until they held a referendum or who "have no position of leadership except by this method." The media now launched a campaign against the very idea of a plebiscite or of its application to Husayn. *Al-Jumhuriyya*, for instance, wrote that the real heroes and leaders of history had not been chosen by plebiscites but had come to the fore "through the sufferings and the hopes of the people." Many rulers had rigged the results of plebiscite, but history hardly remembered them. It concluded by saying: "We ought to be ashamed of ourselves, and in front of our children, for even the passing thought" of making Husayn's leadership dependent on a referendum. The weekly *Alif Ba'*, too, rejected the idea, asserting that Husayn was the "choice [*istafaynak*] of the people." (*Istafa* differs from *intakhaba*, the common word for "elect," in that it indicates a divine choice. Mustafa—i.e., one chosen by God—was one of the attributes of Muhammad.) A *bay'a*, wrote *al-Thawra*, was more authentic than a referendum that would predictably result in 99.99 percent affirmative votes; it would express the people's rebuff of the mere thought of an alternative leadership.[33] When the *bay'a* was held, the media spoke of it as "a spontaneous plebiscite on Saddam Husayn['s leadership]." Referring to the original proposal, the demonstrators in Baghdad shouted: "No third, no two-thirds; we all want Saddam Husayn."[34]

Although he could easily have doctored the results of a referendum, Husayn probably did not wish either to test his public standing or to establish a precedent. But other reasons must be considered, such as his perpetual search for authentic roots and historical continuity. For this purpose, *bay'a* had a truer ring than "referendum," a practice and a word taken from the West. A plebiscite was, after all, a momentary reflection of public feeling; unlike the *bay'a*, it did not establish a lasting obligation on the part of the people. As for the ruler, the *bay'a* implied a more flexible obligation: he was entitled to ask for its renewal, particularly at times of crises. Moreover, a comparison with Muhammad was more desirable to Husayn than a parallel with Western election procedures. The *bay'a* allowed for no reservations, it was addressed to him personally, and it remained valid for as long as he lived. Husayn added a unique feature to it: the use of blood to write the *bay'a* deed. Not only did the members of the national assembly do so, but many people and numerous organizations continued to send Husayn *bay'a* documents written with their blood. The documents, sent by people from all walks of life, including soldiers and religious scholars, were always unilateral. They pledged the people's obedience and loyalty but did not hold the leader to any conditions. One such document said that the *bayʿa* to Husayn was like a *bayʿa* to all of Iraq. Another said that the Iraqis had decided to go with Saddam Husayn until the end, "whether to die with honor . . . or live as victors in their land."[35]

The original *bayʿa* ceremonies lasted for a week. From then on, their anniversary became a national holiday in Iraq. These anniversaries were considered renewals of the oath, but they were not the only dates serving that purpose. Husayn's birthday was another such occasion; so were military defeats or victories. A special anthem was written for these repeated festivities, and a long-distance running competition for members of the armed forces was called the *bayʿat al-qaʾid* race.[36] Attempts were made to persuade the public of the *bayʿa*'s historical significance. After a particularly bloody battle in the war against Iran, a newspaper wrote that the army had fought "like the *sahaba* [Muhammad's companions] who had sworn allegiance to the messenger of God under the tree."[37] This was meant to evoke an echo of a qurʾanic passage: verse 18 in the sura *al-Fath*, which speaks of the oath "under the tree."

Language, Husayn said, was the Arabs' "constitution"; in the past, it had been enough for people to say *bayaʿnak* (we have sworn allegiance to you) to make a man caliph. He was to remind Iraqis of this again during the uprisings of 1991. On a visit in July 1991 to Basra—the city that had given the signal to start the uprisings—he said that in the past pronouncing the *bayʿa* had put an end to all discussions. Those who thought otherwise were "transgressing" against their oath, and "nobody will agree with [them] and nobody will go with [them]."[38] This was one more qurʾanic allusion, in this case to verse 10 of the same sura, which speaks of transgressors against the prophet's *bayʿa*. Odd as such attempts to transpose seventh-century concepts to the twentieth century may look to an outsider, it seems likely that such constant repetition of ancient themes had a cumulative effect on the way Iraqis conceived of their political experience.

The Myth of Saddam Husayn

"Myth has an impressive quality: it is expected to work immediately. . . . Its influence is much stronger than the rational explanations which are likely to invalidate it later on."[39] Clearly, myths, appealing to emotions and instincts as they do, overcome or lull the intellect. From the start, the men in charge of shaping Husayn's image were keenly aware of this, and they strove to make him a living legend. Muʿalla's novel *The Long Days* was only one link in a long chain. Layer by layer, his image was created in poetry, prose, and the arts, all of which were made subservient to this aim. The more distressing realities were, the more the myths abounded. The shapers of Husayn's myths combined the ancient and the modern in remarkable ways. The images and the symbols were taken from the past, most often from the distant past, but the means employed to market them were the most modern available to the mass media. The press became a subcontractor of sorts for the propagandists; at times, half the space in the papers was filled with pictures and sayings of Husayn and with descriptions of his activities. Commercial advertising hardly exists in the Iraqi newspapers, but when it appears, it takes the form of a picture of Husayn, accompanied by greetings or congratulations on the part of the advertiser. Altogether, Iraqi propaganda methods recall modern marketing techniques, always thinking up new gimmicks to sell the product.

Husayn himself directed these campaigns, whether directly or indirectly. In 1988, *The Political Dictionary of Saddam Husayn* was published. It contained 500 entries of his political expressions, collected and interpreted by the poet Muhammad Salih ʿAbd al-Rida. *The Complete Writings of Saddam Husayn* was published in eighteen volumes.[40] Another method— one with the advantage of brevity—was to collect his witticisms and bons mots (*idaʾat*) and place them at the top of newspaper pages. One such saying was "Democracy is the source of strength of the individual and of society." Politicians and journalists acquired the custom of weaving such sayings into their speeches and articles. Their endless repetition eventually gave them currency among the public at large.

One method used consistently was to equate Husayn with Iraq, with the Iraqis, and with Arabs everywhere. This led to an interesting and novel use of political language meant to underline the bond between the man and his country: ʿIraq Saddam Husayn (the Iraq of Saddam Husayn), a use or misuse of the Arabic genitive case to indicate an inseparable link. Similar expressions were *Saddam al-ʿArab* (Saddam of the Arabs) and *Saddam al-Fath* (the Saddam of conquest). The poet Ghazay Dirʿ al-Taʾi took this method a step further; in a song for children, he wrote:

> We are Iraq and its name is Saddam;
> We are love and its name is Saddam;
> We are a people and its name is Saddam;
> We are the Baʿth and its name is Saddam.[41]

Another approach to the same goal used terms taken from family life: *Abu-l-ʿIraq al-jadid* (the father of the new Iraq) or *Baba Saddam* (Daddy Saddam, perhaps recalling the name of Ataturk, father of the Turks).[42] At other times, he was spoken of as the son or the elder brother of the Iraqi people. The theme of fatherhood was first employed by Husayn himself. In a speech in January 1981, he told his listeners that over the last few months he had received thousands of letters from children and old people, and all had called him "our father and begetter" (*waliduna*). At times, he was addressed as *Saddamuna* (our Saddam). "Saddamism" as a term for a historical phenomenon was used as an overall reference to all that was good in the Arab character.[43]

While such images were meant to evoke feelings of closeness, others were used to place Husayn far from the common people, in a realm of the superhuman, not to say the supernatural. He was likened to light and rain, to the sun and the moon, to the sea and to a river, to a flower and to a tree in paradise. He was like a lion or an eagle, like gold, or like a fortress. All these metaphorical images are found in the descriptions of medieval Islamic rulers, and the writers working for Husayn used them just as the court poets of earlier times had.[44] Of particular interest are images taken from the earliest Arab-Muslim cultural environment: *khayma* (tent), *kufiyya* (the traditional desert headdress), *sayf* (sword) and *faris* (knight). The last two terms are in special favor with Husayn. He is called *sayf al-Islam al-battar* (Islam's sharp sword)[45] and *faris al-ʿarab* or *faris al-umma al-ʿarabiyya* (knight of the Arabs or Knight of the Arab nation).[46]

Husayn gave instructions to research the historical significance of these terms, and the army organ *al-Qadisiyya* wrote an article explaining that, in ancient times, the word "sword" had been the synonym of strength, might, and honor. Arabs would keep their swords by their sides day and night, and compose poems about them. Muhammad had said: "He who girds his sword for the sake of Allah, Allah will gird him with a belt of honor"; his grandson, the Imam ʿAli, had spoken of the sword as a "blessing"; and—the article goes on to say, as if it were a perfectly natural transition—Saddam had said: "The sword is the weapon of the strugglers who defend the land, [their] principles, and sovereignty."[47] The sayings here attributed to Muhammad and ʿAli are not found in any of the accepted *hadith* collections I have been able to consult. This is significant in two ways. It attests to the need to rely on old authorities, and it shows that the production of new *hadith* items goes on today as it did at so many earlier stages of Muslim history. Husayn ordered a "sword of *Qadisiyya*" made, produced from parts of the weapons of soldiers who had fallen in combat against Iran and from jewelry donated by Iraqi women for the war effort. It was awarded to war heroes.[48]

The army newspaper *al-Qadisiyya* also examined the historical concept of *faris* (knight) and found that it was used to denote all that was good in the Arab character: manliness, tolerance, knowledge, talents superior to all other mortals, and the capacity for revenge. Such a man, the article proclaimed, was Husayn. "After the Arab nation had become detached from its past and ancient glory, God sent it one of its sons [Husayn]," who possessed all the qualities of knighthood and who remade Iraqi history. Through his genius, he linked the present with the past.[49]

Husayn's Role Models

In August 1990, a few days after the invasion of Kuwait, Husayn sent a message to Egyptian president Muhammad Husni Mubarak, attacking him for making common cause with the United States and Saudi Arabia against Iraq. He reinforced his political argument by referring to Mubarak's lowly origin from a peasant family not connected with the families of Egypt's former rulers. He contrasted this with his own origin from a most illustrious family that traced its origins back to the Qurayshis, the tribe of Muhammad; he claimed descent from the prophet's grandson Husayn, the son of 'Ali bin Abi Talib and Fatima.[50] This was not his only reference to his genealogy, whether actual or imaginary. On the contrary, it was part and parcel of the buildup of his image among Iraqis and among Arabs everywhere. This pride in ancestry (*al-mufakhara bi-l-hasab wa-l-nasab*) goes back to the most ancient period of desert culture. It remained a vital element in Islamic political culture because descent from the tribe of Quraysh (and even more so from its Hashim subtribe, to which Muhammad's family belonged) was one of the means of establishing the legitimacy of a Muslim ruler. Descent from 'Ali, the prophet's cousin, son-in-law, and closest associate, would of course lend a leader a potent claim to legitimate leadership. Moreover, Shi'is would consider any leader not descended from 'Ali a usurper (even if the leader came from Quraysh).[51]

The claim to such lineage was only one aspect of Saddam Husayn's endeavors to liken himself to the great leaders of the Arab and Muslim past. There was probably an element of compensation in such effort, for in fact Husayn was born into a simple farmer's family in the village of 'Awja near the town of Tikrit. But an aura of greatness derived from an affinity with great figures of the past was more likely to arouse the imagination of Iraqis and engage their loyalty than being a Tikriti. The historical figures Husayn wished to liken himself to varied with changing circumstances. His small army of poets, writers, and journalists made the changes required by the course of events and by Husayn's varying preferences.

Among the first model figures Husayn wished to equate himself with was of course 'Ali bin Abi Talib. The timing of Husayn's first use of 'Ali as a personal model was not coincidental. It came some time after Khomeini's Islamic Revolution in Iran (February 1979) and Husayn's own final takeover (July 1979) and was intended to achieve three goals: to ingratiate himself with the Shi'i population of Iraq; to counter the contagion likely to spread to them from Iran through Khomeinist propaganda; and to give Husayn the image of an "authentic" Shi'i in contrast with Khomeini's non-Arab, hence "false," Shi'ism. In a speech in August 1979, Husayn praised 'Ali as representing "the spirit and the meaning of the Islamic message." The present Iraqi leadership was likewise seeking such "godly values." He went on to establish his own link with 'Ali by saying: "We are the grandchildren of the Imam Husayn [bin 'Ali]." But since everybody knew he was a Sunni, this seemed not enough. After a while, he published an "official" genealogy to "prove" his descent from 'Ali.[52] One of his establishment writers, Amir Ahmad Iskandar, took the matter a step further, explaining that, precisely as in the manner approved by tradition, Husayn's family tree established his descent "link by link" (*jidhr ba'd jidhr*). Iskandar went on to say that Husayn had not mentioned this point previously because he did not wish to dwell on his own historical and religious roots in front of those who had none.[53]

The employment of professional "image-builders" and writers to ac-
quaint the widest possible public with Husayn's genealogy exemplifies the
technique of taking up a remark of his—originally perhaps a quite inconsequential one—making it common knowledge, and eventually turning it
into a "fact." Did the publication of the family tree give Husayn's claim
greater credence among Iraqis? Perhaps, as had often been the case with
tribal genealogies, the ambitious pretension behind it was accounted more
important than the facts; legend counted for more than reality. One way
or another, Husayn was a past master of building up such myths layer by
layer until they became an established part of the Iraqi political discourse.
Since no one publicly questioned the official genealogy, it was perfectly
easy to go on reinforcing it and even to export it beyond the borders of
Iraq. 'Izzat Ibrahim al-Duri, a senior Ba'th functionary and Husayn's right-
hand man, declared with a ring of inner conviction that "the values of the
Imam 'Ali are being renewed in the leader of our revival."[54] As we have
seen, Husayn did not hesitate to cite the point in his note to Mubarak as
if it was beyond question.

At a later stage, Husayn placed the caliph al-Mansur at the center of
his historical image–building effort. The purpose here was to create an
impression of political and military greatness rather than of moral rectitude. Al-Mansur was the second Abbasid caliph, reigning from 754 to 775.
His name is linked with the suppression of Shi'i opposition to his dynasty
and with the elimination of the remaining supporters of the Umayyads
(who had preceded the Abbasids). He expanded Abbasid territory to the
north and the east; he built Baghdad and made it the splendid, even legendary, imperial capital as which it is remembered. He was thus a fine
role model to use in wartime.

In 1985, while the war against Iran was at one of its peaks, an establishment writer wrote (in a piece that was half poem/half article):
"Saddam Husayn al-Mansur will continue to be [our] moon and Iraq
will be the flag of victory."[55] "Al-Mansur" is used here with a twofold
meaning: the literal meaning of "victorious by the grace of Allah," and
the added connotation of the caliph so named. A year or so later, the
first meaning was made more explicit by calling Husayn *al-mansur b-i-llah*,[56]
but here again we find an echo of the names of past rulers, such as al-
Mustansir b-i-llah, al-Mustanjid b-i-llah, and al-Muntasir b-i-llah. In
order to underline the continuity between Mansur I (the caliph) and
Mansur II (Husayn), *al-Jumhuriyya* used the expression *Baghdad
al-Mansurayn* (the Baghdad of the two Mansurs), "the one bearing witness to Mansur's wondrous foundation, the other bearing witness to
Mansur Saddam Husayn's wondrous rebuilding of it." The paper thought
it significant that the date of the foundation of Baghdad, the anniversary of the formation of the Ba'th, and Husayn's birthday all fell in the
month of April. For one of his birthdays, the inhabitants of Baghdad
gave Husayn a model of the caliph's city made of pure gold. The use of
al-mansur was not discontinued at the time of Iraq's severe defeats at

the hands of the Iranians. A journalist spoke of the Iraqi soldiers in the field as "millions of al-Mansur Saddam Husayn."[57]

Another suitable role model was Saladin who, although a Kurd, was a native of Tikrit. Quite apart from his historical achievements against the European crusaders, he could therefore be a useful symbol for Arab-Kurdish unity—a symbol much needed in the modern era of prolonged warfare between the two peoples in Iraq.[58] His successful reunification of the Muslims in consequence of his victories over the crusaders was taken as a signal to the Arabs that they, too, could unite, provided a new Saladin stood at their head. It is not clear when Husayn first began to model his own image after that of Saladin. The uncertainties of Husayn's birth may have had something to do with his choice; the accepted version held that he was born in 'Awja near Tikrit, but others believed that he was born in Tikrit itself. Furthermore, the population register of the ministry of the interior records the year of his birth as 1939, while his official biographies give the year as 1937.[59] There have been several attempts to explain the difference.[60] The most plausible is that he wished to appear as having been born precisely 800 years after Saladin (1137/1937).[61] In fact, Husayn did have a point in common with Saladin: both had a vast propaganda machine working for them. Just as, according to some historians, Saladin was driven to fight the battle at Hattin by his own propaganda claims, so Husayn's own propaganda methods dragged him into the Gulf War.[62]

Primary targets of Ba'th propaganda were children. From a tender age, they were exposed to official indoctrination and taught to admire Iraq's leader. In this particular context, comparing Husayn with the great figures of Arab history was a useful device. In 1987, a Baghdad publisher of children's books printed a booklet entitled, *The Hero Saladin*. Its cover picture showed a portrait of Husayn, with sword-wielding horsemen in the background. The first, shorter, section was a presentation of Saladin's life, with the accent on his reconquest of Jerusalem and of "Arab Palestine." The second and longer part was devoted to the "new leader," whom it called "the noble and heroic Arab fighter Saladin II Saddam Husayn." Throughout the booklet, Husayn was referred to as "Saladin II," and his life story was told in a manner meant to establish the similarity between the two. To do so, Husayn's "heroism" in the war against Iran was given particular salience. It was Husayn, the booklet said (addressing itself to its "young friends"), who "personally coordinated most of the battles, so as to demonstrate to the Arab and the international world that a leader must be at the head [of his forces]." So also Saladin had done. Again, like Saladin, Husayn was spoken of as the leader of the Arab nation in its entirety. The booklet concluded with greetings and blessings from the children to "Saladin II."[63]

Sometime later, *al-Qadisiyya* published a long article written at the insistence of Husayn and entitled, "Saladin, the Liberator of Egypt, Syria [*al-Sham*] and Palestine." There was no specific reference to Husayn's affinity with Saladin, but the article began by speaking of the "real" hero who was " a glowing star . . . [that] melts the snows of despair." In July 1987, a colloquium on Saladin was held at Tikrit under the title, "The Battle of Liberation—from Saladin to Saddam Husayn." Latif Nusayyif al-Jasim, the minister of culture and information, dwelt on the "wonderful coincidence" that Saladin and Husayn were born in the same district, "two sons of Iraq and of the Arab nation with its glorious history." A newspaper spoke of the line linking the original battle of Qadisiyya to Hattin and again to the modern Qadisiyya (the war against Iran).[64]

The mythology equating Husayn with Saladin continued after the war against Iran and may have served (whether intentionally or not) as a sort of preparation of public opinion for the "liberation of Jerusalem" and, in consequence, the encounter with the world of the infidels (i.e., the Gulf War, in terms used in Iraq). Characteristic of this trend is an article in *al-Qadisiyya* under the heading, "Our Saddam Is the Saladin of the Arabs and the Kurds." It said that just as history had caused the rise of "our grandfather" Saladin, so it would witness the rise of Husayn, "the best of sons to the best of fathers."[65] The following day it elaborated on the theme, saying that "Palestine is embracing Baghdad" because the latter was the spring of hope for the Arabs and hope would erupt from it despite its enemies, who were trying "to stop the light shining [from there] on the Arab lands." Or, as another newspaper put it: "For the first time since Saladin" Arab hearts were beating with hope—the hope given them by Husayn.[66]

Little wonder, then, that in some people's minds the Gulf War took on eschatological dimensions. At the height of the war, a newspaper wrote: "We smell the smell of Hattin and of the battle for the innermost sanctum." The "campaign of oppression" against Iraq had really started back in 1987, recalling that Hattin had been fought in 1187. Just as Saladin had foiled an attack by the crusaders in 1191, so his modern embodiment would defeat the "new crusaders" in 1991.[67]

Unlike with Saladin, no direct affinity with the prophet Muhammad could possibly be established without being interpreted as blasphemous. Only indirect and cautious hints were at all admissible, and only veiled, evocative expressions could be used. We have seen that the fictitious hero of *The Long Days*—Husayn's "double," as it were—was called Muhammad. After the invasion of Kuwait, Husayn took the additional name of 'Abdallah, possibly an allusion to the name of Muhammad's father, possibly to be understood in its literal meaning of "servant of God," possibly both.[68] Somewhat more tangible was the use of the word *rasul* (messenger) in connection with Husayn: he was at times called *rasul al-shams* (messenger of the sun) or *rasul al-ʿArab* (messenger of the Arabs). Even though *rasul* was often enough used for "messenger" in the day-to-day sense, such titles could hardly fail to evoke an association with Muhammad's appellation of *rasul Allah*.[69] Moreover, it had become customary to describe Muhammad as *al-rasul al-qaʾid* (the messenger and the leader). This was an anachronistic use, since the word *qaʾid* in the sense of "leader" did not exist in the seventh century, but it established an affinity between the prophet and Husayn, the leader. Calling Husayn's annual birthday celebrations *mawlid al-qa'id* also had some similarity with the prophet's birthday, called *'id al-mawlid al-nabawi al-sharif*.[70] Another hint lies in the stress on Husayn having been born an orphan on his father's side and having grown up in his paternal uncle's house, just as Muhammad had grown up in the house of his paternal uncle Abu Talib.

A long time passed between Muhammad's death and the appearance of the first written account of his life (called *sira*, or more specifically *al-sira al-nabawiyya*).[71] Husayn, for his part, had a biography of himself written in his lifetime and called it *sira*. Late in 1990, the national assembly passed a law establishing a special committee to oversee the writing of what might be called Husayn's official biography. The assembly rejected a proposal to call the biography *sifr* (book, large volume), preferring *sira*, notably because of its association with the prophet. It explained its choice by saying that the biography was intended to keep Husayn's memory alive "for hundreds of years."[72] To call his biography *sira* was one way of establishing a link with the prophet; another was calling his personal aircraft *al-Buraq*, the name given to the legendary animal that bore Muhammad from Mecca to Jerusalem and back in a single night (the "night's journey" that became a Muslim holiday). *Al-Jumhuriyya* spoke of Husayn's "special relationship" with his plane, adding: "Who said that an aircraft is a [mere] thing bereft of understanding?"[73]

Breaking the otherwise cautiously observed taboo on direct comparisons between Husayn and Muhammad, a scholar named Ahmad Sawsa wrote that Husayn was following in the prophet's footsteps and turning his teachings into realities. That was so, he explained, because "the purpose behind the appearance of the prophet in his time was to accomplish the unity and rebirth of the nation." There had, he went on, never been an Arab leader like Husayn; even Saladin had only begun the work of unification but had not completed it.[74] Even more daring was a poet, Ghazay Dir' al-Ta'i, who wrote:

O our lord Saddam
You have brought the light of God
To the Arab tribes
And broken their idols
In times long past.[75]

In a similar vein, the poetess Shafiqa al-Daghistani wrote that the Arab chosen from on high to carry the torch of the mission of mankind was the very man (Husayn) who was now standing guard on Iraq's eastern frontiers. "Just as the paths of Mecca . . . knew him, so the borders of the homeland know him today, as he stands firm against the gods of evil." *Al-'Iraq* compared Husayn's war against the "apostates and the ignorant" of Iran with Muhammad's wars for the true faith. Amin Jiyad wrote that the man now living among us "has become a prophet."[76]

Muhammad's name is never mentioned without adding the blessing *salla Allah 'alayhi wa-sallam* (God's prayers and peace upon him). If Husayn resembled him, it was natural to link his name with a blessing of his own. And indeed, the words *hafizahu Allah* (may God preserve him) became almost a part of Husayn's name. Some, wishing to enlarge upon the theme, began saying, *Hafizahu Allah wa-ra'ahu* (May God preserve and protect him). The first to use this blessing was 'Abd al-Ghani 'Abd al-Ghaffur, director-general of the ministry for youth affairs, in 1981. He wrote of Husayn that he resembled the caliph 'Umar in his search for justice and 'Ali in the firmness of his principles; he then added, "*hafizahu Allah.*" Three years later, having served in the meantime as minister of religion and of religious endowments and having become a member of the top party leadership, he published an "open letter to the President, the leader Saddam Husayn, may God preserve him."[77] From then on, members of the armed forces, party men, writers, and journalists, as well as people from the public at large who understood which way the wind was blowing, added the blessing to each and every mention of Husayn. This was particularly noticeable in times of crisis or when Saddam Husayn seemed to be in danger, or else when the user of the phrase felt threatened. One such time was the Gulf War and its immediate aftermath. Even scholars followed suit: the historian Hasani wrote of "the beloved leader Saddam Husayn, may Allah preserve him."[78]

Do these things have a significance beyond being indications of the prevalent personality cult? They became current under the pressure of circumstances, but they teach us something about how political language is shaped through the interrelationship between the ruler and the ruled, with the latter learning to sharpen their senses to pick up the new usages as quickly as possible. Do they do so as a protective screen a defense mechanism? Or is there an element of inner persuasion? These questions must remain moot.

I I I

Unity and Separatism

Iraq is one of those states that lack a most vital element in social life: likemindedness and ethnic and religious unity. . . . This is a point which fills my heart with grief. In my opinion, there is not yet an Iraqi nation; rather, there are human blocs without any national or patriotic feeling, full of superstitious religious traditions and with nothing to unite them. They listen to councils of evil, incline to anarchy, and are ready to rise against any government whatsoever. This being so, we endeavor to form from these blocs a people which we shall educate, guide and teach.
—Memorandum by King Faysal I, quoted in 'Abd al-Razzaq al-Hasami, *Ta'rikh al-wizarat al-'Iraqiyya*

Iraq is unique in that each of the three main groups that make up its population—Sunni Arabs, Shi'is, and Kurds—is torn between two affinities: an Iraqi and a supranational affinity. For each group, the two are incompatible and, often enough, conflicting. The Iraqi idenity they all share is the most recent and least rooted; the supranational orientation has much deeper roots and much greater historical weight. Moreover, the latter has a transnational character, linking each group with a different region outside Iraq geographically, historically, or ideologically. The Sunnis feel part of the wider world of Sunni Arabs everywhere; the Shi'is have a certain affinity with the Shi'is across the border in Iran; and the Kurds feel linked with their Kurdish conationals in Syria, Turkey, and Iran. The second trend not only impeded the emergence of an Iraqi nationalism but also created dilemmas of self-identification and made relations between the three groups problematic. This was aggravated by the fact that, compared with the combined numerical strength of Kurds and Shi'is, the Sunni Arabs are a minority. Yet it is they who dominate and virtually run the state. The other groups' strength of numbers therefore forced the Sunnis to placate them to some extent to counter the constant threat of separatism and division.

Understandably, these problems became more severe whenever modern Iraq passed through one of its many crises. How would Sunnis rate their "Iraqiness" against their all-Arab nationalism? How would Shi'is balance being Arabs and Iraqis against their affinity with their coreligionists? And what would be more important to the Kurds: being Iraqi citizens or belonging to the (extraterritorial) Kurdish entity? Or perhaps the focus of their identity was a separate, though presently oppressed, Kurdish entity within the Iraqi borders? Such questions could not fail to create mutual suspicions. They also raised vital issues of principle: Was one of the three groups superior to the others, and if so, why? Were the Sunni Arabs entitled to foster links with Arabs across the border yet deny the other two groups such cross-border identifications? What implications did this situation have for the domestic consolidation and ultimate strength of the state? All these questions were amply reflected in the political language used to speak of them—a language in which loaded terms abounded. As we shall see, terminology created stark black-and-white pictures, and one group often described another in terms that were a mirror image of the way the latter spoke of the former.

6

The Sunni Arabs
An Issue of Double Identity

Guardians of "the Iraqi Tent"

Among the many new terms that have entered the Arabic political dictionary since the late nineteenth century, *wataniyya* and *qawmiyya* have a particularly strong emotional impact. Both words, though from Arabic roots, were first used in Turkish. Both connote the loyalty of the individual to a larger social frame. *Watan* has to do with soil and territory, originally meaning "place," often in the sense of house, locality, or even cattle fold. In modern times, *wataniyya* has come to mean "patriotism" or loyalty to a territorial unit. *Qawmiyya*, by contrast, refers to a community of people; *qawm* originally meant a group, a tribe, or a faction. From the beginning of the twentieth century, it came to mean a group of people of common ethnic and linguistic origin possessing common characteristics.[1] Wherever nation and territory are coterminous, the two words become nearly interchangeable (cf. *nationalisme* and *patriotisme* in French). In the Arab world, where speakers of Arabic are divided into many states, *wataniyya* has come to mean loyalty to one's territorial state, and *qawmiyya* or *qawmiyya 'arabiyya*, loyalty to the Arab nation—that is, the entirety of Arabs, regardless of their belonging to one Arab state or another.

The post–World War I division of the Arab lands into several states was a national trauma, and this may explain the almost obsessive use of the word *qawmiyya*, particularly in political rhetoric. But beyond rhetoric,

89

the term evokes the strong fellow-feeling among Arabs grounded in their ethnic origin and their common language. These have remained potent factors despite the many years that have passed since the establishment of the Arab territorial states. But the constant evocation of Pan-Arab nationalism creates, in turn, a commitment on which the territorial states find it difficult to encroach. At certain times and in certain places, *qawmiyya* and *wataniyya* coexist; at other times and elsewhere, they compete with and struggle against each other.[2]

If this is true of the Arab states in general, it is doubly true of Iraq, and most especially of Ba'thi Iraq. This is partly because of the ideological commitment of the Ba'th party to all-Arab nationalism and partly because of the ethnic composition of Iraq. On the domestic scene, the Ba'th strove to create an Iraqi people (*sha'b*), a policy that if it had succeeded would have reinforced the Iraqi territorial entity at the expense of the all-Arab affinity of Iraq. In a different way, but with much the same effect, the Ba'thi desire for hegemony in the Arab world placed the interests of Iraq above those of other Arab states, regardless of the all-Arab verbiage with which such claims were usually put forward. Ba'th leaders understood the dilemmas thus created but still clung to both policies. The change in the frequency with which one or the other of the above two terms were used provides us with something like a seismograph measuring tensions at home or indicating fluctuating domestic or inter-Arab priorities.

When Iraqi media spoke of *wataniyya*, they meant to stress Iraqi patriotism or "Iraqiness." In using the word, they were appealing to an existing or hoped-for consensus encompassing Sunnis and Shi'is, Arabs and Kurds, communists and nationalists. At such times, the Iraqi territorial state was spoken of as a superior value. The non-Arab component of the population, the Kurds, joined the authorities in adopting an attitude of Iraqi patriotism—at times because they considered it politic to pay lip service, at other times because they hoped to head off the development of stronger all-Arab ties.[3] Well aware of such motives, the Ba'th stressed its *watani* character with great frequency, trying to impress actual or potential allies (the communists, the Kurds) and making it appear that the fall of the Ba'th would be a great *watani* disaster.[4]

From the early 1970s, the Ba'th spoke of *al-qiwa al-wataniyya*—Iraq's "patriotic forces." These were not named, but Iraqis understood very well that the term applied to the communists and the Kurds with whom the authorities wished, at various times, to form a coalition. Even though the Ba'th protested from time to time that it had no monopoly on patriotism, it claimed the right to pass judgment on who was or was not *watani*. These definitions were subject to change. As Husayn put it: "He who was a patriot in the 1950s will not be so considered in 1968." Patriotism, in his view, was to be measured by the way certain people related to the burning issues of the moment.[5] When the alliances with the Kurds and the communists broke up (the former in 1974, the latter in 1978), acknowledgment of the patriotism of the erstwhile allies was withdrawn and they became "traitors." When some of them "repented," they were "taken into the Iraqi tent [*khayma*]." Husayn declared occasionally that "Kurdishness" did not detract from "Iraqiness," provided the Kurds were ready to remain within "the big Iraqi tent" (i.e., did not want to secede).[6]

The expression "tent" in the political context, apparently first used by Husayn himself, of course stems from the Bedouin tradition and was intended to convey the sense of a common fate and a feeling of togetherness in the face of external difficulties. A communist turned pro-Ba'thi, 'Aziz al-Hajj, seems to have followed in Saddam Husayn's footsteps when he likened Iraqi *wataniyya* to a "tent in which all the loyal sons of great Iraq find shelter, regardless of their [political] affinities." At the time of the Kurdish uprising in 1991, a pro-Ba'th Kurdish newspaper wrote that despite the rebellion, the Kurds continued to add a "brilliant color to the Iraqi tent" and kept regarding Iraq as their homeland (*watan*).[7]

Since the Ba'th regime saw itself as being in charge of the tent, it wished to lay down more precise definitions of Iraqi patriotism. One way to do so was through elimination. For instance, the right to the title of patriot was taken away from the leaders who had preceded the Ba'th. After they had tried to liquidate all patriotic organizations and parties, "power passed to the *watani* party [i.e., the Ba'th]." Henceforth, loyalty to Iraq was measured by loyalty to the party. In Husayn's words: "What we demand of the Iraqis is to be patriotic and not deviate from [our] path [*masira*]." Another yardstick was whether citizens placed their Iraqi identification above all other loyalties. The political report of the 1982 party congress laid down that "*wataniyya* . . . means the practical preponderance, in times of crisis, of loyalty to the homeland, should it conflict, in given circumstances, with the loyalty . . . to religion, to a religious school [*madhhab*], or to a tribe." Patriotism, it went on to say, was no longer a shallow feeling but rather a "deep, strong and solid emotion of love of the fatherland, loyalty to it, and action for its sake."[8]

From its inception, the Ba'th regime considered schools prime instruments for instilling patriotism. President Ahmad Hasan al-Bakr said that the most important task of schoolteachers was "to arouse sentiments of *wataniyya*." Husayn formed a national (*watani*) education committee and discussed with its members ways and means of strengthening patriotic feelings among the pupils. The Iraqi flag was to be raised in schools every Thursday morning. Curricula were to give salience to *watani* culture. The minister for youth affairs, Ahmad Husayn al-Samarra'i, said that youth centers all over Iraq were busy "developing feelings of patriotism and Arab nationalism [*qawmiyya*]." During the war against Iran, special hymns were composed for schoolchildren. They were given such titles as "My Homeland is the Friend of the Sun," or "The Defenders of Our Frontiers."[9]

The army was expected to act as a melting pot, helping the various groupings in the population overcome religious and ethnic divisions (see Part 4). Husayn spoke of Iraq's "national" (*watani*) armed forces, which alone were capable of guaranteeing *watani* independence. The political report of the 1982 party congress similarly referred to the army's "historical opportunity" of proving its patriotism in the war.[10]

All this could have been fairly uncomplicated if everybody had understood *watan* to mean Iraq. But according to Ba'th doctrine (and other ideologies in Arab countries elsewhere), *watan* could also refer to the Arab world as a whole, as for instance in the common phrase *al-watan al-'Arabi al-kabir* (the great Arab homeland). In similar fashion, Palestine was called *al-watan al- salib* (the stolen homeland) or *al-watan al-muhtall* (the occupied homeland). When the entire Arab world was subsumed under the same concept habitually applied to Iraq alone, ambiguities (though possibly intentional) were bound to result. When a daily newspaper used the slogan, "A man who does not shoulder his responsibility of defending the *watan* is not entitled to live," what precisely did it mean?[11] To defend Iraq? Or Palestine? We find a similar question mark attached to the wording of the new national hymn introduced by the Ba'th in 1981. It is entitled "Land of the Two Rivers," a term readily understood as connoting Iraq in its modern borders. But the text itself gives a different impression. The words, "the homeland reaching the horizon with its wings," clearly convey a much broader meaning.[12] Throughout the hymn, there is an attempt to make "Iraq" and "Arab homeland" coincide and to equate Iraq's ambitions with the will of the Arab world at large.

Though *wataniyya* is generally equated with "Iraqiness," there are clearly significant uncertainties here. These derive chiefly from the ambiguous and blurred language used by the Ba'th party itself. In the early years of its rule, the Ba'th promoted the myth of Babylon, expecting that recourse to it would be helpful as a means of creating common historical antecedents that all Iraqis could share.[13] But these attempts were made mainly in a literary and cultural context and hardly spilled over into politics. They were intended to show the historical greatness of Mesopotamia/ Iraq and draw inspiration from its ancient culture. But whether such concepts could serve as a substitute for the necessary drawing together of the country's heterogeneous components by means of a slow and natural process remained an open question.

Standard-Bearers of Arabism

Qawm as the collective name for a tribe, people, or other grouping is a word with deep roots in Arabic. It occurs in a great many suras of the Qur'an.[14] *Qawmiyya*, by contrast, in its modern sense is a nineteenth-century term, the early use of which coincided with the reception from Europe of the idea of nationalism. It became common in Arabic only at the beginning of the twentieth century. At first, it was used both in the meaning of the nationalism of a territorial state (e.g., *qawmiyya misriyya*; Egyptian nationalism, etc.) and in the sense of all-Arab nationalism. But it was the second interpretation that became dominant, as did the ideology of Pan-Arabism linked so closely with its use.

Iraq considered itself the cradle of Pan-Arabism. Already in 1927, officers of the Iraqi army (established in 1921) formulated a *mithaq qawmi 'Arabi* (a Pan-Arab covenant) with the aim of "purging elements harmful to the Arab cause, and of uniting the Arab states in a manner encompassing politics, the economy, education, and the military." As a sop to the Kurds, they added that the "Kurdish problem" would not conflict with Arab nationalism, as long as the Kurds strove to "expand into states bordering with Iraq [meaning Turkey and Iran]."[15]

Sami Shawkat turned *qawmiyya* into the highest Arab value, higher even than religion. Declaring that his time was the era of *qawmiyya*, he wrote that "religion was being defeated by nationalism which was superior to it in the sphere of politics and policy-making" and which would bring happiness to every Iraqi. To make sure that he was properly understood, he added that "no Iraqi concept is more powerful than [all-]Arab *qawmiyya*." Other non-Arab peoples, too, needed to go into "the Arab melting pot."[16] Michel 'Aflaq went to the length of saying that *qawmiyya* was the modern dress in which Islam was being revived. *Qawmiyya* sanctified human love and rejected arrogance, chauvinism, and isolationism. At an earlier stage, however, 'Aflaq had held very different views: *Qawmiyya* would be successful, he had said, if it "inspires hatred to the point of death against anyone expressing opinions conflicting with it." Those with conflicting opinions were men "destined for liquidation" so that their views would be liquidated with them.[17]

While this is not the place to recount the history of Pan-Arabism in the Arab world as a whole, it needs to be said that in modern Iraq there was hardly a politician or ideologue who did not take it up, a fact attesting to its strength. The Ba'th party congress of 1982 included a section on *qawmiyya* in its report, in which it said: "It is false to assume that *qawmiyya* entered the Arab homeland as the result of the confrontation with Europe and through deriving ideas from European nationalism." On the contrary, it had "deep roots in Arab society."[18] It is possible to ignore the apologetic note in this statement and still say that, once received, the idea became powerful in Iraqi, and most particularly Ba'th, thinking.

If *qawmiyya* such as the Ba'th conceived it needed enemies to keep it going, it also needed positive goals. A long series of government actions were therefore described as having been undertaken for the sake of all-Arab nationalism. Among them were the nationalization of the oil industry in 1972; the 1975 decision to grant Iraqi citizenship to any Arab who desired it; and most particularly the war against Iran, consistently described as having been undertaken to "defend" the Arabs and their cause. Arab unity and Iraqi leadership of the Arab world were extolled by means of the rhetoric surrounding *qawmiyya*, as was the invasion of Kuwait. It was the Ba'th, it was claimed, that upheld the principles of *qawmiyya*; it was Iraq that had returned them to their rightful place in political thought and practice; and it was Husayn who step-by-step had made the "dream of *qawmiyya*" come true.[19]

There were, however, leaders in other Arab countries who in the Ba'thi view were acting against *qawmiyya*. Chief among them were President Hafiz al-Asad of Syria and the Libyan leader Mu'ammar al-Qadhdhafi, both of whom sided with Iran during the war. Their Arabism, Ba'th spokespeople declared, was "a fraud," while Iraq's was "authentic." Soon after the outbreak of the war, the internal party organ wrote that the war was being fought to enable people to tell "real Arabs" from *al-mutajanissun bi-l-'arabiyya* (those who had [merely] become Arab citizens). Another newspaper article recalled that in the past the bonds of kinship had been supreme, but today the "citizenship Arabs" were giving their all to foreigners for them to fight fellow Arabs. Other such "citizenship Arabs" were burying their heads in the sand, having failed to grasp what was going on around them.[20] (The allusion is to the Gulf states and their vacillating policies during the war.) Other Iraqi writers used the term *'Arab al-lisan* (speakers of Arabic) with the same intent. Such people had only one attribute of Arabism: their language. But they did not act like real Arabs. The term was often applied to Asad and Qadhdhafi, whose "traitorous conduct" was worse than the open hostility of the enemy.[21] Eventually, however, victory would go to *qawmiyya* because it was set to "accomplish the all-Arab human revolution."[22]

Another pejorative, as old as Islam, was *a'rab* (plural of *a'rabi*). It meant Bedouin: ignorant people and men of the *jahiliyya*. In the Qur'an (*sura al-Tawba*, v. 99) it takes on the additional meaning of blasphemer or of one sitting on the fence with respect to religion. *Lisan al-'Arab* explains that *a'rab* were Bedouin whom Allah called thus because they had come to see Muhammad at Medina to seek material benefits rather than accept Islam. Shortly before the beginning of the Gulf War, the Revolutionary Command Council issued a proclamation addressed to "all believers" and informing them that a plot against Iraq was afoot, concocted by the "heinous *a'rab*" and the infidels. Needless to say, the first term applied to all those Arab states who had joined the wartime coalition against Iraq. The theme of the collaboration between *a'rab* and infidels remained current for some time after the war.[23]

These "non-Arab Arabs" were contrasted with Iraq, the standard-bearer of Arabism who defended Arab honor, soil and security. Iraqis came to be called *ya'arib*, as opposed to *a'rab*. Unlike the latter, the former meant true and genuine Arabs. The word seems to be derived from the name of Ya'rib bin Qahtan, the common ancestor of all Yemenis and considered the first man to have spoken Arabic.[24] Iraqis fighting in the war against Iran were called *ya'arib*; Husayn himself was awarded that honorific and described as the commander of the "battle of the honor of *ya'ribiyya*."[25]

The new Iraqi national anthem of 1981 said the following of the country:

> The desert has bequeathed us the prophet's flag
> And the glory and the character of *ya'ribiyya*.
> Be glad and rejoice, O country of the Arab.[26]

The Dialectics of "Iraqiness" and Arabism

The inherent strength of both *qawmiyya* and *wataniyya* and the complexity of their interrelationship posed a dilemma to each of the rulers of modern Iraq (just as it did to Arab regimes elsewhere). Were the two capable of coexisting? An Iraqi politician, aware of the heavy ideological load, gave a graphic description of what it meant to promote them both simultaneously: It was like carrying two watermelons with one hand.[27] This was particularly true of Iraq's Sunni Arabs. At times, for instance under Bakr Sidqi (1937–1938) or Qasim (1958–1963), "Iraqiness" was put first, but as a rule the dominant trend was to try to balance and reconcile the two.

In light of the Ba'thi ideology and given the realities of Iraqi politics, it is not surprising that the party was especially preoccupied with this issue. This is well brought out by their recourse to the words *qutr* and *qutriyya*, in either a neutral or a negative sense. The literal meaning of *qutr* is "region" or "area." In Ba'th parlance, the term was made acceptable by the particular meaning it assumed in describing the party structure. Its highest organs were called *qawmi*, in particular *al-qiyada al-qawmiyya*: the all-Arab command composed of Ba'th representatives from all Arab countries where the party was able to operate. In the individual countries, the leading body was called *al-qiyada al-qutriyya* (the regional command). Their very existence was tantamount to a recognition of "particularism." As Ba'th domination consolidated in Iraq, the *qutri* bodies (the command, the congress, etc.) became in fact supreme. The *qawmi* command, headed by 'Aflaq until his death in 1989, retained no more than a rather ritual importance, though it continued to be thought of as the highest party forum. In consequence of this use within the party, *qutr* came to be used as the most current word for "country" or "state," replacing earlier words such as *bilad*.[28]

In a different context, *qutr* could be used in an altogether negative sense to describe the antithesis of Arabism and unity and to connote divisiveness, isolationism, and the promotion of narrow state interests rather than the all-Arab cause. In the past, 'Aflaq had frequently attacked *qutriyya* in this latter sense, calling it a "sickness." Appeals for the *qutri* independence of an individual Arab state, he wrote, were fundamentally wrong. He rejected the "mentality of *qutriyya*" and held that this phase was nearing its end. Years later, while heading the *qawmi* command in Baghdad, he continued to pronounce against *qutriyya*, thereby indirectly venting his disappointment with *qawmi*'s diminished status.[29] Other party spokespeople or journalists also came out against it from time to time, describing it as the embodiment of separatism (*infisal*), dissent, fanaticism, and egotism, all of which militated against the all-Arab cause.[30]

To illustrate: the internal party organ wrote that it was the *qutriyya* mentality that had caused the Arab defeat of 1967. A party document warned of two dangers of *qutriyya*: One was that a single Arab state might aspire to the role of Arab leadership; the other was that each Arab country might place its narrow interests above the *qawmi* interest of all.[31] While the party thus attacked other Arab countries, it described Iraq's own policies as being in total conformity with *qawmiyya*. Husayn's "Pan-Arab declaration" of 1980, for instance, was described as stemming from Iraq's all-Arab (*qawmi*) responsibility "which rises above all narrow *qutri* interests." Iraqiness was not a matter of *qutriyya* but rather should be thought of as the "central current" strengthening the country's affinity with Arabism.[32] The changes undergone by the term *qutriyya* thus show that despite originally being neutral, it picked up a heavy load of emotion along the way. They also illustrate the capability, characteristic of Arabic, of giving a single word the connotations of two opposites.[33]

The polemics surrounding Iraqiness and Arabism were not merely, perhaps not even chiefly, a matter of denigrating Arab leaders abroad; they were a most important weapon in domestic struggles.[34] The need to find more clearly defined guidelines by which young people could be educated without exposing them to ambiguity led to a doctrine of having the best of both worlds. The relative weight of *wataniyya* or *qutriyya* against *qawmiyya* might change according to circumstances, but the tendency to balance them persisted. More than that, there were attempts to bring them together in a dialectic link by describing *wataniyya* as a bridge leading to *qawmiyya*.

The tendency to stress both aspects simultaneously is clearly brought out by the name chosen for the front the Ba'th set up with the communists in 1973: al-Jabha al-wataniyya wa-l-qawmiyya al-taqaddumiyya (The Iraqi National and all-Arab Progressive Front). The report of the 1973 party congress spoke of the need to balance Iraqiness and Arabism and warned of the dire consequences likely to ensue if one or the other was given undue weight. Iraq's tasks, it went on to say, coincided in large measure with the vital tasks of the Arab world as a whole, and the two sets of responsibilities were interwoven dialectically, so that "in the present phase, the promotion of Iraqi tasks . . . forms a bridge leading to all-Arab tasks."[35] The next congress, ten years later, stressed *wataniyya* rather more—a fact readily accounted for by reference to the war then going on. Its report said: "For the first time in centuries, Iraqi nationalism [*wataniyya*] is becoming the first loyalty of the people and is turning into a symbol in which Iraqis take pride to the point of being prepared to sacrifice themselves for it." But the reports hastened to add that, nonetheless, *qawmiyya* continued to be "firm."[36]

Saddam Husayn himself spoke frequently of the interconnection between the two concepts. Addressing a colloquium on school reform, for instance, he said: "When we speak of the Iraqi people . . . and when we mention the [greater] Arab homeland, we must not cease to educate the 'Iraqi' to take pride in his plot of soil, in *al-qutr al-'Iraqi* . . . which, legally speaking, is his homeland." One must not exaggerate, he went on, by upholding the entire Arab region as the "homeland in principle [*al-qawmi al-mabda'i*]," nor neglect the "immediate" homeland (*al-watan al-mubashir*), but the opposite was equally inadmissible. This was so, he explained, because the complex Iraqi society contained both Arabs and non-Arabs. Exaggerating the *qawmi* approach would antagonize the non-Arabs. Yet from their "little plot of soil," Iraqis were looking out at "the greater Arab homeland." The right way to deal with the issue, he concluded, was to stress that Iraq was part of the Arab homeland rather than say that the Iraqi people were part of the Arab nation.[37] The whole equivocal passage was clearly intended to tone down Kurdish opposition to the Pan-Arab approach.

Husayn gave a somewhat less blurred version when he spoke about the teaching of history and geography in Iraqi schools. There were, he said, advocates of *qawmiyya* who unduly "detracted from Iraq's greatness." Others stressed Iraqiness and "detracted" from *qawmiyya* and from the greater Arab homeland. What was required was a "scientific and objective" balance between the two. At the same time, any sign of racism or secessionism must be uprooted. "Trends capable of enhancing the unity of the Iraqi people must be reinforced; but so must those tendencies that strengthen the solidarity of the Arab nation in its various states, with a view to the future, hoped-for Arab unity."[38]

On another occasion, Husayn defined the principles of the Ba'th party as demanding the consolidation of authentic Iraqi *wataniyya* just as much as they required Iraq to be at the disposal of the struggle of *qawmiyya*. The Iraqi-Iranian war was, according to him, a great Iraqi battle, just as it was a great Arab battle. Shortly before the outbreak of hostilities in the 1991 war, he described the coming war as a "merger of *watani*, *qawmi*, and human aims."[39] A newspaper wrote that Husayn was the first man ever to "unite *wataniyyya* and *qawmiyya* in a perfect, organic, and effective fusion."[40]

Evidently, then, Ba'thi Iraq did try to carry "the two watermelons in one hand." The Ba'th considered this juggling act altogether mandatory. Both the domestic consolidation of Iraq and the ideological link with the Sunni Arab world abroad were existential requirements for the perpetuation of Ba'thi power.[41] They were all the more vital as support of the party became more and more restricted to the Sunni Arab sector of the Iraqi population and as that sector's numerical strength (as a percentage of the total population) steadily declined.[42] The Sunnis' sense of isolation and of being overrun by the hostility of the other components of the population surfaced in many public expressions in the wake of the Gulf War. Commentators, for example, spoke of the Arab world as Iraq's "strategic depth."

To sum up, it may be said that even today no single formula has been found that is capable of rallying all parts of the population. The Sunni Arabs, as the political elite of the country, are caught in an identity dilemma but are pragmatic and practical enough to always adapt their political discourse to the requirements of changing circumstances. The ensuing vagueness is often enough calculated and meant to conceal real intentions; at other times, it results from a method of trial and error in the search for a formula that would at last be all things to all people.

7

The Shi'is
Loyalty to the Community or the State?

*I*n the Ba'thi view, the groups endangering Iraqi national cohesion and all-Arab unity (i.e., militating against both *wataniyya* and *qawmiyya*) were chiefly the Shi'is and the Kurds. In the political language referring to them, there was usually a great deal of circumlocution. Hints and code words were in common use. These were often indicative of the regime's attitude to Shi'is and Kurds or of official suspicions relating to them. Some such words were general and might refer to Shi'is, Kurds, or others, as for instance *shu'ubiyya*. Others were specific to one particular group. This is true of *ta'ifiyya* (communalism, sectarianism), used almost only for the Shi'a.

Our discussion of the Shi'is' issue should be prefaced by saying that an analysis of Shi'i attitudes toward either Iraqi or Arab nationalism is a most difficult undertaking. First, the Shi'is have not been exempt from the broad process of secularization that has taken place in the Middle East, and it is hard to say just how strong the hold of the Shi'i religion over its believers presently is. Second, the Shi'is have no representative political organization, nor even a newspaper that openly expresses their views. Clandestine organizations do exist, such as al-Da'wa (the Call) or Munazzamat al-'amal al-Islami (the Islamic Action Organization), and they have their own publications abroad (e.g., *al-Jihad*, *al-Tayyar al-Jadid*, *Liwa' al-Sadr*, *Baghdad*, and the English-language *al-Da'wa Chronicle*). But there is no telling how well or how fully these reflect the real views of Shi'is at home. Each has the financial and other support of one particular foreign state

(Iran is one of them) and may well reflect its sponsor's attitudes more faithfully than it claims to. Furthermore, since they are all published abroad, there is no way of knowing how much, or whether at all, they influence the local Shi'i population. This is also the reason why it is more difficult to pinpoint Shi'i input into the political discourse of the Ba'th era than it is, for instance, to single out the communist or Kurdish ones.

Yet we may make use of two unusual facts. One is that the Ba'th exploited the writings of the most noted Shi'i cleric in Iraq, Ayatollah Muhammad Baqir al-Sadr, in order to attack the communists. One such step was to publish (in a censored version) Baqir's well-known book *Iqtisaduna* (Our economy) in which he criticized communist economic doctrine. His usefulness in the fight against communism did not, however, prevent the regime from executing him in 1980 in order to curtail the religious and political influence of the clerics over the Shi'i population and to prevent al-Sadr from turning himself into an Iraqi Khomeini.[1] The other example is that of the Shi'i journalist Hasan al-'Alawi, who was for many years a faithful court writer but escaped from Iraq in the early 1980s. Once abroad, he wrote a book entitled *Al-Shi'a wa-l-dawla al-qawmiyya fi-l-'Iraq, 1914–1990* (The Shi'a and the national state in Iraq, 1914–1990). His book is important because, as a former establishment figure, he had access to a wide range of information and because, as a recent political expatriate, he was able to attest to trends in Shi'i thought. Furthermore, he was a forceful exponent of the views of secular Shi'is whose sentiments had not previously found expression. Finally, he employed the Ba'th terminology with which his career had made him familiar but turned it against its originators. Yet as a general rule, it must still be said that the Shi'is of Iraq are, by and large, a silent majority. The following account is therefore based almost entirely on Ba'th sources and reflects the Ba'th's views.

Ba'th considered the Shi'i question so sensitive that, at times, it imposed a news blackout on the whole issue—to the point of even avoiding the very word "Shi'i." Unlike the Kurdish problem that, for all its ups and downs, was referred to in public, the Shi'a was almost taboo. If the word "Shi'i" was used at all, it was with reference to the Shi'is of Lebanon or Iran.[2] If mention of the Iraqi Shi'is could not be avoided, the Ba'th preferred to call them *al-madhhab al-Ja'fari* or *al-Ja'fariyya*. This expression was introduced in 1736 by Nadir Shah of Persia at a time when he was trying to bridge the gap between Sunnis and Shi'is by declaring the Shi'a a *madhhab* alongside the four orthodox Sunni *madhahib*. The name refers to the sixth Imam, Ja'far al-Sadiq, who is considered the chief author of Shi'i religious laws and precepts.[3] *Ja'fariyya* was a more convenient term for the Ba'th because it did not stress the communal difference as much as the word "Shi'a" (which originally meant "party"—i.e., the party of 'Ali). At times, the word *madhhab* alone stood as a code for "Shi'a." The Shi'is sometimes referred to themselves as the *Ja'fariyya*, perhaps for the very same reason.[4] Another term was *al-rafida* or *al-rawafid* (the refusers), which had become current in the eighteenth and nineteenth centuries.[5]

During this period, a number of tribes in southern Iraq went over to the Shi'a and the process was called *taraffud* (similar to *tashayyu'*).

Ta'ifiyya: Part Sectarianism, Part Racism

The most common Ba'thi term used to refer to the Shi'a was *ta'ifa* (community or sect) or *ta'ifiyya* (sectarianism). Originally, the word had a neutral connotation, meaning part of a whole or a group of people. It is in this sense that it appears in the Qur'an (for instance, sura *al-Tawba*, v. 84). As late as the nineteenth century, it still retained its early neutral coloration and was used widely for ethnic groups, religious schools, parties, military units, and even knighthood orders.[6] It was the Ba'th party that gave it an exceedingly derogatory note, using it in the contexts of racism, tribal fanaticism, and civil strife. The party used it to attack the Shi'a without naming it or else to send a signal to the Shi'is without publicly referring to a potentially embarrassing problem.[7] The use of *ta'ifiyya* was meant to convey to the Shi'a that loyalty to the Iraqi state must be placed above loyalty to their religion—otherwise there was a danger that in times of crisis Iraqi Shi'is would look to their coreligionists in Iran rather than act in conformity with Iraqi interests.

The Ba'th held that *ta'ifiyya* had deep roots in history and that there were always certain quarters interested in fanning it, so as to exploit it against Iraq in general or against the Ba'th in particular. Some such quarters were domestic, others were foreign, such as "imperialism" or Iran. One of the first Ba'th pronouncements on this issue came after riots in the Shi'i holy cities of Najaf and Karbala' in February 1977. An ideological guide issued by the party, *Al-Minhaj al-thaqafi al-markazi* (The central cultural program), devoted a whole chapter to the matter. True to form, it did not make a single reference to the riots but spoke of *ta'ifiyya* being aroused by imperialism. It said that the "sectarian game" (*lu'bat al-tawa'if*) played by imperialism and by "sectarian elements" was intended to attach people's loyalty to their community rather than to their country, to undermine national unity (*wataniyya*), and to slow down the all-Arab, socialist revolution of the Ba'th. Community leaders were exploiting the *'uqda ta'ifiyya* (the sectarian complex) left over from earlier reactionary regimes. But these existed no longer, and the Ba'th did not persecute groups or individuals, except if they were acting against it. Neither did it discriminate between citizens on religious grounds. The only community known to the party was that of "the nation and its struggling masses." To overcome such problems, a distinction must be drawn between the community as a political current and the community as a social reality. What needed to be fought was not the community but rather sectarianism. The "sectarian complex" of the "simple masses" and their feeling of being persecuted and disadvantaged must be done away with.[8]

After the Islamic Revolution in Iran and after Tehran had started to try to export the revolution to Iraq, the accusations of inciting sectarianism were naturally directed against Iran. Persia, it was claimed, had not ceased to do so since the sixteenth century. Part of the Persian method was to maintain schools in Iraq, starting in the seventeenth century. Fadil al-Barrak, who wrote a book about them, claimed that while the names of Iraqi schools reflected the national spirit, the Persian-run schools were given names reflecting "racism and communalism." A school at Najaf, for instance, was called al-Madrasa al-'Alawiyya after the Imam 'Ali; another, in Kazimiyya, was called Shahrabani after the wife of the Imam Husayn. Iran, he went on, had made these schools into "hothouses" of *ta'ifiyya* and propaganda centers for Iran, and their curricula were drawn up to serve that purpose. It was here that the cadres of the Da'wa and 'Amal organizations had been trained.[9] Syria and Israel also came in for their share of accusations of fostering sectarianism in Iraq.

Most dangerous of all, however, were various domestic quarters including the regimes of Qasim and the 'Arif brothers, which persisted in clinging to the spirit of sectarianism. The Communist Party did not escape similar charges. Worst of all was the Shi'i political party, al-Da'wa. Its origins dated back to the Qasim period, but it surfaced at the time of Khomeini's rise to power. The report of the 1982 party congress referred openly to it, saying that it was the most active group among the advocates of sectarianism. It was attempting, the report went on, to reach out to confused young people and to turn them against the Ba'th. At a later stage, the Da'wa leadership moved to Iran and urged its followers in Iraq to engage in acts of terror and destruction in the hope of launching a sectarian civil war *(fitna ta'ifiyya)*.[10]

In the face of all these hostile forces, the Ba'th for its part asserted that it rejected sectarianism and fought it tooth and nail. One way to do so, according to Saddam Husayn, was to write and teach history in a manner that would not arouse sectarian sentiment but on the contrary uproot it.[11] To make society immune to sectarianism, however, was not enough. Most of all, the Ba'th party itself needed to be protected against the "sectarian infection." To allow sectarian ideas to infiltrate into the minds of the party's rank and file would imperil its "ideological principles."

Reading between the lines, one sensed that it was especially among Shi'i party members that a feeling of uneasiness was taking hold. They felt discriminated against, both with regard to their personal careers and with regard to the standing and welfare of their community as a whole. The article continued: "A party member who has nothing better to do than count the number of officials in offices and institutions according to their community is sinning gravely against his principles." There might be party members who thought that canceling broadcasts of the *'ashura'* mourning ceremonies (in memory of the murder of the Imam Husayn, the main rite of the Shi'i calendar) ran counter to "the legitimate rights of [their] community and family." But such thinking only showed the weakness of their faith in the party and pointed up their being strangers there. Rather than disregarding the rights of the communities, the party went out of its way to protect its members against "puny sectarianism" (*ta'ifiyya sughra*), such as preferences for people from one particular town, from some special group, or from a certain tribe. As if to drive home the point, a law regulating the licensing of parties, issued in 1991, prohibited the establishment of "sectarian" parties.[12]

The goal of *ta'ifiyya*, as the Ba'th saw it, was to cause the breakdown of its regime by means of sowing domestic discord. Iran was in the vanguard of this campaign and had gone to the length of "raising the standard of Islam as a substitute for nationalism." Tehran was seeking to undermine both Iraqi and all-Arab (*watani* and *qawmi*) security. The call to replace nationalism by Islam was intended to enable Iran to expand; to "change the old political map of the Arab homeland" and to replace it with a new one, including "sectarian and reactionary states." The Arab world was to be carved up and each Arab state split into "ministates" (*duwaylat*). Establishing such "states of sects" (*duwal al-tawa'if*) was to blur the Arab identity.[13] In Iraq in particular, the "sectarian poison" was to cause the state to break up into three small units that would be permanently at war with one another. The later *intifada* of the Kurds and Shi'is in 1991 was adduced as proof of that. Hasan al-'Ali, a Shi'i, and then a member of the Iraqi (*qutri*) party leadership, vehemently attacked the Shi'i uprising in the Dhi Qar area and said that the Shi'is there were betraying their homeland and their Arab identity. He, too, said that their aim was "to split up Iraq."[14]

Hasan al-'Alawi's book contains scathing criticism of Ba'thi policy, both overt and covert. He starts out by refuting the customary concept of the Shi'is as a sect. Such usage was meant to harm them and was as groundless as calling the Spanish a Catholic sect or the English a Protestant one. Sectarianism, he went on, was the most constant feature in Iraqi history. Yet no Iraqi scholar has dared to tackle the issue, and the Shi'is themselves were exceedingly cautious in trying to avoid the accusation of sectarianism, a charge they were so easily exposed to. The regime had enacted a "conspiracy of silence" around the issue of the Shi'is, lest they might have to share power with them. All Iraqi regimes—and the Ba'th most of all—discriminated against the Shi'is, and the rulers (rather than the Shi'is) should therefore be called sectarian. 'Alawi invented a neologism to connote turning into a sectarian: *tatayyuf*. In Iraq, he said, sectarianism was not a characteristic of the man in the street but a matter of "official policy." The regime had made itself into the "*madhhab* of the ruler" and thus had institutionalized discrimination against "the *madhhab* of those being ruled."[15]

Those Shi'is who were coopted into the establishment were not authentic members of the Iraqi Shi'a because they themselves joined the others in discriminating against their own kind. 'Alawi calls them by the contemptuous name of *shi'at al-sulta* (approximately, government Shi'is). The worst type of discrimination, he says, was "secular sectarianism" as practiced by the regime whose own adherence to all-Arab nationalism (*qawmiyya*) was the most extreme case of sectarianism. The Ba'th, he goes on to say, took discrimination a big step further by claiming that the Iraqi Shi'is were really Persians. This definition had enabled the regime to expel "many thousands of Iraqis."[16]

The Evils of *Shu'ubiyya*

Another derogatory term for the Shi'is, though not exclusively for them, was *shu'ubiyya*. This is an old word with a multitude of historical and emotional overtones. It dates back to the Abbasid period, but some historians use it anachronistically to describe certain aspects of pre-Islamic society.[17] It is derived from *shu'ub* (singular, *shu'ubi*), which originally seems to have connoted tribes or tribal confederations of non-Arab (*'ajami*) origin. This was contrasted with *qaba'il* (Arab tribes). There is no consensus about whether the first *shu'ubiyya* in Abbasid times was a purely literary movement or a political movement. Some thought of it as a religious sect, others as a *madhhab*.[18] It is widely agreed, however, that under the Abbasids it was opposed to the superior standing of the Arabs and demanded an equal status for all Muslims, regardless of their ethnic provenance. Ethnic and religious affinities, the advocates of *shu'ubiyya* argued, were two altogether separate things.

Some historians thought that *shu'ubiyya* not only denied Arab superiority but also claimed superiority for non-Arabs. This, they asserted, was particularly true of the Persians who launched the *shu'ubiyya* campaign in the first place. They quoted passages from early Arab history to bear out their arguments, such as the saying by a Persian military commander under the Abbasids: "The Arab is like a dog: throw him a piece of bread and hit him over the head with a club." The poet al-Mutawakkili (himself of Persian origin) wrote in a poem that all "sons of Hashim" ought to return to where they had come from: "Return to the Hijaz to eat fog and mind your flocks," he told them. During the war against Iran, *al-Jumhuriyya* quoted this poem on two occasions and also printed a reply by the Iraqi poet al-Shaykh al-Najafi.[19]

Originally, *shu'ubiyya* did not have a derogatory connotation; those who adhered to it thought of it as a perfectly legitimate, even just, struggle for equality. They used to quote a well-known verse from the Qur'an: "O mankind, We have created you male and female, and appointed you *shu'ub* and *qaba'il*, that you may know one another. Surely the noblest among you in the sight of God is the most godfearing of you."[20] At first, *shu'ubiyya* was interchangeable with *taswiya* (equality). But the negative connotation came into use at almost the same time; since *shu'ubiyya* was a Persian claim for equality with the Arabs, the latter rejected it emphatically.

In modern times, *shu'ubiyya* became current again and entered the political lexicon, but in the derogatory sense alone. It became one of the

most sharply barbed terms to attack the enemies of the Arabs, whether
real or imaginary, foreign or domestic, Arab or non-Arab. The Baʿth writer
ʿAbd al-Hadi al-Fukayki wrote that the *"shuʿubi* bloc" was composed of
many races and the adherents of many and varied schools of thought: "The
only thing they have in common is their hatred of the Arabs and their
rejection of Islam." They were an "international" crowd, made up of
"Iranians and Turks, negroes and Indians, Spaniards and Romans . . . and
the rest of the riffraff of peoples."[21] Perhaps under Fukayki's influence,
two other researchers, Sami Hanna and George Gardner, made a special
study of *shuʿubiyya* over the entire course of Islamic history. They distinguished between various forms of *shuʿubiyya* at different times—in the
periods of the caliphs, the crusaders, the Ottomans, and under Western
domination—or else of the local kind. The common denominator was the
desire "to suppress the uniqueness of the Arabs."[22]

In Iraq, and most especially in Baʿthi Iraq, *shuʿubiyya* was used to vilify
a multitude of enemies and applied to practically all adversaries or rivals
of the Baʿth or to anyone suspected of resenting the political domination
of Sunni Arabs or of opposing Arab unity. A *shuʿubi* was now "anyone
who works against the idea of liberating Arab nationalism and anyone
opposing Arab comprehensive unity. He must be liquidated, regardless
of his race or national identity."[23] This sense of being surrounded by a
vast *shuʿubi* conspiracy reveals the extent of the Baʿth party's perception
of its isolation, its fortress mind-set, its constant fear of losing its monopoly
of power, and the concomitant need to delegitimize all rivals. Under Qasim
as well as under the first Baʿth regime, the charge of *shuʿubiyya* was lev-
eled mainly at the Iraqi communists, then strong adversaries of the Baʿth
and always staunch and consistent opponents of Arab unity. Thus, in 1963,
the newspaper *al-Jamahir* coined the expression *"shuʿubi* communism."
Qasim himself, who was opposed to Pan-Arabism, was called "the *shuʿubi*
despot" or *qasim al-ʿarab* (the divider of the Arabs).[24]

During the second Baʿth regime, the accusation of *shuʿubiyya* was diverted from the communists, who were no longer dangerous, and instead
applied to other domestic or foreign adversaries: imperialism, Zionism,
the Syrian regime of Asad, and Khomeini or the Iranians in general. The
main domestic group now so called were the Shiʿis and, to a lesser extent,
the Kurds. In 1971, for instance, *al-Jumhuriyya* spoke of *"shuʿubi* pens"
filling the columns of the Kurdish paper *al-Taʾakhi* with poison.[25] A
notable critic of *shuʿubiyya* at that time was Saddam Husayn's uncle
Khayrallah Talfah. *Al-Taʾakhi* came out against his view that "Islam
without Arabism is *shuʿubiyya*" and quoted a traditional saying of Muhammad to refute it that read: "There is no difference between Arab or non-
Arab [*aʿjami*] except with regard to their fear of God."[26] On the eve of
the war against Iran, Talfah wrote an article about *shuʿubiyya* in which
he called it "a political idea concocted in the minds of non-Arabs" whose
only thought was to "harm the standing of the Arabs and detract from
the value of Islam." Talfah went back to the events of 1936 to describe

Bakr Sidqi's takeover as *"shuʿubi* collusion against Arab nationalism"* that had originated at a secret meeting at the home of Sasson Khadduri.[27] (Sidqi was of Kurdish origin; Khadduri was a Jew.)

After the outbreak of the war against Iran, the theme of *shuʿubiyya* occupied a central place in public parlance. It served to demonize both the Iranian enemy and Shiʿi fundamentalist quarters in Iraq and was primarily intended to prevent Iraqi Shiʿis from becoming sympathizers of either, let alone activists for them. The report of the 1982 party congress stated that Iran's first expansionist aim had been "to weaken Iraq, to cause damage to its *watani* and *qawmi* regime, and to bring a *shuʿubi* [i.e., Shiʿi] leadership to power in Iraq." Referring to the al-Daʿwa party, the report stated that "Persians and would-be-Persians [*mutafarrisun*]," driven by racialism and *shuʿubiyya*, had always been the most active among political-religious movements.[28] Husayn also said that, if Arab rule was strong, the *shuʿubiyya* strove to prevent it from exercising power; if it was weak, *shuʿubiyyun* attempted to fill the power vacuum themselves.[29]

During the war and at its conclusion, Husayn was praised for having stopped "the great *shuʿubi* storm—the strongest and most hostile ever to blow across the Arab region." But even when the war was over, the press continued to exhort Iraqis to remain on guard against *shuʿubiyya*, as it was still being employed by "political, sectarian, and racist organizations" who feared and opposed the Arab "civilizing mission" among the peoples of the world.[30] To make the point even more forcefully, the 1990 constitution contained a clause to the effect that "Iraqi society must reinforce the values of brotherhood . . . and prevent the spread of communal, racist, programs and ideas . . . or of *shuʿubiyya*." Similarly, the 1991 party law banned parties that acted according to the principles of *shuʿubiyya*.[31]

The constant attacks on *shuʿubiyya* eventually elicited a reaction from two Shiʿi figures who understood their impact and wished to refute them, though at times their efforts seemed rather defensive and apologetic. In two books published abroad, they criticized the Baʿth for its Pan-Arab ideology and for its suppression of Iraqis in general and its discrimination against Shiʿis in particular, for which the term *shuʿubiyya* was a mere cover. Al-ʿAlawi's book explained that when the Baʿth was speaking of *shuʿubiyyun*, it meant Shiʿis. The intention behind the use of the word was to equate, in the minds of ordinary Iraqis, Iraqi Shiʿis with Iranian Shiʿis. Al-ʿAlawi rejected this approach emphatically, stressing that Iraqi Shiʿis were authentic Arabs loyal to their Arabism. The Shiʿa had, after all, risen among Arabs, he went on, and to make Iraqi Shiʿis appear as Persians (*ʿajam*) was no more than an attempt to "detract from the value of the Arab majority [in Iraq] whose right to representation in government had been taken away."

Al-ʿAlawi singled out some Shiʿi personalities accused of *shuʿubiyya* who in fact had only been guilty of opposing discrimination. In particular, he mentioned the Shiʿi poet Muhammad Mahdi al-Jawahiri, who had started writing poems on this subject back in 1921 and was in turn attacked by nationalists such as Sati' al-Husri and Fukayki. Al-'Alawi also observed that the term *shu'ubiyya* was being used in Iraq more frequently than anywhere else in the Arab world. This was not because *shu'ubiyya* was stronger there than elsewhere but rather because of the perpetually "strained nerves" of the Ba'th leaders.[32]

The expatriate Shi'i writer Kanan Makiyya published his book *Republic of Fear* under the pen name of Samir al-Khalil.[33] He, too, was severely critical of those Arab nationalists who spoke of the *shu'ubiyya* as the antithesis of Arab nationalism. Khalil, whose personal sense of hurt and of suffering in exile is unmistakably present in his writings, wrote that by *shu'ubi* the Ba'th meant people who had chosen to place themselves outside the Arab camp—an act tantamount to treason. In this way, the party wanted to impart a "satanic" character to minorities, Shi'is, and communists. This was the idiom of hatred and arrogance. It was the language of people whose ideology constantly needed to create domestic enemies in order to extract Arabism from its vicissitudes.[34]

Iqlimiyya: The Enemy of Unity

After *ta'ifiyya* and *shu'ubiyya*, the third enemy of unity was *iqlimiyya*. It derives from the Greek root *klima* and meant "climate" in classical Arabic. Early Arab scholars taught that the world was divided into seven climates. Later, the meaning changed to "region" or "territory."[35] In modern usage, it retained that meaning but was used most frequently in the sense of "subregion"—part of a greater whole. During the merger of Syria and Egypt (1958–1961), Syria was called *al-iqlim al-shimali* (the northern region) and Egypt *al-iqlim al-janubi* (the southern region). In Iraq, the Kurds demanded that their area be called *iqlim* rather than *mintaqa*, as preferred by the Ba'th. The latter also means "region," but the former carries a more distinct connotation of a clearly delineated geographical entity.

Iqlim itself sounded neutral, but *iqlimiyya* was an extremely negative term. In the eyes of Pan-Arabists, particularly of the Ba'th leaders, it came to indicate regionalism or narrow local interests and was used to denote the opposite of Arab unity. It was taken to mean that small and separate Arab territorial entities were legitimate, placing local interests above the all-Arab cause. As with some of the terms we have already discussed, this was true of various Arab countries, but it acquired a special acuity in Iraq. Already in the 1930s, Shawkat came out against *iqlimiyya* and considered it directed against all-Arab nationalism.[36] Under the Ba'th, *iqlimiyya* became a synonym of communalism or sectarianism, racism and *shu'ubiyya*. *Iqlimiyya* meant divisiveness with regard to the soil, *shu'ubiyya* with regard to the components of the population. The former was used in such combinations as *kiyanat iqlimiyya hazila* (contemptible regional entities); *iqlimiyya mustana'a* (artificial regions); *iqlimiyya dayyiqa* (narrow regionalism). There were also such expressions as "*iqlimi* deviation" or "*iqlimi* mentality." Organizations, foreign regimes, or alliances could be held up to contempt by having the adjective *iqlimi* applied to their names. Both Bakr Sidqi's and Qasim's regimes were so called. But the Ba'th also blamed the Shi'is and the Kurds for seeking to give Iraq a "regional" character at the expense of its Pan-Arabism.

Al-'Alawi puts the boot on the other foot: it was precisely the Sunni Arab leadership, he asserts, who turned Iraq away from a Pan-Arab to an *iqlimi* orientation. He adduces as proof the 1937 Saadabad Pact between Iraq, Turkey, Iran, and Afghanistan that, he says, was "the first *iqlimi* axis to isolate Iraq from the Arab arena." The Ba'th regime, too, he goes on, tends to shut itself off from other Arab regimes. He reminds his read-ers that Abu Khaldun Sati' al-Husri, the noted ideologue of Arab nation-alism, accused the Ba'th of *iqlimiyya* and of hostility to Arab unity. (This did not prevent him from attacking al-Husri for discriminating against the Shi'is.) Al-'Alawi coins a new phrase to describe Ba'thi conduct: *ta'aqlum al-sulta* (making the government provincial). True, the Ba'th preached comprehensive Arab nationalism, and its criticism of Qasim and of the communists had homed in on the point of *iqlimiyya*. Yet it was the Ba'th that actually practiced *iqlimiyya*. According to al-'Alawi, this was seen in the way in which the party restricted the very concept of loyalty to only a single *madhhab* (the Sunnis). The Ba'th made this *madhhab* coincide with the Iraqi state as a whole. By doing so, he goes on, the party created what he calls "the loyalty of the small geography" at the expense of Iraqi (*watani*) nationalism.[37]

By contrast, he wrote, the Shi'is were the real Iraqis. They had given proof of that back in 1920 when they led the uprising against the British. They might perhaps resign themselves to discrimination, but they would never suffer a slur on their "Arabism, nobility, and honor, or their loyalty to the state and the homeland which have arisen on the dead bodies of their sons and their saints." To equate Iraqi Shi'is with Iranians would only help Iran, which in any case was eager to see all Shi'is everywhere under its own protection and influence. Iran would like nothing better than to expand into Iraqi territory and to annex the Shi'i holy cities there. If that happened, he adds ironically, Iraq's own Arabism would become questionable and the Arab League would have to reconsider Iraq's membership.[38]

While al-'Alawi made a good case in arguing that the Shi'is were loyal to Iraq and were as good Iraqi nationalists as the next person there, he could not make the same point about all-Arab nationalism. He tried to distinguish between two concepts that the Ba'th considered interchange-able: *'uruba* (Arabism) and *qawmiyya* (all-Arab nationalism). The former, he argued, could be either secular or religious; the latter was always secu-lar. *Qawmiyya*, he considered, could be questioned on religious or on Marxist grounds; *'uruba* could not. It was after all impossible to hold a people's descent against them. *'Uruba* was thus better capable of serving as the common denominator of various components in the population than *qawmiyya* was. Those who fought for Iraqi independence in 1920 were *'urubiyyun* rather than *qawmiyyun* and as such differed greatly from nationalists of the type held up as models by al-Husri or 'Aflaq. Iraqi nationalism was not identical to *qawmiyya*.[39] Al-'Alawi's words clearly reflected the Shi'i malaise with Arab unity, which would turn the Shi'i community in Iraq into a small island in a vast Sunni sea.

Attempts to isolate the Iraqi Shi'is altogether from their Iranian coreligionists seem, however, rather artificial. They may have reflected the Shi'is' identity crisis and their apologetic trend of writing but were hardly a real option. This is borne out by declarations made by Iraqi Shi'i fundamentalist clerics in Iraq during the war against Iran. To them, Iraqi defeats were victories for the Shi'a. To give a single example, in June 1982, after the Iranians reconquered the town of Khorramshahr, Muhammad Taqi al-Mudarrisi, leader of the Islamic Action Organization, wrote: "Today, . . . the Islamic army has started to march forward for the first time after six hundred years of continuous decline . . . [and has] delivered this heavy blow to the Saddamist *jahiliyya*."[40]

8

The Kurds
Autonomy or Secession?

Ba'th Ambiguity toward the Kurds

In a clash between two peoples or ethnic groups, the terminology employed by one side or the other is a barometer—even more accurate than in other areas—of the changing stages, the slightest nuances, and the mounting or diminishing sensitivities in their relationship. Fears, suspicions, overt or covert aspirations and intentions are all reflected in the choice of words. This is most certainly true of the struggle of the Kurds against the dominant Arab Sunni group in Iraq. The clash was basically a confrontation between two quite recent national movements, historically speaking. Since their struggle followed a very convoluted course, the terms used with reference to it changed greatly, too. The very names the Ba'th gave to the Kurdish movement are a case in point, ranging from "that rebellious pocket of [foreign] agents" to "a liberating national [*qawmi*] movement." Under a regime like that of the Ba'th where every public expression is subject to strict and searching censorship, such usage is most instructive. An example of the "effectiveness" of Ba'th censorship is the fact that during a whole year of bloody fighting against the Kurds (in 1974–1975) the Iraqi media had hardly a word to say about it. The Iraqi public did nonetheless get wind of what was really going on, and the chasm between the media version and actual reality contributed a great deal to the abysmal distrust of official news and its habitual replacement by whispered rumors that is so characteristic of life under the Ba'th regime.

The Kurds, an old ethnic group speaking an Indo-European rather than a Semitic language, have lived in their particular area since ancient times. Iraqi rulers perceive their very existence as a challenge to both Iraqi and all-Arab nationalism, and every single modern Iraqi regime has had to deal with them in one fashion or another. Attitudes have ranged from the desire to assimilate them to a readiness to recognize their national rights. The Baʿth regime alone had, over the years of its existence, moved through the entire gamut of policies lying between these poles. To make it easier to follow the discussion below, here is a brief list of the principal stages in Baʿth-Kurdish relations:

> 1968–1970: hostilities alongside internal deliberations leading to the proposal of autonomy
> March 1970: autonomy proclaimed
> 1974: breakdown of negotiations on its implementation
> 1974–1975: war and defeat of the Kurds
> 1975–1990: renewal of the Kurdish struggle for autonomy
> 1991: Kurdish uprising in the wake of the Gulf War, with the Kurdish region under international protection.

One of the first to advocate assimilating the Kurds into Arab nationalism was Sami Shawkat. "Every nation seeking revival," he wrote, "must use all possible means to merge [*damaja*] into its nationalism every minority living on its soil." The Arab nation, he went on, was suited to, and capable of, digesting (*hadama*) and representing races and peoples subject to it. This was because of the exalted qualities of the Arabs, which caused other peoples to love them and to want to become part of them, and because of the Arab language, which let others "intoxicate themselves with the sounds of the Qurʾan and to subject themselves willingly" to those who spoke Arabic.[1]

A more subtle way was simply to "Arabize" the Kurds. This had been done in the 1947 Baʿth party statutes that laid down that an Arab is anyone "who speaks Arabic or *lives on Arab soil* or aspires to live there or believes in his belonging to the Arab nation" (emphasis added). The full meaning of this was brought out by an additional clause saying that "Arab soil" extended from the Taurus and Pusht-i Kuh Mountains, via the Basra Gulf and the Indian Ocean (here called "the Arab Ocean"), the Ethiopian mountains, the Sahara, and down to the Mediterranean Sea and the Atlantic Ocean.[2] That, of course, made the Kurds into Arabs. During the Qasim period, *al-Thawra* preached for amalgating the Kurds in the melting pot of the Arab nation, by force, if necessary. The mouthpiece of the Kurdistan Democratic Party (KDP), *Kha-bat*, replied in a series of articles that called assimilation a "fascist" device.[3] Muhammad Rashid al-Fil wrote a book entitled *The Kurds in the Eyes of Science* (published in Najaf in 1965) in which he claimed that the Kurds were of Arab origin and had migrated to their present area from the Arabian Peninsula.[4]

Michel ʿAflaq, who as we shall see was the prime mover in bringing about a change in the Baʿth ideological attitudes toward the Kurds, could not bring himself to think of the Kurds but as Arabs. For centuries, he stated, the Kurds had been Muslim and Arab "citizens [*muwatinun*]," just like other Muslim Arabs. A later Ba'th document took a similar line. It conceded that the Kurds had a separate local and national (*qawmi*) existence but went on to say that "it would be wrong to consider them a nation different from the Arab nation, like the Persians or Indians are different." The reason was that the Kurds lived on lands on which "Arab states [*duwal*] have grown for thousands of years."[5] Saddam Husayn's uncle, Khayrallah Talfah, declared that "anyone who dwells [*yaskun*] in the Arab homeland and speaks Arabic is an Arab, regardless of his ethnic origin."[6] Husayn himself, during a visit to the province named after the Kurd Saladin, asserted that Saladin had been an Arab and that there was no contradiction "between the Kurdishness of a Kurd" and his being part of the Arab nation.[7] The same line was followed with regard to the Yazidis (the "devil worshipers") who, according to one researcher, were Kurds. Today's Kurds, he held, had been Yazidis before they became Muslims. The Ba'th, however, claimed that they were "Umayyad Arabs," perhaps after the name of Yazid, one of the Umayyad rulers.[8]

Alongside the attitudes sketched above, there developed another line: a sweeping recognition of Kurdish national rights. The years 1968 to 1970 may be thought of as the period of gestation of the plan for Kurdish autonomy within Iraq. The reasons for this temporary change in Ba'th thinking and for the autonomy plan put forward are too complex to be detailed in a book that is not a historical narrative. Suffice it to say that they were the result of stringent domestic constraints, including a power struggle between the civilian and the military wing of the regime, growing pressures from the Kurds themselves, short-term tactical considerations, and perhaps (a possibility to be mentioned with great caution) a conviction here and there that only a revolutionary approach was capable of settling the Kurdish problem once and for all. One way or another, it took great efforts for the new approach to be accepted by the party establishment and even more for it to be translated into action. There was much soul-searching, and when the new course was eventually set, it was done half-heartedly and with great reluctance.

Already in the earliest days of its regime, the Ba'th had begun to speak of the Kurds as a nation (*qawm*) possessing national rights and aspirations. The party press explained that, since the Ba'thi revolution was a progressive one, it recognized the national rights of others, had freed itself from overbearing attitudes, and rejected the idea of assimilation. The Kurdish people (*sha'b*) had their national privileges by right and had no need to "receive" them from the Ba'th. Kurdish national rights, Ba'th spokespeople declared, encompassed "the economy, culture, ethics, and politics."[9]

In putting forward such arguments, the Ba'th occasionally went to the length of mentioning "self-determination" (*taqrir al-masir*). This may have been done inadvertently and without fathoming the full meaning of the

term, but the few occasions on which it was used were enough to provide
the Kurds with valuable ammunition for later rounds. *Al-Thawra*, which
had taken the lead in setting forth the new ideological line, asked why
self-determination should not be granted to the Kurds since they understood perfectly well that "their fate lies with that of the Arabs." But even
while arguing in favor of the Kurds, *al-Thawra* still felt compelled to make
some sneering remarks about Kurdish "feudalists" and "chauvinists."[10]

Al-Thawra also referred to the fact that the Kurdish population spread
over areas belonging to several states; they were "dispersed," it wrote,
living among Arabs, Persians, and Turks. "Thus they suffer from the same
problem [of being divided] that the Arab nation is suffering from." Hence,
Kurdish unity (*wahda*) was one of the "basic aims of every genuine national [*qawmi*] movement."[11]

A New Framework for Identity: The 1970 Autonomy

From among all the various expressions used between 1968 and 1970,
"self-government" (*hukm dhati*) or "autonomy" seemed most innovative
and likely to present the greatest challenge.[12] Kurdish autonomy was first
spoken of by 'Aflaq in 1969 when he said that "the party is not opposed
to the right of the Kurds to some kind of autonomy." The Kurds themselves had used the term since the early 1920s. So had the Communist
Party.[13] The novel element was the Ba'th party's readiness to go along
with it. But, well aware of the dangers inherent in providing a new point
of reference for the Kurdish identity, the Ba'th added an important rider:
"Since the Ba'th party is a nationalist Arab party, it cannot, in its attempt
to resolve the Kurdish issue, neglect Arab national interests."[14] A second
reservation was perhaps even more important: Recognizing a Kurdish
identity must not harm the uniform all-Iraqi identity; on the contrary, it
must reinforce it. It became a constant theme of the Ba'th idiom to state
that Kurdish rights were being recognized within the boundaries of the
"unity of the Iraqi people" and of the "integrity of the Iraqi territory."

The endless repetition of these phrases attested to Ba'thi anxieties over
the possible consequences of such a coexistence of two frameworks. It also
demonstrated a compulsion to proffer apologetic arguments directed not
only at the party establishment but also at the non-Kurdish population at
large. The latter did not favor recognition of Kurdish rights, sensing that
its ultimate consequences were unpredictable. For years after autonomy
had in fact been established, the leader of one of the Shi'i fundamentalist
movements continued to object to it strenuously. "Iraq," he said, "must
be a single state and a single people. Any idea of dividing the homeland
into a northern, a southern, and a middle part is lacking in logic, since
Iraq is not a large country, neither with regard to its area nor its resources."[15] The need to ward off criticism turned Ba'th apologetics about
the Kurds into an integral part of its political discourse. Even before au-

tonomy was instituted, Saddam Husayn declared defensively that the recognition of Kurdish rights did not detract from "the integrity of Iraqi soil or the unity of the Iraqi people."[16] This was meant not only to reassure the Arabs (Sunnis as well as Shiʿis) but equally to warn the Kurds and let them understand how far they would be allowed to go.

Despite all the inner conflicts in the minds of the Baʿth leaders, Kurdish autonomy was eventually proclaimed on 11 March 1970. The proclamation contained two important clauses relating to Kurdish uniqueness on the one hand and the Kurds' place in the Iraqi state on the other. The first, which took the form of proposed amendments to the draft constitution and was indeed incorporated in the provisional constitution of July 1970, read: "The Iraqi people is made up of two main nationalities [*qawmiyyatayn*]; the Arab nationality and the Kurdish nationality. The constitution recognizes the national rights of the Kurdish people and the rights of all other minorities within the framework of Iraqi unity." The second spoke of the "Kurdish people's possibilities for the exercise of their overall national rights, including autonomy."[17]

As for the real meaning of autonomy, there were many rather convoluted explanations of its significance and its possible ramifications. The inner struggle of the Baʿth was reflected in the fact that the word "autonomy" did not even appear in the heading of the proclamation entirely devoted to it. Instead, it was curtly called "The March Proclamation [*bayan adhar*]." The clause on national rights was worded cautiously, almost in an offhand manner, and mentioned only "possibilities." Oddly enough, it was the Baʿth rather than the Kurds who had pushed for autonomy, and both sides acknowledged this. A senior member of the KDP, Dara Tawfiq, explained later, somewhat apologetically, that full autonomy had indeed long been a strategic aim of his party but that in the initial talks with the Baʿth the KDP had sought to steer a middle course that would gain the Kurds the minimum acceptable to them yet fall short of provoking civil war.[18] As for the Baʿth, it had hardly issued the March Proclamation when it began a long campaign of denials and attempts to revise what had been done and to control the damage caused. If until March 1970 and for a short while after, the Baʿth had spoken with a measure of restraint, its later language was indicative of barely suppressed fury, misgivings, and suspicions.

The autonomy plan had emerged as the result of prolonged military confrontation and drawn-out negotiations between the Kurds and the government. Yet the Baʿth had insisted on the use of the term *bayan* rather than *ittifaq* (agreement).[19] This was no mere quibble: the choice of the term by the Baʿth was meant to demonstrate that it constituted the sovereign state power and that, as such, it was unilaterally awarding certain benefits to one particular group in the population (comparable perhaps to the way *millet* status was awarded in the Ottoman Empire). This being so, the sovereign was of course equally entitled to withdraw such benefits at any time. The Baʿth insisted on the use of *bayan* as if one single word rather than another was capable of obscuring the magnitude of its concessions to the Kurds and the dangers inherent in them. It is worth remembering that in 1966, Prime Minister 'Abd al-Rahman al-Bazzaz, who had reached an earlier accommodation with the Kurds, had also adamantly refused to use the terms "agreement" or "negotiations" because, he said, these were not words applicable to contacts between the inhabitants of one and the same country.[20]

The recognition of the Kurdish right to autonomy triggered a severe identity crisis in the ranks of the Ba'th. This accounts for the constantly widening gap between what the March Proclamation had originally said and how it was later interpreted and implemented. Initially, both sides had understood that the proclamation put far greater stress than in the past on what marked off the Kurds from the rest of the Iraqi population. Among other things, the proclamation spoke of the use of the Kurdish language as one of the two official languages of the Kurdish area (alongside Arabic). It provided for separate Kurdish organizations such as an association of Kurdish teachers and a Kurdish students organization. More than that, it provided for the eventual establishment of separate administrative, quasi-governmental organs—a Kurdish legislative council and an executive that would give life to the concept of self-government.

The scope of these concessions inevitably triggered increased Ba'thi efforts to conceal them behind a spate of talk about Iraqi unity. *Al-Jumhuriyya*, for instance, wrote on the morrow of the proclamation's issue: "The Revolutionary Command Council has registered an important revolutionary achievement for the sake of national [*watani*] unity in the [Iraqi] state by settling the Kurdish problem peacefully." Saddam Husayn himself summed up the autonomy plan by saying that it meant "the reinforcement of Iraqi unity and the absolute rejection of partition [*tajzi'a*]."[21]

The gravest anxiety of the Ba'th was that autonomy might prove a stepping-stone to secession and thus to the partition of Iraq. A year after the proclamation, Husayn (its principal author) declared that "autonomy is given to a people, not to the soil." This was a restrictive reinterpretation, turning the autonomy into a matter of personal status rather than applying it to an area. On another occasion, an unnamed "senior party official"—probably Husayn himself—was quoted as saying that a demand for territorial boundaries for "such minorities" would signal "their wish to secede from the Arab homeland."[22] The adamant oppositon of the Ba'th to demarcating the boundaries of the autonomous region was expressed again in 1975, after the Kurdish uprising had been suppressed. At that time, Husayn warned that administrative divisions must not be allowed to turn into "a 'Chinese Wall' separating Arab from Kurd."[23] Consistent with this approach, the name "Kurdistan" (commonly used by Kurds when referring to their region) was rarely used by the Ba'th. Instead, it used terms like *al-mintaqa* (the region or the zone), *al-shimal* (the north), *al-mintaqa al-shimaliyya* (the northern region), or *shimaluna* (our north), as well as *mintaqat al-hukm al-dhati* (the autonomous area).[24]

The appearance of legitimacy given to the Kurdish people and their national rights also faded quickly. If, for a moment, the Baʿth had recognized that the Iraqi Kurds were part of a larger Kurdish nation, it soon went back on its word and presently became exceedingly hostile to the idea or any mention of it. About a year after the proclamation of the autonomy, *al-Jumhuriyya* reminded its readers that the provisional constitution had proclaimed Iraq to be part of the Arab nation but "did not say that the Kurds are part of a larger Kurdish people who inhabit an area between Iran and the Soviet Union." The March Proclamation also had not affirmed such a thing, since doing so "would signify an openly secessionist attitude and put an end to the partnership" between Kurds and Arabs. Autonomy, it went on, meant that the Kurds remained within "the Arab unity we are struggling to implement." Kurds "outside this national [*qawmi*] formula" were simply foreigners.[25] Two decades later, the 1990 constitution laid down that "the Iraqi people are made up of Arabs and Kurds" rather than being "two peoples," Arab and Kurd, as the provisional constitution had said.[26]

Another example of the restrictive interpretation of earlier promises has to do with the Kurdish legislative council. The 1974 autonomy law had spoken of an "elected legislative council [*majlis tashriʿi muntakhab*]." But this was a dangerous thing: It would have given the Kurds something that was being denied the Arab population, and it would thereby stress their separate and special status; it would also have set a new precedent in Iraqi politics: the holding of elections. A further law, enacted only days later, therefore stated simply that the first council might be set up by nomination (*ikhtiyar*) rather than by elections.[27] The difference in wording was crucial: *intikhab* connotes a formal procedure of electing representatives, while *ikhtiyar* meant that a body or person selected nominees as the body or person saw fit. The composition of the first legislative council was indeed determined by nominations. Later, when elections were held, they were under full Baʿth control so that its elected members were all approved in advance by the government and the elections were turned into a propaganda show.[28]

The most severe reversal of Baʿth attitudes occurred in the party's assessment of the Kurdish national movement under the leadership of Mulla Mustafa Barzani, with whom the Baʿth had first fought and then negotiated. At first, and until about two years after the March Proclamation, the Baʿth used some of the most complimentary terms in its lexicon to refer to it: *haraka taharruriyya* (liberation movement) and *haraka taqaddumiyya* (progressive movement). Gradually, these were replaced by derogatory names: first, *al-haraka al-musallaha* (the armed movement) and later, after the renewal of hostilities in 1974, *al-haraka al-mutamarrida* (the rebellious movement), or worse, *al-jayb al-ʿamil al-mutamarrid* (the rebellious pocket of agents—"agents" being used solely to connote a person in the service of the enemy).

As we have seen in Chapter 1, words such as *intifada* or *thawra* were used mostly with positive meanings; *tamarrud* (rebellion) by contrast, was nearly always used in a pejorative sense. In classical Arabic, *marid* is a bad person, rough and allied with the devil. In modern language, the verb *marada* means "to tarnish the honor of the family," and *tamarrada* means "to be arrogant, overbearing, or defiant." But it also means "to rise up against legitimate authority"—an act to be utterly condemned.[29] When the Ba'th used the term with reference to the Kurds, it did so in the most negative sense, implying treason and collaboration with the enemy, often alongside expressions such as "the reactionary uprising in the north of the homeland."[30]

Kurdish Nationalism versus Arab and Iraqi Nationalism

The above account makes it clear that the years 1970 to 1974 occupy a unique place in the political discourse of Iraq in general and the Ba'th in particular. A dialogue between the regime and the Kurds existed during this period. Though often sharp and heated, it differed greatly from the customary monologue on the part of the government. The Kurdish paper *al-Ta'akhi* (Brotherhood), organ of Barzani's movement, took the lead in starting and maintaining the dialogue. It had been licensed after the March Proclamation and not only took up the cause of the Kurds but also wrote critically of many general political, social, and economic issues. *Al-Ta'akhi*'s outspokenness dragged the establishment press into a discussion of controversial subjects that it was palpably reluctant to take up. The mere mention of these themes ran counter to the usual Ba'thi practice and discredited the picture of quiescent harmony that the regime wished to project. Nonetheless, as long as the Ba'th was committed to the March Proclamation, it had to put up with *al-Ta'akhi*'s criticism. As long as that was the case, the only thing the Ba'th could do was to use its own newspapers to put up the best arguments it could against *al-Ta'akhi* and to try to keep the latter's circulation down, despite the popularity it was acquiring throughout Iraq, precisely because of its provocative tone. In 1974, however, when hostilities broke out again, the Kurdish movement decided to close down its paper since it was being published in Baghdad and would not be able to continue along the same lines. *Al-Ta'akhi* was thereupon taken over by a group of Kurdish collaborators with the regime. In 1976, the Ba'th completed the process of *Gleichschaltung* by changing the name of the paper to *al-'Iraq*.

As the Ba'th strove, by this and other means, to stress Iraqi unity, the Kurds emphasized their uniqueness all the more. The most important way for them to do so was to insist on using the term "Kurdistan" (land of the Kurds). This term had first been used by the Seljuks in the twelfth century to refer to a large region of today's eastern Iran.[31] Later, it was applied to the whole area populated by Kurds. Throughout the history of modern Iraq, whenever any regime endeavored to avoid the use of "Kurdistan," the Kurds insisted on it all the more. If they wished to speak of the Kurds of Iraq only, Kurds would say *Kurdistan al-'Iraq* (the Kurdistan of Iraq) or alternatively, *Kurdistan al-janubiyya* (southern Kurdistan) in order to distinguish between Iraqi Kurdistan and Kurdish areas in neighboring countries. Most Kurdish parties, even those who collaborated with the Ba'th, used "Kurdistan" as part of their names (thereby stressing the territorial aspect rather than just the national one as calling themselves "Kurdish" would have done). We have seen this already in the name of the KDP. But the party that had collaborated with the Ba'th since 1973 did likewise: it called itself *al-hizb al-thawri al-Kurdistani* (the Kurdistan Revolutionary Party).

Use of the name "Kurdistan" engendered much suspicion on the part of Baghdad governments. During an earlier round of negotiations in 1964, for instance, the prime minister, Tahir Yahya, said that it was "impossible to call northern Iraq Kurdistan without paving the way to secession." His Kurdish interlocutor, Ibrahim Ahmad, replied that Iran was using Kurdistan as the official designation of the Iranian Kurdish area and that this had not done Iran any harm. For the Kurds, he went on, this was not a matter of rhetoric but a substantive issue on which their future depended.[32] Jalal al-Talabani, a Kurdish intellectual and a veteran political leader, explained that "Kurdistan" was an old, historical name for the geographical area of the Kurds. It had been current in the Ottoman Empire and was used at present in land-registration documents. There were, however, he went on, certain "racists" and "fanatics" who considered the name artificial and who claimed that the mere mention of it was a proclamation of "heretical" secessionist intent.[33] The Ba'th press attacked the Kurds for using the word, but the internal Kurdish monthly *al-Kadir* argued that using the expression "the homeland Kurdistan" was not chauvinism.[34]

The Ba'th found it easier to reconcile itself to *Kurdistan al-'Iraqiyya* (Iraqi Kurdistan) because it showed more clearly that Kurdistan belonged with Iraq. The Kurds themselves were used to speaking of "Kurdistan in Iraq," "Kurdistan in Iran," and so on. The term "southern Kurdistan" (turning around, as it were, the Ba'th expression "northern Iraq" for the same area) was particularly unacceptable to the Ba'th. It had been used by a Kurdish author, 'Ali Sidu al-Kurani, who lived in Jordan and had published a book in Cairo in 1939 entitled *From Amman to 'Amadiyya: A Journey through Southern Kurdistan*. An Iraqi officer, Mahmud al-Dura, who had fought against the Kurds and later had written a book about them, considered the title to be an emphatic declaration of Kurdish expansionist desires.[35] The Kurdish nationalist movement continued to use the term "southern Kurdistan," though mostly in internal publications. But the Ba'th scanned these and then condemned them publicly for having used the expression.[36]

The controversy over naming the Kurdish region touched implicitly on issues of principle: How were Kurdish ambitions to be defined? What was the geographical and political framework in which Kurds sought their identity? What precisely was the nature of their link with the non-Iraqi Kurdish regions, with Iraq, and with the Arab world? Talabani defined the Kurds as people (*sha'b*) with their own legitimate national (*qawmi*) rights, including self-determination. The latter, he said, "includes the right to set up an independent state" of their own. But, he added, at the time of writing (1970–1971), Kurdish national interests made it preferable not to exercise that right and to refrain from secession (*infisal*) from Iraq. In the existing circumstances, he maintained, autonomy was the optimal solution. As for the future, this would depend on changing conditions and on "the attitude of the Arab people to their fraternal people, the Kurds."[37]

The right to self-determination was apparently accepted by a broad section of the Kurdish population, and the internal organ of the KDP, *al-Kadir*, reaffirmed it repeatedly.[38] The same monthly took the argument a step further, saying that the implementation of the right to secession depended on the Kurds alone. If at present the Kurds demanded autonomy and opted for a "voluntary union" (*ittihad ikhtiyari*) with Iraq, this was their own free will and not a decision dictated by fear.[39]

At various times in the history of modern Iraq, the Kurds raised demands ranging from independence to federal union with Iraq to the "liberation and unification of Greater Kurdistan."[40] But autonomy was the middle ground on which the majority of Kurds met and on which, for a while, they were joined by the Ba'th. But the principle of autonomy had barely been accepted by both sides in 1970 when serious differences emerged almost simultaneously about its interpretation and the language to be used with reference to it. As we have seen, these started with the term to be used for the projected settlement. The Kurds were careful to call it *ittifaqiyya* (agreement) and stressed that it had been reached as a result of ten years of revolutionary struggle.[41] In substance, they conceived of autonomy as a status only a little short of independence. Elected bodies were to exercise the self-government agreed upon. The Kurdish language was to play a greatly enhanced role, and Kurdish culture was to be strengthened and was to serve as a dam capable of containing Arab cultural domination. Again and again, when the Ba'th regime changed or reinterpreted the March Proclamation, the Kurds accused it of "chauvinism," "racism," and "arrogance," of attempts to absorb and merge the Kurds into the Arab population, and of engaging in the "Arabization" of their region by settling Arabs there.

Arabization was closely connected with the question of fixing the boundaries of the Kurdish region. The Kurds urged the Ba'th to give the autonomous region a well-defined territorial character, and originally an official body was to be set up to demarcate the boundaries of the Kurdish "entity." But the Ba'th consistently shirked the question, and when the agreement eventually broke down in 1974, it was over this issue.[42] One of the reasons was that the Kurds wanted oil-rich Kirkuk included in their region. But beyond that, there was an objection in principle by the Ba'th to legally recognized boundaries within Iraq and to the augmented Kurdish feeling of separateness that was bound to result from the existence of a borderline.

The Kurds called themselves by names that seemed to mirror the descriptions the Ba'th regime used for the Iraqi people: *al-qawmiyya al-Kurdiyya* or *al-umma al-Kurdiyya* (the Kurdish nation), *al-sha'b al-Kurdi* (the Kurdish people), *al-watan al-Kurdi* (the Kurdish homeland), *al-watan al-Kurdi al-kabir* (the great [or greater] Kurdish homeland), or *Kurdistan al-kubra* (Greater Kurdistan). If the Kurds had a "natural" homeland, as they asserted, then why should it be included in the "artificial" state of modern Iraq? The question was hinted at in a passage in *al-Ta'akhi* reading: "Modern Iraq, in its borders and with its peoples, consisted until World War I of three Ottoman *vilayets* with different names. The name Iraq [by contrast] has no geographical or historical antecedents, neither in history books nor in atlases." It had appeared only two years after the British had occupied what had been the area of ancient Mesopotamia.[43] If this was enough for *al-Jumhuriyya* to conclude that *al-Ta'akhi* had threatened Iraq with partition into three parts, one can understand the resistance of the Ba'th to marking a borderline. In fact, however, the question mark the Kurds applied to the name of Iraq was no more than an argument to counter the government's earlier questioning of the separate status of the Kurds. Talabani wrote that a "chauvinistic nationalist current in the Arab liberation movement" held that the frontiers of the Arab lands ran along the Taurus mountain range. Its adherents thought that any non-Arab peoples living to the south of it were minorities within the Arab world. Therefore, he concluded, "if these caused trouble to the Arab nation, they could be evacuated across the border." According to the Ba'th, Kurdistan existed only in Iran and Turkey, not in Iraq.[44]

But if there were occasional (and rather feeble) reservations about the territorial integrity of Iraq, the usual line taken by Kurdish spokespeople coincided with that of the Ba'th: Kurdish autonomy, they repeated over and over again, would work within Iraqi unity. However, they often made that point in a form that contained a hidden protest. They spoke of *ittihad ikhtiyari* (voluntary union), an expression that could also be understood to connote "federation." This was greatly objectionable to Baghdad. Even just to say *ittihad* instead of *wahda* seemed to stress the existence of two parts of equal status that had been joined together, while *wahda* was taken to signal an organic whole. *Ikhtiyari* was worse. It implied that the Kurds were free to decide whether to remain part of Iraq or secede from it. The furious reaction of the Ba'th to its use caused *al-Ta'akhi* to hold up the Soviet Union as a model. There, federal states with demarcated boundaries did exist, but this had not caused the Soviet Union to disintegrate. Why then should Baghdad object to borderlines or self-determination?[45] (This, of course, was said before the collapse of the Soviet Union.)

Even when agreeing to the principle of Iraqi unity, the Kurds did not conceal their malaise over the concept of all-Arab unity or their suspicion of any Arab unity scheme Iraq might be part of. Any such plan was liable to change the Kurds from being a sizeable component of the Iraqi population into being a diminutive minority in a wider, almost exclusively Arab, entity. In the 1950s, when such union schemes were the order of the day, Kurdish leaders sought a formula to redefine their links with Iraq should such an eventuality come about. Their point of departure was to question the definition of Iraq as "part of the Arab homeland," since it ignored the Kurds and their history. There was no way of subsuming Iraq's non-Arab population under the heading of "the Arab nation." The proper way to speak of Iraq was to say that it consisted of two parts: Iraqi Kurdistan and the Arab areas of Iraq. The latter alone, so the Kurdish spokespeople asserted, could be considered part of the Arab homeland.[46]

During the 1963 Syrian-Egyptian-Iraqi unity talks, the Kurds—in keeping with their basic attitude—demanded that if a federal union came into being between the three states, their own area should be given full autonomy. However, if there was to be a merger into a unitary or central state, then the Kurds must set up a separate region (*iqlim*), to be linked in some fashion with the new Arab state.[47] While no such union scheme was ever implemented, the discussion about such a possibility did not quite cease. Iraq's insistence on including a clause in the 1970 constitution to the effect that "Iraq is part of the Arab nation" once more brought it to the fore.

Kurdish definitions of their identity in terms of belonging to Greater Kurdistan further complicated the issue. The two Kurdish parties active in the 1930s and the 1940s—Hewa and Ruzgari—advocated the unity of all areas inhabited by Kurds.[48] During the period dealt with here, that demand was no longer put forward. But there were still unmistakable echoes in statements by Kurdish leaders of the belief that the division of Kurdish territory was a historical injustice. The term *wahda wataniyya Kurdiyya* (Kurdish national unity) was still employed, and the influence of Kurdish movements in Iraq, and of the leadership of Mustafa Barzani, extended to Kurdish areas outside Iraq. As *al-Ta'akhi* put it: "The Kurdish movement in Iraq is the movement of Kurds anywhere. It is a national [*watani*] movement, not any different from the national movements of other peoples."[49]

9

The Baʿth Facing Particularism and Secession

Rather than attesting to the strength of the Baʿth, the Baʿthi vision of Iraqi and Arab unity was indicative of internal weaknesses and constraints within the Iraqi society. The Sunni Arabs promoted the concept of unity because they hoped to turn it into a means of strengthening their own position at the expense of the other groups in the Iraqi population and that of Iraq at the expense of other Arab countries. The collective memory that, not so long ago, Iraq had been made up of three separate Ottoman *vilayets* remained alive, much to the displeasure of the Baʿth rulers, for whom it conjured up partition. Even more powerful, and much more traumatic, was the collective memory of the fragmentation of the Arab world into small states after the collapse of the Ottoman Empire.

The Baʿth idiom possessed many expressions that, while applied to current events, elicited an echo of that painful experience. Examples were *tajziʾa* (meaning "division" but evoking a picture of something being cut into pieces); *taqsim* (division or partition); *tamziq* (carving up); *infisal* (secession); and *duwayla* or *duwaylat* (statelet, ministate). This last term is the diminutive of *dawla* (state) and, in this context, connotes contempt and frustration. This is brought out very strongly in remarks by Salah al-Din al-Sabbagh, one of the leaders of the Rashid ʿAli al-Kaylani movement. He wrote: "There is no wolf so deadly to the Arabs, and no such sworn enemy of Islam as Great Britain; as for the Arabs, it carved up their body into ministates [*duwaylat*], parties, and tribes, for them to fight each other while [Britain] picks up the spoils."[1] The theme recurred for a long time. When

the Ba'th party was already in power, *al-Jumhuriyya* wrote that imperialism had not been able to weaken the Arab nation until it "tore its natural
unity to pieces and turned them into contemptible little entities."[2]

The most telling symbol of the small, laughable state was Israel. It was
habitually referred to as *duwayla, al-duwayla al-maskh* (monster statelet),
or *duwayla al-'isabat* (the ministate of gangs).[3] In the Ba'th view, Israel
had only succeeded in surviving because of the fragmentation of the Arab
world and because of the existence of Arab "ministates with weak and
despicable regimes." This ministate, Israel, the Ba'thi argument ran, was
a threat to Arab unity because it was perpetuating the tactics of imperialism, intimidating the Arab nation, sowing despair in its ranks, and trying
to harm the Arab "liberation current." In this endeavor, Israel and the
imperialist powers had later been joined by Iran. What Iran hoped to gain
was Middle Eastern hegemony; what Israel hoped to gain was to become—
militarily, economically, and technologically—the strongest among the
small states.[4]

Iraq (which all along equated "big" with "strong") felt similar contempt
for the plan to set up a Palestinian state. This, its spokespeople and press
writers said, would be no more than a *duwayla mustana'a* (small artificial state). In the Persian Gulf, too, Arab public opinion (as the Ba'th saw
it) rejected the narrow borders and the petty dynasties of the *duwaylat*
and was waiting for a change of regime there.[5] In the case of Kuwait, the
appellation *duwayla* served as justification (one of several) for annexing
it. A few days after its occupation, Saddam Husayn said that imperialism
had "set up small and weak states and had placed at their head families
who had been of service to it. By setting up such repulsive small oil states,
it robbed the majority of their people as well as of the [Arab] nation of
their wealth." These families had begun "gnawing at the body of the
nation and cause corruption to permeate it. In such circumstances there
remained no choice but to apply radical remedies."[6]

Contempt and presumptuousness turned into anxiety when the focus
turned to Iraq itself and when the specter of partitioning the country into
Sunni Arab, Shi'i, and Kurdish parts appeared, or seemed to appear, on
the horizon. The Ba'th itself conjured up this apparition as a propaganda
theme to be used against Kurds and Shi'is or to rally Sunni Arabs around
it. It could also be employed to gain inter-Arab support or to impress foreign countries outside the region who were always afraid of territorial
change and the instability that would come with it. But, as happened more
than once in Ba'th discourse, the propaganda effects were like a thin film
spread over a multitude of genuine fears and painful weaknesses. More
than that, these seemed frequently to hover at the edge of self-fulfilling
prophecy.

Husayn himself often addressed these problems. On one occasion he
likened Iraq to "a huge ship for all Iraqis, Arabs, and Kurds" and warned
that he would not allow anyone "to drill a hole in this ship, lest it fall
apart and sink." On another occasion, he said he was opposed to any plan

that might help "Iraqi particularists or secessionists" and that he would "draw his sword against it and fight it, regardless from which quarter it comes."[7] Such talk about the danger of Iraq disintegrating occurred in three contexts: the scheme for Kurdish autonomy; the Islamic revolution in Iran; and the Kurdish and Shi'i uprisings after the Gulf War. In the first context, an unconscious parallel may have been drawn between the Israeli *duwayla* and the potential *duwayla* of Kurdistan. In this case, the fear of secession was indeed fed by some Kurdish statements and attitudes, whereas with regard to the Shi'is, there were hardly any real grounds for it. Nonetheless, the party congress report of 1982 spoke of "the south and the separatist danger [existing] there."[8]

If there was at any time a real danger to the territorial integrity of Iraq, it was during the Kurdish and Shi'i uprisings in the spring of 1991. Iraq had never before faced the challenge of simultaneous rebellions in the south and the north, encouraged by the twenty-eight-member wartime coalition that had fought the Gulf War and still kept some of its forces on Iraqi soil. The Kurds and the Shi'is gave their uprising the heroic-sounding name of *intifada*, while the Ba'th called it *safhat al-ghadr wa-l-khiyana* (the chapter of treachery and treason) or *fitna* or *mihna*. The last two connote situations of crisis or of a supreme test. And indeed, the uprisings were a period of the most serious test since the establishment of modern Iraq of the cohesion of the Iraqi state and the identity of Iraqi citizens. *Fitna*, however, carries additional connotations, all extremely negative. In the Qur'an, it can mean heresy, arson, an act of Satan, torture, and civil strife within the Muslim community.[9] The "Great *fitna*" is the name given to the civil war that broke out in the wake of the murder of 'Uthman, the third caliph, in 656. From then on, it acquired the meaning of an abortive attempt to challenge legitimate authority or to overturn the ordered life of the community. In preferring it to the most common word for civil war, *harb ahliyya*, the Ba'th wished to evoke a distant past, common to all Muslims, and to express its rejection of current events by means of an ancient term known to all.

After Husayn had suppressed the uprisings—also called *fitnat al-shaytan* (Satan's civil war)—the Ba'th press praised him for having prevented the partition of Iraq. As *al-Thawra* put it: "The knight is the valiant leader whose name is linked with the unity [*wahda*] of Iraq. . . . All our brothers and all our good friends and even our enemies know this very well and say: 'But for Saddam Husayn, Iraq would have been divided into ministates [*duwaylat*] and into small satellite states.'"[10] But success in 1991 did not spell safety from future attempts against Iraq's territorial integrity. The subsequent evacuation of the Iraqi army from Kurdistan and the establishment of an autonomous Kurdish entity there in 1992 gave a new momentum to Kurdish separatism. The involvement of neighboring and Western governments in Iraqi Kurdish affairs ever since have further deepened Ba'thi apprehensions about the breakup of the Iraqi state. Where this will lead cannot be assessed today.

IV

Cycles of Enmity and Violence

The existence of a real, live enemy imparts vitality to our doctrine and makes our blood circulate.
—Michel ʿAflaq, *Fi sabil al-baʿth*

There is something beyond money and knowledge which preserves the honor of peoples and protects them from bondage and humiliation—and that is force . . . and that means: to excel in the art of death.
—Sami Shawkat, *Hadhihi ahdafuna*

One of the most striking characteristics of the Baʿthi political discourse is its constant emphasis on threats from ever-present and dangerous enemies and, simultaneously, on strength, force and the use of force, and violence and its application. Closely linked with each other, these two themes provide the regime with its raison d'être. The invocation of fear and anxiety and the glorification of the use of force attest to the influence of fascist thinking on the Baʿthi worldview, regardless of the fact that the Baʿth itself presents them as springing from the Arab political tradition.

The urge to magnify the image of enemies derives from three main sources: the residual sediments of the period of the British mandate and the collective memory of colonial domination; the "Zionist menace" and the commitment of the Baʿth to the Palestinian cause; and the immediate danger from Iran, kindled by Iraqi-Iranian competition for hegemony in the Persian Gulf. There are, however, additional enemies, both foreign and domestic, and they, too, are exploited to escalate tension, intensify suspicions, and augment the constant sense of being menaced. Saddam Husayn described this by means of a telling metaphor: He likened Iraq to a man living in an isolated house in the forest. Even though he has a handgun, he must still lock the door. On another occasion, he spoke of Iraq as a man ill with malaria, pursued by a wolf. Despite his fever, he must run ever faster to get away from the wolf.[1]

Underlying all these dangers and threats is a vast conspiracy (*muʾamara*). Originally, *muʾamara* meant to conspire to kill a person. The prevalence of the sense of a plot being woven or an act of underhand collusion being concocted has been attributed to the fact that in most Arab states underground plotting in total secrecy has indeed been the only course open to the opposition.[2] Such *mu'amarat* were being plotted by all of Iraq's enemies, each in turn. Even actions that were indisputably Iraqi initiatives (such as launching the war against Iran in 1980) were described as being undertaken in response to, or for the purpose of foiling, a conspiracy. Husayn said (perhaps rather more revealingly than he had meant to) that Iraq had known since 1977 that in 1980 "a great *mu'amara* would be planned [against Iraq] since that was the year when Iraq's stance was to be translated into action."[3]

Genuine anxiety and propaganda effects become intertwined to an extent that make it difficult, if not impossible, to unravel them. Propaganda created an atmosphere of permanent crisis, and this in turn enabled the regime to mobilize greater support for the Ba'th and rally the population behind it. In this fashion, it became possible to divert anger and frustration away from the regime and toward external enemies, to lend legitimacy to the liquidation of domestic adversaries, and, most important, to underpin the Ba'th ideology of force, violence, and aggrandizement.

That ideology had its antecedents among like-minded thinkers in the Arab worlds in the 1930s and the 1940s, but it differed from them by translating fiery slogans into meticulously organized day-to-day action. The party set up a vast propaganda machine with the primary aim of dominating every aspect of social life, reaching out to people in all walks of life, and directing them toward one single aim: the admiration of force. Establishing ideological predominance went hand in hand with the building of a vast military infrastructure and the creation of a war machine the like of which Iraq had not known before. The military buildup, together with the salience given to the (real or imaginary) hostility of (real or imaginary) enemies, dragged Iraq into a series of domestic struggles and foreign wars that the Ba'th eventually could no longer control. The regime ended up a prisoner of the machinery of force it had created itself. This apparatus grew and was perfected throughout the years of Ba'th rule, concealing rather than correcting the country's grave internal political and social weaknesses. This was illustrated in stark colors by the events of 1991, when, as soon as the war machine was seen to falter, there was an outburst of violent opposition on the part of the Shi'is and the Kurds.

10

Three Cycles of Hostility

Imperialism: "An Antediluvian Dinosaur"

In 1973, at a colloquium on Iraqi schools' curricula, Saddam Husayn declared that the central task of national education was to define the country's traditional enemies and to teach the children hatred of imperialism (*karahiyya li-l-istiʿmar*). This, he added, should be done not only by the traditional methods of instruction but also in many indirect ways: through proverbs and adages, the wording of exercises in arithmetic, and various visual teaching aids. If the regime indeed aimed at radically changing society, teaching must not be detached from politics. Another aim of education, he said on a different occasion, must be to impart to pupils habits of discipline and order. This requirement, too, was explained by reference to imperialism or other foreign enemies: in later life, students may have to bear arms and to "oppose an imperialist or [other] hostile landing [*inzal*]." They would then do so even under the most difficult conditions "because they have become accustomed to discipline and order from an early age."[1]

The fullest exposition of "imperialism" is found in a voluminous book devoted exclusively to it. It reviews imperialist aims and policies from 1840 to 1960. During these 120 years, the authors found, the word "imperialism" had changed its meaning no fewer than twelve times. At first, it was used as a neutral or even positive political term and was linked with the idea of Europe bringing progress and development to backward peoples.

After passing through further stages, it acquired a heavy emotional charge and turned altogether negative, not only connoting policies of expansionism and of seeking economic, military, and strategic advantages but also embodying all that was, ideologically speaking, negative, even satanic, conspirational, and aggressive. In the Third World, including the Arab countries, imperialists were believed to engage in constant plots to undermine the independence of states and to prevent their social, economic, and political development.[2]

The concept of imperialism entered Arab discourse after World War I, with the division of the Middle East and the establishment of British and French mandatory regimes there. Arabic had three words to refer to it: *isti'mar*, *imbiryaliyya*, and *istikbar*. *Isti'mar*, a relatively new term found only since the beginning of the twentieth century, is the most literal translation Arabic has for "colonialism." The root, however, already occurs in the Qur'an, in the sura *Hud*, verse 64: *huwa ansha'akum min al-ard wa-ista'marakum fiha* (it is he who produced you from the earth and has given you to live therein). Its meaning later expanded to indicate the settling of some area by foreigners. *Imbiryaliyya* is, of course, no more than a loanword. In this particular case, unlike so many other political terms, the Arabic *isti'mar* appeared earlier than the "imported" word *imbiryaliyya*. The former was prevalent in Iraq from the end of World War I until the 1960s. From then on, both were often used side by side or interchangeably.[3] Since *isti'mar* was used initially to describe the British and French mandates and became a synonym of bondage and oppression, when the mandates were terminated and the overall influence of Britain and France was diminishing, a new term was needed to shift the stress from the old kind of direct domination to the new brand of indirect imperialism. The typical representative of the new imperialism was the United States.

Istikbar is derived from *istakbara*: to be proud or arrogant or to consider oneself great. *Istikbar* became current in the 1980s and was used to connote the two superpowers, jointly or severally. Its use originated in Shi'i fundamentalist quarters that in turn had taken it over from the regime of Khomeini. In Iran, it was used in conjunction with Khomeini's slogan: "Neither East nor West" and marked the opposite of another term often used by Khomeini, *al-mustad'afun* (the oppressed). In his book *'An al-'Iraq*, Muhammad Taqi al-Mudarrisi (see Chapter 7) speaks frequently of global *istikbar* and its plots against Islam. In his view, the Islamic movement in Iraq had been growing rapidly and was gaining momentum when international *istikbar* decided to give unlimited support to the Ba'th regime, having chosen it to stop the Islamic trend. Mudarrisi warned that "the *mustakbirun* would end up forcing their will upon us . . . and sell us at a public auction sale." Later, another Shi'i leader, Muhammad Baqir al-Hakim, also condemned global *istikbar* for its collaboration with the Ba'th in suppressing the 1991 *intifada*.[4]

In the rare cases when the Ba'th regime itself employed the term, it was done scornfully, as for instance in *al-Jumhuriyya* when it wrote: "Khomeini purports to fight the international *istikbar* powers." However, in the period just before the Gulf War, the use of the word became more frequent, just as the use of other Islamic terms became current at that time (see Part 5). Thus, for instance, an article published in December 1990 asserted that Iraq would not let itself be intimidated, nor would it contemplate capitulation "because we attribute no importance to those who think themselves great [*istakbaru*]."[5]

Alongside these three terms there existed a popular expression in Iraq that was a personification of imperialism: Abu Naji. This goes back to the period of the British mandate when "imperialist Britain" was referred to as Abu Naji. The literal meaning of the expression is "the savior," and it was apparently used among the Jews of Baghdad as a code word for the British, whom they so regarded from the moment the British first entered the capital in World War I.[6] Over time, it turned into a common expression, but since it was used by people who did not know its origins, it acquired all the negative connotations of "imperialism." Recalling childhood memories, the Iraqi journalist Mazhar 'Arif wrote of the fear and hatred evoked by the name of Abu Naji, "the evil and the accursed" who would "devour children and grown-ups and towns and cities and anything that moved" and who had turned all of Iraq into his "private estate." Later, he had witnessed a demonstration calling for "the fall of imperialism, of [the leading statesman] Nuri Sa'id, and of Abu Naji." It was then that he understood what this imaginary name really stood for. Today, 'Arif went on, Abu Naji had gone from the region, but the methods of imperialism were still being applied indirectly since "Great Britain has not rid itself of the spirit of the old imperialism." However, some twelve years later, in 1992, *Babil* wrote: "Abu Naji has gone and we don't remember his bad deeds any more."[7]

Three types of imperialism can be discerned in the Ba'thi political idiom: the actual imperialism exercised by the great powers and guided by their ambitions in the region; "imperialism on behalf of" a third party, like that carried out, for instance, by the Kurds, the Zionists, or Iran; and a rather amorphous kind that could be attributed to any foe, domestic or foreign, real or imaginary. As we shall see presently, Ba'th spokespeople and writers who used the catchword *isti'mar* were not always careful to explain which of the three they were referring to. This helped to increase tension and reinforce the sense of threats and perils lying in wait for Iraq and thus to appeal for greater internal cohesion.

The man who did most to make Iraq a symbol of resistance to imperialism was Salah al-Din Sabbagh, a central figure in Rashid 'Ali al-Kaylani's military coup of 1941, who was executed in 1945 for his part in it. His book *Fursan al-'Uruba fi-l-'Iraq* (The knights of Arabism in Iraq) was a scathing attack on British imperialism and its Iraqi supporters, and it became a basic text of antiimperialist education. On the eve of the Kuwait crisis, for instance, *al-Qadisiyya* cited it as an indictment of European imperialism. In doing so, however, it did not quote verbatim from the book but rendered its gist in simplified Arabic, obviously assuming that Sabbagh's original language went above the head of the common reader, in particular the rank-and-file soldier to whom the passage was primarily addressed.

Throughout the book, Britain is likened to a wolf out for prey, deadly for the Arabs and for Islam. In Sabbagh's opinion, British imperialism was the most "cunning and bitter" of all. This was so because it first set out to study the weaknesses of the Arabs and then dealt with them according to the qur'anic verse, "Kings, when they enter a city, disorder it and make the mighty ones of its inhabitants abased." In order to secure their important strategic interest in the Arab region, the British had turned to certain local Arab quarters and to the Jews and made them the pillars of their regional policy. Sabbagh concluded: "I detest Britain and all those who help it to enslave [*yastaʿmir*] my people because I am a Muslim and Islamic law lays down that no infidel shall rule over me . . . and because I am an Arab and Arabism forbids a foreign army to corrupt my country." He attacked Nuri al-Saʿid, the virtually permanent strongman of Iraq from the end of the British mandate until the fall of the monarchy in 1958, saying that he and his supporters "pretend to be Arabs, yet they kill the sons of my homeland at the instance of the enslaver [*mustaʿmir*]."[8]

Sabbagh was not alone in using antiimperialist slogans in order to attack domestic rivals, first and foremost Nuri al-Saʿid; many other nationalists did so. Nuri and the court establishment paid them back in the same coin. But in their idiom, it was the Soviet Union rather than the West that represented the dangers of imperialism. Just as the Soviets had established their ascendancy over Egypt's Nasir, so they were out to place Iraq in their orbit.[9]

Much like many other Arab ideologues, Michel ʿAflaq came out repeatedly against imperialism and its local helpers. But he also called on the Arabs not to blame imperialism for all that was wrong with them. On one occasion, he went as far as saying that the Arabs themselves had brought about imperialism through their failure to put their own house in order.[10] But the Iraqi Baʿth ignored that approach altogether. It became common practice to exploit fear of and hatred for imperialism—or rather, to stimulate them intentionally. In particular during the first decade of its rule, this was done frequently to rally the public behind the party and to mobilize mass support. The targets were various opposition groupings at home and Israel, Iran, and the United States abroad.

The difficulties the Baʿth party encountered in consolidating its hold on power during these years led it to seek the greatest possible number of "imperialist" enemies. The officers who had collaborated with the Baʿth in mid-July 1968, only to be removed from power two weeks later, were then described by the Baʿth media as the representatives within Iraq of the "new imperialism." So were the "spies" hanged in January 1969. The suppression in 1975 of the Kurdish uprising was also described as "the liquidation" of "the haven of imperialism" in Iraq.[11] In the long struggle against Iran, which grew particularly acrimonious between 1969 and 1975, Iran was habitually referred to as an agent of imperialism and often enough as the imperialist country par excellence. Reference was made to Iran's imperialist aspirations in the Persian Gulf and throughout the Arab region.[12]

The rapprochement with the Soviet Union that culminated with the signing of the Treaty of Friendship between Iraq and the USSR in 1972 caused the Ba'th to adopt some of the Soviet language of opposition to U.S. imperialism. A joint Soviet-Iraqi communiqué in 1970 spoke of the common "resolution to finally liquidate both the new and the old imperialism."[13] Similar joint statements were made frequently, both before and after the signing of the treaty. It would be wrong to think of them as mere lip service by Iraq to a powerful ally; rather, they reflected authentic and deeply rooted Ba'thi attitudes. Expressions of this kind grew in intensity and became more strident as relations between the United States and the Shah of Iran grew closer. The 1973 party congress stated that the Ba'th "confronted the imperialist countries fundamentally, directly, and most sharply, because they stand in the way of the realization of our national [*qawmi*] dream." It also made clear that the principal imperialist power was the United States. Husayn warned of imperialist plans to attack Iraq or to "open new fronts" against it and added that it was therefore necessary to make the country's borders "razor sharp." The aims of imperialism were to make Israel stronger and to take control of the region's natural resources. Iraq would fight imperialism not only in Iraq but also wherever it was found in "the length and breadth of the [Arab] homeland." Imperialism, he concluded, might make gains in the short run, but eventually the Arabs would win.[14]

The most comprehensive statement of Ba'thi antiimperialism was *Al-Minhaj al-thaqafi al-markazi* (The central educational program), issued in 1977. It contained a special chapter devoted to this issue, entitled "Al-'Arab wa-l-imbiryaliyya" (The Arabs and imperialism). Its importance lay in the fact that it was meant to be the textbook for the education of a whole generation of young party members or sympathizers. It was not just a collection of slogans but purported to analyze the problem of imperialism scientifically. In retrospect, it can be seen as having helped prepare public opinion for the "confrontation with imperialism" in the Gulf War. The document defines imperialism as an "aggressive ideology" adopted by the Western powers. As such, it had passed through four stages: (1) the period of its peak, with the establishment of "political, military, and economic ascendancy," lasting until World War I;[15] (2) the interwar years during which the first "cracks" appeared; (3) the decline of the "traditional" form of imperialism, from the end of World War II to the Bandung Conference of 1955; (4) the rise of the "new" imperialism, led by the United States. The United States aimed at maintaining imperialist influence by perpetuating the small Arab "entities" set up between the two world wars to divide the Arabs and to keep them weak; by "planting artificial entities" in the region, such as the "Zionist entity"; by maintaining the global division between strong and large and weak and small states; and by using covert methods to ensure imperialist predominance in culture and education.

The document enlarges on the global strategic importance of the Arab region and goes on to say that demographic strength, geopolitical advantage, and vast economic resources would enable the Arabs to turn themselves into a great progressive power of the first order, provided that they united.[16] But it was precisely that unity or union that the "new imperialism" sought to frustrate. A pivotal reason for this policy was the dependence of U.S. imperialism on Arab oil. To maintain its grip on the oil sources, the West built up Israel's strength and encouraged it to threaten its Arab neighbors with nuclear war. For the same purpose, it armed Iran and gave it the green light for acts of hostility against Iraq. It also reinforced Arab reactionary quarters, first and foremost Saudi Arabia. The United States placed the "Arab nation under military siege" by deploying its navy close to Arab shores. And finally, it manipulated oil prices with a view to reestablishing its ascendancy and holding down European and Japanese influence in the Middle East. According to the document, it was the U.S. view that the road to absolute control of oil resources passed through the Arab capitals, which the United States must first force into "political, military, and domestic" subjection.

What can the Arabs do to stand up to these schemes? The document outlines several courses: work for the liberation of Palestine and reject peace with Israel; augment feelings of unity among the Arab masses and between the Arab states; plan a broad counteroffensive against imperialism rather than continue with a merely defensive line, as had been the case until then; and adopt an independent economic policy and build up a powerful infrastructure for military industries. In a sideswipe at Saudi Arabia, the document demands that no further moneys from oil income should be deposited in the United States: the present deposits were like "a huge gift to our enemy and the enemy of the peoples." These deposits were helping the United States overcome its economic crisis. Instead, such funds should be used for development projects in Arab countries. In conclusion, the document forecasts that the *last quarter of the twentieth century* would witness a "frontal struggle between global imperialism" and the Arab masses. This would eventually put an end to imperialism as a "historical phenomenon." This outcome was inevitable because already imperialism had become a "senile devil . . . to be likened to an antediluvian dinosaur. By contrast, the Arabs are a young, revolutionary, and rising force—a force capable of striking a devastating blow at U.S. imperialism."[17]

Such great hopes faded somewhat in the course of the second decade of Ba'th rule, and *imbiryaliyya* and *isti'mar* were used a great deal less frequently. They came back into fashion again in 1988, after the end of the war against Iran. *Al-Jumhuriyya* published an article entitled "The Hatred of Imperialism Has Reasons of Its Own" that stated: "By liquidating Iranian aggression, Iraq has done away with the fictitious pillar of support of imperialism and Zionism on which Washington and Tel Aviv had leaned for many years in order to frighten and terrorize peoples."[18] In 1989, *al-Thawra* repeated what Saddam Husayn had said in 1973 about educating young people to hate imperialism and added Zionism as another target of hatred.[19] But it was Husayn himself who imparted a new kind of élan to the revival of its use. In his well-known speech in February 1990 that marked the beginning of the Kuwait crisis, he said that at the time when the United States had "occupied the imperialist bases" in the Middle East at the end of World War II, Washington had also decided that its interests coincided with Israel's and had concluded that U.S. strategy "required [existence of] an aggressive Israel." (On a later occasion, Husayn added that he had long refrained almost entirely from employing the term "imperialism," but had resumed it after senior U.S. State Department officials had asked Iraq to drop it altogether.)

A closer look at the February 1990 speech reveals that in many of its parts it is a replay of the 1977 party document. There is, however, one difference. While the document refers to the United States by circumlocution, using various descriptions of imperialism to do so, the speech names it directly. Both the document and the speech stress the importance of Arab oil for the U.S. economy; both speak of Washington's desire to control the Persian Gulf and to dictate oil prices; both make much of the strategic link with Israel. Furthermore, both emphasize the duty of the Arabs to confront and face up to the United States, whether by attacking and liquidating Israel, by forcing the U.S. fleet out of the Gulf, or by withdrawing Arab deposits from American banks. To succeed in all this, the Arabs must unite among themselves as well as find outside support.[20]

From then on, while the Iraqi army was being readied for action, the media relaunched the verbal campaign against imperialism, reviving old themes and adding new ones. As in Sabbagh's writings, the United States (and President George Bush personally) were likened to a wolf out for prey and ready "to sink its dirty claws" into the body of Iraq. But Iraq would not succumb; on the contrary, it would be up to its task of being "the strong pillar of the Arabs and the Muslims in standing up to its true enemies—imperialism and Zionism." The old theme of the impending great attack on Iraq and on the Arab nation, now being planned by imperialism and Zionism, was sounded again. The approaching liquidation of imperialism was again predicted.[21] Needless to say, all these slogans became even more strident during and immediately after the Gulf War. When in 1992 Iraqi flights over southern Iraqi territory were banned, a new term was invented to refer to the ban: *isti'mar al-sama'* (imperialism in the sky).[22]

What lessons can we draw from the changing frequency with which "imperialism" was used? First, we find that it is quite a reliable barometer for the status of U.S.-Iraqi relations. The period of its falling into abeyance coincided with the years of a U.S.-Iraqi rapprochement (marked by the renewal of diplomatic relations in 1984). The renewed use of the term a few years later attested to the Ba'thi assessment that, though ostensibly outmoded, it had retained a powerful emotional appeal and was still capable of rallying people behind the regime to face "the enemy." It also shows that the resumption of enmity toward the West was a deliberate Iraqi policy choice. This is borne out by the fact that propaganda preparations for a new round (including the stepping up of talk about imperialism) preceded political action for quite some time. That still leaves the question of whether the party document quoted above was in effect a contingency plan for political action, to be taken out of the drawer and implemented at the appropriate moment, or whether it was just one more piece of long-winded official verbiage that happened to become important in a rather fortuitous manner at a much later stage in Iraq's volatile history. There is no cut-and-dried answer; one way or another, the document described deeply rooted Ba'thi convictions that could easily be recalled to duty in the context of new political requirements. In the words of Koebner and Schmidt, "The greatest evil of imperialism as a political slogan has been wrought in the minds of men, because it was so often employed as a toxicant. It could whip up emotions, but at the same time it diminished reason and judgement. It obscured the genuine political problems."[23]

Israel: "The Monstrous Entity"

Much like "imperialism," Israel was made a target of hatred, but comprehensively, more thoroughly, and for a longer time. It must be said, though, that just as with attacks on "imperialism," exploiting slogans about Israel was not the exclusive preserve of Iraq; it existed abundantly in other Arab countries. Perhaps, though, it took up a more central position on the political scene and did so for a longer time than in most other countries. Whereas there were two or three common words used to vilify imperialism, we find a much greater variety of derogatory terms employed to deny the legitimacy of Israel's existence and to express contempt—mixed with fear—for Zionism. One of the most characteristic features of the Iraqi press was the use of quotation marks around the word "Israel." The practice began in the first year of Ba'th rule (1969) and continues in the 1990s, though not as consistently.[24] The quotation marks are meant to indicate that the very existence of Israel is open to doubt. Their use replaced earlier terms during Qasim's regime, such as "the so-called Israel" or "[the entity] pretending to be Israel" (*Isra'il al-maz'uma*).

Another frequent term was *al-dahkila* or *al-kiyan al-dakhil*. The term means a stranger or a person seeking or enjoying protection and is taken from Bedouin life, where it was an age-old practice for weak or pursued persons to ask for the protection of the strong. The appeal for protection is taken as a measure of the importance and strength of the tribe to which the person appeals. Tribes were therefore careful to observe the custom. What is important in the context of Israel, however, is that *dakhala* is granted for a specified time: strong and warlike tribes allow the claimant two months and ten days, others allow a period ranging from three days to one month. In every case, the *dakhil* must give up all weapons as soon as protection is awarded and must leave at the appointed time; the *dakhil* can never become a member of the tribe. Obviously, in relation to Israel, it is not the quality of Arab hospitality and generosity that is evoked but rather the *dakhil's* status as a stranger and the short duration of the stay. Just as the *dakhil* cannot be accepted into the tribe, so Israel can never be accepted into the Arab region.[25]

Another expression used frequently also plays on emotional associations and unpleasant historical memories: *wujud shadhdh* or *kiyan shadhdh* (an irregular or deviant body or entity). The period of the British mandate over Iraq (1920–1932) was called *al-wad' al-shadhdh* (the irregular or abnormal situation). To use the same word for Israel is to point to its "deviant" nature and at the same time, by association, to allude to its links with "British imperialism." Furthermore, it makes the reader or listener expect the demise of that "entity" within a short period of time, as with the mandate.

Other expressions used with similar intention were *Isra'il al-laqita* (Israel the stray, picked up, as it were, from the gutter), *walida fasida* (freak), and *kiyan mazru'* (foreign implant). The latter word, taken from modern medical practice, suggests strangeness, artificiality, and, above all, the possibility of rejection. The presence in the body of an implant rejected by its surrounding tissue is bound to endanger the whole organism. At other times, a more direct language is used: Israel is not a real state but a *'isaba muhtilla* (an occupying gang), a "state of gangs" or a "robber state" (*dawlat al-ightisab*), or a "raping state" (*dawla ghasiba*). The most frequent way of denying Israel's statehood is *al-kiyan al-Sahyuni* (the Zionist entity) or *al-kiyan al-Isra'ili*.[26] *Kiyan* is usually a neutral word connoting status or existence, but coupled with "Zionist" or "Israeli" it becomes a term for something illegitimate or unnatural.

Another series of expressions is used to arouse fear and create a sense of permanent menace: "poisonous snake," "octopus," "dragon," "monster" or "monstrous state," and "cancerous growth."[27] "International Zionism" is described as "a beast of prey thirsty for Arabs." Israel is the "state of war" (*dawlat al-harb*) or the "government of war" (*hukumat al-harb*); its defense minister is a "minister of aggression" (*wazir al-'udwan*). Its area was "a single vast arms store"; it was "the fortress of aggression and expansionism.[28]

It was not, however, only a matter of selecting various pejorative terms. A lot of explanatory writing was also done to describe Israel's nature and analyze its policies. The internal party organ, *al-Thawra al-'Arabiyya*, took up the Israeli issue frequently. The primary aim of the "Zionist entity," it wrote, was to "liquidate the [Arab] national existence surrounding it and to set up microscopic sectarian states" incapable of standing up to it. The same idea was present in the accusation that Israel worked for the "Balkanization" of the Middle East. Failing this, Israel aimed at weakening the military presence around it, particularly that of the Palestinians and the Iraqis. Israel's strategy had become dangerous for all the Arab countries because of the Israeli concept of a "security belt" stretching from North Africa as far as Pakistan.[29] In a speech given a short time before the invasion of Kuwait, Husayn warned of Israel's drive for expansion, which he compared with Adolf Hitler's theory of *lebensraum*. *Al-Jumhuriyya* unearthed "The Protocols of the Elders of Zion" (well-known as a forgery written by the czarist secret police) and summarized its contents.[30] In short, Israel was depicted as a danger to the very existence of the Arabs, thereby forcing them to maintain a constant state of military preparedness. The war with it would be everlasting.

The gravest danger of all stemmed from the Gordian knot tying Zionism and imperialism together, a perception leading to the adoption of the term *sahyu-imbiryaliyya* (Zio-imperialism). The establishment of Israel was described as the opening move in a new crusade and as tantamount to setting up an imperialist bridgehead on Arab-Muslim territory. References to the crusades elicited a strongly emotional reaction of mixed pain and anger, but at the same time there was some comfort in them for the Arab listener. After all, the crusader state had not lasted long; being similar to it, neither would Israel.

Ba'th doctrine declared that the idea of setting up an "artificial Zionist state" had been conceived by imperialism early in the nineteenth century, at the time of Muhammad 'Ali's rise in Egypt. At the same time, Ba'th ideologues went on to say, the Zionists with their imperialist ideology wished to foster an entity in Palestine that would serve the aims of imperialism. This had resulted in a veritable Zionist-imperialist symbiosis. *Al-Thawra al-'Arabiyya* explained that the aim of imperialism was to "dominate the Arab area, keep it divided, backward, and dependent, exploit its natural resources and their marketing, and benefit from the [region's] strategic positions"; therefore it needed an "aggressive base" in the Arab region.[31] As imperialist interests in the Middle East spread out, so the link between "international imperialism" and "international Zionism" grew closer. Israel therefore needed to be made "strong," "aggressive," and "terrorist." As a reward for acting as a "forward guard post," Israel became the "spoiled child" of imperialism. It turned into a "state of military colonies" (*dawlat al-musta'marat al-'askariyya*) and into a "province" of the United States and Europe and served them as a "deadly weapon" against the Arab nation and its unity.[32]

In the Ba'thi view, Jewish-Persian links were much older than the Jewish connection with imperialism; indeed, they went back to antiquity. While the Zionist-imperialist alliance was based on common interests, the Jewish-Persian link was based on a shared hatred of Arabs in general and Iraqis in particular. Khayrallah Talfah wrote an article entitled "Iranian-Zionist Relations throughout the Ages." He stated: "Iran has been linked to the pro-Zionist Jewish movement by deep and lasting ties for thousands of years, and despite the course of generations and the changes in government, these ties have remained close and cooperation assumed various shapes." *Al-Jumhuriyya* wrote similarly about the "historical continuity" of Jews and Persians weaving joint plots against Iraq. These began with "Cyrus the Persian" enlisting a mostly Jewish fifth column in Babylon, which enabled him to conquer the city, and continued up to the days of Zionist-Khomeinist cooperation.[33]

Zionist-Persian conspirational ties formed the subject of two books published in 1980s: Fadil al-Barrak's *Al-Madaris al-Yahudiyya wa-l-Iraniyya fi-l-ʿIraq* (Jewish and Iranian schools in Iraq) and Saʿd al-Bazzaz's *Al-Harb al-sirriyya, khafaya al-dawr al-Israʾili fi harb al- khalij* (The secret war: the mysterious role of Israel in the Gulf War [the Iraqi-Iranian war]).[34] The first dwells on the "dangerous" and "destructive" role of Jewish and Iranian schools played in Iraqi society. The second deals with Iranian-Israeli cooperation, placing particular stress on the first years of the Iraqi-Iranian war, including the bombing of the Iraqi nuclear reactor in June 1981. It says that the *israʾiliyyun* (Jews or Israelis) "never hated any town as much as they hated Babylon, and this hatred is still burning in them 2,500 years later." The Jews never forgot their hatred of Nebuchadnezzar, who exiled them in 586 B.C. It was no coincidence, the book went on, that Shah Muhammad Riza celebrated the memory of Cyrus, "who saved the Jews from the Babylonian captivity." This earned him the appreciation of the Israeli prime minister at that time, David Ben-Gurion. What most infuriated both Persians and Israelis, the author continued, was the building of the nuclear reactor and the name given to it: Tammuz. Iraq had chosen the name after a god-shepherd from the ancient Babylonian legends who fought wild boars and other predatory animals and became a symbol of renewal, fertility, and perseverance in the face of adversity. The name alone was enough to arouse the hatred of the Israelis. They felt they were reliving the ancient legend, with themselves cast in the role of the boar.[35]

Apart from their abysmal hatred of Iraq and of all Arab countries, Iran and Israel also had some interests in common. Both were agents of imperialism and sought to strengthen it; both were hostile to Palestine; and both "planned to divide the Arab homeland between them and to place it under their tutelage."[36] This was the foundation of Iranian-Israeli cooperation under the shah, particularly in the economic field. Cooperation grew even more intense under Khomeini. The latter was motivated by "the deeply rooted Persian hatred of the Arab revolution" and by the tradition of *shuʿubiyya* (see Chapter 7).

Al-Thawra al-ʿArabiyya spoke of the way Israeli prime minister Menachem Begin and Khomeini had allotted tasks to each other: Iran was to fight Iraq on the ground and, by forcing it to concentrate on its eastern border, remove it from the Arab arena; Israel would bomb the reactor and, a year later, launch a war in Lebanon. Israel and international Zionism assisted Iran in all possible ways. Israel provided Tehran with military-planning experts, supplied it with weapons, and pushed it into war. Zionist propaganda meanwhile gave the Iranians good press, spread lies about the course of the war, and made the world press ignore "Iraq's victories." At times, Israel took action on behalf of Iran, particularly in areas in which the latter was weak, such as foreign-policy influence and propaganda, as well as in the military field. However, it did not do so for the love of Tehran but to prevent Iraq from playing a role in the Palestinian conflict. As long as the war between Iraq and Iran lasted, Israel enjoyed "temporary security." The overall idea was for Israel and Iran to undertake a pincer movement against the Arab world and break it apart. But Iraq would prove stronger than its enemies.[37]

Al-Jumhuriyya published an article entitled "Tajir al-bunduqiyya wa-tajir al-bazar" (The merchant of Venice, or, alternatively, The arms dealer and the merchant of the bazaar), which discussed the "organic" ties between the "Jewish merchant whose greed extends to blood" and "the Persian merchant whose vengefulness and rancor" led toward aggression. "Just as the Jewish merchant of Venice was defeated by the cleverness and wisdom of one of his contemporaries, so the aggressive Persian will be defeated by the heroism and resistance of the Iraqis, and a new Shakespeare will sing of the Iraqi victory and will make it a model for future generations."[38] A similar idea underlay the building of the great "victory arch" in Baghdad in 1989 to mark the first anniversary of the end of the war against Iran. It is made of two huge swords crossing at the top and forming an arch between them. The artist who designed it, Khalid al-Rahhal, said the sword pointing eastward was directed against Iran, the other against Israel.[39]

Describing Israel as "monstrous" implied a commitment to do away with it. In the Ba'th idiom, fighting Israel is not depicted as a war about frontiers or territories but rather as total political, economic, social, and cultural (*hadari*) warfare. Therefore, preparations for it must also be comprehensive: scientific, technological, political, social, economic, cultural, and military. Husayn, who had dwelt on this theme in the 1970s, said that the strategy against Israel must be comprehensive and allow for various intermediate stages; it must appeal to the quality of *sabr* (patience or endurance, implying the capacity for a long haul), but it must be the patience of the revolutionary, not of one who has despaired. In 1978, he predicted that within twenty years Israel would find itself at a dead end; the same period, he added, set the latest limit for the Arab struggle against it. He, and following him Tariq 'Aziz, asserted that the Arabs were capable of destroying the "legend" called Israel. Their numerical superiority, the vastness of their territories, and their oil power would ensure their success.[40]

The Iraqi political discourse has many terms to connote the destruction of Israel. In the party's first decade in power, the most frequent terms were *tasfiya* (elimination), *izala* (destruction), *inha'* (termination), *jala'* (evacuation), and *maqtal* (killing, murder). Later, more "colorful" expressions were added to the lexicon. In a series of articles entitled "The Last Days of 'Israel,'" *Al-'Iraq* wrote that the strength of "the Arab body would break the strength of the body of 'Israel' and will [eventually] drive the last nail into 'Israel's' coffin." Another expression was *wa'd al-mashru' al-Sahyuni* (literally, the burial of the Zionist project), which was evocative of the pre-Islamic practice of parents burying daughters alive, whether from economic distress, for the honor of the family, or to keep the parents' inheritance intact.[41]

Husayn went further. In an address to army personnel, he said that "Tel Aviv must be ground into dust by bombs." He added that "the Zionist entity" had come to perceive the Iraqi army as the combat force that would eventually "eliminate it and cleanse the Arab soil from its presence." The Iraqis sought to have the honor of being the first Arabs "to smell gunpowder in the Arab land of Palestine." On another occasion, he said Iraq was at the head of those Arabs who meant to strip Israel of its clothes (*ta'riya*).[42] His most memorable statement on Israel was made in April 1990 when he said, "We have sworn by Allah to burn half the state of Israel by fire, should it do anything against Iraq." Should the "hornet" try to sting, "we shall tear off its head and its tail." Israel, he concluded, was "built on a lie." In keeping with such statements, when Iraq dispatched missiles against Israel, *al-Thawra* wrote that "the countdown for the destruction of so-called Israel has begun. The missiles of our great Iraq, the leader of the community of believers, have paved the road to Palestine."[43]

Iran: "The Yellow Storm"

The third side in the triangle of Iraq's enemies was Iran. Zionism and imperialism were distant clouds on the political horizon, but Iran was seen as the close, immediate enemy, always ready to attack Iraq. This perception was fed both by historical reminiscences and by the events in the recent past, some of which had occurred after the Ba'th had come to power. In 1969, Tehran unilaterally revoked the Shatt al-'Arab agreement of 1937 (which had acknowledged Iraq's sovereignty over that waterway); in 1971, it had seized three small islands at the mouth of the Persian Gulf, threatening Iraqi oil exports; with U.S. encouragement, it had made itself the "policeman" of the Gulf; it had given direct and indirect support to the Iraqi Kurds in their struggle against Baghdad; and, worst of all, the regime of Khomeini threatened to export its Islamic revolution. In Iraq's perceptions, all these steps menaced Iraq with the danger of partition or of a stifling encirclement. More than that, they stood in the way of Iraq's own plans to build up its strength and assume regional hegemony. Whereas the earlier propaganda attacks aimed at delegitimatizing Iran and its regimes, wartime propaganda aimed at its demonization.

One way to throw doubt on the legitimacy of Iran was to call it Persia, in disregard of the fact that the country had called itself Iran at least since the sixteenth century.[44] In times of tension—and of course during the war—Iran was habitually referred to as Persia by Baghdad; however, when Iraq sought to improve relations, it used the name Iran (for instance during the October 1973 war against Israel or on the eve of the Gulf War).[45] At the peak of the war against Iran, the internal party newspaper addressed the point directly: "What is called the contemporary state of Iran is an artificial state established by force, oppression, and national bondage. The name Iran has replaced expressions like *bilad Fars* [the country of Fars; Fars is a province of Iran] or Khorasan [the name for northeastern Iran in classical Arabic historiography] or the Safavid dynasty [which ruled from 1501 to 1722]. The name of Iran "has been chosen to give the [various] peoples of Iran common racial roots as members of the Aryan race."[46] (During the period of the last two shahs, Iran had claimed to be the country from which all Aryans originated.) The almost exclusive use of "Persia" in clearly derogatory contexts began six months before the outbreak of the war and may be seen as a verbal preparation to arouse public support for the war.[47]

By preferring "Persia" over "Iran," the Ba'th wanted to point up the "racial" character of Iran and stress its expansionist nature; such usage was to convey that the region of Fars had subjected neighboring peoples by force and had occupied their territories. To conceal what it had done, Persia had called the larger area Iran, as if it was a country in its own right. But Tehran had no right to represent the non-Farsi minorities, the Kurds, the Azeris, the Baluchis, and the Arabs in the southwest who had come under Iranian rule. Such Ba'th assertions conveyed a barely disguised appeal to the minorities to rebel. Furthermore, they evoked historical memories of the seventh-century Muslim-Arab victory over the Sassanians, the last pre-Islamic dynasty of Persia. The emphasis on linguistic and racial differences and the evocation of ancient history were meant to give the Iraqi-Iranian struggle a dimension of historical depth in terms of a longstanding, almost perpetual, national conflict between Arabs and Persians rather than a mere Iraqi-Iranian dispute. It was tailored to arouse emotions of hostility to "Persians" among Sunni and Shi'i Arabs in Iraq.

Another "war of names" was conducted over the Persian Gulf. Here it was Iran that wanted to perpetuate the use of the word "Persian," while Iraq used Khalij Basra or al-Khalij al-'Arabi (the Gulf of Basra or the Arab Gulf).[48] Again and again, Ba'th spokespeople declared the Gulf "an Arab lake." Tehran's use of "Persian," they asserted, attested to its old dreams of hegemony and empire, with the Gulf at its center. They stressed Iraq's commitment to protect the Gulf against such aspirations and to keep it Arab. Iranian policy with regard to the Gulf, they claimed, was one of *tafris* (Persianization) and could lead to the establishment of "a second Palestine." In 1977, as if to underline its commitment, the Iraqi Revolutionary Command Council set up an Arab Gulf Office, headed by Saddam Husayn himself (who was then still deputy chairman of the council)."[49] Another aspect of *tafris*, according to the Ba'th, was the change of a number of geographical names in Iran, removing names with Arabic roots and replacing them with others of Persian linguistic origin. Most salient in this context were the changes of the name of the southwestern region until then commonly known as Arabistan to Khuzistan and of the town names Muhammara and ʿAyn Dimashq to Khorramshahr and Andimeshq.[50]

The Shatt al-ʿArab (the stretch of river between the junction of the Euphrates and the Tigris and down to the Gulf) also became the subject of a semantic dispute. The precise border along its course depended on agreements between Iran and Iraq that had been contested for generations. Iraq demanded that the frontier ran along the eastern bank; Iran insisted that it ran along the deepest line in the river, the so-called Thalweg. The Iraqis clung to the name Shatt al-ʿArab (literally, the coast of the Arabs) but sometimes used Shatt al-ʿIraq as well; the Iranians renamed it Arvand Rud (the beautiful river). In 1969, when the shah unilaterally revoked the 1937 agreement on the Shatt, *al-Thawra* wrote that the very existence of the name Shatt al-ʿArab was "decisive proof" that it belonged to the Arabs. The "evil" Persians had hoped that the spring floods would carry away "the mother and her child [i.e., the Baʿth and its revolution] and wash their bodies onto the shores of the Shatt al-ʿArab or the Shatt al-ʿIraq."[51]

At the beginning of the war against Iran, the issue was judged important enough to be the subject of a special booklet for children. It was written to make the children feel that Iran had been out to steal the river. It asked, "Have you ever heard of a thief trying to steal a whole river?" The "aggressive Persians" were trying to do just that by claiming that the "Arab Iraqi" river was theirs.[52] In fact, however, Iraq was the first to consider diverting the Shatt into Iraqi territory. According to an Iraqi government publication, Sabbagh had investigated the possibility of changing the course of the river because he had understood "the gravity of the danger menacing Iraq from the east" and sought to "set Iraq free from Iranian pressures." The idea was then revived during the war with Iran. The river itself was not diverted, but a huge drainage canal, 565 kilometers long, was dug in 1992 from Baghdad to the Gulf and was called "the third river" or "Saddam River."[53]

The central motive in the Baʿth discourse about Iran was thus meant to make Iraqis sense the everlasting hatred and hostility of Iran toward all Arabs and toward Iraq in particular. This was true of almost the entire period of Baʿth rule, with only short interruptions during which it was thought politic to halt propaganda against Iran. At all other times, various names were used to describe Iran's attitude: "the strategic hatred," "the black hatred," or "the hatred stretching over generations." *Al-Jumhuriyya* wrote that it had existed for 2,500 years, from Cyrus the Achaemenid to the Ayatollah Khomeini. ("Achaemenid" and "Khomeini" are more similar in Arabic than is apparent from the English spelling.) The attack on Iraq by Cyrus was later made a festival in the Jewish calendar. (Needless to say, the actual story of the Purim festival alluded to by the newspaper is quite different.) From the Achaemenids to Khomeini, the paper went on, the Persians had plunged a knife "into the back of the Arabs whenever their guard was down." Instead of being good neighbors, Persia had been aggressive and had "stolen from the Arabs whenever there was an opportunity." It had fought the Ottomans to conquer Arab lands, had befriended the British in order to weaken the Arabs from the rear, and had later collaborated with the Americans "to stab the Arabs in the back."[54]

Iran's perpetual hostility toward Iraq was "documented" in a book published shortly before the outbreak of the war against Iran. It was entitled *Ta'rikh al-hiqd al-Farsi 'ala al-'Arab* (The history of Persian hatred of the Arabs). The same topic was serialized at the end of the war in *al-Qadisiyya* under the heading "Judhur al-'ada' al-Farsi li-l-umma al-'Arabiyya" (The roots of Persian hostility toward the Arab nation). The series had been prepared by the army's Directory of Research and of Psychological Services. It found environmental, geographical, and geopolitical reasons for this hatred but kept stressing the "Persian destructive mentality [*'aqliyya takhribiyya*]."[55] Iranians were also described as the standard-bearers of *shu'ubiyya*. Whenever the "waves of *shu'ubiyya* struck the Muslims so as to harm Islam, the Persians formed the vanguard."[56]

Given the hatred of the Persians, the next step was to convey a sense of danger and menace to the public. The principal means to do so was the use of the phrase "yellow storm" (*'asifa safra'*), or alternatively "yellow wind" or "yellow wave." These expressions were coined by Husayn in a speech in 1982 following the withdrawal of the Iraqi forces from Iranian territory and to warn of Iran's aggressive aims. It had been incumbent, he said, on "the Iraqi people, the guardians of the eastern gateway of the Arab world, to stand up to this yellow wind, just as our forefathers had stood up to the incursions of the Persians and the Tatars for hundreds of years." Khomeini, he went on, had kindled the yellow wind in Tehran at the instance of imperialism and Zionism; if Iraq had not stopped it, "the Khomeinist and Zionist wind would have swept away and destroyed all the states of the east."[57]

On another occasion, Husayn called on all Iraqis to trust their heroic compatriots, "who, with their solid bodies, defend modern Iraq against the new Hulagu."[58] By referring to Hulagu, the grandson of Chingiz Khan, Husayn had intended to evoke the most traumatic event in Arab history: the Mongol conquest of Baghdad in 1258, the collapse of the Abbasid caliphate, and the destruction of thirteenth-century Iraq—events so devastating that it took Iraq until the twentieth century to overcome their aftereffects. The adjective "yellow" was used to characterize the Mongols (as in the phrase "the yellow peril," once current in the West), to conjure up images of evil, cruelty, and destruction, and to depict today's Iranians as the descendants of the Mongols. In time, other adversaries of the Ba'th were also called "yellow-faced." Mu'ammar Qadhdhafi's "Green Book," for instance, setting forth the main tenets of his ideology, was called "the yellow doctrine"; Syrian president Asad was referred to as "the yellow serpent"; and Khomeini's seizure of power became known as "the yellow revolution."[59]

The equation of the Iranian threat with the Mongol invasion remained a prime motif for the mobilization of mass public opinion during and after the war. In 1982, *al-Jumhuriyya* gave one of its articles the headline, "Above All: To Stop the Yellow Wind." Similarly, Talfah spoke of the "merciless" yellow wind.[60] A poem by Rashid Majid, entitled "The Mongols," read in part:

> Each period has its own Mongols;
> They come, laden with hatred
> Wearing different masks
> and behind every mask
> is the face of the new Hulagu
> and other Mongol faces . . .
> The yellow pest coming
> from the east
> has passed but [its disappearance]
> has not brought peace.[61]

After the war, references to the "yellow wind" served the purpose of retroactively extolling the magnitude of Iraq's success in the field. As Husayn put it soon after the end of the war: "The merit of our achievements is all the more salient if we contrast them with what was bound to happen unless we had defeated the villainous yellow wave so thoroughly." He reverted to the theme after the Gulf War, saying that the Iranian danger had been a "miserable yellow dust storm" and the war of the United States and its allies "a dark gale."[62]

At times, the description of the Iranians as Mongols, Tatars, or barbarians was spelled out in greater detail. The "Persian character" was described as aggressive, domineering, prone to war, and bloodthirsty. Persians, and in particular their rulers, were fanatics and likely to engage in the "collective killing" of thousands of people. Husayn said that Iraq must at all times keep one eye open to the east, "where the treacherous, the heretical, and the bloodthirsty are found." The Iranians would "cut off the breasts of Iraqi women unless their sons fought" to protect them.[63] Their cruelty was expressed in a well-known adage repeated over and over again: *Ma hann a'jami 'ala 'Arabi* (A Persian will not have mercy on an Arab).[64] True, the sense of *a'jami* gradually broadened and the word eventually came to mean "stranger" in general, but its original connotation was "Persian." (Persia was often called *bilad al-'ajam* [land of *'ajam*].) *A'jami* not only was used to stir fear but also contained an element of scorn: one of its meanings is a person who does not speak Arabic, or speaks it poorly or with a bad accent, or even a dumb person.[65]

The creation of Iran's fearful image was completed by the personal demonization of Khomeini.[66] He was compared with Hitler, called bloodthirsty, insane, ignorant, deceitful, a dwarf, and a sorcerer. The worst accusations, however, were reserved for his self-ascribed Islamic mission. Khomeini's doctrine of exporting the Islamic revolution and the anxiety of the Ba'th that he might succeed in doing so in Iraq caused the regime to make the most strenuous efforts to depreciate his image as a pious believer. Ba'th spokespeople and media therefore declared Khomeini unfit to represent or preach Islam because he himself was a *majusi*—that is, one of the fire worshipers of ancient Persia. As such, he was an infidel (*kafir*) and a blasphemer who claimed divinity for himself.

Another name by which the Ba'th called Khomeini was *hubal*, after the name of one of the idols that stood inside the Ka'ba in pre-Islamic times. He was also called Abu Lahab after the uncle of the prophet who had rejected Islam and had become an enemy of Muhammad. The sura *al-Masad* speaks of Abu Lahab as condemned to hell: "He shall roast at a flaming fire and his wife, the carrier of the firewood, upon her neck a rope of palm-fiber." *Al-Qadisiyya* published a long poem that took its inspiration from the sura beginning with the words: "Perish the hands of Abu Lahab, and perish he." The war Khomeini had started was now burning his hands, thus making the prophecy come true.[67] The most offensive name of all was *taghut*, a qur'anic expression for heretic, idol, or the devil.[68] Khomeini's religion was a faith of hatred toward the Arabs who were the true messengers of Islam, and his hatred of them marked him with the stamp of *shu'ubiyya*.

If Khomeini himself was not a good Muslim, neither were the Iranians as a body: they were all *majusis*. In Iran, the Ba'th media stated, Islam was not a faith but a means to an end. Its instruments might change shape occasionally, but the aim remained to gain imperialist advantages at the expense of the Arabs.[69] *Al-Thawra* wrote: "The Persians . . . do not fight except to occupy Arab soil, to injure Arab honor and diminish Arab pride. . . . This was true of Khusraw [the great Sassanian king] who made war in the name of fire; of Pahlavi the greater [Riza Shah] in the name of the English; and of Pahlavi the lesser [Muhammad Riza Shah] in the name of the United States and of the Zionists; but Khomeini [pretends to do so] in the name of Islam."[70]

Khomeini could not possibly export Islam to the Arabs, for Arabism and Islam were coterminous concepts. Saddam Husayn himself, as well as the Iraqi media, repeated again and again that Allah had chosen the Arabs and none other to be his messengers and that the duty to spread the faith was theirs and theirs alone. The Qur'an had come down to them in Arabic, and one of its verses said so explicitly: "We have sent it down as an Arabic Qur'an."[71] Only the Arabs were genuine and authentic Muslims, and only they fully understood the Qur'an and knew how to live up to its precepts. Khomeini was not fully conversant with Arabic and could thus not be a good Muslim. Nor was his revolution truly Islamic, for it was built on hostility toward the Arabs. An enemy of the Arabs could not call himself a true Muslim, let alone aspire to export his brand of revolution. In Husayn's words: "A Muslim who hates the Arabs cannot be a Muslim, because the Arabs are the leading force of Islam as they are of all heavenly religions."[72]

Faced with these three pernicious dangers, how was Iraq to deal with them? Against whom should it turn first? As far as we can tell, the decision to turn first against Iran was made in April 1980. At that time, Talfah wrote: "Many people say that Palestine must be dealt with first. That is true—and yet I say: Iran is a dagger in the heart of the Arabs, therefore it must be removed so that the Arabs can regain their health and recover their strength, and only then can they face up to foreign enemies. As the old proverb has it: 'He who lives with us is the worst thief'."[73] But even after the decision had been made, the regime still needed to conduct a lengthy information campaign, explaining why fighting Iran was more urgent than liberating Palestine. The case was most fully argued by the foreign minister, the Shiʿi Saʿdun Hammadi, sometime after the outbreak of the war. He asserted that if Iraq had not made war, Iran would have invaded it; as a matter of fact, since Iran thought of the Gulf as its own particular *lebensraum*, it was planning war against all the Gulf littorals. In defending its own soil against Iran, Iraq was also defending all other Arab, and indeed all other Muslim, countries. Khomeini, "greedy for power and influence," had interfered in those countries' domestic affairs. In conclusion, he quoted the Imam ʿAli as saying, "The wise man is not he who can tell good from bad but the one who can discern the lesser evil."[74]

Referring to Palestine, Hammadi said that it was indeed a major Arab issue, but that could not be taken to mean that other problems need not be dealt with as they arose. The "stolen land" in Palestine was not any more sacred than the land stolen along the Shatt al-ʿArab, Iraq's exit to the sea, vital to its existence. Iraq could not possibly go to war in Palestine before its eastern border was quiet. The numerical and qualitative improvement of the Iraqi army realized for the war against Iran would eventually benefit the struggle over Palestine. Finally, the Palestine issue was a matter of the long haul and required lengthy preparations.[75] The same point was made in a more simplified form in a children's book entitled *Katibat dabbabat raʾiʿa* (A glorious tank regiment). It includes a story of a pupil telling the class that his father had brought down an Iranian fighter plane. The teacher comments on the story by saying that just as the father downed the Iranian plane, so "tomorrow, when you grow up, you will bring down a war plane as you go out to liberate our Arab soil in Palestine."[76]

In the Iraqi view, the nightmare of the three circles of hostility closing around Iraq came true during the Gulf War. Husayn described the frightening vision when he said, "They lay in ambush for us in three positions." But after Iraq's victory over Iran, Zionism, imperialism, and Tehran built a single, common trench "combining in it all the forces of evil, unbelief, and cruelty. . . . They all shot their treacherous arrows at us, whether collaborating with each other or acting directly."[77]

11

The Ethos of Force

A Vision of Strength and Greatness

Focusing on dangers and threats went hand in hand with a stress on force, a vision of greatness, and the fostering of a military ethos of honor and self-sacrifice. Together, they came to form a self-fulfilling prophecy that was acted out three times: in the Iraqi-Iranian war, in the invasion of Kuwait, and in the Gulf War. While speaking of the Khomeinist danger to Iraq, Saddam Husayn also delineated his vision of Iraq: in our vision, he said, "we draw a large picture of Iraq. We want Iraq to possess a weight like that of China, a weight like the Soviet Union, a weight like the United States, and that is indeed the factual basis of our actions."[1] Though he went a great deal further along such lines than any of his predecessors, Husayn was not the first to dream of a mighty Iraq. We find him influenced by the thinking of Sami Shawkat, the noted educator of 1930s (see Chapter 1). Shawkat was in turn influenced by European fascist doctrines and gave them expression in his book *Hadhihi ahdafuna*. There are frequent echoes of his language in the Ba'th idiom, yet the party never acknowledged its debt to him and never held him up as a thinker of the first rank, possibly because of the striking fascist provenance of his ideas, possibly because he "deserted" from the nationalist camp at the time of al-Kaylani's coup in 1941.[2]

We can discern some specific points in Shawkat's teachings that influenced the Ba'th in general and Husayn in particular. One is the way he draws inspiration from the periods of Arab and Muslim glory, especially from the time of Muhammad and the first four caliphs, and from Harun al-Rashid.[3] Another point is his emphasis on military strength: Iraq, he argued, must have an army of 500,000 men and hundreds of warplanes (as indeed it did under Husayn) and should place itself at the head of a vast Arab state. Both led him to the glorification of force as the most important element in the history of nations. Force was tantamount to justice, he held, and young people must be educated from an early age to apply force and to turn themselves into disciplined soldiers. To gain strength was such a supreme aim that one should "excel in the art of death" for its sake. Iraq must always prepare for war, he concluded. Even Husayn's personal style carries echoes of Shawkat's; when he said, "He who does not fight heroically in the defense of his people, the hooves and the boots of the foreign army will trample on him," he was paraphrasing a similar sentence by Shawkat. He did the same in asserting that "justice without force is merely a vain vision." In an apparent imitation of Shawkat's phrase *sina'at al-mawt*, Husayn speaks of *sina'at al-shabab*. Both are strange combinations of words and may, with difficulty, be rendered as "the art of death" or "creating death" and "creating youth."[4]

Another source of inspiration was Salah al-din al-Sabbagh (see Chapter 10). Unlike in the case of Shawkat, Ba'thi sources often referred to al-Sabbagh as an authority, quoted from his writings, and held him up as a role model. This no doubt had to do with the fact that al-Sabbagh devoted his major book to the Kaylani uprising; his coup had long been a highlight of Iraqi history as seen by the Ba'th and had served as a paradigm of resistance to a foreign power. Al-Sabbagh, too, had extolled power and had found authority for doing so in a verse from the Qur'an that was taken up by the Ba'th as a sort of motto: "Make ready for them whatever force and strings of horses you can, to terrify thereby the enemy of God and your enemy."[5] To gain strength and apply force, al-Sabbagh argued, mobilization must be both material and spiritual and must encompass the fields of science and technology. Iraq must develop industries and set up institutes where scientists and inventors could "devote their lives to research and try to reach the moon."[6]

The concept of force was thus established firmly at the core of Ba'thi discourse. To illustrate, a proclamation of 1973, issued by the Revolutionary Command Council, said that bitter and prolonged experience "has taught us that the only language capable of safeguarding our rights, our honor, our welfare, and our interests . . . is the language of force and of struggle, based on scientific revolutionary planning." Husayn took up the same theme when he said that no state had ever reached peace without moving along "the road of force."[7] Even before he reached the presidency, he said reassuringly that the Arab "sister countries" need not worry about the growth of the Iraqi army; a day would come when Iraq would properly be entitled to boast of its strength, but it would then use it "only for war against the enemy," never against an Arab country. In the light of later events in Kuwait, we can recognize Husayn's method of using threats and reassurances in the same breath, hinting at future action while camouflaging it in contradictory phrases.[8]

Iraq's military buildup went on throughout the Ba'th years, and its representatives eventually spoke of Iraq as a great power. *Al-Jumhuriyya* called the country a "growing power [*quwwa muta'azima*] in every field and on every plane." *Al-Thawra* described it as "a genuine and active great power taking its stand against domination and aggression."[9] One of Husayn's writers spelled out Husayn's share in building a strong Iraq; Husayn, he said, had understood that unless the Arabs were victorious in the field, unless they hoisted their flag in the east and in the west, and unless they were militarily strong, they would not gain in status and not be honored among the nations. Therefore, "with perseverance and resolve," he had built "a strong Iraq, [proving] that only the strong and the victorious will be listened to and respected by the world."[10] Not surprisingly, one of Husayn's biographers tells us that Husayn had gone about with a gun strapped to his belt since the age of ten.[11] This gesture is a kind of modern imitation of the caliph's habit of appearing in public leaning on a sword.

A Military Society

With the constant glorification of force and the use of force, Iraq turned into a military society in which martial virtues took pride of place. Ba'thi language attests to the penetration into ordinary speech of expressions and phrases taken from the military way of life. This process was described as *'askarat al-tarbiya* (the militarization of education), *'askarat al-sha'b* (the militarization of the people), *taslih al-sha'b* (arming the people), and creating *al-sha'b al-musallah* (the armed people). Iraq, Husayn said, was "all one army, from one end to the other."[12] The armed forces were *taj al-sha'b* (the crown of the people) or *masna' al-abtal* (the factory of heroes). In addition to being taught in the army, "military thinking and culture" was (according to a decree issued by Husayn) to be taught to all civilian Ba'th party members and to all government officials. The report of the 1982 party congress noted the extent to which military terms had entered people's everyday language. This had given rise to the spread of the "love of militarism," given the inhabitants greater pride, and made young people in uniform more highly regarded. However, the report went on, that did not mean that "the new Iraqi society" had developed "aggressive inclinations"; the contrary was true.[13]

The nurturing of the military spirit was done by various means: an army theater (*masrah 'askari*) was set up even before the war against Iran; an Iraqi composer wrote an "army symphony"; an encyclopedia on the Iraqi army since its inception in 1921 was commissioned in 1977 and filled thirty-nine volumes.[14] When, in the course of the rocket exchanges in 1987, an Iranian rocket hit a school in Baghdad, Husayn decided to award the title of *jaysh balat al-shuhada'* (the courtyard's army of the martyrs) to every child born after the event. With this in mind, *al-Jumhuriyya* wrote that Iraqi women were different from the women of other countries: they had "started to give birth to an army, to victory and heroism." An Iraqi mother taught her baby to shoot, fight, and take revenge while still carrying it; by the time it was born, "it bears arms which will not be laid aside without being used, and has the decorations of exalted heroism on its chest."[15]

For all we know, a higher percentage of the population was mobilized and put into uniform in Iraq than in any other Arab country. There were three types of military or paramilitary frameworks: the armed forces, the so-called popular army (originally a kind of party militia set up for internal security duties but later used in the field against Iran, and a paramilitary youth organization. Already in 1977, the army started accepting volunteers between the ages of fourteen and twenty-five (apart from those conscripted by law at the age of eighteen).[16] The mobilization of volunteers was stepped up during the war. By the end of the war, the army numbered 1 million men, four times as many as it had when the war began.[17] The Ba'th stressed over and over again that the army was not a professional body but an "ideological army" (*jaysh 'aqa'idi*); it was made up of "fighters who, besides their weapons, were armed with a solid ideology." "Ideological" of course meant Ba'thi, and a series of measures were taken to "strengthen the control of the party and of the revolution over the army."[18] One of these was the setting up in 1973 of the Directorate of Political Guidance (*Mudiriyyat al-tawjih al-siyasi*) for the army. It replaced a pre-Ba'th body (in existence since 1964) that had had the more restricted role of building up army morale.

The objectives of the armed forces were redefined in the light of the principles of Ba'th rule. Initially, under King Faysal I, the army's task had been defined solely as the maintenance of internal security. (External security was still a matter for the British.)[19] Under Husayn, the Ba'th laid down the following objectives for it: the defense of the regime; the defense of the Iraqi borders; and the defense of the Arab nation as a whole. Addressing the first battalion of the Republican Guard a few days after assuming the presidency, Husayn put it this way: "We do not want the Iraqi army to defend Iraq's borders alone; rather, we want it to be the armor of the Arab nation and its sword, drawn against the enemies."[20] Militant statements of this kind grew in stridency until they shaded over into the wartime usage of the Iraqi-Iranian armed conflict.

In another address to military men, given a few months before the launching of the war, Husayn likened the Iraqi soldiers to "knights" (*fursan*), thus evoking the title of Sabbagh's book. Each soldier, he went on, was ready to die for the sake of "the honor of his sword, the honor of his spear." He said he wanted the 13.5 million Iraqis to assume the same weight as a nation of 40 million (then the population of Iran) and added:

"I believe unquestionably that our weight will bring down the scales in our favor—whether in war or in construction." A month or so later, he asserted that Iraq did not want war with Iran but again stressed that the Iraqi armed forces were capable of measuring up to every foreign force: American, Soviet, French, Turkish, or Iranian. The following day, he was even more specific: "We are ready to face the biggest army in the world and fight it on Iraq's soil."[21] All the while, the Iraqi army had been made stronger than it had ever been and stronger than any other Arab army. Husayn revealed that during the first year of the war, Iraq had spent billions of dollars on arms and had found "new avenues" of supply everywhere, including "the black market." The sole exception had been the "Zionist entity."[22] Rearmament fed the dynamics of war just as much as rhetoric did. When it eventually came, the war in turn vastly reinforced the ongoing militarization of Iraqi society.

The slogan *'askarat al-sha'b* did not remain idle talk. Soon after taking power, in February 1970 the Ba'th tried to put it into practice by setting up a party militia, the "popular army" (*al-jaysh al-sha'bi*, or PA). The cue seems to have been given by Michel 'Aflaq, who had said a year earlier that carrying arms must no longer be confined to an organized body (i.e., the army). The magnitude of the dangers threatening Iraq was such that "the entire Arab people must be called up."[23] The new PA was the direct successor of *al-haras al-qawmi* (the national guard) set up during the first, short-lived Ba'th regime. But the new name attested to a new conception: the present body, though still primarily an instrument of the party, was to be a veritable army operating alongside the regular armed forces.

During the very first days of the second period of Ba'th rule, the party started training "groups from among the people" in the use of arms. A commission was formed to lay down the objectives of the new force. Husayn (then still a comparatively unknown figure) was appointed chairman. Its recommendations led, in 1970, to the establishment of a general headquarters for the PA, with Taha Yasin Ramadan (al-Jazrawi) as its commanding officer.[24] Ramadan indicated the broad ambitions he had for the PA by saying that "the revolution will arm *all* [emphasis added] citizens and train them to defend [the revolution]." The party stated the rationale of setting up the PA by asserting that in an emergency, this would "enable the masses to defend the revolution and its achievements, as well as the homeland." Ramadan gave another explanation, saying that Iraq's sparse population (compared to Iran or Turkey) required a PA to complement the regular armed forces.[25]

Al-Thawra al-'Arabiyya listed the characteristics that marked off the PA from ordinary militias elsewhere: (1) the PA, being trained for internal and external defense, had become a "firm pillar" of the regular armed forces; (2) its ranks were drawn from all walks of life: students, farmers, and—an important innovation—women;[26] all members were trained in the use of many types of weapons, including tanks and antiaircraft artillery; (3) "the training the revolution gave the masses" enabled PA members to keep their weapons at home and to use them promptly, in case of need, according to orders from their superiors; (4) until 1977, only party members were admitted into the PA; from then on its ranks were thrown open to others from among many various sectors of the population.[27]

The new, broader recruiting policy was part of the process of the overall militarization of Iraqi society, noticeably stepped up in 1977. In the decade beginning that year, membership in the PA grew from some 75,000 to 1 million.[28] During the war against Iran, people over sixty-five years old were called upon to join it, and special commando and *fida'iyyun* units were formed from its ranks. When asked about the task of the latter, Ramadan replied: "We don't need these fighters [for combat duty], but we want to know who is unreservedly ready to fight. This is . . . a sort of plebiscite to disprove claims that the Iraqi people are tired of the war."[29] The information minister, Latif Nusayyif al-Jasim, claimed that by 1982, 2 million people had enrolled as *fida'iyyun*.[30] Though the figure was certainly vastly exaggerated, it still attests to the regime's objectives and is therefore evidence that should not be dismissed.

Originally a voluntary body, the PA increasingly turned into a second conscript army during the war, operating alongside the regular units. Service was by rotation for three months at a time. At times, PA units were sent on combat missions at the front instead of performing their usual internal-security duties. Not only party members but also many other popular sectors, notably students, were conscripted. The latter were clearly unenthusiastic. Husayn censured them for this, reminding them that service in the PA was a "national duty"; anyone failing to fulfill it would be dragged from his home and told to "do his duty." Others, too, resented having to serve in it, and in some sectors of the population, it came to be referred to as *al-jaysh al-la-sha'bi* (the unpopular army).[31]

The ambition to turn the Iraqis into an "armed, fighting people" (as Ramadan put it) turned out to be a two-edged sword.[32] At the Iranian front, the PA failed to do any serious fighting alongside the regular army; a great deal worse than that, many of its members deserted to the enemy. Worse still, during the Kurdish and Shi'i uprisings of 1991, many members seem to have used the government arms they had been allowed to keep at home to fight in the ranks of the rebels. The party promptly disbanded the PA, but the fighting spirit it had taken such care to impart was probably still there, at the service of the regime's opponents.

Apart from setting up the PA, the regime set up a youth organization under the name of *futuwwa*, also called "the homeland's reserve army."[33] It was officially set up in 1978 but had been active unofficially since approximately 1973.[34] Its members were between the age of twelve and fifteen. Its main expansion occurred during the war years: in 1982 it had some 127,000 members; three years later, it numbered 1,120,000.[35] Between 1974 and 1980, the budget allocation for youth organizations grew by a factor of 120. *Al-futuwwa* was primarily a body for the ideological training of youth according to the party's doctrine. Children and youth,

Husayn declared, had no natural class identification or political orientation; therefore the party had to become their "mother and father." But alongside the ideological schooling, there was military training, including camp life away from the family; arms training for individuals and units; development of the fighting spirit (*jundiyya*) and of manliness; and "implanting the spirit of sacrifice for the sake of the homeland."[36]

Beyond all this, a deeper motive seems to have been at work: to revive historical reminiscences and to educate young people as well as Iraqis of all ages to adopt values derived from the (distant or recent) past. The name *futuwwa* recalled two distinct periods in Iraqi history: the late Abbasid period and the 1930s. The word comes from *fata* (boy, youth). In its broad sense, *futuwwa* connotes the entirety of good qualities found in a youth, just as *muruwwa* does for a grown man. Muslims think of 'Ali as the ideal youth, as expressed in the adage *La fata illa 'Ali* (There is no youth except 'Ali). In a narrower, more specific sense, the word connotes members of the *futuwwa* movements that existed at various times in various Islamic countries. Regarding Abbasid times, the word *futuwwa* is linked with the caliph al-Nasir li-Din Allah (1181–1223) who tried to bring together and formalize various groupings of that name and make men of religion, military men, and administrative officials join the unified body. The *futuwwa* was to educate its members and provide a religious and social frame of reference for them. Members had first to serve as candidates or novices. They were then promoted into the ranks of the organization by means of a special initiation ceremony that included drinking a glass of salt water. A full member was called *rafiq*, wore distinctive clothing, and carried a sword.[37]

The modern organization so called was officially inaugurated in 1936 and combined medieval Islamic inspiration with an imitation of the Nazi youth organization in Germany. Similar bodies were formed in other Arab countries at about the same time with the same mixed antecedents. The Iraqi *futuwwa* demanded that all high-school students wear uniforms and receive military training. Army officers taught military subjects at high schools. Students who did not qualify in these subjects were not admitted to colleges or other institutions of higher education. Salah al-Din al-Sabbagh was in charge of physical education in the *futuwwa*.[38]

The Ba'th not only took over the name *futuwwa* but also set its media to work to remind the public of its historic precedents. Newspapers published stories about the activities of the *futuwwa* in the 1930s and enlarged upon its contribution to the struggle against the British and to al-Kaylani's coup. Nor was the medieval *futuwwa* neglected. *Al-Qadisiyya*, for instance, published the text of caliph Nasir's decree establishing it, including the caliph's reference to 'Ali as "the source of *futuwwa*."[39] The press also extolled the part young people played in the wars in ancient Arab society. Boys (*fityan*) used to volunteer for the hardest combat duties, willing to die at the head of their units. An article quoted the caliph Abu

Bakr as writing to the *"fata"* Khalid bin al-Walid that Allah was watching over him, hence "when you confront the enemy be bent on death."[40]

Glory, Honor, and Death

The systematic promotion of perceptions of hostility threatening from all sides combined with the vast military buildup made war likely, if not inevitable. When it came, a huge propaganda apparatus was created to glorify war as such, to justify the inordinate duration of the fighting against Iran and the heavy casualties, and to foster the ideals of glory, honor, and self-sacrifice. The glorification of war found its echo in the wartime idiom. Alongside the common word for war (*harb*), other supposedly rousing terms were used, such as *malhama* (epic of war);[41] Husayn himself preferred the word *munazala* (wrestling bout, joust), particularly when speaking of the Gulf War. The name given the Gulf War to make it appear superlative, *umm al-ma'arik* (mother of battles), had its precedent during the war against Iran. Right at its start, the poet Radi Mahdi Sa'id published a poem in which he called the war *umm al-suyuf* (mother of swords) and *umm al-butulat* (mother of heroism); he also called Husayn *Abu al-'azamat* (father of great decisions).[42] Similar expressions were added later: *umm al-malahim, umm al-amjad,* and *umm al-intisarat* (the mother of epics, of glories, of victories). After Iraq's defeat in the Gulf War, cynically minded Iraqis added *umm al-mahalik* (mother of defeats) to the list.

Hand in hand with the glorification of war went the denigration of the enemy. Verbal violence became part and parcel of the wartime language. A few examples from an abundance of instances may suffice. During the war with Iran, the commander of the third army sent a message to Saddam Husayn, saying: "Great sire, we gladly inform you of the annihilation of thousands of harmful magi [*majusi*] insects that carried out an abortive offensive late last night. These [Iraqi] forces turned the magi into black masses piled up on our pure land. . . . We will turn what is left of these harmful insects into food for the birds of the wilderness and the fish of the marshes."[43] When later asked about the use of chemical weapons, the same commander replied: "If you give me a pesticide to use against those swarms of insects . . . I shall use it."[44]

The language used here by a field commander addressing his commander-in-chief was given nationwide currency when the message was read out over radio and television. The press, too, took up the fashion. *Al-Jumhuriyya* wrote of Iranian bodies being "rubbed" into the earth of Basra: "We shall tear them to pieces and chop them up and cut off their feet so that they will not defile the pure earth of Basra and we shall shout at the top of our voices: Remain standing, noble Basra . . . despite the yellow storms."[45] For hours, television broadcasts showed Iranian bodies, or parts of them.

Motifs of violence appeared frequently in cartoons, particularly in *al-Thawra* and *al-Jumhuriyya*. Their captions were often in the Iraqi colloquial, thus driving the message home even more starkly. Usually devoid of humor and sophistication, such cartoons were meant to instill fear, depict cruelty, and appeal to a sense of honor. In most of them, the figure of Khomeini was used to personify Iran. One drawing showed an Iraqi hand holding a sword and cutting into Khomeini's body; another pictured Iraqi soldiers from various corps at play, with Khomeini's body as their football; a third showed smiling Iraqi rockets on their way to split (*falasha*) Khomeini's skull. Yet another showed an Iraqi flag with a portrait of Husayn hitting the scorpion Khomeini over the head while Iraqi children watched, jumping with joy. Some cartoons showed Khomeini roasting Iranian soldiers over a fire or crouching on all fours before a giant Iraqi soldier.[46] The 1987 Iranian offensive against Basra was called "the great harvest," and a cartoon showed an Iraqi farmer "reaping" a crop of Iranian heads and arranging them in heaps, over the caption: "We have won the battle by means of the great harvest of heads of the guards of Khomeini, the hyena."[47] Even if one cannot pinpoint precisely how verbal and physical violence interconnect, some kind of interaction evidently exists.

Another aspect of the same syndrome was the endeavor to extol military virtues, particularly in terms taken from the Arab past. Many words lent themselves especially to such use: *rujula* (manliness), *furusiyya* (knighthood), *butula* (heroism), and *shaja'a* (courage, valor). Husayn himself was held up as the model embodying all these virtues. The tendency to play up such qualities found expression in the award of decorations for valor to tens of thousands of officers and other ranks. Husayn personally awarded no fewer than fifteen decorations for valor, including "the Qadisiyya sword," to the commander of the Republican Guard, after his units had recaptured the island of al-Faw in 1988. By the time of the ceasefire later the same year, he had awarded him another twenty-three medals.

Honor was another motif sounded again and again in many variations. *Sharaf* was used to indicate the honor of noble descent and social status; *karama*, the quality of generosity and goodness;[48] *'izz*, strength and greatness; *ghayra*, jealous self-respect; *shahama*, knighthood and nobility; *majd*, glory and prestige; *wajh*, power and riches;[49] *waqar*, dignity; *'ird*, family honor. The inspiration for what we might call the ideology of honor came from ancient Arab society, where honor was often more important than friendship, tribal obedience, or life itself. In old Arab poetry, the quest for honor and glory and the avoidance of shame were often the main themes.[50] The cult of honor persisted until the present century, mainly among Bedouins but also in urban society. Honor was a matter not for the individual alone but for the group; it was a lever of social predominance and was instrumental in preserving the delicate balance within the group. Honor in the collective sense meant the defense of the tribe, the group, or the society as a whole against its challengers. Lost honor must be retrieved by violence. Tribal raids both augmented the honor of those who carried them out and diminished the honor of their victims.[51] Saddam Husayn may have intuitively applied in later life a value system in which he grew up as a youth, but he was surely not blind to the manipulative advantages of the motif of honor as an instrument of mass appeal. It could serve to spark emotions, camouflage true intentions, and, if need be, cover up failures.

A few illustrations will demonstrate this. Addressing a unit of the Republican Guard, Husayn proclaimed that the honor (*sharaf*) of the Arab nation could not be secured unless "Iraq's arm reached out [beyond Iraqi territory] to every point in the Arab homeland." On another occasion, he said that the time had come to revive the glories (*amjad*) of the Arab past, so rich in heroic deeds. One of his sayings was, "Your honor is your rifle—keep it and use it to give back to [the term] honor the meaning for the sake of which your fathers fought." Honor surpassed material satisfaction: "When one defends honor (*karama*) one must keep the stomach down so it will not remain open [to demand satisfaction]." A few months before the outbreak of war against Iran, he declared that anyone not ready to act for the recovery of the glory (*majd*) of Iraq and of the Arab nation would be accounted a traitor. Present-day Iraq, he said, had all the means to achieve glory: a great party, manpower potential, the land of the two rivers, and oil.[52]

References to honor became even more frequent during the war. For Iraqis, Saddam Husayn said, as for all mature nations, honor ranked higher than bread; it was their highest value.[53] The defense of honor and the achievement of glory were the most salient arguments used to justify prolonging the war against Iran. Iraq was fighting not only for "its geography" but also for its sovereignty and its honor (*karama*). Since it could not renounce the latter, it could not stop the war. Rather, it was Iran that must end the war, since it was abusing Iraqi honor. The war had to go on so that "the Iraqis could hold their heads high with honor ['*izz*] and so that the honorable [*shurafa'*] Arabs would continue to be masters rather than slaves."[54]

The same line of appeal was employed during the Kuwait crisis and the subsequent war. Indeed, it was broadened to encompass the entire Arab world. It was even used to appeal to the United States: America would lose nothing if it stopped its aggressive moves, while the Arabs stood to lose their honor, their humanity, their present, and their future. Only the loss of honor was worse than war. "If the Arabs and the Iraqis were to be afraid of war and thereby lose these values [i.e., honor, sovereignty, and peace], . . . they will lose their very existence."[55]

Husayn's appeal to the other Arab rulers resembled the old tribal competitions in which each tribe measured its strength, heroism, and honor against those of the others and prided itself on its exalted qualities. Husayn compared his noble descent to President Husni Mubarak's humble origins; berated the rulers of Kuwait, who, he said, were greedy for money but forgetful of the honor of their women; mocked the rulers of Saudi

Arabia because they were asking to be protected by U.S. women soldiers; and in general attacked all Arabs who, by joining the U.S.-led coalition, had forsaken their manly honor. But Iraqi men and women would keep their honor intact and would not retreat before "American women."[56] In words reminiscent of al-Samaw'al's *mu'allaqa* (pre-Islamic Arabic poem) extolling the honorable few facing the despicable multitude, Husayn said that Iraqis would not yield even to "the largest states in the world," for, regardless of their small numbers, their moral standing was superior.[57] Iraq was ready to go to war and continue fighting for any length of time until the fighting came to "an honorable close" and Iraq gained honor from Allah. More and more, "honor" became a word to conjure with. Its use ranged from the honor of the uniform, the flag, and the sword to "bread with honor," "sweets accompanied by honor," and finally "death with honor."[58]

If honor fails, shame (*'ar*) takes over. Originally, shame meant a man's failure to uphold the honor of the family and protect women or to fulfill his duty as a fighter. Shaming people was used to make them obey their military draft notices. The press, for instance, printed the story of a father who killed his son with his own hands for having shirked military service in the war against Iran. Husayn awarded the father a special decoration for his "exemplary" conduct. The Iraqi national theater performed a play in which a mother burns her son alive for having deserted from the army, accompanying her action by a song entitled "Al-Nar wa-la al-'ar" (Better death by fire than shame).[59]

Closely related to the notion of death with honor was the traditional concept of death for the sake of Allah: *istishhad* or *shahada*. Since the beginning of Islam, *istishhad* (i.e., becoming a *shahid* or martyr) opened the way to paradise. This was the interpretation of sura *al-'Imran*, verse 163: "Count not those who were slain in God's way as dead, but rather living with their Lord." Explanations of the word *shahid* supported this exegesis. One of them stated that the word meant that Allah and his angels had borne witness (*shahidu*) for the departed. Another interpretation averred that a *shahid* was so called because, despite his death, he was *shahid*, meaning "present" (i.e., alive).[60] Originally, the appellation *shahid* was reserved for fighters fallen in a war against infidels. Later, it came to include people who had fallen for the sake of their people, their homeland, or their regime. During the war against Iran, the Ba'th used *istishhad* to connote a soldier's death both in fighting the Iranian "infidels" and for the homeland. One source of inspiration for these attitudes may have been Shawkat's writings about the "art of dying" as an integral part of the art of living. Hence his phrase: "There is no greater sanctity than the sanctity of the *shahid* who sheds his blood for the homeland."[61]

Saddam Husayn started speaking of *istishhad* as early as 1975. At a colloquium about historiography, he asserted that the writing of history must prompt people to excel and arouse them to self-sacrifice. A man practicing *istishhad* was giving his all to his society and his homeland and was therefore entitled "to leave a good and salient mark on his people and on history."[62] The ground was thus prepared for the massive use of the concept of *istishhad* during the war against Iran, when the coffins started coming back from the front in thousands and Iraqi families had to be persuaded to resign themselves to their fate. The salience given by the Ba'th to *istishhad* was in part a response to the centrality of that concept in Khomeini's Iran. Thus, in Iraq, too, *istishhad* became a veritable ritual, frequently with macabre overtones. As often before, it was Husayn himself who set the tone. He coined a phrase that became a wartime motto: *al-shuhada' akram minna jami'an* (the "martyrs" are the most honored of us all). The war against Iran, he said, was a holy war; those who fought in it were entitled "to great glory" if they lived and to "meeting their God" honorably if they fell. Coining a strange neologism, he called the Iraqi fighter *mashru' li-l-istishhad* (a project for *istishhad*). "Many Iraqis," he said, considered "themselves candidates for *istishhad*" and envied those who had already achieved it.[63]

The first play staged by the army theater after it was set up early in the war dealt with the theme of *istishhad*. The officer in charge explained his choice by saying that *istishhad* was the "dream" of every fighter who possessed honor. The civilian stage fell in line: a play called *Dancing on the Shoulders of Death* extolled heroic death for "the existence of an independent people." *Al-Jumhuriyya* spoke of soldiers who were "in love with death for the glory of the state."[64] The same newspaper enlisted history for the cause of the present. It printed for its readers a message from the first caliph, Abu Bakr, to his field commander Khalid bin al-Walid enjoining him not to wash the bodies of the *shuhada'*, for their blood would be "their light" on the day of the Last Judgment.[65]

Istishhad was even preached to young children. Within a month of the outbreak of the war against Iran, *al-Jumhuriyya* began publishing a special supplement for children that was to appeal to them "in the language of heroism and *istishhad* . . . without which Iraq would be headed for ruin." Many of the stories subsequently printed in the supplement indeed dealt with *istishhad*.[66] Even the draft constitution of 1990 had a clause reading, "*Istishhad* for the sake of the homeland, the nation, and the people's principles is an honor and a supreme value that society and the state seek to reinforce in its patriotic, nationalist, social, and moral meaning."[67]

An integral part of these comprehensive endeavors were the various forms of memorials and commemoration ceremonies for the fallen. After the Iraqi reconquest of al-Faw in 1988, the Ba'th ordered little glass bottles to be filled with sand from al-Faw that was mixed with the blood of the *shuhada'* and topped by an Iraqi flag. They were distributed to public figures who came to visit Faw after its reoccupation.[68] The central commemorative project was the memorial site for a *shahid* erected in Baghdad in 1983 and considered the most impressive of many of its kind.[69] At its center was a huge turquoise-blue cupola (*qubba*), forty meters high. Its middle section was open, dividing it into two parts. The designer, Isma'il Fattah al-Turk, explained that the overall design had been inspired by Abbasid architecture, but its opening was symbolic of *layla al-qadr*, the night during which the heaven opened and the Qur'an was first revealed to Muhammad. The *shahid*, al-Turk went on, was not the body that remained on earth but the soul that rose to heaven through the opening of the cupola. Among the decorative inscriptions on the wall was a verse from the Qur'an that had also been turned into a wartime motto: "Count not those who were slain in God's way as dead, but rather living with their Lord." Husayn's maxim quoted above was also inscribed there. There was a fountain playing in time to music, a device meant to convey that the death of the *shahid* was "reason for joy" stemming from the pride in *istishhad*.[70] The Ba'th thus tried to turn *istishhad* into a festive occasion. In the same spirit, a radio broadcast describing the funeral of a war victim spoke of the mother of the fallen following the coffin "as if going to his wedding."[71]

The first of December was made "*Shahid* Day" and was marked with festive ceremonies throughout Iraq. On one such occasion a poem was published under the title "The *Shahid*'s Wedding Day [*'urs*]." It called on young men throughout Iraq to dance in the streets to honor the heroes on their holiday. One verse spoke of an Iraqi mother asking for the *istishhad* of all her children in gratitude to Allah for granting them this honor and for bringing them to the gates of paradise. During one such ceremony, the wives, mothers, and sisters of the *shahid* "wore their wedding dresses a second time" to bear witness to their faithfulness to the departed who had "upheld the honor of the homeland which is their [own] honor." The press published pictures of the women in their dresses.[72]

The salience given to *istishhad* was only one means of the broad quest for roots capable of justifying the war and of giving it a religious and spiritual meaning. The return to the past carried striking Islamic symbols and an abundance of ancient motifs into Ba'thi political discourse. This process will occupy us at greater length in Part 5.

V

Epic and Apocalypse

In the name of God, the Merciful, the Compassionate
Hast thou not seen how thy Lord did with the Men of the
    Elephant?
Did he not make their guile to go astray?
And he loosed upon them birds in flight,
Hurling against them stones of baked clay
and He made them like green blades devoured.

—sura *al-Fil*

The Ba'th party differed from all its predecessors in that it came to power possessing a full-fledged doctrine it thought capable of guiding it unerringly through the maze of power. It began its rule resolved to make that doctrine into a firm guide applicable to each and every aspect of life in Iraq. Yet despite—or perhaps because of—the existence of such a set of cut-and-dried dogmas, its concepts clashed starkly with Iraqi realities. Ba'thi precepts and Ba'thi discourse were strange to large sectors of Iraqi society and alienated them. This was true in particular of the Kurds and the Shi'is. But neither did the Ba'th tenets of secularism and "leftism" elicit any real enthusiasm in the ranks of the party's natural reservoir of potential supporters. This applied even to some party members and certainly to many people whose interests prompted them to identify with the ruling elite. The Ba'th idiom was foreign to their life experience and their worldview. Speaking its language was usually no more than a ritual for them. The well-known slogans were repeated over and over again but failed to assume any personal significance.

The real test of the strength of Ba'th doctrine occurred at times of crisis and challenge, such as the Shi'i riots of 1977, the Islamic revolution in Iran in 1979, the war against Iran (1980–1988), and the formation of the international military coalition against Iraq in 1990. It was at such times that the doctrine was found wanting. Gradually, the party had to drop the political discourse with which it had come to power and replace it with, or at least range alongside it, a different kind of public language. The latter drew on themes of historical, above all Islamic, provenance. In some measure, this process was intentional and guided from above; in part it was forced on the regime by specific circumstances; and in part it sprang spontaneously from deep layers of the Iraqi collective experience.

Pivotal to this development was the "reliving" of the past: the public preoccupation with historical subjects, their relevance, and their implications. This was not a matter of theory, scholarship, or intellectual pursuit. Rather, it was a highly political and altogether deliberate discourse with a clear purpose: to implant a heightened feeling for, and an intensified consciousness of, myths from the recent as well as the more distant past. The aim was not so much to glorify the past (though this was done constantly, as a sort of by-product) but to inculcate certain attitudes with regard to the present that the Ba'th had failed to bolster with its traditional arguments.

Modern history provided the myths of "the Great Revolution of 1920" and of al-Kaylani's "Revolution of 1941." The main accent, however, was placed on myths from early Islamic and even pre-Islamic times. During the 1980s, the greatest salience was given to an event from actual history, the al-Qadisiyya battle, which gradually became embroidered with symbols of an altogether epic character (see Chapter 12). In the late 1980s and during the early 1990s, another event, partly historical, partly legendary, took up the center of the public stage: the so-called War of the Elephant (see Chapter 14). This belonged to the pre-Islamic period but had a markedly Islamic significance. Each of the two had a distinct, clearly discernible task: the first, to prepare the ground for the war against Iran and, once it had started, to keep up the momentum of popular support for it despite its duration; the second, to provide, through its eschatological aspects, a haven or safe refuge to fall back on in the face of adversities and to hold out hope for an apocalyptic cure of all earthly ills.

The advantages of a myth over a cold and cerebral ideology are obvious, most of all in times of crisis. The myth appeals to emotion and addresses itself to the deepest layers of the mind. It engenders enthusiasm and is capable of manipulating the masses. It can provide role models and serve as a source of emulation. In the words of Emmanuel Sivan, its efficiency "becomes most evident when an analogy is drawn between it and a contemporary event, because [then] it supplies explanations and interpretations for the anguish of the present, it summons men to action and to heroic deeds, it provides a vision and imparts hope for a better future. Myth is superior to intellectual explanation and does not require proof; those who use it must spread it . . . among the masses without raising questions or allowing for second thoughts." In Iraq, the media played a primary role in spreading "myths of mobilization." In doing so, they could rely on a characteristic of Arab society in general: its deep affinity with the past.[1]

Taking these processes as a whole, one may speak of the "Islamization" of political discourse. In other words, over time the regime came to use religion as an instrument of its rule, allotting it two cardinal tasks: that of a safety valve releasing pressure that otherwise might conceivably lead to a genuine religious revolution and that of providing a means of mass mobilization for clearly defined ends. True, such use of religion looks like a pragmatic and functional method, coldly applied by the regime; none-theless, it attests to the deep religious beliefs and instincts of society at large—and perhaps of the leaders as well. Ideally, the regime would like to ride the crest of the "Islamic wave" and lead it in the direction it de-sires without ever letting the forces of Islam come to dominate them. But in doing so, the regime is wielding a double-edged sword, and there is no telling which way it will cut.

12

History as a Lever of Politics

Recherche du temps perdu

"History is the most dangerous concoction the chemistry of the mind has produced. It sets peoples dreaming, intoxicates them, engenders false memories, exaggerates their reflexes, keeps their old wounds open, torments their leisure, inspires them with megalomania and persecution complexes."[1] These words by Paul Valéry might come from a textbook teaching the Ba'th how to look at history. Whether known to Ba'th ideologues or not, they tally with the party's almost obsessive preoccupation with *ta'rikh* (history), a preoccupation fully shared by Saddam Husayn personally. By his own testimony, history had penetrated his whole being and was present in all his thinking.[2]

We have already had occasion to mention, in different contexts, that he participated in—indeed, laid down the guidelines for—conferences on education. In 1973, he told a colloquium of educators that, just as past rulers had guided earlier generations of historians in their writings, so the Ba'th would lay down how today's authors should write history. Contemporary historiography, he said, must have one single aim: "To fortify the citizen's pride in the history of his people and his nation [i.e., Iraq as well as the Arabs in general] and to make it the principal source of inspiration for his actions, his creativity, and his sacrifice."[3] Two years later, during a similar meeting on the reform of school curricula, he spoke in particular about how to write history textbooks for pupils in the lower grades: history, he said, must "directly permeate" young brains in an "absolute fashion," without theoretical or philosophical explanations or analyses that might confuse them. He gave the matter even fuller treatment in 1978 when he made a speech on "rewriting history." The speech was followed by a series of public debates and commented and elaborated on by the press. Various contributions by historians, writers, and party functionaries who had participated in the debates were collected in book form and published shortly before Husayn's assumption of ultimate power in July 1979 under the title *Hawl kitabat al-ta'rikh* (On writing history). Although most contributions came from others, Husayn was named as the author. Similar events occurred in 1987, under the theme of "rewriting Arab history."[4]

Let us look at the development of the term *ta'rikh*. It means a definite time, a date, as well as history and historical science. There are various versions of its derivation. *Lisan al-'Arab* suggests that it might come from *irkh* (a newly born calf), and thus signify something newly come into the world.[5] *Kitab muhit al-muhit* avers that the letters of the radical have changed places and that the word derives from *ta'khir* (returning backward in time). The most commonly held view is that the word derives from an old Semitic root, *warakh* (moon; hence, month). The literal meaning of *ta'rikh* would then be the fixing of months and of days within the month by observation of the moon (the Arab calendar being lunar rather than solar).[6] The simultaneous connotation of "date" and "history" by a single word may have to do with the practice of Arab historians, down to the tenth century, of arranging their material in a strictly chronological fashion.[7]

Be that as it may, past and present are flexible concepts in Arab society, with one shading over into the other. In the words of Morroe Berger: "History and the present are intimately related in the Arab world." Arab historiographers, being part of the society they live in, follow the same pattern and their writings often move from the past to the present without a clear delineation.[8] Saddam Husayn exemplifies the same trend: he speaks of the "inner cohesion" (*iltiham*) of the mind with history, of contact (*tawasul*) with it, of the "revival" (*ihya'*) of history, and of the return (*istirdad, i'ada*) to its glories. In an unusual simile, which also has a somewhat apologetic ring to it, he stressed that "we do not seek to return to history but rather to move history toward us." He has also used the phrase *al-shahid al-ta'rikhi* (the historical witness or the historical figure present with us)—in other words, a character from the past now living with us, as it were, and influencing present-day people.[9]

Husayn's views found a ready echo with many party functionaries as well as with some Iraqi historians (though not, it must be said, with all). Ilyas Farah, a member of the highest party forum, spoke of a "legitimate meeting" between the past and the present and between the past and the future. The historian 'Abd al-'Aziz al-Duri wrote that certain historical events "are still alive in the thinking and in the soul of the Arabs." Another historian, 'Imad 'Abd al-Salam Ra'uf, developed a whole theory on the matter: History was not a matter of the past but was existing and at work in the present. The "revolutionary interpretation" of history was different from "objective historical research" because it signified "penetrating" (*taghalghul*; literally, "infiltration") into "the historical experience and coinciding with it—however distant that experience may be." The Arab revolutionary historian differed from his Western colleague committed to objectivity; the former's task was to "to draw close to the historical event in his intellect, his emotions, and his sensations." His aim was "uniting and fusing" with the occurrences of the past. Such fusion was necessary, for only the historian who achieved it was capable of making history a living part of the present.[10]

We must thus ask ourselves what this overly intense preoccupation with history signifies. What is it that gives rise to the blurring of the line dividing the past from the present, and what needs does it cater to? One partial answer, somewhat theoretical in nature, may have to do with the very name of the Ba'th party, which means "renaissance" and implies bringing back to life events and attitudes seemingly lost in the recesses of antiquity. Such a commitment is bound to lead to a fruitless search after an unattainable *recherche du temps perdu*. This is all the more frustrating because the further back the search leads, the more sublime its objects look and thus become all the more impossible to revive. Instead of looking forward to the future with its promise and its uncertainties and with the lure of the unknown, society is urged to look back to, and emulate, highly familiar paradigms and role models from an ideal (or idealized) past. Something of this frustration seems to underlie Husayn's words (at a ceremony awarding wartime decorations) when he said that Iraqis and Arabs reading books of Arab history did so with a sense of pride but also with a choking feeling in their throats. Undoubtedly, the choking feeling was that of envy and of the frustration of not being able to live up to the models of the past.[11]

Another way of accounting for the preoccupation with the past is the failure of modern values and the frustration accompanying it. The sharper the disappointment, the more idealized the past appears. Closely related to this is the rejection of the source of these values: Western civilization and the process of Westernization. Both force Iraqis (and Arabs in general) into a permanently apologetic stance. Sami Shawkat, comparing Western and Arab history, wrote, "Our Semitic-Arab history reaches back to a depth of thousands of years, [to a time] when Europeans lived in forests, marshes, and caves." Elsewhere he wrote: "Throughout the Middle Ages, we were the only carriers of the torch of civilization and of light in the entire world, unlike other peoples who were stagnating in ignorance; it was we who carried into modern Europe the science on which it built its material and cultural accomplishments."[12] The same points were made by Husayn in endless repetition: Iraq had created culture when other peoples were shrouded in "deadly darkness." Iraq was the cradle of all important civilizations, and the Arabs were the first to proclaim a universal faith.[13] Such points were argued with increasing forcefulness during the Kuwait crisis, when Husayn dwelt constantly on the comparison between Iraq's 6,000-year-old civilization and the shallow, superficial, and materialistic civilization of America. Iraq, Husayn said, "harbored within it the entire history of Arab glories and of its great men"—an altogether unwarranted appropriation of the past of other Arab countries.[14]

Yet another aspect of the same theme can be seen in the ideological, political, and didactic use made of history. Hauling it into the present was to give back to the Arabs (and to the Iraqis in particular) their sense of mission (*risala*) to mankind. Like the forefathers of today's Iraqis who, according to Shawkat, had carried civilization abroad during the Middle Ages, so the latter must now resume that "historical role" (*dawr ta'rikhi*). Husayn and other establishment figures were wont to speak of their country's "debt" to history, which was owed not so much to present and future generations but to history itself. Addressing a gathering of soldiers shortly after the outbreak of the war against Iran, Husayn said, "By Allah, you are fighting for the sake of history—its past, its present and its future—because you are defending its glories and its values." In a 1978 address to a military gathering, he had said he could not promise the army a quiet life. He reminded them that their ancestors had reached Andalusia, China, and southern France and added, "We have the right to aspire to make the shape of the present reflect the splendor of the past." History, he said, must be reconstructed, revived, and even relived (*haya*). In looking at the achievements of the past, for instance those of ancient Babylon or of the period of the Muslim conquests, Iraqis must learn to attain the same accomplishments.[15]

Yet another use to which history was put was that of generating hope, building confidence, augmenting motivation, and raising morale. During one of the Iranian offensives against Iraq, for instance, *al-Jumhuriyya* published an article headed by the words the ancient Babylonians had inscribed on the walls of their capital: *ayn yabur shabo*, meaning "the enemy shall not pass."[16] At the start of the Gulf War, Husayn sent U.S. president George Bush a reproachful message, reminding him of the Iraqi uprisings of 1920 that had been carried out with the simplest of weapons: the *fala* and the *migwar* (pitchforks and clubs). How, then, could the Iraqis of today, with their most magnificent tanks—better even than the American ones—recoil or show fear. He told a questioner that it was impossible for a civilization 6,000 years old to be defeated by the forces of evil.[17]

Husayn's preoccupation with history also has a personal aspect: He wants to enter history and be remembered as one of its great men. One of the laudatory books about him dwells at length on Husayn's attitude toward history. For him, reading history is not entertainment, a waste of time, or even just an expansion of knowledge but rather a matter of drawing lessons and forming a worldview. Husayn, the author goes on, has an "appointment with Iraqi history" because "a country with a great history" always needs a great historical leader. The real history of modern Iraq began with Husayn; other leaders might end up in the "trash bins of history" (*mazabil al-ta'rikh*), but Husayn was inscribed in its annals by "the pen of history" itself. The author goes to the length of describing his own meeting with Husayn as "an encounter with history."[18]

On Writing History

If such is the role of history, it goes without saying that its writing cannot be left to historians alone and that scholars must not be allowed to deal with it in a manner detached from the realities of modern Iraq. Shawkat had already shown the way. There were, he wrote, two ways of writing history—one for research, the other for education and guidance (*tawjih*). The educational authorities must concern themselves with the latter and impart a love of history to the young generation. "Regarding history for history's sake, our society is not concerned with it; it is only for experts and researchers." In revising history textbooks, he stated, the ministry of education had eliminated all that was "inconsequential" and "unimportant" in history.[19] Whether following Shawkat's line of thought or relying on its own totalitarian instincts, the Ba'th regime interfered massively in the writing (or rewriting) of history and in the didactic messages it was meant to convey. Husayn declared that history was not being written for the dead, it was there to guide the living. Failure to do so would mean the loss of its "effectiveness, its vitality, and its dynamics." Historiography must accentuate the ideal and heroic figures—not so much to do them justice but rather to make them into role models and sources of inspiration for the people of today, and in particular for those among them who were cut out to become heroes. Here, too, Husayn followed in the footsteps of the educators of the 1930s, when the teaching of history centered around a list of thirty to forty Islamic and pre-Islamic heroes.[20]

Not only were individual historical figures given special salience, but also certain general aspects and particular periods of history were either played up or toned down as the regime's didactic aims required. Husayn was of the opinion that in teaching the period of the Muslim conquests, teachers must not stress the material aspect (i.e., the quest for war booty), for this would lead the students to think that their ancestors went to war for the sake of material gain rather than for exalted values. *Al-Thawra* echoed his words, writing that national (*qawmi*) history must speak of "the positive aspects, the lofty qualities, and the cultural achievements so that the [young] generation will follow the straight path and will struggle for the sake of exalted aims." The teaching of history must guide the emotions and sensations of students and must influence them intensely.[21] Obviously, then, periods of eminence and splendor must be taught; others need hardly be mentioned.

It seems to follow that Arab history must be extended into the past in order to include a greater number of glorious episodes. Several generations of researchers, historians, educators, and politicians—among them Shawkat and Husayn—proclaimed the Sumerians, the Babylonians, and indeed all Semitic peoples to be Arabs.[22] They perceived the rise of the early civilizations and the rise of the monotheistic religions as a single continuum in which the Arabs formed the links between cultures and creeds. Husayn declared:

> For thousands of years, you have given mankind great civilizations . . . *and you have taken part, together with the sons of your glorious Arab nation, in spreading the great divine faiths* and you have also lived in previous periods of decline, . . . and your enemies have therefore thought that your hour of historic opportunity is over, never to return. But you have given proof . . . that your people lives and your nation lives and renews itself and that you are the descendants of the great ancestors who excelled in history as your leaders.[23] (emphasis added)

Such an approach clashes, of course, with the traditional Islamic view that considers all periods preceding Islam as the "time of ignorance" (*jahiliyya*) and thinks of the rise of Islam as the real beginning of Arab history. But Husayn maintained that it was an error "to look at our history as if it had been empty or shameful before Islam." If the Arabs really had been so ignorant, oppressed, and evil, they would not have succeeded in accomplishing the divine mission with which they were entrusted. Allah chose the Arabs not because they were base and sinful but because they possessed the inherent capability of becoming "the leaders of mankind and changing its face." Before the advent of Islam, the Arabs already had honor, nobility of mind, and rectitude. When in the thirteenth century, under the blows of the Mongols, "glory departed [from Iraq], this did not reflect [the Arabs'] real condition, but was no more than an interlude." To understand their real capabilities, one must look at their contribution to mankind before that time, when others, including the Americans, were still living in caves.[24]

Fame did not, however, reside in the distant past only. Iraqis had also written glorious pages in the book of recent history by their uprising in 1920 and by the 1941 "May movement" of al-Kaylani. Husayn complained of the injustice done to the "May movement" by Iraqi historiography, which had either ignored it or not recognized its heroic qualities. After all, it had flown in the face of Britain—the same Britain that, he went on to say, was still causing many Third World states to "shiver" and "bow" before it.[25] The reappraisal of the al-Kaylani episode and its elevation to a symbol of gallantry and unflinching courage in confronting the outside world was only a small item in the overall rewriting of history (*iʿadat kitabat al-taʾrikh*) that Husayn instructed Iraqi historians to undertake. The writing of history, he said, needed to "express our worldview" and be in keeping with Baʿthi ideology. But to interpret history in the Baʿth way did not mean "falsifying it or re-creating it by artificial means." In any case, historians were divided into schools, and everyone was entitled to "bring up from the depths of history those elements that are bound to reinforce his [particular] doctrine or ideology."[26]

Who, then, was to be entrusted with the writing of history so defined? Husayn, as well as the Iraqi historians involved in the debate, rejected writings of the Western orientalist school (*mustashriqun* or *musta'ribun*), or indeed of any foreign writer dealing with Arab history. The principal reason for rejecting them was that they wrote under the influence of "imperialist and racist concepts." Husayn said that they were enemies of the Arabs and kept stressing "that the Arab brain is not complex [enough]" and incapable of dealing with complicated matters. As one historian put it, Western orientalists, taking a negative view of the Arabs, picked from history only what seemed to support their prejudices. Another complaint, also aired during the public debates, was that Western historians looked at Arab history merely from an analytical point of view but failed to grasp the inner spirit that moved it. Being foreign to that spirit, they failed to fulfill a historian's foremost task: that of providing inspiration and a vision to the young generation. Another historian accused Western orientalists of "ignorance" and "bias" and pointed to their inability to free themselves from Western patterns of thought. Their narrow studies of narrow themes gave a distorted and even harmful picture of the Arab past. Another participant acknowledged the great Western contribution to Arab historical, cultural, and linguistic studies but deplored it, saying that the time had come to raise a new generation of historians from among the Arabs who would no longer rely on the work of foreign orientalists.[27]

Making History Known

Under the Ba'th, teaching history—in the widest sense of the word—became a primary tool of political influence and indoctrination. Its means varied. The appeal to the educated classes was through books, articles, and public debates. For the wider public, more easily digested (often visual) methods were used: films, popular festivals, the erection of statues, postage stamps, et cetera.[28]

One of the pioneers of writing history along the lines laid down by Husayn was Fadil al-Barrak, director general of intelligence from 1984 to 1988. His most important book deals with "the role of the Iraqi army in the [1941] government of national defense and the war against Britain." It can serve as a model for the new, purpose-oriented, and didactic method of writing history. Al-Barrak chose a period that Husayn had demanded be revised, centering around the army as a symbol of strength and of a daring spirit of confrontation with forces stronger than itself. He also dwelt at length on the Pan-Arab ideology then prevalent in the ranks of the military. In a second book, published a short time later and incor-

porating the reactions of historians and public figures to the earlier publication, al-Barrak explained frankly the purpose of the first book. With
a flattering aside in the direction of Husayn (who had just become president), he wrote that none of the historians who had lauded Husayn's
approach had then proceeded to apply it. That was why he had felt the
need not only to "reread history" but also to rewrite it "with the aim of
using its contents to accelerate cultural processes in our noble nation."
Al-Barrak explained that, in following Husayn's recommendations, he had
not acted from personal motives; he also had not wished to add yet another book to the shelves of historical writing. Rather, he wanted his book
to let readers learn lessons for the present and the future. He quotes Husayn
over and over again about the need to do justice to the events of 1941
and to bring their heroes alive in the minds of today's Iraqis. The story of
1941, he went on to say, was an "epic worthy of the [highest points of]
glory in our history" and a symbol of the greatness of the Arab revolutions in the first half of the twentieth century. Al-Barrak rejected charges
that the "May movement" had had pro-Nazi sympathies. Rather, it had
been a national liberation movement that had faced its defeat with honor,
had turned a new page for later Arab generations, and had been a most
important event in the emergence of the Ba'th.[29]

Since al-Kaylani's movement was considered by the Ba'th as a paradigm
of heroism,[30] the press frequently dealt with its course and its heroes—
first and foremost Salah al-Din al-Sabbagh. This was particularly noticeable on the eve of the invasion of Kuwait. At that time, *al-Qadisiyya*
published a series of articles about British plots against Iraq in 1940 and
1941, using British Foreign Office documents released in the meantime.
It continued by printing a series of day-to-day Iraqi police reports from
the same period, describing among other things the British air attacks.[31]
The timing of the publication of the documents, which had remained
untouched for forty-nine years, was, of course, not coincidental and was
intended as an incitement against Western imperialism and perhaps to
prepare public opinion for what was to follow. After the Gulf War, the
Ba'th marked the fifty-first anniversary of al-Kaylani's coup by awarding
al-Sabbagh the *rafidayn* order and three other decorations for valor. Three
other officers who had participated in the movement and had been executed were also awarded posthumous decorations for valor.[32]

Ba'thi preoccupation with history peaked twice, each time in circumstances that attested to its functional and instrumental purpose. The first
wave, in the 1970s, was intended to elaborate on the place of the hero in
society and in history. This was part of Saddam Husayn's preparations
for his takeover of exclusive personal power and for shaping his eventual
historical image (see Chapter 5). The second wave, in the late 1980s, was
meant to play up the horrors of Western imperialism, its many interven-
tions in Arab affairs, and the injustice it had inflicted on the Arabs. Its
purpose was to prepare public opinion for a confrontation with the West
in general and with Kuwait in particular. Of special interest is an article

published by *al-Jumhuriyya* in 1987 under the heading "Rewriting Arab History" that was strongly critical of the existing historical literature on the "Arab Gulf," blaming it for relying exclusively on foreign sources and on "biased imperialist and orientalist" writings "hostile to the Arab nation and to Islam." These failed to reflect historical truth and needed to be discarded or at least "examined carefully before being circulated or quoted from."[33]

At about the same time, a book on King Ghazi was published in Baghdad. Its very publication was an act of historical revisionism, since both the king's person and his reign (1933–1939) had, from the time of Qasim's takeover onward, been thought of as flawed and distasteful and had therefore been neglected by modern Iraqi historiography. The sudden rehabilitation of Ghazi and his elevation to the rank of a national hero had a twofold purpose: to recall his part in opposing the British and to remind the public of his many and persistent efforts to "return" Kuwait to Iraq.[34] But apart from sketching a portrait of Ghazi and describing the events of his short reign, the book presaged a general revision of history with a view to rehabilitating the period of the monarchy, the royal family, and some of the figures most closely associated with it.

One book expressing this new line was on Faysal I. *Al-Qadisiyya* commented that Iraqis had become accustomed to thinking of the entire period of the monarchy in terms of *al-'ahd al-ba'id* (the era that had passed away) without distinguishing between the role of Faysal I as founder of the modern Iraqi state on the one hand and the unpatriotic stance of certain politicians in the 1940s and the 1950s on the other. The time had come, the paper added, to correct this unbalanced picture.[35] Husayn himself used the opportunity to state that political and intellectual writing in Iraq must be "free" and not "look as if it expressed the view of the rulers or of the ministry of information." He also said that he had no objection to books being written about Qasim (regardless of the fact that he himself had taken part in an attempt on Qasim's life in 1959). Two such books were indeed written at about that time.[36]

The rewriting of history reached a peak a month after the invasion of Kuwait when almost simultaneously three studies were published, each containing "documentary proof" that Kuwait was an integral part of Iraq. Their titles bear witness to their thrust: *Al-Kuwayt 'Iraqiyya* (Kuwait is Iraqi); *Kuwayt al-'Iraq* (Iraq's Kuwait); and *Al-Huwiyya al-'Iraqiyya li-l-Kuwayt* (Kuwait's Iraqi identity). Shortly afterward, a fourth book was published under the title *Kuwayt al-'Iraq: al-nidal fi sabil al-wahda* (Iraqi Kuwait: the struggle for the sake of unity). Its title page showed a crowd of demonstrators carrying a banner with the slogan: *Al-Kuwayt 'Iraqiyya damman wa-lahman* (Kuwait is Iraqi in its flesh and blood). The last book enlarged on the role played by three pre-Ba'thi Iraqi leaders in pressing for the "return" of Kuwait: King Ghazi, Nuri al-Sa'id, and Qasim.[37] Thus, their rehabilitation during previous years now served to legitimize Iraq's conquest of Kuwait. Indeed, during the period between the invasion and the Gulf War, it became a pivotal Iraqi argument, supported by quotations from these three, that the country had never relinquished its claims to Kuwait.

If this message of historical revisionism was expected to appeal to intellectuals, newspaper readers, and people involved in party affairs, a different method was needed to reach out to simple, uneducated people and to the rank and file of the army. This was done by using historical symbols and heroic figures from the past known to the public at large, firmly ensconced in the collective memory, and considered capable of inspiring enthusiasm. An instructive example is provided by the names of Iraqi army units or of sectors of the front. Just as in the 1930s and the 1940s, when history was taught with reference to a list of heroic figures from the past, during the Iraqi-Iranian war such names were used in the army. From among some forty unit names mentioned in the press during the war, about thirty were names of heroes, battles, or other major historical events. Thus, we find units named after Muhammad, Saladin, and Khalid bin al-Walid, after al-Muthanna bin Haritha, Qaʿqaʿ al-Tamimi, and Saʿd bin Abi Waqqas, and after Tariq bin Ziyad and ʿUqba bin Nafiʿ. A term used frequently in naming units was that of the battle of Hattin (1187). *Al-Qadisiyya* published a poem on the thread linking that battle—with all the mythological overtones it had since acquired—with today's events. Part of it read:

> History is returning;
> Yesterday the Crusaders' war,
> Today the Zionist offensive,
> And tomorrow the coming victories.[38]

History Is Returning: Qadisiyya as a Parable

In January 1980, the filming of a giant screen production called *al-Qadisiyya* was begun in Iraq. Work on the film was personally supervised by ʿIzzat Ibrahim al-Duri, deputy chairman of the Revolutionary Command Council and then the regime's number-two man. During one of his visits to the filming site, he explained that the purpose of making the movie was to present history as a living thing, just as it had happened 1,400 years earlier, and to let it inspire modern viewers. The actresses starring in the production had a most important task: to arouse enthusiasm among the women who would urge their sons, husbands, and brothers to fight and to sacrifice themselves for the sake of the nation. He went on: "We are most certainly moving toward decisive battles. Our present position forces upon us decisive battles against the enemies so as to open the arduous road leading to the renewal of our glory and our civilization."[39] Nine months later, with the outbreak of the war against Iran, the film became reality. Iraqis became accustomed to call the war "Saddam's Qadisiyya" or "The Second Qadisiyya" (*al-Qadisiyya al-Thaniya*).

The battle of Qadisiyya, which became a symbol of Muslims prevailing over infidels and of Arabs defeating Persians, took place in 636 or 637, south of the city of Najaf (today a stronghold of Iraqi Shiʿis). Al-Tabari devoted no fewer than 200 pages of his classical history of the Muslims to this battle alone. Legendary appendages soon attached themselves to the account of the battle, and it is not easy to separate historical truth from later accretions. The Arab-Muslim forces were under the command of Saʿd bin Abi Waqqas, whom the caliph ʿUmar had sent out to reinforce the units of al-Muthanna bin Haritha already fighting in Iraq. The latter had died of war wounds before the reinforcements reached his army. The Persians were under the command of Rustum, who was reluctant to face the Arabs but had to follow the wishes of young King Yazdajird III. The battle lasted for three days and four nights and ended with a disastrous defeat for the Persians. Rustum was killed. The battle and a series of subsequent engagements put an end to Sassanian rule in Iraq and led to a vast eastward expansion of Muslim rule.

Some details particularly impressed later generations. Among them was the fact that the Persians had battle elephants, a "weapon" not found on the Muslim side, but the Arabs succeeded in putting them out of action, apparently by blinding them. Fighting poets, among them al-Qaʿqaʿ and Abu Mihjan, played an important role in keeping Muslim morale high. Some 30,000 Persians were said to have chained themselves to each other during the fighting so they would not give way or flee from the battle. But they could not withstand the assault, retreated, and met their death in a canal at the rear of their lines. Their bodies filled the canal and made it possible for the Muslims to reach its far side.[40]

The myths woven around al-Qadisiyya are a most instructive example of the Baʿthi technique of using an event with a core of historical truth that is deeply etched into the collective memory in order to further the party's ideology of Arab nationalism and to appeal to the public by means of a challenge of great emotional power. At the same time—whether intentionally or not—it served to further blur the borderline between the past, the present, and the future.

After Husayn's assumption of the presidency in 1979, the use of the Qadisiyya myth reached its peak. The gradual and methodical way in which it was spread by the media and other means (such as the film) were a central part of the preparation of public opinion for the war against Iran. *Al-Jumhuriyya* wrote about the heroes of the battle and added that they had now been born again and that the original Qadisiyya had become a model for today's "wars of liberation" (*maʿarik al-tahrir*). Today, there were many Qaʿqaʿs and thousands like Qadisiyya.[41] For the same purpose the regime called on youths and adults to attend camps named *abtal al-Qadisiyya* or *fursan al-Qadisiyya* (heroes or knights of Qadisiyya). Their express purpose was to hold up the battle as a model for the present. During a visit to these camps, Husayn praised the "descendants of Qadisiyya" present there and said he was proud of them, just as he was proud "of the pure blood of every struggler and soldier [that was being] shed for the sake of the soil of the nation." On the eve of the war, the commander of one of the units about to go into action declared that his men were "ready to revive the spirit of al-Qadisiyya. . . . If the Persians have forgotten al-Qadisiyya, or have caused it to be forgotten, we shall remind them and relive [the battle]."[42]

As the war continued for eight years, it became necessary to invent new ways of renewing the Qadisiyya message—both that of the original battle and that of Husayn. The two were becoming nearly indistinguishable. New stamps on the theme of Saddam's Qadisiyya were issued. Later, when government bonds were sold to finance the war effort, the bond certificates bore portraits of Husayn shown against the background of a map of the Arab world. The film on Qadisiyya was finished in 1981 and screened in every movie theater. It was also sent to Cannes as Iraq's entry in the film festival there. In the district of Mada'in, a huge special outdoor "panorama" was erected at a cost of 7.5 million dinar. Using the most modern equipment, it produced audiovisual displays of "the eternal battle of al-Qadisiyya that had liberated the soil of Iraq from Persian domination." A Baghdad square was named "Saddam's Qadisiyya" and an eighteen-meter-long wall was put up with a relief called "The Two Qadisiyyas." It showed elephants, swords, flags, and horses, as well as seventh-century fighters alongside soldiers in modern uniforms.[43]

The sword was made yet another symbol of al-Qadisiyya. We have already described the victory arch with its two swords (see Chapter 10). Its designer revealed that at some time during the war, it had been decided to replace the customary sword by a special, curved "sword of al-Qadisiyya" as "a symbol of the liberation of the Arabs through the two Qadisiyyas." The "Qadisiyya sword," made from parts of the weapons of the fallen and from jewelry Iraqi women had handed over as contributions for the war effort, became one of the highest wartime decorations. Its recipients had to take the following oath: "I swear . . . to uphold the ideals of this Iraqi-Arab sword. . . . I declare that I am fully resolved not to let this sword fall from my hand." Beginning in December 1981, a "Week of Saddam's Qadisiyya" was celebrated each year. The newspaper *al-Qadisiyya*, originally a supplement to an army weekly, became an independent daily and soon equaled the other dailies in importance.[44] On the first anniversary of the outbreak of the war, a book on "Saddam's Qadisiyya" was published; so was a series of children's books under the same heading.

The use of the Qadisiyya myth could only be rendered effective if the parallels between 636/637 and 1980–1988 were made sufficiently apparent to the public at large. The internal party organ *al-Thawra al-'Arabiyya* explained that the appellation "Saddam's Qadisiyya" had been chosen "because there are so many similarities between the Qadisiyya of Sa'd [bin Abi Waqqas] and of Saddam that even the passage of time and the change of generations could not obscure them." Both battles had been fought on

Iraqi soil; both had taken place after a period of "revolutionary ferment" (caused first by Islam, then by the Ba'th); and in both, the "Persian army" was much better equipped and several times more numerous than the Arab forces. The inevitable conclusion, the paper went on, was that, just as the Persians had been broken by Sa'd the first time, they would soon be broken by Saddam. *Al-Jumhuriyya* already drew the same conclusion at the end of the first month of hostilities. It gave the number of men in the field as 36,000 Arabs and 120,000 Persians (roughly the proportion of the size of the populations of the two countries in modern times). Another point conveyed by the parallel was Iraq's criticism of the other Arab states, who stood by idly at a time of such an epic struggle. In a broad hint in the direction of Syria, *al-'Iraq* recalled the role of al-Qa'qa', who had led Syrian reinforcements into battle at the original Qadisiyya, and described the heavy blows he and his men had dealt the Persians. Husayn contrasted the "holders of Arab identity cards" (i.e., Arabs in name alone) with eight blind men from the province of Qadisiyya who had volunteered for the army, following the example of a blind man who had carried a flag at the original battle.[45]

An indirect way of drawing such parallels was the profusion of newspaper stories on the period of the first Qadisiyya and its heroes. *Al-Qadisiyya* outdid all others in that respect. It devoted a long article to the life and deeds of Waqqas, quoting at length from sayings and letters of the caliph 'Umar to him. It enlarged in particular on the role of women in encouraging the men, with special reference to the well-known poetess al-Khansa', who urged her four sons to seek fame and booty and did not shed a single tear when all four fell in the battle.[46]

13

The Manipulation of Islam

Ba'thi Convolutions over Islam

The employment of Islamic themes in Ba'thi discourse has covered the entire gamut from ignoring them in the beginning to their abundant and eventually strident use during the regime's later years. It needs saying, however, that there was no basic change in the content of Ba'thi thinking; rather, the use of Islamic themes was stepped up or toned down as circumstances seemed to require. It is possible to discern several distinct phases in this process and to point to domestic and external developments that influenced it. From 1968 until 1977, the Ba'th regime was silent on the topic of religion; between 1977 and 1980, there were indications of an impending change; the war years, from 1980 and well into the first postwar year 1989, constituted the phase of toeing the Islamic line; the last phase, from 1989 onward, was one of deliberate Islamic flag-waving.

The first phase was in keeping with the overall ideology of the Ba'th, such as it had consolidated before the party's rise to power. These were the years of applying socialism, the domestic alliance with the Iraqi Communist Party, and the foreign alliance with the Soviet Union. These were the years when the party attempted to base its rule on the secular principles of its original doctrine. Some researchers maintain that from the outset there had existed an affinity with Islam too strong to allow for a truly secular approach.[1] But it can be shown that the party discourse as well as its actual policies were in essence secular. The 1947 party stat-

176

utes, for instance, made no mention whatsoever of Islam or of its place in the projected polity. More than that, clause 15 of the statutes declared: "The national bond [*al-rabita al-qawmiyya*] is the only bond existing in the Arab state and it is this bond that promises harmony among the citizens and their fusion in a single melting pot while struggling against all other loyalties: religious [*madhhabiyya*], communal, tribal, racist, and regional [*iqlimiyya*]."[2] Michel 'Aflaq's writings reveal an inner conflict between his need as a Christian to demonstrate fidelity to Islam and its legacy and his political convictions about the place of religion in the state. The former placed him in a defensive position vis-à-vis the majority, as it required a constant effort to demonstrate that his Arabness was not tainted and his attitude toward Islam was without blemish. This led him to portray Islam in a heroic, idealistic, and romantic mold—an approach not devoid of authentic conviction.

'Aflaq spoke of Islam as if it were a heroic war epic and of Muhammad as a heroic figure worthy of emulation by every Arab (regardless of faith). His best-known saying on the point was: "Muhammad was all the Arabs; all Arabs should therefore be Muhammad." Every Arab could live a life like Muhammad's in the present, even if perhaps on a smaller scale. Christian Arabs, too, must take pride in Muhammad and acknowledge that "Islam is the national culture that they must absorb and nurture just as they nurture all [else] that is most dear to them in their being Arabs." In 'Aflaq's view, Islam is a universal and eternal revolution and an integral part of being an Arab.[3] As against this, he rejected any link between state and religion and was critical of "religious movements" and of present-day religiosity (*tadayyun ra'ij*). "A religious state [*dawla diniyya*]," he wrote, "was something attempted in medieval times and . . . [it] ended in failure." Religious movements were sustained by "negatives": "communal hatred, fear, and other negative emotions." Today's piety, he went on, stemmed from opportunism and ignorance. It had lost its pristine spiritualism and could no longer "impart vitality to the nation or raise it up." There was no room in the Ba'th doctrine "for any religion unless it had faith in ideals [*iman mithali*]."

Such statements were not the end of 'Aflaq's tortuous road. Elsewhere, he wrote that the Ba'th, being a "positive spiritual movement," could not dissociate itself from religion or clash with it, but it could disassociate itself "from stagnation and opportunism, and from sitting on the fence." He rejected the charge that the Ba'th promoted heresy (*ilhad*) but repeated over and over again that the party sought a secular (*'ilmaniyya*) state that would grant freedom of worship to all religions and all denominations.[4] Trying to square the circle led him to an even more radical statement that attests to the great inner struggle of this Christian ideologue. At a party conference almost a decade after the Ba'th takeover, he returned to the theme of the "organic link" between Islam and Arabism and repeated that the Ba'th conceived of Islam as a spiritual, ideological, and social revolution and had placed it at the center of Arab nationalism. Therefore, he went on, "there is no Arab who is not a Muslim; . . . every statement to the contrary is misleading."[5]

It was this baggage of ambivalent concepts that the Ba'th party brought with it when it came to power—a baggage widely seen as shot through with Christian notions and heretical teachings. It began its rule with the strong urge to turn its doctrine into the ideology of the masses, believing it capable of resolving all existing conflicts within Iraqi society. Its first instinctive reaction, therefore, was to shy away from everything to do with religion. While the provisional constitution adopted soon after the take-over laid down that "Islam is the religion of the state and the principal fundament of its constitution," the second provisional constitution (1970), which was formulated by the Ba'th alone without political allies, left out the second part of the clause.[6]

For almost a decade, there was hardly any reference to religion in the regime's public discourse. When necessary, the media carried short and dry notices on such things as the date of the pilgrimage and the procedures for participating in it. Public silence did not, however, prevent the Ba'th from quietly seizing control of the religious establishment. This "creeping annexation" of previously autonomous religious bodies began in 1974. For example, starting with the academic year of 1974/1975, the religious colleges (*kulliyyat al-fiqh*) in Najaf and Baghdad were put under state control, under the jurisdiction of the Ministry for Higher Education.[7]

Public discourse changed after the outbreak of Shi'i violence in Najaf and Karbala' in 1977. Briefly, the riots occurred against the background of what Shi'i men of religion saw as an accelerated secularization of the state and as a reaction against the assumption of state control over hitherto autonomous Shi'i religious institutions. The violence caused a serious crisis, and harsh punishment was meted out. The events forced a change in the public idiom of the Ba'th.[8] Its first sign came six months later when Husayn addressed a small gathering at the Ministry of Information. He said that the Ba'th party was not neutral between faith and irreligion; rather, though not itself a religious party, it was always on the side of faith. But when Husayn began to speak of "religious quarters," he used warlike terminology. He warned of "confusing the trenches" between the party and such forces. He called the latter "enemies," adding that such confusion made it more difficult to tell friends from enemies and could cause "the revolutionary gun" to hit friends as well. To fight the enemy and to aim true, the field of fire must be open and broad. Put in less allusive terms, the party must not employ religious terms in order to come to a temporary accommodation (a "momentary encounter," as he called it) with the religious elements. To do so would undermine the party's ideological fundaments and its political power base.

Husayn admonished party members against being carried away by religious sentiment and warned religious quarters against the "politicization of religion [*tasayyus al-din*]," which would divide the people between being religious or secular. As for those who sought to use religion for political aims, the regime would hit them with an "iron fist." Yet the party's over-all approach ought to be balanced; it should not lean toward irreligion, nor should it put on a "religious cloak." The Ba'th, Husayn went on, must allow religious ceremonies to be performed but must not get involved in them. He repeated several times that the party's doctrine was not a "copy" of some religious teachings "but a doctrine of life for Arabs." Husayn went on to draw a line between heritage (*turath*) and religion. The party and the state were entitled to take pride in the "spiritual heritage"—in the glories of the past and the great national leaders, as well as in religion—but they must not follow religious patterns of action nor stray from the path of "changing and rebuilding society" according to the party's guidance.[9]

This approach—implying the secular character of the state and the sepa-ration of state and religion—remained official policy for only a few years, until the early 1980s. Cracks started to appear in it even earlier, caused by the pressures of domestic developments. The above warning against the politicization of religion notwithstanding, the Association for Religious Guidance (*Jam'iyyat al-tawjih al-dini*) "in the light of Ba'th principles" became active in the middle of 1977, if not earlier. Set up by the party, it apparently served as an instrument of domestic intelligence gathering in religious quarters. Later, it was renamed the Committee for Religious Indoctrination (*Lajnat al-taw'iya al-diniyya*).[10]

Husayn himself soon transgressed the rules he had laid down, under-taking a series of visits—covered in detail by the media—to the Shi'i holy places and taking part in religious rituals. It was at one of these visits that he first hinted at his personal descent from Husayn, the son of 'Ali (see Chapter 5).[11] At about the same time, Husayn began gradually and cau-tiously to touch on religious themes. Husayn's speech above was not pub-lished until a year after he made it.[12] The delay attests to the sensitivity the party attributed to the subject as well as to the pressures causing its publication. When it eventually appeared in print, it was meant to guide party members in dealing with the issue.

The 1977 riots did not long remain the only, or even the main, reason for the Ba'th's being "dragged" into the religious issue. Khomeini's Islamic revolution in 1979 was a much graver event for the Ba'th and forced greater changes in it. It gave rise to much anxiety, at first because of the party's fear of its indirect reverberations and later because of the deliberate ap-peal by Iran for Iraqis to act likewise. Ba'thi reactions attested to the party's dilemma: on the one hand, it was resolved to put down religious trends, oppress religious activists, and act against any signs of the "politicization of religion"; on the other hand, it was drawn willy-nilly toward the lines of the "enemy," to the point of adopting the image of its adversaries.

A turning point in this respect was a speech Husayn made barely ten days after his final takeover of exclusive power. The speech was intended to settle accounts with personal adversaries in the ranks of the Ba'th and with the Communist Party, as well as reject pressures by the illegal Shi'i al-Da'wa (the call) party and refute the principles of Khomeini. Husayn opened his speech with a reference to early Islam and to the importance of faith, such as that of the men who had followed Muhammad from the outset. He phrased his speech in a manner intended to make the listeners draw a parallel between those early believers in Islam and the longtime Ba'th party members who now must have similar faith in their leader Husayn. He deplored the fact that, during the 1960s and the early 1970s, the party had allowed its original "heritage" to weaken and criticized party members for letting elements of liberal and bourgeois thinking, as well as communist teachings, penetrate their worldview and their political debates. This, however, he emphasized, had now stopped.

He then attacked the Communist Party, dwelling on the differences between it and the Ba'th, especially over their attitudes toward history and early Islam (a line of reasoning attesting to the importance he attributed to the interpretation of history). Unlike the communist ideology, which was a foreign implant brought to Iraq from the West, the Ba'th doctrine had its roots in history and in Islam. "Historically speaking," he said, "we precede them, because their history goes back [only] to the nineteenth century, while ours began 1,400 years ago, and because the history of the Arab Socialist Ba'th Party is the direct continuation of the history of the Arab nation." Ba'th doctrine was not an innovation because it was "not detached from the [Arab-Muslim] heritage but rather stemming from it." It formed "a connecting link between the stage of the first renaissance that was grounded in the principles of Islam, and the new renaissance that our party and our revolution represent today." His rather obscure conclusion was that "what is needed now is to turn the entire society into a 'generally Muslim' one; that is to say, into a generally Ba'thi one." [13]

These tactics of fighting off the Islamic wave and at the same time trying to ride it became a great deal more salient with the outbreak of the war against Iran and unfolded fully during its course. Many regarded the use of Islamic terminology as no more than a propaganda gimmick, yet it would be wrong to ignore the genuine dilemma underlying it. There was genuine soul-searching over the proper way to measure up to the challenges of religion. Pressures were mounting for several reasons: Shi'i religious activists threatened to undermine the party's power, at least in the Shi'i areas; Iran made religion its main weapon for maligning Ba'thi Iraq, proclaiming it a heretical regime; events in Iran had made the Baghdad leadership recognize the sweeping power of religious sentiment and its capacity to impart an enthusiastic fighting spirit to Iranian soldiers. Against this, the weaknesses of Ba'th ideology in emotionally motivating Iraqis and keeping their morale high in a seemingly endless war were becoming starkly apparent. Hence the emergence of Husayn's new line, which required party members to toe the traditional party line with regard to religion but gave much wider rein to Islamic rhetoric and Islamic symbols in the ranks of the army.

The line for party members was confirmed and spelled out more clearly at the 1982 party congress. Its report—the first official Ba'th statement to probe explicitly into the question of religion—reaffirmed the distinction between faith as a positive characteristic and the "religious-political phenomenon" (*al-zahira al-diniyya al-siyasiyya*) as a harmful deviation. The latter trend, according to the report, was led by the al-Da'wa al-Islamiyya party, which was being urged on and encouraged by Iran. Its line was to exploit religious sentiment for political purposes and to cast the present in the mold of religious "anachronism." The report went on to criticize certain Ba'th party members who had assisted the religious-political trend by demonstrating their religiosity, at times going to the length of stressing "religious concepts at the expense of Ba'thi concepts." The report warned of the ideological and political dangers likely to spring from this and declared that such a politicization of religion would not be tolerated in the future. Party members who had erred must return to the line laid down by Husayn.[14]

This rearguard action against religious sentiment in the ranks of the party continued for a long time. But all the while the use of Islamic motifs and symbols grew in frequency and significance in the regime's appeals to the men at the front. Husayn himself was quick to don the religious mantle himself and used a broad scale of terms with Islamic associations. He was careful at all times, however, to preserve a note of ambivalence, hiding or revealing his underlying aims as circumstances seemed to indicate.

Husayn's Islamic Rhetoric

Husayn ordered the publication of a book called *Saddam Husayn's Political Dictionary* and had parts of it serialized in the press, beginning in 1988. It contained an entry on religion that was reprinted in *al-Thawra* in the summer of 1990. The entry bears witness to the predominance of religious terms that had emerged in Husayn's idiom by that time. It also attests to his basically defensive stance vis-à-vis Iran over the issue of religion. The entry had a sentence that read: "The Iranians adhere to a new religion that has nothing to do with Islam. The only thing the two have in common are some outward features."[15]

While Iran's attitude toward Islam was thus being devalued, the regime increasingly emphasized the value of "true" Islam such as practiced in Iraq. Husayn himself began developing his image as a pious Muslim ruler. The Iranian and the Iraqi leaders were, so to speak, going in the opposite direction: Khomeini, the religious professional, turned into a political leader; Husayn, the professional politician, sought a religious role. Under the former, religion overpowered politics; under the latter, politics overpowered religion. But unlike in Iran, Iraqi politicians and functionaries continued to be barred from participation in religious discourse. Only Husayn had the right to make statements on religious issues and to take action on them. As a rule, other officials or party figures kept silent on the issue of Islam except in Husayn's presence or with his prior permission. Husayn had two reasons to insist on his monopoly: he wanted to stop party members from being carried away by the Islamic wave, a development likely to have utterly unpredictable consequences; and he wanted to be seen in the tradition of Arab-Muslim rulers who combined religious authority, political power, and military command in a single person. A senior army commander, Mahir 'Abd al-Rashid, said that just as Muhammad had been both prophet and commander, so Husayn, his descendant, combined spiritual with military leadership.[16]

In adopting a more explicitly Islamic stance, Husayn had been influenced not only by the political developments we have mentioned but also apparently by the approach of his uncle Khayrallah Talfah. Talfah had been like an adoptive father to Husayn and had been one of his early role models. He had taken part in al-Kaylani's revolt and had subsequently been jailed for five years. His influence on Husayn, both ideologically and with regard to religion, was strong. By 1976, Talfah had published nineteen books, among them a work in five volumes called *Kayf al-sabil ila Allah?* (What is the road to Allah?). There seems to have been some sort of inner struggle in Husayn's mind between the views of 'Aflaq, the author of *Fi sabil al-Ba'th*, and Talfah and his *Sabil ila Allah*. Over time, the latter won out. This was well borne out by Husayn's personal style and usage as they developed and changed after his assumption of the presidency and especially after the outbreak of the war against Iran. Thus, in one of his wartime speeches, Husayn said: "We seek and aspire to strengthen the spiritual and religious direction [*al-ittijah al-dini*] in this country." The term *mutadayyin* (pious, religious), originally a negative word in the Ba'th dictionary, was rehabilitated by Husayn. In May 1987, for example, he declared: "Our Arab nation is a religious [*mutadayyina*] nation and is obliged to carry [the call of] its religious mission to the peoples of the earth."[17]

The inclusion of Islamic terms in Husayn's personal idiom and the perfection of their use as an instrument of war reached their peak during the Gulf War. The *basmala* (in the name of God) became a constant invocation at the beginning of his speeches.[18] Quotations from the Qur'an became very frequent, the verses selected to reinforce Iraqis in their belief in the justice of their cause and to encourage them to march on. On one occasion, Husayn referred to the famous battle of Badr (in 624), in which a small band of Muslims defeated a force of infidels three times as numerous as themselves, and reminded his listeners how Muhammad had blinded the enemy by throwing sand into their eyes while asking for God's succor against them. He quoted from the sura *al-Anfal*, most of which speaks of the battle at Badr, especially verse 17, reading: "You did not slay them, but God slew them."[19]

A similar practice, noticeable earlier but standard practice in wartime, was to end his speeches with the words *Allah akbar* (God is most great). At other times, he concluded his addresses by repeating *Allah akbar* three times, a practice expected to elicit enthusiasm and augment motivation. During the Gulf War (but at no other time), he signed messages and letters with the words *'Abd Allah al-mu'min* (God's believing servant).[20] Stressing his own piety was meant to make him appear as the defender of Muslims against the unbelievers, whether these were the Western powers or those Arab leaders who acted in collusion with them. Naturally, the defender of Islam would prove superior to the infidels.

Husayn thus seemed to have abandoned the traditional Ba'th discourse and reverted—in a single leap, as it were—to the idiom of early Islam. The world was no longer divided between the Arabs and imperialism but between Muslims and infidels. The principal expressions in the new lexicon were *mujahid* (discussed later); *kafir* (unbeliever); *mu'min* (believer); *iman* (faith); *haqq* (justice); *khandaq al-kufr* (the trench or the position of heresy); *hashd al-mu'minin* (the community of the believers); and *al-da'wa* (the call [to Islam]).

An example of Husayn's Islamic manner of speech came in an interview with a CNN reporter in November 1990, at the height of the Kuwait crisis: "It is impossible for us to capitulate to those who bring together 400,000 soldiers against us, because we put our trust in Allah." Speaking of himself in the third person, he went on: "Saddam Husayn is an Arab citizen, a servant from among God's believing servants; he struggles [*yujahid*] for justice [*haqq*] and rejects oppression [*zulm*] and fears only the one God." On another occasion, he spoke in a reassuring vein (whether he was reassuring the Iraqi public or himself has to remain moot). He said, "Do you know why the Iraqis are confident? Because they are people who believe in God, and they are sure that justice is on their side. He who walks along the path of justice, God is with him; and he who has God at his side, what would he fear?"[21] At about the same time, Husayn started speaking of party members as "believers" (*mu'minun*) and of the "mission" of the Ba'th as *da'wa*.

The use of *da'wa* is indicative of the way the Ba'th (especially during the two wars) remade itself in the likeness of its enemies. As noted previously, al-Da'wa was the name of an illegal Shi'i party of religious activists. It first became active under Qasim, but it was only after the rise of the Ba'th that it began clashing with the regime. Its underground activity peaked in the late 1970s, ending with its decisive defeat at the hands of the regime sometime before the outbreak of the war against Iran. Though suppressed, it left the Ba'th marked by the conflict, particularly in its discourse.

The word *da'wa* has many layers. It is used to connote the call for the dead to rise from their graves on the day of the Last Judgment; it may connote the call of Allah and his prophets for men to believe in the true religion; it may mean the mission of the prophet (*da'wat al-rasul*); and it may connote the call to pagans to adopt Islam, lest the forces of Islam make war on them. The Ba'th appropriated the word a short while after its first significant clash with the al-Da'wa party in February 1977. A party document said among other things that the Ba'th had the right to call itself al-Da'wa because its program was a call for national unity and for fighting anyone who was trying to obstruct it. Later, Husayn reasserted some of the word's original religious overtones, saying, "The party need not grant membership to all applicants. What is incumbent upon us is to select 10 from among 100 *believers* [emphasis added] to conduct the *da'wa*, and *da'wa* here means the Ba'th." Elsewhere, he stated: "For the *da'wa* to turn into a real popular mission, we must test the sincerity of . . . [those who engage in it]; as for our enemies, they wish to put an end to your *da'wa* and to your mission [*risala*]."[22]

Of particular interest in this context is a speech made by Husayn on the first anniversary of the Gulf War. Its main burden was a comparison between his own days and the period of Muhammad and between his war against a "coalition" of thirty "pagan" states and Muhammad's war against the infidels. What both wars had in common, he said, was the victory of faith over godlessness—a victory achieved by the aid of God. "If in those days there was hubal [the pre-Islamic Meccan idol whose image Muhammad shattered upon his return to Mecca], today there is the human *hubal*. . . . God willed it that . . . 18 million believing and God-fearing Iraqis stood up to a billion citizens of the aggressive states." Despite the disparity in numbers and equipment, "there was the miracle of the battle. . . . Faith vanquished godlessness and truth prevailed over falsehood." Husayn went on to quote verse 69 of the sura *al-Anbiya'* describing how God saved Abraham from the fire in which the idolaters wished to burn him: "We said, O fire, be coolness and safety for Abraham."[23]

Islam in the Service of the War

The use of Islamic terminology was most conspicuous in the Ba'th discourse about the war. The prolonged fighting against an army of religiously motivated Iranian Shi'is made it necessary to address Iraqi soldiers—themselves mostly Shi'is—in terms commensurate with Iran's appeals to its own men. In the clash between Iran's Islamic ideology and the secular ideology of the Ba'th, the latter was palpably inferior. Husayn seems to have discerned this weakness at a very early stage of the conflict. The three basic catchwords of the Ba'th—unity, freedom, and socialism—were no longer capable of motivating Iraqi soldiers and keeping their morale high. The longer the war lasted and the longer the casualty lists grew, the more evident this became. New slogans were needed, and if they were to serve as badges of identity and to relate to recognized elements in the depths of social and historical consciousness, they could only be taken from the domain of Islam.

The sense of being, religiously speaking, on the defensive found expression in *al-Jumhuriyya* only a few days after the outbreak of the war. Under the heading "Allah akbar," the paper emphatically denied a statement by an Iranian "ignorant man of religion" that the Iraqi army was putting to death every soldier found to adhere to the commands of Islam. Next to a picture of a praying Iraqi soldier, the article stated: "Every Iraqi soldier is entitled to regard such ignorant talk as a bad joke as he watches his comrades and his superiors turn to God five times a day, fulfilling the commandment of prayer and giving thanks for the great victory over the heretic enemy who falsifies religion." Major-General Hisham Sabah al-Fakhri, considered one of the most brilliant Iraqi field commanders, told an interviewer that Iraqi soldiers repeatedly shouted *Allah akbar* before going out on a night attack, thereby petrifying the enemy. Fakhri later wrote a book on Iranian psychological warfare, asserting that Iran's religious wartime propaganda had failed to shake Iraqi morale.[24]

At the center of the Ba'thi employment of symbols of Islam stood the "epic" of al-Qadisiyya. As we have seen, it signified snatching victory from seemingly certain defeat and placed Arabs opposite Persians and Muslims opposite infidels. Al-Qadisiyya became even more pivotal for Iraq when Iran countered it by reference to Karbala' (the place where Husayn bin 'Ali was murdered). Revolutionary Iran had turned Karbala' into a public symbol of heroism and self-sacrifice.[25] Each country thereby "prevented" the other from using its particular symbol: Iran could not make use of al-Qadisiyya because it had been turned into an Arab badge; similarly, Iraq could not make reference to Karbala' because the Iranian Shi'is had made it their own. Moreover, Karbala' spoke of failure and defeat, while the Ba'th was searching for symbols of victory. Both, however, made use of the figure of 'Ali. The Iraqi evocation of his name is best illustrated by the words of Hamid Sa'id, then director-general of Iraqi radio and television. Speaking at the time of a major Iranian offensive at the end of 1981 that would eventually push Iraqi troops from positions on Iranian territory they had occupied earlier in the war, he said that when 'Ali was retreating, he did not ride on horseback or wear armor on his back. When asked why, he replied: "I am not being pursued like a coward and therefore I need no horse, and I am not fleeing from anybody, therefore I need not cover my back." Sa'id went on to comment: "When there is no alternative except retreat . . . you must retreat forward [*tataraja' ila amam*]."[26] The lesson was that retreat as such was legitimate, though it still had to be wrapped up in linguistic absurdities.

Another term appropriated by the Ba'th for its particular wartime purposes was *jihad* (today commonly translated as "holy war"). It was a word with a long history. Its earliest, pre-Islamic meaning (as rendered in *Lisan al-'Arab*) was of making an effort or investing one's energy, even to the point of exaggeration, whether in speech or action. An associated meaning was that of loyalty in war. Its principal connotation, dating back to the days of Muhammad and still prevalent today, was that of warfare for the sake of Allah against infidels or those who refused to accept Islam. The Qur'an itself uses the word frequently in this sense.

In classical Islam, an elaborate body of rules was laid down about the collective duty of the believers to wage holy war against the domain of unbelief.[27] Though originating in the idea of war by Muslims against infidels, the term was later also applied to warlike action by Muslims against other Muslims of a different persuasion. The Wahhabis of the Arabian peninsula, for instance, not only proclaimed *jihad* against non-Wahhabi Muslims (whom they considered heretics) but also used the word for internecine warfare within the Wahhabi community. To speak of *jihad* was useful in that it gave the conflict in question the appearance of historical depth and helped to obscure its actual causes; it deprived the opposite side of legitimacy by implying that it was heretical or infidel; it augmented the fighters' motivation; and it made it easier to win Muslim states as allies, since joining a *jihad* was acting in the defense of faith.

Quite soon after the beginning of the war against Iran, Saddam Husayn addressed a gathering of soldiers with the words: "This is the day of your *jihad*." *Al-Jumhuriyya* redefined *jihad* as a "liberation war" because it coincided with the "Arab-Muslim concept of liberation war." The paper began another article by stating that "the Arab nation is the nation of *jihad*," explaining that the Arabs had adhered to the idea of *jihad* from the dawn of history and were "justly considered its pioneers." Imam Husayn bin 'Ali had taught Iraqis to "resist despotism and deviation" through *jihad*. In similar fashion, the term *mujahid* (one engaged in *jihad*) entered the Ba'thi idiom. The first to be so named was Saddam Husayn, the honorific bestowed upon him by a progovernment Shi'i cleric, Kashif al-Ghita' in mid-1982.[28] From then on, his name was habitually coupled with that appellation. The commander of an army corps opened a message to Husayn thus: "The *mujahid* for Allah for the sake of the nation, the builder of the new and magnificent Iraq, the deviser of its victories and its protector, the master, president, and field marshal Saddam Husayn, the supreme commander of the armed forces, may God protect him."[29] Placing *mujahid* first in the list of titles attested both to the depth of the Islamization of military discourse and to the scale of priorities set by Husayn. It is significant that *mujahid* now replaced *munadil*, the former title deriving from the original revolutionary ideology of the Ba'th (see Chapter 3).

Next, Husayn began awarding the title of *mujahid* to others—not to military men (as was the practice in Iran) but to men of the Iraqi military industries. They were, he told them, the real *mujahidun* because they saved billions of dollars in arms purchases abroad that would otherwise have to have been "scraped off the skins of the Iraqis and spared from their food." Such work was *jihad* "in its most exalted form." From then onward, the men of the military industries were always called *mujahidun*.[30] Addressing them as *rijal al-iman* (men of faith), Husayn, in words sounding like some kind of premonition, said, "If all the satanic forces on earth come together against us, they will not be able to make Iraq budge from its true positions."[31] The final consecration of the word *jihad*—equating Ba'th with it—came with the publication of the 1990 draft constitution. One of its clauses read: "The men of the Ba'th formed the vanguard of the *jihad* that ended with the victory of the [1968] revolution." At the same time, the Revolutionary Command Council took the additional name of *al-mu'assasa al-qiyadiyya al-mujahida* (The leading *mujahid* institution).[32]

All this was later to appear as no more than a general rehearsal for the great *jihad* of the Gulf War. In the war against Iran, it was a rather laborious procedure to define the enemy as heretic and to consider Iran as part of the *dar al-harb* (the domain of war; the traditional designation of territories outside the Muslim world). In the Gulf War, by contrast, all the elements of *jihad* as the Ba'th understood them were clearly present from the start. The war placed Muslim Iraq opposite the "infidel Christian" world led by the United States. One of Iraq's declared war aims became the liberation of the holy places of Mecca and Medina, which had "fallen into the hands" of Christian infidels with the aid of Muslim "collaborators." These, first and foremost the Saudis, were in reality no more than *munafiqun* (hypocrites). Calling them and other Arabs by that name immediately evoked the original seventh-century *munafiqun*—those inhabitants of Medina who sat on the fence regarding Muhammad's mission. Muhammad had regarded them as unbelievers destined for the fires of hell.[33] The liberation of the Muslim holy places in Palestine was also made a declared aim of the war.

If the war against Iran became a *jihad* only during its course, the Gulf War, by contrast, was declared a *jihad* immediately after the invasion of Kuwait, quite a while before hostilities erupted. This was first done by Husayn, who quoted from verse 74 of sura *al-Tawba*, and next by the National Council (Husayn's parliament), which resolved:

> The National Council has declared a *jihad muqaddas* [sacred holy war] to defend the values and the honor of Arabism and Islam and to rescue venerable Mecca and the tomb of the Arab prophet Muhammad, God's prayer and peace be upon him, from being defiled by the invaders. . . . For *jihad* is our destiny and *jihad* is one of the pillars of our religion. . . . *Jihad* is the duty of all Muslims. The Most High has said: "O Prophet, struggle [*jahid*] with the unbelievers and the hypocrites, and be thou harsh with them, their refuges shall be Gehenna and evil homecoming."[34]

From then on, *jihad* was the key word used by Husayn and the media when referring to the Gulf War. Husayn, for instance, proclaimed: "There is no slogan other than victory. *Jihad, jihad* for the liberation of *al-haramayn al-sharifayn* [the two sanctuaries; i.e., Mecca and Medina]!" To strengthen the fainthearted and those who thought the battle lost, he quoted verse 66 of sura *al-Anfal*: "O Prophet, urge the believers to fight. If there be 20 of you, patient men [*sabirun*], they will overcome 200; if there be 100 of you, they will overcome 1,000 unbelievers."[35] Al-Qadisiyya compared Muhammad's *jihad*, undertaken to remove the barriers obstructing "the spread of Islam," with Husayn's and concluded that the latter was the direct continuation of the former. Even *al-Thawra*, the official organ of the party and as such the guardian of its original ideology, was not behind in adopting Islamic terminology. Heading an article with the words *hayya ʿala al-jihad* (hurry to perform *jihad*) it asserted that the war was being fought so that "religion shall be God's alone"; on the day of "the great battle," the fighters would raise the cry of *Allah akbar*.[36]

The warlike terminology was then gradually transferred to other areas. Efforts to raise agricultural production in response to the embargo came to be called *al-jihad al-ziraʿi* (the agricultural *jihad*); the suppression of the Kurdish and Shiʿi *intifada* after the Gulf War was proclaimed a *jihad*. The high point came with the 1991 party congress, which was named *muʾtamar al-jihad wa-l-binaʾ* (the congress of *jihad* and construction). The congress for its part crowned the entire Iraqi people with the title of *mujahid*. Did this mean that the word had reverted to its original meaning of effort and of investing energy, this time in the reconstruction of Iraq? Or was it meant to presage the renewal of war at some uncertain future date? Or perhaps the reference was to the perseverance and endurance of "the 100" facing "the 1,000"?

The first signs of the Islamization of public discourse came appropriately in military communiqués during the war against Iran. The very first wartime communiqué by the armed forces opened with the *basmala*. This then became the constant practice. Announcements by the Revolutionary Command Council, which had never done so in the past, now also used the *basmala* fairly frequently.[37] After the loss to Iran of the island of al-Faw in 1986, references to Allah and the use of other religious elements in speech increased. Such references reached a peak during the Iraqi spring and summer offensives of 1988, as reflected in the names of the army corps. The Special First Corps (the last to be formed, after seven others) was named Quwwat Allah Akbar (the forces of God the Most Great).[38] It had been assembled rather hastily after the fall of al-Faw. It was "special" in that it was manned largely by officers and men who had previously retired. It never played much of a role in the actual fighting, and its formation was mainly of symbolic value, as a challenge to Iran.

After 1988, the names of units and weapons alluded to Iraq's military recovery and the transition from the defensive to the offensive. The missiles used against Iranian cities (a turning point in the conduct of the war) were named al-Husayn and al-ʿAbbas. (The latter was Imam Husayn's stepbrother.) Saddam Husayn, who conducted the naming ceremony himself, meant to signal to the Iranians that, after they had used names symbolic of the Shiʿa throughout the war, it was now his turn to do likewise.[39]

"Husayn" was used with a twofold association: the Imam Husayn, the victim of Karbala' and role model of the Shi'is, and Saddam Husayn. A Shi'i expatriate noted that this was not the first time that an Iraqi Sunni regime had cynically attached Shi'i symbols to weapons of destruction directed against Shi'is. Thus, the first Iraqi brigade, which was named Musa al-Kazim (after the seventh Shi'i imam), was employed in suppressing the Shi'i population of Iraq.[40]

In 1989, when Iraq announced that it had built missiles capable of lifting satellites into orbit, the missile was named al-'Abid (Worshiper of God). Husayn was reported to have chosen the name "to express to the creator, be he praised and exalted, his gratitude and worship for the success and achievement he has, by his grace, granted to Iraq and the Arab nation." *Al-Qadisiyya* headlined an article about the missile: "Al-'Abid Does the Impossible." "Arab superiority," it went on to say, would soon "bury the U.S.-Zionist foolishness of strength." Arab honor would now emerge cleansed from the period of weakness into which it had sunk. Al-'Abid would set the "Arab-foreign" or the "Arab-Zionist balance" right. From now on, "space will speak Arabic." Other headlines proclaimed: "Through al-'Abid, the Iraqis Have Placed Themselves on the Moon."[41]

Military operations and offensives were also given Islamic titles. Thus, a series of offensives against the Kurds in 1988 were code-named *al-Anfal*.[42] The literal meaning of *anfal* was "booty." In the Qur'an, sura *al-Anfal* deals with the battle of Badr.[43] S. D. Goitein has called the battle, fought on 17 Ramadan AH 2 (16 March 624), "one of the most decisive battles in world history": it led to the establishment of the "Muslim theocracy," and Muhammad's success at the head of his men made him the "unquestioned authority" in Islam then and since. Muhammad and his 300 Muslim fighters faced 900 men from Mecca, and at one point the Muslims had grave doubts about the outcome. However, the battle ended with a resounding victory for the Muslims, who killed many of the Meccans when they attempted to flee and took much booty.[44]

In his book *Kayf al-sabil ila Allah*, Talfah devotes a whole chapter to the battle of Badr, calling it "the first battle in which faith fought unbelief and atheism." With an eye to the present, he observes that the Muslims won because they loved their leader; they overcame a superior force through the strength of their faith and because they followed the precept, "Seek death so that you may live." Talfah wrote that angels were fighting at the side of the Muslims at Badr, adducing as proof verses 9 and 10 of sura *al-Anfal*: "I shall reinforce you with 1,000 angels riding behind you. . . . Help comes only from God." He added that in those days "faith divided father from son, brother, from brother and husband from wife," proving that faith was above all else.[45]

The progovernment Kurdish newspaper *al-'Iraq* reported that Saddam Husayn had personally planned the *anfal* campaigns against the Kurds.[46] In doing so, he clearly had Badr in mind. The units carrying out the campaigns were called *quwwat Badr* (the Badr forces), and the offensive began on the anniversary of the battle of Badr (16 March 1988). But Husayn added his own macabre touch to the old model. The campaign started with a poison-gas attack against the Kurdish village Halabja, killing about 5,000 of its inhabitants.[47] The attacks against the Kurds were described as decisive, and inasmuch as they cleared the way for the subsequent series of successful offensives against Iran that led to the cease-fire of August 1988, such a claim is indeed justified. Husayn may also have wished to demonstrate that the end sanctifies the means, as verse 60 of sura *al-Anfal* reads: "And if thou fearest treachery any way at the hands of a people, dissolve it with them equally; surely God loves not the treacherous."

In public, the campaign was lauded, even by some Kurds (who undoubtedly hoped thereby to save their skins). The following verses, entitled "Muhammad rasul Allah" (Muhammad the messenger of God), illustrate the point:

> The curse of history on the heads of the evil
> May stones thunder over them
> From the most select of the prophets
> The fighters hurried to and fro . . .
> Hope sprang up
> and shouted from the top of the mountain
> together with [all] Iraq
> the words of "sura *al-Anfal.*"[48]

Al-ʿIraq commented that after the conclusion of the *anfal* campaigns, the Kurdish "terrorists" (i.e., the antigovernment rebels) were now "condemned to political death," just as the fighting had "condemned them to military death throughout the length of Iraqi Kurdistan."[49]

Beginning with *anfal*, all subsequent operations were given code names with Islamic connotations. The operation that ended with the reconquest of al-Faw, for instance, was called *Ramadan mubarak* (the blessed [month of] Ramadan).[50] Husayn appears to have launched it in Ramadan because the conquest of Mecca by Muhammad in 630 had taken place in that month (in disregard of the treaty of Hudaybiyya of 628). Immediately after the victory at al-Faw, Husayn underlined its religious significance by going to Mecca and Medina for the ʿumra—the minor pilgrimage performed at any time between *hajj* seasons.[51] Further campaigns, undertaken to clear the mountainous areas of Kurdistan, were code-named *Muhammad rasul Allah* and *sayf Allah* (the sword of God). Four operations against the Iranians for the reconquest of Iraqi territories held by them were called *tawakkalna ʿala Allah* (our trust is in God), words taken from verse 89 of sura *al-Aʿraf*. A cartoon showed an Iraqi holding high a large rock, about to bring it down on a helpless Iranian stretched out before him. The caption read *tawakkalna ʿala Allah*. Saddam Husayn's family was now called *al-ʿaʾila al-mutawakkila ʿala Allah* (the family who trusts in God).[52]

Saddam Husayn spoke frequently about trust in God, mostly in addresses to military men but also in his appeals to the public at large. Just before the beginning of the Kuwait crisis, he said: "I am sure the Arabs will not need guns to liberate Palestine, because if they trust in God that will suffice."[53] A good illustration of the change from the traditional Ba'th idiom to the Islamic language of the period of the two wars is a 1990 announcement by the Revolutionary Command Council concerning the dismissal of the defense minister, 'Abd al-Jabbar Shanshal. It, too, opened with the *basmala* and then quoted verse 61 of sura *al-Anfal*: "And if they incline to peace, do thou incline to it; and put thy trust in God."[54] A decade earlier, let alone in the early years of the Ba'th regime, such a style in an announcement from the highest body of the state would have been unthinkable.

During the war against Iran and even more so during the Gulf War, the words *Allah akbar* (God is most great) came to be used with great frequency. The phrase (the use of which is called *takbir*) does not occur in the Qur'an; instead, we find, for instance, *rabbuka fakabbir* (Thy Lord magnify) (sura *al-Muddathir*, v. 3).[55] The cry *Allah akbar*—the shortest way to enunciate God's greatness—became central to Muslim life and is used on numerous occasions to give thanks to God or to ask for his succor. Muhammad himself used the words in speaking of people who had died during the *hajj*. They are repeated four times at the beginning of the *adhan*, the call to prayer, and are said five times during each prayer.[56]

Allah akbar turned into a slogan used constantly in military announcements and in the media. Thus, a military communiqué said, "*Allah akbar* is with the great Iraqi people, *Allah akbar* is with the Arab nation, the nation glorying in its prophets and messengers. *Allah akbar* is against the enemies of Iraq and against the enemies of the Arab nation."[57] In one of its announcements, the Revolutionary Command Council said, "Iraq has risen in the name of God and drawn its sword together with those who believe in religion. . . . Nothing is great except justice and our God. . . . *Allah akbar*, and contempt upon the contemptible."[58] A short while before the beginning of the Gulf War, *al-Qadisiyya* quoted Husayn as saying that the battle would be fought "under the flag of *Allah akbar*." The Islamization process peaked on the eve of the Gulf War when Husayn, at a meeting of the army high command, ordered the words *Allah akbar* to be inscribed on the flag of Iraq. The minister of information, Latif Nusayyif al-Jasim, explained that when "his Excellency [Husayn] grasped the flag of Iraq, his eyes were sparkling . . . and he showed with his noble hand that the words *Allah akbar* were to be embroidered on the flag of Iraq." *Al-Qadisiyya* commented that the country had nothing but Allah and "his gift, Saddam Husayn."[59] In every subsequent edition, the paper then showed the new flag at its masthead. By contrast, the party newspaper *al-Thawra* continued to appear with the old Ba'th slogan, "Unity, freedom, socialism," as if to demonstrate the split mind of the regime.

14

From Islamic Rhetoric to a Vision of Apocalypse

"A Mission to the Nation and to Mankind"

The year 1989 witnessed three events that greatly changed Saddam Husayn's concepts of religion and its role in impending developments: the death of Khomeini on 3 June; the death of Michel 'Aflaq on 23 June; and, over the year, the collapse of the Eastern European regimes. Seemingly unrelated, all three signaled to Husayn the collapse of an ideology. The demise of Khomeini implied the demise of Khomeinism, which had so gravely threatened Iraq. To Husayn, it seemed a sign from on high that the scales in the long struggle were being tipped in his favor. 'Aflaq's death appeared to signal the end of the secular Ba'thi ideology as he had originally shaped it. This was underlined by the Ba'th when it announced that (at an unspecified time) 'Aflaq had converted to Islam. (He had been born a Greek Orthodox Christian.) There is no way of confirming or denying his conversion, but it appears odd that he did not make it known in his lifetime. Party circles explained that this had not been done in order to not "attribute political significance" to the matter.[1] Whatever the truth, the posthumous disclosure was a resounding admission of the party's apologetic stance with regard to Islam and of its desire to rid itself of the burden of its secularist (not to say atheist) antecedents. It was much like proclaiming that the Ba'th had joined the Islamic mainstream. Developments in Eastern Europe likewise conveyed the message of an ideology having reached the end of its tether. Husayn had loathed communism but also pondered the political void it had left behind. If one adds Husayn's conviction that the West was declining, it is possible to understand his sentiment that changes of an almost apocalyptic magnitude were at hand and that he himself, Iraq, the Arabs, and Islam were now called upon to assume worldwide roles.

Already in August 1989, Husayn spoke of Iraq's victory over Iran in terms of a primordial experience. He linked it with the *isra'* and *mi'raj*—Muhammad's night journey to the Temple Mount in Jerusalem and his ascent to heaven: "This day, a year ago, the fire of *isra'* and *mi'raj* was lit and a fine odor was spreading—the scent of the mission of glorious Iraq."[2] A much clearer statement came in October of that year, in Husayn's speech on the prophet's birthday. At its core was the idea that God had given the Arabs a new and universal mission, inspired by and continuing that of Muhammad. Husayn spoke of Muhammad's birth and the prophetic mission given him forty years later at almost the same time that the Persian kingdom of Khusraw was on the point of collapse. He went on to say that Muhammad's being the last of the prophets did not mean that God had let the Arab mission to lead mankind lapse. On the contrary, God had chosen "the angel of leadership" so that he would "always dwell among the Arabs." The Arabs themselves must not forget the mission imposed upon them, "for what is required of us is to be inspired by the heavenly mission which the true angel Gabriel enjoined upon Muhammad."

God had once again given the Arabs the task of redeeming mankind and leading it out of the grave crisis into which it had slipped. It was, he went on, a crisis that had befallen both the capitalist West and the communist East. Alluding to Khomeini's Iran, he said that a catastrophe was about to strike mankind unless "the Arabs showed [the world] the right way," just as God had shown the way to wipe the kingdom of Khusraw from the face of the earth. Trying to reconcile the traditional view that there could be no prophet after Muhammad, he said that the rebirth of the nation did not signify a direct mission (*risala*, the qur'anic term for Muhammad as God's messenger) but rather "an inspiration by the contents" of the original mission "to the nation and to mankind." Obviously, Husayn was casting himself in the role of some kind of modern prophet combining the qualities of spiritual, political, and military leadership and possessed of a universal mission, like Muhammad.

As if Husayn's own words had not sufficed, his biographer, Fu'ad Matar, commented on them in an article attached to that of Husyan's. As someone who had followed Husayn's development closely, he wrote, he understood that Husayn's words were not a simple comparison between two historical periods but rather a statement "that the ground is being prepared for something novel." They were not just a further step in the development of Husayn's thinking on religion but a new doctrine (*nazariyya*) trying to "bring together religion and this world [*al-din wa-l-dunya*]" and to supply a novel alternative both to the trend toward religious extremism among Arabs and to the ideologies now visibly collapsing all over the world. He added that some people were likely to conclude that Husayn was comparing himself to Muhammad. After all, he contended, both had faced the Persians when they reached the age of forty, and both had defeated them. (This was a rather forced comparison: Muhammad at forty had received his first revelation; Husayn at forty had entered into his confrontation with Khomeini.) Matar concluded by saying that Husayn was unlikely to wait until the prophet's next birthday to spell out many things that he had now left unsaid.[3]

Indeed, about half a year later, in February 1990, Husayn added a further layer to what he had said in 1989. He came out against "the only great power in the world," the United States, demanding that it "remove" itself from the Middle East. It seems hard to understand Husayn's subsequent provocation of the United States over Kuwait and his war against the twenty-eight-member coalition without considering the eschatological convictions that had gradually crept into his worldview. With the vast propaganda machine of the Ba'th at his disposal, he found it comparatively easy to give wide currency to the new religious, and eventually eschatological, idiom. The magnitude of the transformation of his attitude toward Islam comes out starkly in his statement on the eve of the invasion of Kuwait: "If there is a clash between the nationalist [*qawmi*] concept and the exalted principles of Islam, then the nationalist concept must be changed or eliminated for the greater good of the exalted law. This is how we understand the link between Arabism and Islam. In short, we here are the party of God, *hizb Allah*, and the party of God is the greatest and strongest of all parties."[4]

If we follow the twists and turns of Husayn's thinking, we can discern the prolonged process, during and after the long struggle against Khomeini, of his adoption (consciously or otherwise) of his adversaries' tenets. The protracted hostilities, the need to mitigate the grave domestic consequences of the war, and the sense of being trapped that had taken hold of the Iraqi public at large required recourse to religion and to a vision of a better future. In such a situation, a political discourse heavily laden with Islamic terms or words evoking Islamic association became a propaganda instrument of the first order. As it took a further turn, sliding over into apocalyptic contents, it was bound to carry with it not only the Iraqis but also the Arab and the Muslim world as a whole, or so Husayn seems to have expected.

The War of the Elephant

> Then Abraha built the cathedral in San'a' such a church as could not be seen elsewhere in any part of the world at that time. He wrote to the Negus saying: "I have built a church for you, O king, such as has not been built for any king before you. I shall not rest until I diverted the Arabs' pilgrim to it." . . . In the morning Abraha prepared to enter the town and made his

elephant ready for battle and drew up his troops. His intention was to destroy the temple and then return to the Yaman. . . . They made the elephant (his name was Mahmud) face Mecca. . . . Then God sent upon them birds from the sea like swallows and starlings; each bird carried three stones, like peas and lentils, one in its beak and two between its claws. Everyone who was hit died, but not all were hit. . . . As they withdrew they were continually falling by the wayside dying miserably by every waterhole. Abraha was smitten in his body, and as they took him away his fingers fell off one by one. Where the fingers had been, there arose an evil sore exuding pus and blood, so that when they brought him to San'a' he was like a young fledgling.

    —Ibn Hisham, *Sirat Muhammad*, quoted in A. Guillaume, *The Life of Muhammad: A Translation of Ishaq's Sirat Rasul Allah*

In *Sirat Muhammad,* Ibn Hisham speaks of occurrences traditionally regarded as the starting point of a momentous chain of events for Arabs and Muslims, culminating in the advent of Islam. They are supposed to have taken place in 570, later called "the year of the elephant." The same year was then made to coincide with the year of Muhammad's birth. The historical background is that of a mighty power struggle between the two great empires of the time: Byzantium and Persia. Byzantium was trying to use the Arabian peninsula as a jumping-off ground to strike at Persia and aided its ally Christian Abyssinia in conquering Yemen in 525. Around 550, Abraha, the Abyssinian ruler of Yemen, tried unsuccessfully to capture Mecca. Abyssinian rule in Yemen lasted for some fifty years, until the Persians seized the area in 575. Their rule in turn was short-lived, lasting until the advent of Islam.[5] The historical core of these events was later covered over by legendary accretion, such as considering the "year of the elephant" the year of the prophet's birth, or the (most probably inaccurate) account of war elephants having taken part in the attack on Mecca. The assault on the city later assumed apocalyptic proportions. It is linked with the name of Abu Righal from Ta'if, who showed Abraha the desert trails to Mecca and has remained the embodiment of the traitor and informer ever since. (It is customary to stone his grave, located at Al-Mughammas near Mecca.)[6]

What has all this to do with Saddam Husayn? Driven by wartime exigencies, urged by his contemplations on history and the possibility of reliving it, and prompted by the conceptual changes in his outlook that we have traced above, he seems to have seen in these events and the myths surrounding them a foreboding of the future. Those who wished to see them could indeed find certain parallels. Iran was the modern Persia; the United States was cast in the role of a new Christian Byzantium; Israel was the "reincarnation" of old Abyssinia, the local power acting in the interest of one of the great powers. Saudi Arabia and the other Arab countries cooperating with the United States were the modern Abu Righals leading the infidels to Mecca. Husayn himself, as well as the Iraqi media, reinforced public awareness of such parallels by using an abundance of terms and expressions evoking the words of sura *al-Fil.*

The short sura itself is obscure. Abraha and Abu Righal are not named in it; they are alluded to by the general expression *ashab al-fil*, or the owners of the elephant whose designs are foiled by Allah. The elephant itself—all the more frightening for not then being known to the Arabs— became the symbol of a strong and threatening outside force. The legend- ary birds, the *ababil* (plural of *ibbala*, meaning a bunch of twigs, indica- tive of the closeness of the birds in flight), turned into symbols of heavenly intervention. The stones they drop to kill the elephant belong in the same symbolic context as the throwing of seven stones at Mina during the pil- grimage to Mecca or the stoning of those guilty of certain offenses. (They are also connected symbolically with the use of stones as weapons during the *intifada* of the Palestinians.) The stones of the *ababil* were made from a material called *sijjil*, literally some kind of dried mud, but understood to mean stones burned in hell and bearing the names of the transgressors.[7] They came to connote both a challenge and a punishment from God. (Sura *Hud* speaks of the stones Allah dropped on Lot's wife to punish her.)[8]

The Ba'th started to make use of the myth with the outbreak of the war against Iran, though it was only during the Gulf War that the theme was developed fully. The first parallels drawn in the 1980s concerned Syrian president Hafiz al-Asad and Libyan leader Mu'ammar al-Qadhdhafi, who sided with Iran during the war. Both were compared with Abu Righal. To give just one example, in a vehement attack on both, *al-'Iraq* wrote that they were "doubtlessly the descendants of that fool who led Abraha and the elephants toward . . . Mecca, but God turned them back by send- ing against them the *ababil* with stones of *sijjil*." Like Abu Righal, all that would remain of Qadhdhafi and Asad would be their names as traitors.[9] Some writers asserted that comparing these modern Arab leaders with Abu Righal meant doing an injustice to the latter. They far outdid "poor Abu Righal." Asad, for instance, was acting as a guide not only to the Zionists but also to Khomeini. Abu Righal must feel sorry in his grave for not having reached the same depth of treason.[10]

Motifs taken from sura *al-Fil* were often used in the wartime propaganda against Iran. For instance, when in August 1985 Iraqi aircraft bombed the Iranian oil terminal on the island of Kharj, a military communiqué declared: "On this blessed day, the aerial hawks burst forth . . . issuing from their bases and trusting in Allah, be he exalted. God having willed it so, they carried the *sijjil* stones and turned against the arteries of evil and the des- pots' outlet for their oil. . . . Oh proud Iraqis! The island of Kharj was de- stroyed and was turned into a field of thistles being burnt by the *ababil* birds."[11] A little later, Salim al-'Azzawi published a poetic piece in which the motif of the *sijjil* stones occurred over and over again.[12] Khomeini him- self came to be called "Abraha" by the Iraqi media. The "new Abraha," *al- Jumhuriyya* wrote, was trying to seize Mecca just as Abraha had done, and he and the Iranians were therefore due for heavy punishment.[13]

The Palestinian *intifada*, beginning in December 1987, served as a turn- ing point for further stepping up the use of imagery connected with the elephant and the *ababil*. This related in particular to the use of stones by Palestinians in their encounters with Israeli soldiers. The clashes were reported enthusiastically in Iraq, and the legend of the *ababil* was used to depict Iraqis and Palestinians as being engaged in the same struggle to fight off evil. This was brought out in a poem by Adib Nasr entitled "I Shall Throw Stones in Your Name, Oh Saddam":

> The missile bursts forth,
> The missile bursts forth,
> And I shall throw stones in the name of Allah,
> And I shall throw stones in the name of Jerusalem [al-Quds, the holy],
> And I shall throw stones in your name, Oh Saddam.
> I am faith,
> I am flint,
> I am stones from the walls of Jerusalem
> [Thrown] at Tehran.

A newspaper article entitled "'Am al-hijara matar min sijjil" (The year of the stones is a rain of *sijjil*) also made the point that there was a profound symbolic connection between the *intifada* and the Iraqi-Iranian war. "The stones fighting against the invader [of Palestine] . . . draw their strength from the iron of the Iraqi weapons that did not grow cool for eight years, until the great victory."[14]

If 1988 was the "year of stones," 1989 witnessed the preparations for the "year of the elephant." A long poem so called contained all the principal motifs linking the ancient themes with the present in an apocalyptic vision encompassing both. It was symptomatic of this outlook:

> The sun will turn dark seven times
> And the earth will burst into flames seven times
> And they will mingle
> And burn
> And go out again,
> And smoke will spread
> And the year of the elephant will begin.
> The way [leading] to it will begin here,
> In Karbala'.
> Who saw Abraha?
> He was not just an army and an elephant
> He was the symbol of an evil era
> . . . .
> That evil time
> That time which devours its prophets
> Was casting about in despair for a message
> Adorned by stones
> The hands of the children are *ababil*
> Their stones are the fire of *sijjil*
> To turn back the elephant
> While Abu Righal
> Leads Abraha's men.[15]

The launching of the al-ʿAbid missile at about the same time gave further cause to develop such a vision. *Al-Qadisiyya* wrote that Iraq was making a gift of the al-ʿAbid to the Palestinians on the second birthday of the *intifada*; it would help them to keep the flame burning. The next missile models were called *sijjil* and *ababil*. Not much later, the story of the Iraqi supergun made headlines. It was being built for Iraq by Gerald Bull, a Canadian ballistics expert, and was expected to enable Iraq to shell targets in Israel. Several of its parts were seized by British customs officials in the spring of 1990. Iraq never acknowledged the existence of such a gun, and only veiled references were made to it. Its huge size led Western media to call it "the judgment-day gun," and this may possibly have been its Iraqi code name, since one Iraqi newspaper, while scornfully denying its very existence, called it *midfaʿ yawm al-qiyama* (the gun of the day of the resurrection of the dead).[16] *Yawm al-din* (the last judgment) and *yawm al-qiyama* are almost synonymous. The latter stresses the apocalyptic aspect: the earth will lose its accustomed shape, the heavens will split open, the sun will be extinguished, the stars will fall down, and the dead will arise. God will reward the just and punish the wicked. If the gun was indeed so called, its appellation was another link in the chain of eschatological myths.

The intense economic, military, and political pressures brought to bear on Iraq after the invasion of Kuwait reinforced the apocalyptic vision. Husayn himself added to it. In an address to all Arab and Muslim countries, he deplored the conduct of King Fahd of Saudi Arabia and President Mubarak of Egypt, likening them to Abu Righal against whom Allah had sent the *ababil* with their *hijara min sijjil*. But their treachery in guiding the infidels to Mecca was of such dimensions that Abu Righal's paled beside it. All Arabs and Muslims must therefore unite in a *jihad* against them.[17] If an appeal to Muslims couched in such terms might be calculated to incite their imagination and elicit their sympathy, a similarly worded appeal to George Bush and Mikhail Gorbachev was unlikely to have such an effect. Nevertheless, in identical messages sent to both in September 1990, Husayn wrote: "More than 1,400 years ago, enticed by the devil and intoxicated by his power to expand and dominate, Abraha the Abyssinian had sought to occupy the Kaʿba whose land is now occupied by U.S. forces. . . . Angered by this attempt, God trounced on him, and so Abraha returned with a bowed head and lowered banners." Allah the Eternal would now strike a similar blow at those acting against the Kaʿba and the tomb of the prophet. "When the battle has taken place, then the Iraqi people, whom God has chosen to be in the forefront will triumph . . . and all the invaders will be defeated. The aggressors' banner will be torn apart. . . . The billion Muslims will be the [strategic] depth of the faithful masses."[18]

The press then elaborated on these themes. *Al-Jumhuriyya* wrote that the United States must understand that "just as the knight of the believers, Saddam Husayn, has predicted," Washington will emerge enfeebled from the confrontation and lose its standing. The paper took up the theme of sura *al-Zalzala* (the earthquake preceding the resurrection of the dead), writing that "all will shake once the fury of this earth breaks forth, and nothing will remain . . . and the future will open [and bring] surprises that the enemies will have no strength to withstand." Some writers referred to the use in America of the elephant as the symbol of the Republican Party, hinting that Bush's elephant would share the same fate as Abraha. That made Bush "the owner of the elephant," just as sura *al-Fil* had it. "The party of the elephant . . . and Bush, the new Abraha, have seized Najd and Hijaz"; thus history was returning. But Bush and his party must re-member what happened to Abraha, for "the same fate" was in store for them. *Al-Thawra* quoted the sura in its entirety and then went on to say, "God defeated the owners of the elephant and their commander, Abraha the Abyssinian . . . and he will defeat the American owners of elephants and their commander Bush . . . for the sanctuaries of the Muslims . . . are protected by God, and the will of one billion Muslims is defending them." Abu Righal had been no king, but Fahd was; having led the Americans to the Kaʿba, he would therefore be punished more severely than "little Abu Righal." The curses that would be heaped on Fahd in this world and the next would be even worse than those that had pursued Abu Righal over fourteen centuries.[19]

In October 1990, wishing to give some substance to such rhetoric, Husayn called one of the Iraqi missiles *al-hijara al-sarukh* (approxi-mately, the stone that is a missile). Like some other favorite expressions of his, this combination of words was not strictly grammatical. But it served to link the missile both with the war of the elephant and the Pal-estinian *intifada*. Announcing the choice of the name, he once again reminded his listeners of the story of the elephant and the stones, add-ing that now the stones could do their work at a distance of hundreds of kilometers and were "capable of reaching the targets of evil on the day of reckoning. How numerous are the stones on the soil of Iraq! I have cried, and am crying now *Allah akbar*, these are the *sijjil* stones, God willing." The weapons of the Zionists and the Americans would miracu-lously be rendered impotent, for "we shall throw sand in their eyes and they will be blinded," thus turning them into "harmless elephants." Husayn found confirmation for his view in sura *al-Isra'*, verse 17: "And when We desire to destroy a city, We command its men who live at ease, and they commit ungodliness therein, then the Word is realized against it, and We destroy it utterly."[20]

Only two days later, *al-Qadisiyya* described the current situation in terms of a vast audiovisual spectacle that it called *hadarat al-hijara* (the culture of the stones). It was unfolding in three places at once: ancient Mesopotamia, modern Iraq, and Palestine. Mesopotamia was represented by Gilgamesh and Nebuchadnezzar, Iraq by Husayn, and Palestine by "the children of the stones." Voices accompanied the images like a refrain and spoke in praise of stones. "We built our first home and our culture with stones." Palestinian children, veiled in an Iraqi *kufiyya* (derived from the name of the Iraqi town of Kufa), were seen throwing stones. Another picture showed Husayn "riding a white horse, wearing a *kufiyya* and passing like lightning to al-Quds [the Holy; i.e., Jerusalem]." There, the Palestinian children received him with jasmine flowers and asked him about Gilgamesh, Nebuchadnezzar, and Saladin, who all came from Mesopotamia, "and Husayn opens his generous hands and awards the children a missile called *hijara*." The concluding comment said that Palestinian poets had spoken of "atomic stones," and indeed Baghdad had now made them so. In this way, Husayn had fulfilled the ancient prophecies, had made the Arab sword mighty and victorious, and had gained fame for himself from Morocco to Palestine.[21]

Naming the new missile *hijara* created a safety valve to let off bottled-up fears and forebodings. *Al-Qadisiyya*, for instance, ran a picture showing a giant Iraqi soldier holding something over his head that resembled both a missile and a legendary bird. It was marked *al-hijara al-sarukh*. The Iraqi soldier is facing an Israeli soldier (identified by a Star of David) who is wedged between the Iraqi missile in front of him and the knife of a Palestinian behind him. A press headline proclaimed: "The *Hijara* Missile is the Message of the Mother of Battles" (i.e., of the Gulf War). The ensuing article described the capabilities of the missile and added that its first act had been to "arouse" the Palestinian stones and "give them [added] strength and faith." Its final act would be to "liquidate every form of aggression and occupation, and every aggressive or occupying entity, on Arab soil." Another newspaper printed a poem headed: "Revenge, Revenge upon the Dwarfs of Zion." (Thirty-nine of these or similar missiles were indeed fired on Israeli targets during the Gulf War hostilities.) In an allusion to the writing on the wall in the biblical Book of Daniel, the author said: "It is time that I dip my finger into your blood and write upon your imaginary wall your last letters. . . . The day has come for the stones to speak."[22]

As tension mounted and no way out was to be seen, the myth of the elephant was stressed all the more forcefully. A month before the beginning of the Gulf War, Husayn addressed a meeting of Muslim leaders he had convened from throughout the Muslim world. Like a compulsive act of magic, he repeated to them once again the story of the elephant, imploring Allah's help.[23] Later, when the war was at its peak and after Iraq had already suffered heavily at the hands of the coalition, he told a gathering of soldiers (in words that sounded as if he was trying to convince himself that a miracle was imminent) that 1,400 years after the advent of Islam, Iraqi fighters had proved the existence of the one God. They had shown that the faith and the faithful were strong and that "when God permits, the oppressed can score victory over tyranny," just as he had "enabled the Ka'ba to triumph over the elephant, which they [the enemies] brought to sabotage God's house, but turned round and retreated upon

God's orders."[24] Unlike Husayn himself, the media toned down their references to the myth during the actual fighting in the Gulf War, as if disappointment and frustration had given them back some sense of reality. Only the firing of missiles against targets in Israel elicited a note of satisfaction. *Al-Thawra* gave an article the headline: "The *Ababil* Grind Down Tel Aviv." It read in part: "Israel, the spoiled, wayward child of the United States, . . . Israel that created a monstrous existence for itself, . . . Israel [now] suffers the blows of Iraq and Iraq is teaching it a lesson and is threatening to destroy half of it, if it does not cease to harm the Arabs. . . . Only during the era of Husayn did 'Israel' come to understand its real size. . . . It is indeed a great victory that Tel Aviv is being pounded by Husayn's missiles."[25]

During the last days of the war, Iraq fired some *hijara* missiles in the general direction of the Israeli atomic reactor near the town of Dimona. The commander of the missile force reported the firing to Husayn in a telegram that, among other things, quoted verse 13 of sura *al-Hashr*, dealing with the subjection of the Jews by Muhammad. He went on to say that his heroic men had hit "cursed Dimona" with long-range missiles designed by brilliant Iraqi brains "to make the Zionists scatter like chaff," thus fulfilling their oath to help the young Palestinian stone throwers. He concluded by quoting verse 8 of sura *al-Jum'a*: "Surely death, from which you flee, shall encounter you; then you shall be returned to the Knower of the Unseen and the Visible, and He will tell you that you have been doing."[26] Another detail testifying to a strange intermingling of myth and reality was the report that Iraqi missile engineers had filled the warhead of the missiles directed at Dimona with cement. This was unlikely to improve their aim, but at this late hour in the war, when the battle was known to be lost, it may have been more important to perform the symbolic act of making the *hijara* (stone) missile like a stone than to score a hit.

This escape into a world of the mythological and supernatural was obviously no more than just one dimension of Iraq's extremely complex and multifaceted reality. But even though it only represented a single strand in a manifold texture, it still pointed to a layer of strongly felt, deep-seated historical contents in the depths of the collective memory—a layer most likely to surface in times of crises and of clashes with a strange and foreign culture. Resorting to such religious, even messianic, messages was one aspect of the search for means to measure up to harsh and adverse conditions. Encouragement came from an old story—part history, part legend—about a sequence of events relevant to the present because it was perceived as a timeless paradigm of a crucial juncture, a sequence determining the shape of the future for a very long time to come.

If difficult conditions nurtured mythology, in a kind of mutual resonance, mythology influenced the country's actual conduct. Iraq would and could not have challenged the powerful coalition ranged against it if the mood of its population had not been sustained by apocalyptic images. Yet we must not forget for a moment that part of this imagery had been created in a cold, calculated, and purposeful manner by a manipulative regime. When the myth was shattered, Husayn was still there, firm and down-to-earth, to collect the pieces and start out again in an even more hostile, arduous environment.

Conclusion
The Rape of Language

*T*wo things stand out in our discussion of the political discourse of the Iraqi Baʿth: the constant presence of the past—that is, the massive intrusion of historical contents, themes, and parallels into almost every aspect of the discourse on current events—and the major shift, over some two decades, from a secular, leftist, and socialist idiom to a language dominated by Islamic terms and religious motifs. These two characteristics impart to the party's language its particular flavor. They make it, at one and the same time, a repository of archaeological relics and a living thing: developing, changing, shedding one shape and slipping into another.

What strikes the researcher right from the beginning is the predominant influence of Saddam Husayn's personal idiom on Arabic usage in Iraq. His utterances are presented directly through every avenue of public expression and indirectly through their echoes in the words of politicians, intellectuals, and newspeople. Husayn's manner of putting things and the notions underlying his choice of words seem likely to have left a profound mark on Iraqi society, which has been exposed to them so intensely and for such a long period of time. Whether propelling the public in the direction of violence or brinkmanship or—at times—in the direction of flexibility, his words have permeated society as a whole. In that respect, Husayn differs greatly from earlier rulers of modern Iraq whose tenure left no more than a feeble residue.

To say so is to point to the powerful effect of Iraq's subjection to a small group of Baʿth ideologues for such a long time. Even though the Baʿthi

203

discourse changed over time, it was still able at every particular juncture to impose a more strictly monolithic character on the public idiom than Iraq had ever known before. No spontaneous expression of ideas was possible, and inasmuch as the discourse changed, it did so only after having passed through the fine filters of the party.

This leads to the most difficult question arising out of this study: How do political speech and political action interrelate? We cannot make an apodictic judgment, but we can point to several possible indications of how such an interrelationship can be understood. They derive from the threefold role of political language: to reflect a political culture; to serve as an instrument of political action; and to be a catalyst of political change. On the role of language subsumed under the first aspect, there will be a ready consensus. We have given many illustrations of this facet, such as with regard to the various terms connoting "honor" or the notion of *shahada*. If the Ba'th regime has exploited such notions for its own purposes, it has done so in the full knowledge that they were firmly rooted in the consciousness of society and capable of arousing strong emotions. Not all value concepts of this sort were of ancient provenance: the use of *thawra*, for instance, had shed its originally negative connotation and acquired its positive one only during the course of the twentieth century.

In its alternating trends, Ba'thi language reflected changes not only in Iraqi perceptions and values but also in regional and global tendencies. The shift to Islamic parlance was clearly accelerated by the Iranian revolution and by the spread of Islamic fundamentalism throughout the region, as well as by the collapse of the communist regimes in Eastern Europe. The flooding of the language with terms indicative of a return to the Islamic roots reflected both the ideological disorientation of society and the resolve of the regime to assert itself in the face of the fundamentalist sentiments emerging in Iraq and the region as a whole.[1]

Like every other totalitarian regime, the Ba'th had, at a very early stage, understood the power of language as a political tool. It differed from other such regimes only in its point of departure: the collective memories of the Arab and the Muslim past and the sediments they had left behind in the language. Like all totalitarian rulers, Husayn used language to justify his policies, even the most heinous ones. what marked him off from others was that (in the second phase of his rule) he used mostly verses from the Qur'an to give legitimacy to whatever he was doing or was about to do. The most conspicuous examples of this practice were the frequent quotations from sura *al-Anfal* (see Chapter 14) that were used to justify even chemical warfare. The sura was cited with a great deal of cynicism in the knowledge that it found a powerful echo in the minds of a basically traditional public. If the regime's actions could be presented as conforming to old patterns of Islamic history—as if by Allah's command they had become applicable to all ages—opposition was bound to decline. That this involved a corruption of the authentic meaning of qur'anic precepts was of no concern to the Ba'th leaders. What mattered was that providence, rather than the leadership, could be held responsible.

Another aspect of the manipulative use of language was the role it was assigned in preparing public opinion for things to come. This became a strategy in itself. Salient examples were the fostering of Husayn's image as a leader for years before he made himself the single ruler; the revival of the collective memory of the battle of Qadisiyya many months before the attack on Iran; and the reminders of Kuwait's status as part of Iraq beginning a number of months prior to the invasion and becoming ever more frequent in the aftermath.

Another way of exercising manipulative power was through the particular style chosen for appealing to the Iraqi public. It was characterized by a great deal of exaggeration as, for instance, when Iraq was equated to the great powers, when the hostilities against the military coalition were termed "the mother of battles," or in the macabre term "the wedding of *shuhada*'." It was a language appealing to emotions and calculated to carry with it large masses of people to make them identify with the regime, hate its enemies, and do its bidding willingly. The endless repetition of slogans, reminiscent of the monotonous clicks of the rosary, came to produce a hypnotic effect. The prevalence of such "packaged expressions" placed the individual mind under tutelage and eventually enslaved people. Studying the Ba'thi discourse leaves the researcher with the overall impression of a deliberate effort to obscure, blur, and eventually distort reality.

Husayn himself was a master of putting up a smoke screen between his listeners and the real world, of calling black white and white black. No one dared to contradict him. On the contrary, his associates and the media repeated his words with devout regularity. Information from the outside was prevented from reaching Iraqis. Everything was done to stop them from using their intelligence, to prevent them from arriving at a balanced analysis of trends and events, to stifle independent thinking, and to nip criticism in the bud. the ultimate aim was to exclude the public from any active participation in politics and make them acquiesce in the total power monopoly of a numerically tiny elite.

This leads to a further question: Is the political effect of language limited to the target set for it by the planners? Or does it go beyond that, drawing on unconscious or barely conscious layers of the mind, which is therefore likely to magnify its catalytic influence many times? Some scholars have argued that language is a cause rather than an effect and that the corruption of language leads necessarily to political degeneracy. Verbal violence, they hold, engenders physical violence. Looking back over this material, one cannot but conclude that language has autonomous powers. Speech and action are linked by a mutual feedback. Verbal violence does indeed produce physical violence; physical violence also shades over into verbal violence.[2]

Ba'th Iraq is a most striking example of this two-way traffic, to the point of making it impossible to tell cause from effect. Arguably, the society of modern Iraq was exposed to political and economic conditions that made it violence prone from the start. But it is equally possible to say that unless the Ba'th had developed its particular doctrine, with its accent on violence and force, physical violence would not have reached the degree it did. there is an element of the self-fulfilling prophecy in this interrelationship. The ruler himself ends up caught inside the cage of his public declarations and commitments, and their unrelenting repetition makes it all the more difficult to reject them, even if expediency demands it. Those who initiate the use of this particular brand of language end up its prisoners. This view is fully borne out by the chain of events leading up to the Gulf War.

Much like using language to mobilize the public, the Ba'th used, or created, political myths. We may distinguish between new myths, ancient myths, and myths "renovated" for current use. All of them are flexible: the manner of their presentation may change according to the demands of the moment, the place, and the audience at which they are directed. Their "production" became an integral part of Iraqi political life, at times making it difficult to distinguish between imagination and reality. Mythmaking became fundamental to the Ba'th regime until it appeared as if its collective and individual survival depended on it. The more badly the policies of the "real" Husayn failed, the more the "mythological" Husayn (belonging to the first of the three categories) flourished and prospered.

In the second category, the frequent recourse to role models from among the heroes of Muslim and Arab history illustrates the twofold—part conscious, part unconscious—nature of their appeal. Their images were alive in semiconscious layers of the public memory and formed part of the cultural and historical tradition; trotting them out to augment and elevate Husayn's personal image meant deliberately exploiting their power for propaganda effects. Yarmuk, Qadisiyya, Hattin, and Saladin were used as slogans by many Arab states, but only Iraq turned their employment into a systematic policy and even into a cult. Only in Iraq was the past incorporated into the present to such an extent; ancient and modern Qadisiyya seemed to coincide and to become indistinguishable.

The "myth of the elephant" (see Chapter 14) illustrates the third category. It differed from all the rest in that it revived events dating back to the pre-Islamic period. Its existence in the collective memory was not nearly as sharply defined as that of Islamic heroes and events. It might well have been forgotten altogether until the Ba'th revived it and presented it as applicable to current circumstances. when it did, it apparently succeeded in making it (to borrow a term from another context) a "virtual reality" for Iraqi society.

The political purposes of mythmaking resembled those of the uses of language. One of them was to prepare the ground for events already in the planning stage and expected to unfold shortly. (We are reminded of

Ernst Cassirer's opinion that in Nazi Germany "mental rearmament" long preceded physical rearmament.)[3] A second aim was to make the public at large act or suffer beyond their natural capacity. Yet another was to make people accept their vicissitudes unquestioningly. Did the myths perform as the regime expected them to? Again, it is extremely difficult to give a clear answer. What we can say with a measure of assurance is this: Employment of one or another item from the reservoir of myths the regime had accumulated over time allows us to understand just where the leaders located a point of weakness or a sense of crisis in society. The frequency of a myth's use was a measure of the acuteness of the malaise. There is no good evidence of how these attempts were received by the Sunni community, but the uprisings of the Kurds and the Shi'is immediately after the end of the Gulf War show that they were not impressed. The insurrections were accompanied by the destruction of some of the most salient emblems of the Ba'th, such as the burning of portraits of Saddam Husayn— sheer sacrilege from the point of view of the regime.

Other areas of malaise are pointed up by such gestures as adding the words *Allah akbar* to the Iraqi flag and to the state emblem and by changing the name of the state from al-Jumhuriyya al-'Iraqiyya (the Iraqi Republic) to Jumhuriyyat al-'Iraq (the Republic of Iraq). Such acts do attest to a degree of flexibility on the part of the regime in dealing with crises and in resisting pressures by partly giving way to them, but they point with even greater forcefulness to the existence of a crisis in the first place. Inscribing the above words on the flag is an instance of the politically oriented, manipulative use of Islamic symbols, but it is also an indication of the severe disorientation both of the regime and of society. Symbols have been said to "connote the coming-together of ideas, approaches, and shared emotions."[4] If so, their frequent replacement attests to cultural crises; the regime was trying to shed the symbols of the past—now seen to have failed to produce social cohesion—and substitute new ones it expected to fare better.

The change in the name of the state in May 1992 is a case in point.[5] Ostensibly an insignificant, merely formal change, it was a great deal more significant than it appeared at first glance. It must be seen in the context of the practice (mentioned in the introduction) of changing the name of a person in danger in the expectation that renaming the person would, as it were, deceive fate and thus avert the danger. Changing the name of the state at that particular juncture, when Kurdistan seemed on the point of slipping out of its control, was expected to work in a similar fashion. Moreover, al-'Iraq had been the name of the country under the monarchy, and the return to it signified a desire to return to earlier times, whether from the fatigue engendered by a series of crises (in comparison with which those of the monarchy seemed puny) or whether from an overall notion that the past was always better than the present.

The name change concluded a series of lesser steps taken to refurbish the image of the monarchy. This extended to a rehabilitation of the social groups that had predominated under the monarchy: the tribes and the tribal shaykhs. The Ba'th had seemingly removed them forever from the scene. But since the Gulf War, Husayn had made much of the shaykhs and of his links with them as a means of reinforcing Ba'thi control over the Shi'i community. On one occasion, he had even described the Ba'th party as *'ashirat al-'asha'ir* (the tribe of tribes).[6] Yet the retention of the word *jumhuriyya* (republic) showed that the Ba'th was not ready to go all the way in divesting itself of its former "assets" but rather wished to create a link between the past and the present.

The revival of the name al-'Iraq at a moment when Kurdistan was very nearly separating from it had its ironic side, which the regime may not have been aware of. The classical Arab geographers had used the word to denote an area extending from the middle course of the Euphrates and the Tigris down to the Persian Gulf. It excluded the Iraqi part of the Jazira (northwestern Iraq in modern terms) and all of Iraqi Kurdistan. Moreover, at least according to some linguists, *'iraq* connoted "seashore" or any stretch of country close to the sea.[7] This old definition could be construed to include Kuwait, but what was happening in reality was the opposite: Iraq was retreating from the seashore and moving inland. The war against Iran and the Gulf War had closed its outlet to the sea. Part of the seashore of Umm Qasr, its only seaport (and that a minor one), had been assigned to Kuwait, and the ban on flights over the Shi'i south had reinforced the Iraqi feeling of being "bottled up" far from the sea. Using al-'Iraq in these circumstances only underscored the chasm between aspirations and achievements, between image and reality, between discourse and action.

The public discussion of the Arabic political discourse (*al-khitab al-siyasi*) is only beginning in the Arab countries. The Arabic press, in Iraq and elsewhere, has started to deal with it since the Gulf War and in doing so has paid special attention to Iraq.[8] the Iraqi daily *Babil* (a recent foundation, owned and published by Husayn's son 'Udayy) has taken a leading part in prompting the theme. In an article on "Saddamism" (*Saddamiyya*), it called on the other Arab countries to adopt the Iraqi cultural and political language and thus to replace "the Nasserite discourse" that had collapsed in the wake of the 1967 defeat. Until then, both politicians and intellectuals had deluded themselves that playing a "starring role" (*nujumiyya*) on the political stage was "enough . . . to snatch a quick victory from the enemy." But, the article continued, "Saddamism"—born from Ba'thism—differed from all other earlier forms of discourse in the Arab world in the following two ways: its "mission" was not limited to a short period but would extend over "hundreds of years," and it represented what *Babil* called "the 'no' project [*mashru' la*]"—that is, saying "no" to the American epoch (*zaman*). The new era of "Saddamism," in turn, was different from the earlier period of being "dragged along" (*tab'iyya*) by foreign influences. This period had lasted from the fall of Baghdad in 1258 to the rise of the Ba'th. Until then, people had said "yes"—fully or partially—to the strangers and had accepted—fully or partially—foreign solutions and foreign projects. By contrast, the Ba'thi national (*qawmi*) discourse had firm foundations of its own, possessed great depth, and had a future-oriented outlook. As such, it deserved complete Arab popular support and had indeed received it during the Gulf War.[9]

Such articles infuriated expatriate Iraqi opposition quarters, which launched a counterattack. The poet Karim 'Abd, a Kurd belonging to one of the opposition groups, published a scathing critique of the Iraqi "discourse of the rulers" (*khitab al-sulta*). Under the Ba'th, he wrote, lying had become heroism, and murder had become polished speech (*fasaha*). "Uncouth language had spread out from the presidential palace, and the ministers and counselors had carried it into the schools and universities. . . . The Arabic language started to groan from the pages of the newspapers and to sound like a death rattle from the lips of announcers and commentators." Arabic, he went on, had become convoluted, enslaved, and oppressed. It had turned self-contradictory because it attempted to suit itself to all conditions and fit all circumstances. The Ba'th regime had taken up the discourse of nationalism and leftist convictions and had gone on to empty it of all content; it was now doing the very same thing to the language of religion. While executing anyone belonging to a religious party, 'Abd continued, it gave military units religious names. It had capped all this by inscribing the national flag with the words *Allah akbar*. This was not foolishness, he felt, but rather a kind of "negative and destructive brilliance": speaking the language of religion would enable the regime to bring Islam under its control and destroy it from within. Husayn had "terrorized" language. His officials had come to believe that language could be used like a net in which the murder victim could be caught and seduced to trust the word of the killer.[10]

The most trenchant criticism came from another source: the Egyptian intellectual al-Sayyid Yasin, who analyzed the political discourse in the Arab world as a whole during the Gulf War. He criticized three aspects of it: the language of the intellectuals; the idiom of the masses; and the discourse of the rulers. The first had become the victim of emotionalism and rhetoric; criticism and objective analysis had become extremely rare in it. The most crucial problem of the intellectuals was, in Yasin's view, their link with the establishment. This placed them between the hammer of threatened oppression and the anvil of financial rewards for making their pen subservient to the ruler. More than that, they were ready to receive some minor "gifts" of ostensible democratization but failed to struggle for real democracy and genuine freedom of speech. They had turned into the kind of intellectuals who exist only to "give the regime their seal of approval."

As for the masses, Yasin asserted that they had become totally enmeshed in the net of Husayn's political rhetoric and identified unquestioningly with

Iraq's official policy. This, he went on, had resulted from the leadership's total control of the media and had enabled the regime to "emasculate" the political consciousness of the masses and to use its propaganda machine to "guide" them in all things. Control of the Iraqi media was reinforced by "levying high customs dues on intellectual and cultural imports" from other Arab countries and by imposing strict censorship on them. This limited and warped the political consciousness of the public at large.

Yasin's most stringent criticism, however, was reserved for the "language of the ruler." He argued forcefully against those who claimed that the very nature of the Arabic language led its speakers away from reality and into a world of dreams. This was a false charge. Like every other language, Arabic was made up of a variety of languages; the language of Islamic radicalism differed fundamentally from the language of secularists. The latter was logical, analytical, and rational. Arabic was perfectly capable of accommodating both. There was no room for blaming the language as such. It was not the fault of the language that Arab rulers distorted it for their political purposes. Small "political elites" had indeed "raped the Arabic language over recent decades and adopted a political idiom that was intended to spread a false consciousness [wa'y za'if]. This language has turned precious terms like democracy, socialism, unity, social justice, and national [watani] independence into hackneyed and meaningless words." Eventually, language had lost its credibility and the masses had ceased to trust it.

Husayn himself, Yasin claimed, had adopted an artificial religious language in which "facts and imagination blended together" and cool political reasoning mixed "with an obscure mysticism closer to the language of derwishes than to the discourse of a modern political conflict. . . . [The latter] is usually clear, sharply edged, and brief and [thus] able to convey its message to the world." For all that, he went on, Husayn had carried the masses with him—proof, he thought, that popularity did not necessarily require cogent ideas or the use of modern terms. On the contrary, at times a certain political idiom was capable of becoming popular precisely because of its "internal contradiction, its structural weakness, its defective style, and its primitive ideas." The atmosphere enveloping the Arab masses and the "state of their mind" had made it possible for the "run-down [mutahafit]" Iraqi political speech to succeed with them.

Finally, Yasin considered the task of the individual word. The language used during the Gulf War, he concluded, had proved the single word to be "primitive and backward" and "without hope of redemption," because it was born from the violent rape of the language. It had given, as it were, a "naive" kind of expression to the thoughts and feelings of

> peoples who do not distinguish between fact and dream and between legend and reality. [They are] peoples who believe that simply uttering a word, or spreading it by means of the political discourse or in military communiqués was a substitute for action, or was indeed action itself. . . . In this manner, the violated language was able, at a time of crisis, to create a forged

and spurious consciousness that sufficed for a while to drug the masses. But the masses woke up to the reality of defeat and [when they did], despair and frustration took hold of them.[11]

Babil, however, was not to be shaken in its convictions: the word, it wrote, was "like a minesweeper," moving ahead to detect negative things and destroy them.[12]

Far removed as they were from each other, the two views had one thing in common: They agreed that the word was the most important instrument for making political culture what it was.

Notes

ABBREVIATIONS

The following abbreviations are used throughout the notes and bibliography.

AAS	*Asian and African Studies*
DR	Daily Report: Near East and South Asia
EI¹, EI²	*Encyclopedia of Islam*, 1st and 2d editions
INA	Iraqi News Agency (Baghdad)
IJMES	*International Journal of Middle East Studies*
MECS	*Middle East Contemporary Survey, 1981–1982, 1993, 1994, 1995* (various publishers)
MEJ	*Middle East Journal*
MES	*Middle Eastern Studies*
SWB	British Broadcasting Corporation, Summary of World Broadcasting: The Middle East and Africa

INTRODUCTION

1. Ernst Cassirer, *Language and Myth* (New York, 1946), p. 9. Throughout the notes, "H" means "in Hebrew." The titles of Hebrew books will be given in translation; those of books in Arabic, in transcription. Unless otherwise noted, all translations from the Arabic are mine; the Qur'an quotations are from A. J. Arberry.

2. On language as symbol, see Terence Hawkes, *Structuralism and Semiotics* (London, 1977).

3. E.g., Genesis 1:3, 1:5.

4. Cassirer, *Language and Myth*, pp. 44–62.

5. Ibid, pp. 48–56.

6. See Ernst Cassirer, *The Myth of the State* (New York, 1955), pp. 355–357; Roland Barthes, *Mythologies* (Paris, 1957), pp. 193–230; Dov Landau, *From Metaphor to Symbol* (H) (Ramat Gan, Israel, 1979), pp. 8–87; Nancy S. Struever, "The Study of Language and the Study of History," *Journal of Interdisciplinary History* 4 (1974): 401–415; Nils B. Kvastad, "Semantics in the Methodology of the History of Ideas," *Journal of the History of Ideas* 38 (1977): 157–174.

7. Cassirer, *Myth of the State*, pp. 355–357.

8. Ibid., p. 350.

9. Jabra I. Jabra, "Arab Language and Culture," in Michael Adams (ed.), *The Middle East: A Handbook* (London, 1971), pp. 174–178, quotation from p. 178; Khalid Kishtainy, *Arab Political Humour* (London, 1985), pp. 11–12.

10. 'Abd al-Amir al-Ward interview, *Alif Ba'*, 24 May 1989.

11. *Al-Hayat*, 12 May 1992.

12. Quoted in Raphael Patai, *The Arab Mind* (New York, 1976), p. 49. For the poetical character of the Arabic language, see Timothy Mitchell, *Colonising Egypt* (Cambridge, 1988), pp. 142–144.

13. R. B. Serjeant, "Arabic Literature," in Adams, *The Middle East*, p. 535.

14. Zahran al-Badrawi, *Fi 'ilm al-lugha al-ta'rikhi: dirasa tatbiqiyya 'ala 'Arabiyyat al-'usur al-wusta* (Cairo, 1988), pp. 34–43; A. F. L. Beeston, *The Arabic Language Today* (London, 1970), pp. 13–14. For a discussion of the connection between Arabic and Islam, see James Coffman, "Does the Arabic Language Encourage Radical Islam?", *Middle East Quarterly* 2 (1995): 51–57.

15. Jabra, "Arab Language," pp. 174–178.

16. Hisham Sharabi, *Nationalism and Revolution in the Arab World: The Middle East and North Africa* (Princeton, 1966), pp. 93–95.

17. Patai, *Arab Mind*, p. 65.

18. Todd Gitlin, *The Whole World Is Watching* (Berkeley, 1980), p. 263; cf. Barthes, *Mythologies*, pp. 128–130. See also Dan Caspi and Yehiel Limor, *The Mediators: The Mass Media in Israel, 1948–1990* (H) (Tel Aviv, 1992), preface, introduction, and chapters 4–6.

19. Hamid Mowlana, "Mass Media System and Communications Behaviour," in Adams, *The Middle East*, pp. 584–598; Ami Ayalon, "Sihafa: The Arab Experiment in Journalism," *MES* 28 (1992): 258–280.

20. For the Iraqi press before the advent of the Ba'th regime and for the censorship and nationalization laws, see William A. Rugh, *The Arab Press: News Media and Political Process in the Arab World* (Syracuse, N.Y., 1979), pp. 52–58, 63. For general background on the Iraqi press in the 1950s and 1960s, see G. al-Gailani, "Iraq's Journalism and Political Conflict, 1956–1963," Ph.D. dissertation, University of Iowa, 1971.

21. *Al-Thawra*, 6 January 1969.

22. Hizb al-ba'th al-'Arabi al-ishtiraki, al-qiyada al-qawmiyya, *Al-Minhaj al-thaqafi al-markazi*, vol. 2 (Baghdad, 1977), pp. 277–283.

23. On the second day of the second Gulf War, sixty planes of the "American-Zionist enemy" were reported shot down. *Al-Thawra*, 18 January 1991. The

journalists' contribution to the war effort won them the title "the corps [*faylaq*] of information." *Babil*, 19 June 1994.

24. The first to introduce cartoons into Arabic journalism was Ya'qub Sannu', in the last quarter of the previous century. Kishtainy, *Arab Political Humour*, p. 73.

25. Recently, however, humorous cartoons have started to be published, aimed particularly at adverse economic circumstances. For example, someone seen buying a carton of eggs is asked whether he has come into an inheritance. *Babil*, 5 March 1992. On Arab political humor, see Kishtainy, *Arab Political Humour*.

26. On nineteenth-century poetry, see Yusuf 'Izz al-Din, *Al-Shi'r al-'Iraqi al-hadith wa athar al-tayyarat al-siyasiyya wa-l-ijtima'iyya fihi* (Cairo, 1965); Ibrahim al-Wa'ili, *Al-Shi'r al-siyasi al-'Iraqi fi al-qarn al-tasi' 'ashar* (Baghdad, 1961). Al-Wa 'ili elaborates on the "court poets" kept by provincial governors but also cites instances of satire and criticism. See, e.g., ibid., pp. 48, 112–113, 158, 176.

27. Roland Barthes, *Le degré zéro de l'écriture: Suivi de, nouveaux essais critiques* (Paris, 1972), pp. 18–22.

28. Husayn's political terms were published by the press in 1988 and in book form in 1989. In 1990, it became known that the author of the dictionary, Muhammad Salih 'Abd al-Rida, was working on an additional dictionary. *Al-Thawra*, 7 June 1990.

29. *Babil*, 17 June 1992. For a discussion of Husayn's linguistic style, see Nathalie Mazraani, "Functions of Arabic Political Discourse: The Case of Saddam Hussein's Speeches," *Zeitschrift für Arabische Linguistik* 30 (1995): 22–36.

30. "Khususiyyat al-kasb al-hizbi," *Al-Thawra al-'Arabiyya*, 1984, pp. 30–31. Some issues of this periodical, available in the archives of the Dayan Center, Tel Aviv University, are undated and unnumbered. I have indicated the available information in the text.

31. C. K. Ogden and I. A. Richards, *The Meaning of Meanings: A Study of the Influence of Language upon Thought and the Science of Symbolism*, 10th ed. (London, 1966), p. 149. See also Haim Blanc, *Human Language* (H) (Jerusalem, 1989), pp. 126–127. Blanc cites the use of "ass" meaning "donkey" as distinct from that meaning "stupid person."

32. For a discussion of this, see the introduction to Richard Koebner and Helmut Dan Schmidt, *Imperialism: The Study and Significance of a Political Word, 1840–1960* (Cambridge, 1964).

33. See Charles Issawi, "European Loan-Words in Contemporary Arabic Writing: A Case Study in Modernization," *MES* 3 (1967): 110–133; Ami Ayalon, "Dimuqratiyya, Hurriyya, Jumhuriyya: The Modernization of the Arabic Political Vocabulary," *AAS* 23 (1989): 25–42.

34. Quoted in Cassirer, *Myth of the State*, p. 187.

35. Ibid., pp. 354–355.

36. Bernard Lewis, *History Remembered, Recovered, Invented* (Princeton, 1975), pp. 24–25.

CHAPTER 1

1. See Hanna Batatu, *The Old Social Classes and the Revolutionary Movements of Iraq* (Princeton, 1978); Stephen H. Longrigg, *Iraq, 1900 to 1950* (Lon-

don, 1953); Uriel Dann, *Iraq under Qassem: A Political History, 1958–1963* (New York, 1969).

2. On this and other terms connected with revolution, see Ami Ayalon, "From Fitna to Thawra," *Studia Islamica* 67 (1987): 145–174; Bernard Lewis, *Islam in History: Ideas, Men, and Events in the Middle East* (New York, 1973), pp. 237–263; A. T. Hatto, "The Semantics of Revolution," in P. J. Vatikiotis (ed.), *Revolution in the Middle East, and Other Case Studies* (London, 1972), pp. 25–29.

3. This word appears in this sense in the fourteenth-century dictionary by Muhammad bin al-Mukarram bin Manzur, *Lisan al-ʿArab*, 6 vols. (Cairo, n.d.), as well as in Edward William Lane's nineteenth-century *An Arabic English Lexicon*, 8 vols. (London, 1863–1893).

4. Ayalon, "From Fitna to Thawra," pp. 158–159, 163–164.

5. Sami Shawkat, *Hadhihi ahdafuna* (Baghdad, 1939), pp. 50–54.

6. Yusuf Ismaʿil, *Inqilab tisʿa wa-ʿishrin tishrin al-awwal* (Baghdad, 1936), pp. 25, 26, 31, 38.

7. ʿAbd al-Fattah Abu al-Nasr al-Yafi, *Al-ʿIraq bayn inqilabayn* (Beirut, 1938), pp. 21, 33, 72.

8. Bashir al-ʿAwf, *Al-Inqilab al-Suri* (Damascus, 1949), pp. 4–8.

9. *Nidal al-baʿth fi sabil al-wahda al-hurriyya wa-l-ishtirakiyya*, vol. 1 (Beirut, 1963), p. 175.

10. See Michel ʿAflaq, *Fi sabil al-baʿth* (Beirut, 1974), which includes articles from different periods of his political activities. I also used earlier editions of 1959 and 1963, but unless stated otherwise, the edition cited is that of 1974.

11. Ibid., pp. 56–58, 76, 84, 101, 281.

12. *Al-Zaman*, 20, 21 July 1958.

13. *Al-Jamahir*, 2 March 1963.

14. *Al-Jumhuriyya*, 31 July 1968.

15. *Al-Thawra*, 20 July 1969; *Thawrat 17 tammuz, al-tajriba wa-l-afaq: al-taqrir al-siyasi al-sadir ʿan al-muʾtamar al-qutri al-thamin li-hizb al-baʿth al-ʿArabi al-ishtiraki al-qutr al-ʿIraqi* (n.p., January 1974), p. 135; Hasan ʿAzba al-ʿUbaydi, *Al-Markaz al-dusturi li-hizb al-baʿth al-ʿArabi al-ishtiraki* (Baghdad, 1982), pp. 82–83; Fadil al-Barrak, *Dawr al-jaysh al-ʿIraqi fi hukumat al-difaʿ al-watani wa-l-harb maʿ Baritaniya ʿam 1941: dirasa tahliliyya wa-naqdiyya wa-muqarina li-l-khalafiyyat al-ijtimaʿiyya wa-l-ʿaskariyya*, 2d ed. (Beirut, 1987), p. 217.

16. *Al-Jumhuriyya*, 2, 8, 27 August 1968; *al-Thawra*, 10, 18 November 1968, 10 October 1971, 2 July 1973, 11 February 1986.

17. Sura *al-Shuʿaraʾ*, v. 227.

18. *Al-Sharq al-Awsat*, 8 March 1989.

19. See, e.g., Muhammad Taqi al-Mudarrisi, *ʿAn al-ʿIraq wa-l-haraka al-Islamiyya* (London, 1988), pp. 16–17, 33, 74.

20. *Al-Jumhuriyya*, 24 March 1979.

21. ʿAflaq, *Fi sabil al-Baʿth*, p. 80.

22. Phebe Marr, *The Modern History of Iraq* (Boulder, Colo., 1985), pp. 112–113; Faʾiq Batti, *Al-Sihafa al-yasariyya fi-l-ʿIraq 1924–1958* (London, 1985), p. 112.

23. "Communiqué, no. 1," quoted in *Al-Jumhuriyya*, 7 February 1969.

24. *Al-Jamahir*, 13 April 1963; *al-ʿIraq*, 5 September 1977.

25. *Al-Jumhuriyya*, 2 August 1968, 30 July 1970; *al-Thawra*, 4 August 1969.

26. Barrak, *Dawr al-jaysh*, p. 152.

27. The Palestinians began using the term presumably about the same time; it is not known who did so first.

28. *Al-Qadisiyya*, 23 January 1990; *al-Jumhuriyya*, 17 August 1990.

29. *Al-Thawra al-Husayniyya*, 22 September 1989.

30. *Al-Kadir*, May 1974. It should be noted that the Ba'th termed the Kurdish insurrection in Iraq a "revolt" and that of the Kurds in Iran an *intifada*.

31. *Al-Tayyar al-Jadid*, 20 July 1987. The Kurds, too, applied this term to earlier events that carried different names. Thus, a book by Jalili Jalil on the 1880 'Ubaydallah revolt was titled *Intifadat al-Akrad 1880* (Beirut, 1979).

32. Ayalon, "From Fitna to Thawra."

33. *Al-Thawra*, 2 May 1976, stated that the May revolution had repercussions on the region and the entire Arab world.

34. *Al-Zaman*, 28 July 1958.

35. *Al-Jumhuriyya*, 14 August 1968; *al-Thawra*, 13 February 1969.

36. *Al-Thawra*, 28 January 1970.

37. *Yedi'ot Aharonot*, 29 January 1992, quoting a journalist of the *Daily Mail* who had visited the secret police headquarters in Kurdistan after it had fallen into Kurdish hands.

38. *Al-Jumhuriyya*, 2 May 1981, 2 May, 21 June 1982.

39. Hizb al-ba'th al-'Arabi al-ishtiraki, al-qiyada al-qawmiyya, *Asbab naksat hukm al-hizb fi-l-'Iraq* (n.p., n.d.), p. 16. This document includes severe criticism of the first Ba'thi regime of 1963.

40. *Al-Thawra*, 10 April 1979. "Communiqué No. 1" was the standard term for announcing coups in Iraq and other Arab countries.

41. Hizb al-ba'th al-'Arabi al-ishtiraki, al-qiyada al-qawmiyya, *Al-Minhaj al-thaqafi al-markazi*, vol. 2 (Baghdad, 1977), p. 105.

42. *Al-Thawra*, 13 May 1977. Saddam Husayn was in turn inspired by 'Aflaq, who thought that the burden of the revolution should be carried by youth.

43. Saddam Husayn, *Al-Thawra wa-l-nazra al-jadida* (Baghdad, 1981), pp. 24, 31, 137–138, 149. The book includes Husayn's speeches from different periods. Those on youth are dated 1976 and 1977. Nazi and fascist influence on Husayn's concept of the role of youth is immediately evident. *Al-Jumhuriyya*, 17 November 1978.

44. *Al-Thawra*, 2, 17, 20 March 1970, 22 September 1971.

45. *Al-'Iraq*, 29 March 1980; *al-Jumhuriyya*, 28 April 1981.

46. *Al-Thawra*, 11 February 1986.

47. Hizb al-ba'th al-'Arabi al-ishtiraki, al-qutr al-'Iraqi, *Al-Taqrir al-markazi li-l-mu'tamar al-qutri al-tasi'*, June 1982 (Baghdad, 1983; hereafter *Regional Report No. 9*), p. 31; Fadil al-Barrak, *Mustafa al-Barzani: al-ustura wa-l-haqiqa* (Baghdad, 1989), p. 263.

48. *Al-'Iraq*, 16 October 1986.

49. Al-Mudarrisi, *'An al-'Iraq*, pp. 60, 64, 71.

50. *Regional Report No. 9*, p. 265.

51. See Hizb al-ba'th, *Asbab*. Written in 1965, this document deals exclusively with the *ridda*.

52. Bernard Lewis, *The Political Language of Islam* (Chicago, 1988), p. 85. For *ridda* in Islamic history, see Muhammad 'Abid al-Jabiri, *Al-'Aql al-siyasi al-'Arabi* (Beirut, 1991), pp. 129–197.

53. *Al-Jumhuriyya*, 18 July 1968, 9 February 1970.

54. *Al-Thawra al-'Arabiyya*, March 1975, pp. 5, 15–16.

55. *Al-Thawra*, 23 February 1976.

56. Hizb al-ba'th al-'Arabi al-ishtiraki, al-qiyada al-qawmiyya, *Al-Taqrir al-siyasi li-l-mu'tamar al-qawmi al-hadi 'ashar* (Baghdad, 1977; hereafter *Eleventh National Congress*), pp. 21–22.

57. *Al-Thawra al-'Arabiyya*, no. 1, 1976, pp. 47–60; no. 5, 1976, pp. 17–19.

58. *Al-'Iraq*, 9 August 1979. See also quotation of Husayn in Shafiq 'Abd al-Razzaq al-Samarra'i, *Saddam Husayn nidaluh wa-fikruh al-siyasi* (n.p., 1982), p. 72.

59. *Al-'Iraq*, 22 August 1981.

60. Ibid., 13 April 1985.

CHAPTER 2

1. The Ba'thi constitution was issued in 1947 in Syria. See *Nidal al-ba'th fi sabil al-wahda al-hurriyya wa-l-ishtirakiyya*, vol. 1 (Beirut, 1963), pp. 172–181. The motto "permanent revolution and the renewal of youth" is from *al-Thawra al-'Arabiyya*, no. 11, 1979, p. 39.

2. John F. Devlin, *The Ba'th Party: A History from Its Origins to 1966* (Stanford, 1976), p. 11. For a discussion on the party, see Olivier Carré, *Le nationalisme Arabe* (Paris, 1993), pp. 39–69.

3. For the term ba'th, see Muhammad bin al-Mukarram bin Manzur, *Lisan al-'Arab* (Cairo, n.d.); Lewis Ma'luf, *al-Munjid* (Jaffa, 1908); and A. S. Tritton, "Ba'th," in *EI²*. The word ba'th appears many times in the Qu'ran in both meanings.

4. Zaki al-Arsuzi, *Al-Mu'allafat al-kamila*, vol. 4 (Damascus, 1972), pp. 197–211. Al-Arsuzi became the leading ideologue of the Syrian Ba'th following the split in 1966 between the Ba'th party in Syria and its former leaders 'Aflaq and Bitar. The Syrian Ba'th party published Arsuzi's writings posthumously. His works deal mainly with the philosophy of language and give some interesting insight into the Arabic language.

5. Michel 'Aflaq, *Ma'rakat al-masir al-wahid* (Beirut, 1963), pp. 34–39.

6. *Al-Thawra*, 12 December 1989, 25 September 1991.

7. Zuhayr Sadiq Rida al-Khalidi, *Al-Qiyam 'ind Saddam Husayn* (Baghdad, 1989), p. 242.

8. *Al-Qadisiyya*, 1 May 1990.

9. Al-Arsuzi, *Al-Mu'allafat al-kamila*, vol. 1, p. 229.

10. Ibid., p. 284; vol. 6, p. 213. According to Ibn Manzur, *Lisan al-'Arab*, al-'anqa' (phoenix), which nobody ever saw, used to appear at sunset, and it is possible to be equated with *tayr ababil* mentioned in the Qu'ran (see Part 5).

11. Said Bensaid, "*Al-watan* and *al-Umma* in Contemporary Arab Use" in Ghassan Salamé (ed.), *The Foundation of the Arab State*, vol. 1 (London, 1987), pp. 149–174.

12. See Ami Ayalon, *Language and Change in the Arab Middle East* (New York, 1987).

13. For Faysal's memorandum, see 'Abd al-Razzaq al-Hasani, *Ta'rikh al-wizarat al-'Iraqiyya*, vol. 3 (Sidon, 1940), pp. 189–195.

14. For instance, *al-Zaman*, 22, 23 June 1958.

15. *Al-Jamahir*, 16 March 1963; *al-Jumhuriyya*, 22 September 1968, 13 January 1978.

16. Some perceive *risala* as the embodiment of God's wisdom. A. L. Wensick, "Rasul," in *EI¹*.

17. Michel 'Aflaq, *Fi sabil al-ba'th* (Beirut, 1974), pp. 86, 98; 'Aflaq, *Ma'rakat al-masir*, p. 55.

18. *Nidal al-ba'th*, vol. 1, p. 173.

19. *Al-Thawra*, 14 July 1978; *al-'Iraq*, 2 April 1980.

20. Saddam Husayn, *al-Thawra*, 7 January 1989.

21. See *al-Jumhuriyya*, 22 June 1986; al-Thawra, 1 January 1989.

22. *Al-Thawra*, 9 May 1990.

23. *Al-Jumhuriyya*, 5 April 1988.

24. *Al-Qadisiyya*, 11 October 1989.

25. *Al-Jumhuriyya*, 15 January 1988; *al-Thawra*, 2 July 1990, 17 September 1991.

26. Al-Arsuzi, *Al-Mu'allafat al-kamila*, vol. 4, pp. 255–257.

27. 'Aflaq, *Ma'rakat al-masir*, p. 18.

28. Sura *al-Baqara*, v. 178.

29. On *hurriyya*, see Bernard Lewis and F. Rosenthal, "Hurriyya," in *EI²*.

30. Fa'iq Batti, *Al-Sihafa al-yasariyya fi-l-'Iraq, 1924–1958* (London, 1985), p. 24.

31. Yusuf Isma'il, *Inqilab tis'a wa-'ishrin tishrin al-awwal* (Baghdad, 1936), pp. 2, 11, 41.

32. Lewis and Rosenthal, "Hurriyya," in *EI²*.

33. 'Aflaq, *Fi sabil al-ba'th*, p. 187.

34. See, e.g., Devlin, *The Ba'th Party*, p. 32.

35. *Nidal al-Ba'th*, vol. 1, p. 173; 'Aflaq, *Ma'rakat al-masir*, p. 17.

36. See Samir al-Khalil, *Republic of Fear: The Politics of Modern Iraq* (Berkeley, 1989), chapters 1, 2.

37. *Al-Thawra al-'Arabiyya*, no. 1, 1976, p. 31.

38. *Al-Jumhuriyya*, 1 January 1980; *al-'Iraq*, 1, 4 March 1989.

39. *Al-Qadisiyya*, 5, 18 March 1989.

40. Sami H. Hanna and George H. Gardner, *Arab Socialism: A Documentary Survey* (Leiden, 1969), pp. 22, 49, 51, 62, 266–289.

41. See P. J. Vatikiotis, "Ishtirakiyya," in *EI²*.

42. Ibid.

43. Al-Arsuzi, *Al-Mu'allafat al-kamila*, vol. 4, p. 258. The word *ishtarak* appears only twice in the Qur'an, meaning participation in another's suffering. Sura *al-Zukhruf*, v. 29.

44. 'Aflaq, *Fi sabil al-ba'th*, pp. 8–9, 229, 307–310; 'Aflaq, *Ma'rakat al-masir*, pp. 15, 38.

45. *Nidal al-Ba'th*, vol. 1, pp. 177–178. On agrarian reform in Syria, see Itamar Rabinovich, *Syria under the Ba'th, 1963–1966: The Army-Party Symbiosis* (Jerusalem, 1972), p. 21.

46. On Nasir's socialism, see Hanna and Gardner, *Arab Socialism*, pp. 98–149.

47. Batti, *Al-Sihafa*, p. 18.

48. On the agrarian reform under Qasim, see Uriel Dann, *Iraq under Qassem: A Political History, 1958–1963* (New York, 1969), pp. 54–64, 357.

49. *Al-Thawra*, 5 January, 18 March, 23 May 1969; *al-Thawra al-'Arabiyya*, no. 5, 1976, p. 40.

50. *Al-Jumhuriyya*, 17 July 1970; *Thawrat 17 tammuz, al-tajriba wa-l-afaq: al-taqrir al-siyasi al-sadir 'an al-mu'tamar al-qutri al-thamin li-hizb al-ba'th*

al-ʿArabi al-ishtiraki al-qutr al-ʿIraqi (n.p., January 1974), pp. 142, 204, 218–220.

51. *Al-Thawra*, 14 April 1977, 21 May 1978; *al-ʿIraq*, 31 October 1977.

52. *Al-Jumhuriyya*, 24 March 1979, 4 July 1980; *al-ʿIraq*, 20 May 1978. In July 1978, Husayn disclosed that the share of the socialist sector (including oil) in the GNP was 97 percent. *Al-ʿIraq*, 23 July 1978.

53. *Al-Thawra*, 24 April, 13 May 1981. In April 1981, the cooperatives were disbanded.

54. Ibid., 28 January 1983.

55. Ibid., 12 February, 10 June 1987.

56. Ibid., 14 February 1990.

57. Ibid., 30 July 1990.

58. Ibid., 17 September 1991.

59. Michel ʿAflaq, *Nuqtat al-bidaya* (Beirut, 1974), p. 135. This speech was delivered in 1969 to Iraqi workers in Baghdad.

60. It should be noted that two opposite meanings of the same word are common in classical Arabic (like *baʿa*, meaning both "buy" and "sell").

61. See Hizb al-baʿth al-ʿArabi al-ishtiraki, al-qiyada al-qawmiyya, *Al-Minhaj al-thaqafi al-markazi*, vol. 1 (Baghdad, 1977), pp. 37–44. For a general article on unity, see Barry Rubin, "Pan-Arab Nationalism: The Ideological Dream as Compelling Force," *Journal of Contemporary History* 26 (1991): 535–551.

62. Al-Arsuzi, *Al-Muʾallafat al-kamila*, vol. 4, p. 258. Saddam Husayn was later to speak of Iraq's desirable image as similar to those of the United States, the Soviet Union, and China. *Al-Jumhuriyya*, January 1980. (See also Chapter 4.)

63. ʿAflaq, *Nuqtat al-bidaya*, pp. 146–147.

64. ʿAflaq, *Maʿrakat al-masir*, pp. 2, 62; ʿAflaq, *Nuqtat al-bidaya*, p. 135; ʿAflaq, *Fi sabil al-baʿth*, p. 259.

65. See Amatzia Baram, "National (Wataniyya) Integration and Exclusiveness in Political Thought and Practice in Iraq under the Baʿth, 1968–1982" (H), Ph.D. dissertation, Hebrew University of Jerusalem, 1986, pp. 450–465.

66. Sami Shawkat, *Hadhihi ahdafuna* (Baghdad, 1939), pp. 32, 38, 44, 46–47.

67. Ahmad Hasan al-Bakr, *Al-Thawra ʿala tariq al-taqaddum* (Baghdad, 1977), p. 11. The speech was given on 1 January 1972.

68. *Al-Jumhuriyya*, 17 July 1970.

69. *Al-Thawra*, 30 March, 25 May 1972.

70. *Al-Jumhuriyya*, 13, 15 January 1975.

71. *Eleventh National Congress*, pp. 230–231, 235.

72. For an analysis of the unity issue during this period, see Baram, "National Integration," pp. 176–242; Eberhard Kienle, *Baʿth vs. Baʿth: The Conflict Between Syria and Iraq, 1968–1989* (London, 1990), pp. 135–151.

73. *Al-Jumhuriyya*, 17, 27 November 1978, 11, 16 January, 24 March 1979.

74. *Al-Watan al-ʿArabi*, 4–10 April 1980.

75. *Al-Jumhuriyya*, 10 September 1982.

76. *Al-Thawra*, 5 May 1986, 7 September 1988.

77. *Al-Thawra*, 1 February 1990; Shafiq ʿAbd al-Razzaq Samarraʾi, *Saddam Husayn nidaluh wa-fikruh al-siyasi* (n.p., 1982), p. 135.

78. *Al-Thawra*, 30 July 1990.

79. *Al-ʿIraq*, 7 January 1991; *al-Jumhuriyya*, 12 August 1990.

80. *Al-ʿIraq*, 9 March 1991.

CHAPTER 3

1. *Al-Jumhuriyya*, 7 February 1969.
2. See the Communist Party organ *al-Thaqafa al-Jadida*, no. 3 (March 1980). Later, the Ba'th also used this term but with positive connotations. *Al-Thawra*, 26 November 1992.
3. *Al-Thawra al-'Arabiyya*, no. 1, 1976, p. 29. In this, the Ba'th is not different from other totalitarian regimes, such as communism, nazism, and fascism, that established one-party systems.
4. *Al-Jumhuriyya*, 1 February 1979.
5. Fadil al-Barrak, *Dawr al-jaysh al-'Iraqi fi hukumat al-difa' al-watani wa-l-harb ma' Baritaniya 'am 1941: dirasa tahliliyya wa-naqdiyya wa-muqarina li-l-khalfiyyat al-ijtima'iyya wa-l-'askariyya*, 2d ed. (Beirut, 1987), p. 162.
6. *Al-Thawra al-'Arabiyya*, no. 11, 1979,
7. Ibid., no. 1, 1976, pp. 49–62. *Al-Thaqafa al-Jadida* wrote that students who refused to join the Ba'th were not allowed to enroll in teachers' seminars or military and other colleges (no. 3 [March 1980]: 171).
8. Michel 'Aflaq, *Nuqtat al-bidaya* (Beirut, 1974), pp. 28, 34, 148, 213; Michel 'Aflaq, *Ma'rakat al-masir al-wahid* (Beirut, 1963), pp. 36–37. In his ideas on struggle and violence, 'Aflaq was most certainly influenced by Georges Sorel; see, e.g., *Reflections on Violence* (New York, 1961), pp. 17, 50, 60, 92, 181.
9. For *Nidal* and *munadala*, see Muhammad bin al-Mukarram bin Manzur, *Lisan al-'Arab*, 6 vols. (Cairo, n.d.), and Reinhart Pieter Anne Dozy, *Supplement aux dictionnaires Arabes*, 2 vols. (Leiden, 1881).
10. *Regional Report No. 9*, p. 30.
11. Hizb al-ba'th al-'Arabi al-ishtiraki, al-qiyada al-qawmiyya, *Al-Minhaj al-thaqafi al-markazi*, vol. 1 (Baghdad, 1977), pp. 167, 171.
12. *Al-Thawra al-'Arabiyya*, no. 11, 1979, pp. 27–37; the quotation is from pp. 34–35.
13. *Al-Jumhuriyya*, 13 September 1968; *al-Thawra*, 19 September 1969, 28 January 1970.
14. Samir al-Khalil, *Republic of Fear: The Politics of Modern Iraq* (Berkeley, 1989), pp. 3–38.
15. Baghdad, 20 December 1991. Another Iraqi writer points out that among other Arabs, too, Iraq's name is associated with violence and intolerance. Khalid Kishtainy, *Arab Political Humour* (London, 1985), p. 96.

CHAPTER 4

1. *Al-Jumhuriyya*, 22 September 1968.
2. Ibid., 17 July 1970.
3. Fa'iq Batti, *Al-Sihafa al-yasariyya fi-l-'Iraq, 1924–1958* (London, 1985), p. 105.
4. Itamar Rabinovich, *Syria under the Ba'th, 1963–1966: The Army-Party Symbiosis* (Jerusalem, 1972), pp. 89–90; John F. Devlin, *The Ba'th Party: A History from Its Origins to 1966* (Stanford, 1976), pp. 211–215; *al-Jamahir*, 24 February 1963.
5. On these attempts, see Haim Shemesh, *Soviet-Iraqi Relations, 1968–1988: In the Shadow of the Iran-Iraq Conflict* (Boulder, Colo., 1992), pp. 22–36.

6. *Al-Jumhuriyya*, 13, 16 August 1968; *al-Thawra*, 11 November 1968, 22 January 1969.

7. See, e.g., Mu'allafat al-rafiq Fahd, *Min watha'iq al-hizb al-shuyu'i al-'Iraqi* (Baghdad, 1973), p. 236.

8. Shemesh, *Soviet-Iraqi Relations*, pp. 24, 66.

9. Saddam Husayn, *Al-Thawra wa-l-nazra al-jadida* (Baghdad, 1981), p. 75.

10. *'Atarid*, a periodical that began in 1934, vehemently attacked those who lived in palaces and ignored the sufferings of the *kadihun*. Batti, *Al-Sihafa*, p. 48.

11. *Al-Jumhuriyya*, 6, 13 August 1968, 22 May 1970; Hizb al-ba'th al-'Arabi al-ishtiraki, al qiyada al-qawmiyya, *Al-Minhaj al-thaqafi al-markazi*, vol. 1 (Baghdad, 1977), pp. 81–82.

12. Batti maintains that the periodical *al-Shabab*, published in 1929, was among the first to use *burjwaziyya*. Batti, *Al-Sihafa*, p. 27.

13. *Al-Jumhuriyya*, 7 February 1969; *al-Thawra*, 2 April, 7 June 1969, 19 March 1973; Husayn, *Al-Thawra wa-l-nazra*, p. 26. The statement was made in July 1977.

14. *Al-Thawra al-'Arabiyya*, no. 5, 1976, pp. 5–7. The political report of the Ninth Regional Congress of 1982 mentioned the notion of "popular democracy" but noted that the Ba'th understood it idiosyncratically. The term *kadih* disappeared earlier. *Regional Report No. 9*, pp. 79–80.

15. *Al-Thawra*, 30 July 1990.

16. There is no Arabic equivalent for the term "democracy." Attempts to render it into *ra'a'iyya* or *shuraqratiyya* from *Shura*, remained semantic curios. Ami Ayalon, *Language and Change in the Arab Middle East* (New York, 1987), p. 108. Zaki Ahmad, "Al-Dimuqratiyya fi-l-khitab al-Islami al-hadith wa-l-mu'asir," *al-Mustaqbal al-'Arabi*, 164 (1992): 112–123.

17. See quotation from *al-Mithaq al-watani* of the Communist Party: "We are struggling for a democratic regime." Fahd, *Min Watha'iq*, p. 123; *al-Jamahir*, 21 February 1963. For the declaration of the Kurds, see *al-Jumhuriyya*, 8 August 1970.

18. Michel 'Aflaq, *Fi sabil al-ba'th* (Beirut, 1974), p. 189. For 'Aflaq's concepts, see Rabinovich, *Syria under the Ba'th*, p. 90.

19. *Al-Thawra*, 29 January 1969. The Kurdistan Democratic Party's mouthpiece later attacked this concept, saying that a free press was a basic pillar of political democracy. *Al-Ta'akhi*, 9 November 1971.

20. For the causes of failure of parliamentary democracy in the Arab world, see Hisham B. Sharabi, *Nationalism and Revolution in the Arab World: The Middle East and North Africa* (Princeton, 1966), pp. 56–64; Elie Kedourie, *Democracy and Arab Political Culture* (Washington, 1992).

21. *Al-Thawra*, 30 April 1972, 20 May 1974, 3 June 1977; *al-Thawra al-'Arabiyya*, no. 10, 1976, p. 31; Hizb al-Ba'th, *Al-Minhaj*, vol. 1, p. 81.

22. Salah al-Din al-Sabbagh, *Fursan al-'Uruba fi-l-'Iraq* (Damascus, 1956), pp. 12–13.

23. *Al-Thawra*, 29 January 1969; *al-'Iraq*, 30 October 1979; *al-Jumhuriyya*, 26 February 1984.

24. *Al-'Iraq*, 30 October 1979.

25. *Al-Thawra*, 22 July 1968; *al-'Iraq*, 20 October 1979; *al-Jumhuriyya*, 1 July 1980.

26. The first saying had already been coined in 1977. Husayn, *Al-Thawra wa-l-nazra*, p. 21. The second was quoted in *al-Thawra*, 16 February 1989.

27. *Al-'Iraq*, 1 March 1989. This *hadith* is not found in the standard collections of al-Bukhari and Muslim, hence its authenticity is open to doubt. Nevertheless, it was widely accepted. Hava Lazarus-Yafeh (ed.), *Studies in the History of the Arabs and Islam* (H) (Tel Aviv, 1982), p. 169.

28. *Al-'Iraq*, 6 March 1989; *Aboth*, chap. 1, v. 14.

29. *Al-'Iraq*, 4 February, 21 March 1989; *al-Thawra*, 1, 2, 6, 11 February 1989, 15 February 1990.

30. *Al-'Iraq*, 15, 25 February, 1 March 1989; *al-Qadisiyya*, 27 November 1989, 19 May 1991; *al-Thawra*, 6 March 1989.

31. *Al-'Iraq*, 6 March 1989; *al-Qadisiyya*, 28 December 1989.

32. *Al-Thawra*, 15 February, in DR, 17 February 1989; *al-'Iraq*, 9 March 1989; *al-Qadisiyya*, 17 September 1991.

33. *Al-'Iraq*, 28 March 1989; *al-Thawra*, 2 March, 3 May 1989.

34. *Al-Tayyar al-Jadid*, 4 January 1989. "Gases" refers to the chemical weapons the Ba'th used against the Kurds in Halabja in March 1988.

35. *Al-Qadisiyya*, 11 July 1990.

36. *Al-Jumhuriyya*, 17 October 1970, 26 July 1979; *al-Thawra*, 19 September 1971, 8 February 1973; *Thawrat 17 tammuz, al-tajriba wa-l-afaq: al-taqrir al-siyasi al-sadir 'an al-mu'tamar al-qutri al-thamin li-hizb al-ba'th al-'Arabi al-ishtiraki al-qutr al-'Iraqi* (n.p., January 1974), p. 100; Hizb al-Ba'th, *Al-Minhaj*, vol. 1, p. 302; Zuhayr Sadiq Rida al-Khalidi, *Al-Qiyam 'ind Saddam Husayn* (Baghdad, 1989), p. 197.

37. *Thawrat 17 tammuz*, p. 143.

38. *Al-Thawra*, 4, 29 January 1969, 23 May 1978, 23 May 1987; *al-Jumhuriyya*, 13 August 1968.

39. *Al-Thawra*, 20 March 1970; Hizb al-Ba'th, *Al-Minhaj*, vol. 1, pp. 167, 194.

40. *Al-Thawra*, 11 February 1977; *al-'Iraq*, 20 October 1979.

41. *Al-Thawra*, 23 May 1987; *al-Qadisiyya*, 12 March 1990; Hasan 'Azba al-'Ubaydi, *Al-Markaz al-dusturi li-hizb al-ba'th al-'Arabi al-ishtiraki* (Baghdad, 1982), p. 235.

42. For vivid portraits of members of parliament, see Hasan al-'Alawi, *Al-Shi'a wa-l-dawla al-qawmiyya fi-l-'Iraq, 1914–1990*, 2d ed. (n.p., 1990), pp. 194–197. On the failure of parliamentary life, see Kedourie, *Democracy*, pp. 25–37, 83–103.

43. See Sharabi, *Nationalism*, pp. 56–59; Devlin, *The Ba'th Party*, p. 214.

44. *Al-Thawra*, 11 November 1968.

45. *Al-Jumhuriyya*, 13 August, 17 September 1968; *al-Thawra*, 11 November 1968, 29 January 1969, 3 June 1977.

46. For the law, see *al-Thawra*, 17 March 1980.

47. *Regional Report No. 9*, p. 83.

48. *Al-Jumhuriyya*, 28 November 1988. Husayn uses the verb *inhashar*, meaning to crowd oneself, to push oneself, which exists only in the Iraqi dialect. See D. R. Woodhead and Wayne Beene, *A Dictionary of Iraqi Arabic* (Washington, 1967).

49. *Al-Thawra*, 2, 14 February, 22 March 1990.

50. Ibid., 2 December 1969, 19 October 1972.

51. *Al-'Iraq*, 1, 4 March 1989; *al-Jumhuriyya*, 1 April 1989.

52. *Al-'Iraq*, 1 March 1989.

53. Ibid., 21 January, 4 March 1989; *al-Qadisiyya*, 12 March 1990.

54. *Al-Thawra,* 8 February 1989.

55. *Al-Jumhuriyya,* 25 April 1991. In an article entitled "Bitter Honey," *Al-'Iraq,* too, called for pluralism—the firm basis of the regime's stability. *Al-'Iraq,* 20 April 1991.

CHAPTER 5

1. *Al-Qadisiyya,* 21 January 1992. On the "benevolent ruler," see Bernard Lewis, *The Political Language of Islam* (Chicago, 1988), pp. 98–102.

2. Ami Ayalon, *Language and Change in the Arab Middle East* (New York, 1987), pp. 124–126.

3. On poetry and propaganda in ancient times, see Lewis, *The Political Language,* pp. 10–11; Hava Lazarus-Yafeh (ed.), *Studies in the History of the Arabs and Islam* (H) (Tel Aviv, 1982), pp. 24–25, 246–249, 336, 349.

4. *Al-Jumhuriyya,* 10 February 1978.

5. His role in the assassination attempt had been given much room in his biographies and even in children's books. In 1981, Adib Makki published a comic-strip album based on Mu'alla's novel. Allen Douglas and Fedwa Malti-Douglas, *Arab Comic Strips* (Bloomington, 1994), pp. 46–59.

6. E.g., E. H. Carr, *What Is History?* (London, 1964), pp. 44–55.

7. *Al-Thawra,* 16 May 1978. The quotation is from sura *al-Ra'd,* v. 17. Usually, no source reference is given for such quotations; the assumption is that the average reader would know where the verse is taken from.

8. Saddam Husayn, *Al-Thawra wa-l-nazra al-jadida* (Baghdad, 1981), p. 60. The article is dated 19 February 1975. An Arab historian, Hisham Sharabi, has criticized the tribal and sectarian relationships that persist in Arab society and reflect the totalitarian character of Arab regimes. *Muqaddimat li-dirasat al-mujtama' al-'Arabi* (Acre, Israel, 1987), pp. 23–26.

9. *Al-Thawra al-'Arabiyya,* March 1975, pp. 10–12; no. 1, 1976, p. 34.

10. Husayn, *Al-Thawra wa-l-nazra,* p. 122. The article is dated 10 February 1976.

11. For Husayn on collective leadership, see *al-Jumhuriyya,* 3 March 1978. He insisted that collective leadership was immune to individual *(fardi)* errors.

12. *Al-Thawra,* 18 October 1971.

13. On *za'im,* see, Lewis, *The Political Language,* pp. 59–60; Hasan al-Basha, *Al-Alqab al-Islamiyya fi-l-ta'rikh wa-l-watha'iq wa-l-athar* (Cairo, 1957), pp. 310–311; Muhammad bin al-Mukarram bin Manzur, *Lisan al-'Arab* (Cairo, n.d.), defines *hakim* as one who prevents oppression and *hukuma* as preventing oppression. Only in the nineteenth century did *hukuma* come to mean government. See Lewis, *The Political Language,* pp. 36–37.

14. *Al-Jumhuriyya,* 28 December 1982; *al-Thawra,* 7 January 1989, 11 March 1990.

15. *Al-Thawra al-'Arabiyya,* no. 1, 1976, p. 49; *al-Jumhuriyya,* 4 September 1981, 10 March 1982.

16. *Al-'Iraq,* 26 September 1985; Sabah Salman, *Saddam Husayn qa'id wa-ta'rikh* (Baghdad, 1986), p. 88; Zuhayr Sadiq Rida al-Khalidi, *Al-Qiyam 'ind Saddam Husayn* (Baghdad, 1989), pp. 173–196.

17. Lewis, *The Political Language,* p. 19; Al-Basha, *Al-Alqab,* pp. 427–428. *Al-qa'ida* in *Lisan al 'Arab* is defined as the leading camel.

18. *Al-'Iraq*, 2 November 1977.

19. *Al-Jumhuriyya*, 1 April 1981; *Alif Ba'*, 28 April 1993. Saddam Kamil (and his brother Husayn) defected to Jordan in August 1995 and were assassinated upon their return to Iraq in February 1996.

20. *Regional Report No. 9*, pp. 216–217.

21. Correct versions would be *al-qa'id al-daruri* (the necessary or inevitable leader) or *qa'id al-darura* (leader by virtue of necessity).

22. *Regional Report No. 9*, pp. 41–42.

23. On *darura*, see Y. Linant de Bellefonds, "Darura," in *EI²*; Lewis, *The Political Language*, pp. 101–102.

24. *Al-Yarmuk*, 28 April 1984.

25. Al-Khalidi, *Al-Qiyam*, p. 227.

26. Ibid., p. 31.

27. *Al-Thawra*, 21 July 1981; *al-'Iraq*, 27 April 1989.

28. *Al-Jumhuriyya*, 14 November, 6 December 1982; *al-Thawra*, 15 November 1982; INA, 13 November, in DR, 16 November 1982.

29. On *bay'a*, see Lewis, *The Political Language*, pp. 58–59; E. Tyan, "Bay'a," in *EI²*.

30. Tyan, "Bay'a," in *EI²*.

31. In Lewis Ma'luf, *Al-Munjid* (Jaffa, 1908), the word *istifta'* means a request for a formal ruling in Islamic law but not yet "referendum."

32. 'Abd al-Razzaq al-Hasani, *Ta'rikh al-wizarat al-'Iraqiyya*, vol. 1 (Sidon, 1940), p. 21.

33. *Al-Jumhuriyya*, 13 November 1982; *Alif Ba'*, 17 November 1982; *Al-Thawra*, 15 November 1982. *Al-Thawra* ridiculed such plebiscites held in other Arab countries, such as Syria. In October 1995, however, a referendum was held to confirm the continuation of Saddam Husayn's presidency. Ofra Bengio, "Iraq" in *MECS 1995*, pp. 321–323.

34. *Al-Jumhuriyya*, 14 November 1982.

35. Ibid., 16 June 1987, 12 November 1988. *Al-Thawra*, 22 June 1989, reported that the "masses" of Basra had sent *bay'a* deeds written with their blood. No such practice is known in Islam. Husayn may have wanted to evoke the well-known Arabic proverb, "Blood doesn't turn into water."

36. *Hurras al-Watan*, 12 November 1989; *al-Qadisiyya*, 25 December 1987. It was also called *raqdat al-dahiya*, an expression found in the Iraqi dialect lexicon and possibly unique to Iraq. See D. R. Woodhead and Wayne Beene, *A Dictionary of Iraqi Arabic* (Washington, 1967).

37. *Al-Jumhuriyya*, 16 April 1983. The reference is to the renewal of the oath, given under a sacred tree at Hudaybiyya in 628.

38. *Al-Thawra*, 2 February 1990; *al-Qadisiyya* 12 July 1991.

39. Roland Barthes, *Mythologies* (Paris, 1957), pp. 216–217.

40. *Al-'Iraq*, 9 January 1989; *al-Qadisiyya*, 28 April 1990.

41. *Al-Jumhuriyya*, 17 July 1987. See also Ghazay Dir' al-Ta'i's book of poetry, *Al-Bahr al-akhdar* (Baghdad, 1988), p. 7.

42. The image of the ruler as the father of the state does not exist in classical Islam; only in Turkey does the word *ata* have political connotations. Lewis, *The Political Language*, p. 17.

43. Shafiq 'Abd al-Razzaq Al-Samarra'i, *Saddam Husayn nidaluh wa-fikruh al-siyasi* (n.p., 1982), p. 72; *al-Jumhuriyya*, 14 November 1988. The newspaper attributed the use of the term "Saddamism" to a Kuwaiti physician heading a

delegation to Iraq. It is ironic that during this period—a year and a half before the invasion—Kuwaiti journalists went out of their way to flatter Iraq in general and Husayn in particular.

44. One can find such metaphors in three poetry books: al-Ta'i, *Al-Bahr al-akhdar*; Kazim Ni'ma al-Tamimi, *Mudhakkirat Basri fi zaman al-harb* (Baghdad, 1988), pp. 63–66; Mahfuz Dawud Salman, *Intazirini bi-thiyab al-qital* (Baghdad, 1988), pp. 39–43. On such honorifics in Islam, see al-Basha, *Al-Alqab*.

45. The prophet Muhammad granted Khalid bin al-Walid the title of *sayf Allah* (God's sword).

46. Two poems dedicated to Husayn shortly before the outbreak of the Iraqi-Iranian war were entitled "Al-faris al-'arabi" (The Arab knight) and "Aba al-fursan" (The father of the knights). *Majallat al-Basra* (n.d.), pp. 71, 101.

47. *Al-Qadisiyya*, 9 July 1986.

48. One of those who received the sword was Iyad Futayyih Khalifa al-Rawi, commander of the Republican Guard during the reconquest of the town of al-Faw in April 1988. Later, he became chief of staff.

49. *Al-Qadisiyya*, 24 March 1988.

50. Radio Baghdad, 23 August, in DR, 24 August 1990.

51. According to most Islamic law schools, the legitimate ruler should be a descendant of Quraysh. Lewis, *The Political Language*, p. 102. Until the fifteenth century, all caliphs were indeed of Qurayshi descent.

52. INA, 8 August, in DR, 9 August 1979. Husayn's family tree appeared in a booklet entitled *Saddam Husayn: Achievements and Life Story* (London, 1981) and also in Amir Ahmad Iskandar, *Saddam Husayn munadilan wa-mufakkiran wa-insanan* (Paris, 1980), p. 21. The latter appeared simultaneously in Arabic, English, and French.

53. Iskandar, *Saddam Husayn*, pp. 17–18.

54. *Al-Thawra*, 8 February 1990. Mudarrisi, the leader of the Shi'i fundamentalist movement Munazzamat al-'amal al-Islami, ridiculed Husayn's pretensions to be a good and upright ruler, saying, "Once, Iraq had a ruler like 'Ali bin Abi Talib and now it has a ruler like Saddam Husayn, and how big is the difference between them." Muhammad Taqi al-Mudarrisi, *Al-'Iraq thawra tantasir* (Beirut, 1983), p. 30.

55. *Al-'Iraq*, 22 September 1985. In Arab society, the moon is the symbol of beauty and goodness. A beautiful girl is called *qamar*; *aqmar al-'ilm wa-shumusuh* is a title used for *'ulama'*.

56. *Al-'Iraq*, 26 October 1986; *al-Jumhuriyya*, 30 December 1986. On the title *mansur*, see al-Basha, *Al-Alqab*, pp. 512–513.

57. *Al-Jumhuriyya*, 21 April, 26 September 1987, 27 April 1988.

58. At the same time—attempting to rewrite history—Saddam Husayn claimed that Saladin had been an Arab. *Al-Thawra*, 22 March 1979.

59. Al-Samarra'i, *Sadaam Husayn*, p. 11; Amazia Baram, "Saddam Hussein: A Political Profile," *Jerusalem Quarterly* 17 (1980): 115; Iskandar, *Saddam Husayn*, p. 17; Fuad Matar, *Saddam Hussein: The Man, the Cause, and the Future* (London, 1981), p. 35. For the registration, see the photograph in ibid., p. 71. He may have obtained the photocopy without its passing Husayn's censorship.

60. Efraim Karsh and Inari Rautsi, *Saddam Hussein: A Political Biography* (London, 1991), pp. 275–276, n. 3.

61. See Sobernheim, "Saladin," in *EI¹*; Andrew S. Ehrenkreutz, *Saladin* (New York, 1972).

62. Emmanuel Sivan, "The Near East during the Crusades," in Lazarus-Yafeh, *Studies in the History of the Arabs and Islam*, pp. 248–249.

63. 'Abd al-Rahman Mustafa, *Al-Batal Salah al-Din* (Baghdad, 1987), pp. 6, 14.

64. *Al-Qadisiyya*, 21 March 1988; *al-Jumhuriyya*, 2, 4 July 1987.

65. *Al-Qadisiyya*, 7 December 1989. The Arabic expression is *khayr khalaf li-khayr salaf*. *Al-salaf* is the collective name for the first generations of Muslims.

66. Ibid., 7, 8 December 1989; *al-Thawra*, 23 April 1990.

67. *Al-Qadisiyya*, 4 February 1991 (quoting the Jordanian daily *al-Sha'b*), 6 March 1988. See also *Babil*, 15 October 1992.

68. The caliphs used to add 'Abdallah to their names; the first to do so was 'Umar bin al-Khattab. Al-Basha, *Al-Alqab*, pp. 393–394.

69. *Al-Jumhuriyya*, 22 November 1980, 24 December 1982.

70. Of the two words for birthday, *milad* and *mawlid*, only the latter is used for the prophet's birthday. It is also in use for other saintly figures. Generally speaking, the mass festivities held to mark Husayn's birthday are an innovation in Iraqi political life.

71. The most ancient *sira* is that by Ibn Ishaq, composed some 150 years after the *hijra*, the emigration of the prophet Muhammad from Mecca to Medina in 622 A.D. Pre-Islamic Arabs had no such custom; the idea of composing a *sira* may originally have been taken from the New Testament. See Y. Rivlin, *The Life of Muhammad* (H) (Tel Aviv, 1936), p. 5; A. Guillaume, *The Life of Muhammad: A Translation of Ishaq's Sirat Rasul Allah* (London, 1955).

72. *Al-Thawra*, 3 December 1990.

73. Of Muhammad's animal Ibn Ishaq wrote: "A white animal, half mule, half donkey; with wings on its sides with which it propelled its feet, putting down each forefoot at the limit of its sight." Guillaume, *The Life of Muhammad*, p. 182; *Al-Jumhuriyya*, 10 September 1987.

74. *Al-Jumhuriyya*, 26 April 1981. On Sawsa and his teachings, see Amatzia Baram, "National [Wataniyya] Integration and Exclusiveness in Political Thought and Practice in Iraq under the Ba'th, 1968–1982" (H), Ph.D. dissertation, Hebrew University of Jerusalem, 1986, pp. 290–304.

75. Ta'i, *Al-Bahr al-akhdar*, p. 13.

76. *Al-Jumhuriyya*, 30 May 1987; *al-'Iraq*, 13 April 1985; *Alif Ba'*, 19 September 1990.

77. *Al-Jumhuriyya*, 4 December 1981, 22 February 1984.

78. *Babil*, 7 August 1991; *al-Jumhuriyya*, 22 January 1987. The blessings appear, for instance, in Fadil al-Barrak, *Mustafa al-Barzani: al-ustura wa-l-haqiqa* (Baghdad, 1989), p. 191; Fadil al-Barrak, *Al-Madaris al-Yahudiyya wa-l-Iraniyya fi-l-'Iraq* (Baghdad, 1985), p. 9.

CHAPTER 6

1. On *watan* and *qawm*, see Muhammad bin al-Mukarram bin Manzur, *Lisan al-'Arab* (Cairo, n.d.). On *watan* and *wataniyya*, see Ami Ayalon, *Language and Change in the Arab Middle East* (New York, 1987), pp. 52–53; Bernard Lewis, *The Political Language of Islam* (Chicago, 1988), pp. 40–41; Bernard Lewis, *The Middle East and the West* (London, 1963), pp. 70–94. *Mawatin* is mentioned once in the Qur'an (sura *al-Tawba*, v. 25), meaning places, lands, or battlegrounds.

2. Sati' al-Husri, one of the leading ideologues of *al-qawmiyya al-'arabiyya*, regarded language and history, but not territory (*watan*), as the essential elements of nationalism. He suggested the term *wataniyya mutatarrifa*, or simply *wataniyya*, for "chauvinism," rejecting other Arab writers' use of *qawmiyya*. Abu Khaldun Sati' al-Husri, *Hawl al-qawmiyya al-'Arabiyya* (Beirut, 1961), pp. 32–42, 99, 293.

3. The communists were the standard-bearers of *wataniyya* and the first (already in 1951) to urge the formation of a *jabha wataniyya*, an Iraqi national front. Fa'iq Batti, *Al-Sihafa al-yasariyya fi-l-'Iraq, 1924–1958* (London, 1985), pp. 135–136. For a similar concept of the Shi'i movement al-Da'wa, see Amatzia Baram, "National [Wataniyya] Integration and Exclusiveness in Political Thought and Practice in Iraq under the Ba'th, 1968–1982" (H), Ph.D. dissertation, Hebrew University of Jerusalem, 1986, pp. 365–389.

4. *Al-Thawra*, 26 December 1968, 10 October 1971.

5. *Al-Jumhuriyya*, 11 January 1972.

6. *Al-Thawra*, 10 March 1983.

7. Ibid., 21 March 1989; *al-'Iraq*, 9 March 1991.

8. *Al-Thawra*, 10, 11 October 1971; *al-Jumhuriyya*, 1 February 1982; *Regional Report No. 9*, p. 172.

9. Saddam Husayn, *Al-Thawra wa-l-nazra al-jadida* (Baghdad, 1981), p. 56; *al-Jumhuriyya*, 16, 26 December 1982.

10. *Al-Thawra*, 1 September 1974; *Regional Report No. 9*, p. 202.

11. *Al-Thawra*, 4 May 1972.

12. Ibid., 21 July 1981.

13. Baram, "National Integration," pp. 236–309.

14. On the other hand, *watan* does not occur there. The word *qawmiyya* is assumed to have appeared first in the early half of the fifth century after the *hijra* in an important missive by Yahya bin Mas'ada. 'Abd al-'Aziz al-Duri, *Al-Judhur al-ta'rikhiyya li-l-shu'ubiyya* (Beirut, n.d.), p. 78.

15. Fadil al-Barrak, *Dawr al-Jaysh al-'Iraqi fi hukumat al-difa' al-watani wa-l-harb ma' Baritaniya 'am 1941: dirasa tahliliyya wa-naqdiyya wa-muqarina li-l-khalfiyyat al-ijtima'iyya wa-l-'askariyya*, 2d ed. (Beirut, 1987), p. 203.

16. Sami Shawkat, *Hadhihi ahdafuna* (Baghdad, 1939), pp. 59–62, 98, 102.

17. Michel 'Aflaq, *Fi sabil al-ba'th* (Beirut, 1974), pp. 111, 119, 128, 130, 181, 182, 199; ibid. (1959), pp. 40–41. The remarks were made in 1941.

18. *Regional Report No. 9*, p. 269.

19. *Al-Thawra al-'Arabiyya*, no. 1, 1976, p. 26; *al-Jumhuriyya*, 4 October 1978; *al-Qadisiyya*, 11 April 1990.

20. Ibid., 11 January 1982.

21. Ibid., 3 June 1982. Ibn Manzur, *Lisan al-'Arab*, gives *'Arab al-lisan* a positive connotation.

22. *Al-Thawra al-'Arabiyya*, 1980, p. 36.

23. *Al-Thawra*, 18 December 1990; *Babil*, 6 May 1992. Another pejorative term was *'Arab Amrika* (the Arabs of America).

24. Such is the meaning of the name in Ibn Manzur, *Lisan al-'Arab*. The word does not occur in other dictionaries.

25. *Al-Jumhuriyya*, 19 June 1987, 1 March 1988; *al-Thawra*, 6 January 1989.

26. *Al-Thawra*, 12 July 1981.

27. Sadiq Kammuna, quoted in Eliyahu Sasson, *On the Road to Peace* (H) (Tel Aviv, 1978), p. 61.

28. E.g., Bakr on the impressive progress of the Iraqi *qutr*, *al-'Iraq*, 30 January 1978. The need to reinforce the fraternity of the *qutrayn*, Syria and Iraq, is stressed in *al-Jumhuriyya*, 26 October 1978.

29. 'Aflaq, *Fi sabil al-ba'th*, pp. 236–238, 242; *Nuqtat al-bidaya* (Beirut, 1974), pp. 128, 166; *Eleventh National Congress*, p. 52.

30. *Al-Jumhuriyya*, 22 October 1969; *al-Thawra*, 7 December 1971; Husayn, *Al-Thawra wa-l-nazra*, pp. 162–163; *al-Thawra al-'Arabiyya*, no. 1, 1976, p. 37; Hizb al-ba'th al-'Arabi al-ishtiraki, al-qiyada al-qawmiyya, *Al-Minhaj al-thaqafi al-markazi*, vol. 2 (Baghdad, 1977), pp. 181, 347.

31. *Al-Thawra al-'Arabiyya*, no. 1, 1976, p. 37; Hizb al-ba'th, *Al-Minhaj*, vol. 1, pp. 180–182.

32. *Al-Jumhuriyya*, 15 August 1968; *al-'Iraq*, 9 February 1980; *Regional Report No. 9*, p. 228.

33. An example is *talahamu*, which means both "to stick together" and "to fight each other."

34. Early in the Iraqi-Iranian war, the party berated those who thought that regaining Iraqi *watani* territory was less important than the reconquest of *qawmi* soil (i.e., Palestine). The point was made in reply to Syrian accusations charging Iraq with ignoring the all-Arab cause. *Al-Thawra al-'Arabiyya*, 1980, p. 18.

35. *Thawrat 17 tammuz, al-tajriba wa-l-afaq: al-taqrir al-siyasi al-sadir 'an al-mu'tamar al-qutri al-thamin li-hizb al-ba'th al-'Arabi al-ishtiraki al-qutr al-'Iraqi* (n.p., January 1974), p. 164.

36. *Regional Report No. 9*, p. 42.

37. Saddam Husayn, *Hawl kitabat al-ta'rikh* (Baghdad, 1979), pp. 16–17. There may be an echo here of Shawkat's words about "the horizon of Iraqi hopes that stretches out over all Arab States." Shawkat, *Hadhidi ahlafuna*, p. 3.

38. Saddam Husayn, *Al-Thawra wa-l-tarbiya al-wataniyya* (Baghdad, 1977), pp. 93–102.

39. *Regional Report No. 9*, p. 256; Husayn, *Al-Thawra wa-l-nazra*, p. 24; Husayn, *Al-Thawra wa-l-tarbiya*, p. 100; *al-Qadisiyya*, 27 June 1990; *al-'Iraq*, 7 January 1991.

40. *Al-'Iraq*, 4 January 1989.

41. As'ad AbuKhalil tried to refute the common view that all-Arab nationalism was disappearing. He argued that that was true only of the "dreamy" kind propagated by 'Aflaq. Instead, a new nationalism was emerging that linked Arab unity with the crucial issues of democracy and Islam. See "A New Arab Ideology?: The Rejuvenation of Arab Nationalism," *MEJ* 46 (1992): 22–36.

42. Estimates for 1931 showed that there were 55% Shi'is, 22% Sunni Arabs, and 14% Kurds. Estimates for 1982–1983 speak of 56–60%, 15–11%, and 25%, respectively. Joyce N. Wiley, *The Islamic Movement of Iraqi Shi'as* (Boulder, Colo., 1992), p. 9. Even if these figures turn out to be exaggerated, the decline of Sunni Arabs cannot be doubted.

CHAPTER 7

1. See Robert Soetrik, *The Islamic Movement of Iraq, 1958–1980*, Amsterdam Middle East Research Associates, December 1991, Occasional Paper, no. 12, p. 11. On Muhammad Baqir al-Sadr's stance against communism, see his *Falsafatuna*, 2d ed. (Beirut, 1969), pp. 25–34, and Chibli Mallat, *The Renewal of*

Islamic Law: Muhammad Baqer al-Sadr, Najaf, and the Shi'i International (Cambridge, 1993), p. 12.

2. E.g., *al-'Iraq*, 16 April 1980, mentions Iranian Shi'is. Exceptionally, *al-Jumhuriyya*, 27 March 1983, spoke of Shi'is in Iraq. Under the monarchy, there was less sensitivity about this. Cf. Faysal's memorandum, 'Abd al-Razzaq Al-Hasani, *Ta'rikh al-wizarat al-'Iraqiyya*, vol. 3 (Sidon, 1940), pp. 189–195.

3. Stephen H. Longrigg, *Four Centuries of Modern Iraq* (Oxford, 1925), pp. 147–153.

4. Ayatollah Muhsin al-Hakim, in *Al-'Ahd al-Jadid*, 28 January 1963; Hasan al-'Alawi, *Al-Shi'a wa-l-dawla al-qawariyya fi-l-'Iraq, 1914–1990*, 2d ed. (n.p., 1990), p. 19.

5. Al-'Alawi, *Al-Shi'a*, p. 42. For *rawafid* in the nineteenth century, see Meir Litvak, "The Shi'i 'Ulama' of Najaf and Karbala', 1791–1904: A Socio-Political Analysis," Ph.D. dissertation, Harvard University, 1991, pp. 52, 138, 176.

6. See Ami Ayalon, *Language and Change in the Arab Middle East* (New York, 1987), pp. 23–25.

7. Previous regimes also used the word *ta'ifi* ("sectarian") for attacking the Shi'a. The Shi'i leader Salih al-Jabr was called *al-ta'ifi* (the sectarian). *Al-Thawra*, 20 November 1962.

8. Hizb al-ba'th al-'Arabi al-ishtiraki, al-qiyada al-qawmiyya, *Al-Minhaj al-thaqafi al-markazi*, vol. 2 (Baghdad, 1977), pp. 157–163. The expressions "sectarian complex" and the "simple masses" echo Faysal's words in his memorandum about "the ignorant Shi'i mob" persecuted by the Ottomans. Hasani, *Ta'rikh*, vol. 3, p. 190.

9. Fadil al-Barrak, *Al-Madaris al-Yahudiyya wa-l-Iraniyya fi-l-'Iraq* (Baghdad, 1985), pp. 9, 106, 116, 123, 133, 143, 146, 176. The Ba'th's desire to identify with 'Ali clearly contradicted al-Barrak's implication that he was a symbol of sectarianism.

10. *Regional Report No. 9*, pp. 291–297. The report of the ninth national (i.e., all-Arab) congress also warned of the situation in the south and of the implications of *al-ta'ifiyya* being fostered by imperialism (p. 37).

11. Saddam Husayn, *Al-Thawra wa-l-nazra al-jadida* (Baghdad, 1981), p. 81 (statement made on 13 November 1973).

12. *Al-Thawra al-'Arabiyya*, no. 5, 1976, pp. 27, 29, 32, 37; *al-Thawra*, 3 September 1991.

13. *Al-'Iraq*, 12 April 1980, 16 March 1989; *al-Jumhuriyya*, 18 June 1980, 9 December 1982; *Regional Report No. 9*, pp. 225, 279, 297.

14. *Al-Qadisiyya*, 17 March 1991; *al-Thawra*, 29 March 1991, in DR, 3 April 1991.

15. Al-'Alawi, *Al-Shi'a*, pp. 10–11, 41, 262–263. During the uprising, al-'Alawi played a leading role among opposition expatriates.

16. Ibid., pp. 259–265, 274. For an account of the formidable expulsion of 240,000 Kurds and Shi'is in the 1970s, see Samir al-Khalil, *Republic of Fear: The Politics of Modern Iraq* (Berkeley, 1989), p. 19.

17. See, for example, in 'Abd al-Hadi al-Fukayki, *Al-Shu'ubiyya wa-l-qawmiyya al-'Arabiyya* (Beirut, n.d.), p. 37.

18. Muhammad bin al-Mukarram bin Manzur, *Lisan al-'Arab* (Cairo, n.d.); D. B. Macdonald, "Shu'ubiya," in *EI¹*; Uriel Dann, *Iraq under Qassem: A Political History, 1958–1963* (New York, 1969), p. 162; Khalil, *Republic of Fear*, pp. 154, 218; Bernard Lewis, *The Arabs in History* (London, 1950), p. 93; Roy

P. Mottahedeh, "The Shu'ubiyya Controversy and the Social History of Early Islamic Iran," *IJMES* 7 (1976): 161–182; Sami H. Hanna and George H. Gardner, "Al-shu'ubiyyah Updated," in *Arab Socialism: A Documentary Survey* (Leiden, 1969), pp. 80–97; al-Fukayki, *Al-Shu'ubiyya*, p. 43; 'Abd al-'Aziz al-Duri, *Al-Judhur al-ta'rikhiyya li-l-shu'ubiyya* (Beirut, n.d.), p. 9. The Egyptian writer Taha Husayn defined *shu'ubiyya* as a *madhhab* whose main proponent was Abu Nuwwas, Harun al-Rashid's famous court poet. Quoted in al-Fukayki, *Al-Shu'ubiyya*, p. 80.

19. Al-Duri, *Al-Judhur*, p. 58, quoting the historian al-Tabari; ibid., p. 85; *Al-Jumhuriyya*, 17 December 1982, 10 January 1983.

20. Sura *al-Hujrat*, v. 13; Macdonald, "Shu'ubiya," in *EI¹*. According to al-Fukayki (who quotes Ibn Qutayba), the first to use the word *shu'ubiyya* was al-Jahiz. Al-Fukayki, *Al-Shu'ubiyya*, p. 31.

21. Al-Fukayki, *Al-Shu'ubiyya*, pp. 20, 52, 111.

22. Hanna and Gardner, *Arab Socialism*, pp. 80–97.

23. Al-Fukayki, *Al-Shu'ubiyya*, p. 98; Hizb al-Ba'th, *al-Minhaj*, vol. 2, p. 162.

24. *Al-Jamahir*, 25 February, 10 March 1963.

25. *Al-Jumhuriyya*, 13 January 1971. The expression "*shu'ubi* pens" is borrowed from al-Duri, *Al-Judhur*, p. 50. See also Barrak, *Al-Madaris*, pp. 48, 192. On the Jewish *shu'ubiyya*, see al-Fukayki, *Al-Shu'ubiyya*, p. 98, and al-Barrak, *Al-Madaris*, p. 9.

26. *Al-Ta'akhi*, 10 November 1971.

27. *Al-'Iraq*, 9 April 1980; *al-Jumhuriyya*, 2 May 1983.

28. *Regional Report No. 9*, pp. 188, 254, 293. *Mutafarris* has two meanings: one who has become a Persian or one who pretends to be a knight or a soldier on horseback.

29. *Al-Jumhuriyya*, 12 May 1987.

30. *Al-Thawra*, 26 January, 17 March 1989; *al-'Iraq*, 16 March 1989; similarly, *Al-Qadisiyya*, 29 March 1989.

31. *Al-Thawra*, 17 July 1990, 3 September 1991.

32. Al-'Alawi, *Al-Shi'a*, pp. 20, 45–49, 225, 275, 370–372, 381. Al-Fukayki described al-Jawahiri as the leading *shu'ubi* poet and propagandist. Al-Fukayki, *Al-Shu'ubiyya*, pp. 78–79.

33. On Makiya-Khalil, see *New Yorker*, 6 January 1992.

34. Al-Khalil, *Republic of Fear*, pp. 153–154, 216–220.

35. Ibn Manzur, *Lisan al-'Arab*; A. Miquel, "Iklim," in *EI²*.

36. Sami Shawkat, *Hadhihi ahdafuna* (Baghdad, 1939), p. 38. He accused foreigners in general of propagating the idea of *iqlimiyya*.

37. Al-'Alawi, *Al-Shi'a*, pp. 246, 295, 316. Here the verb *ta'aqlam* is used differently from its common meaning of "get used to."

38. Ibid., pp. 357, 372–377, 383. Joyce Wiley maintains that most of the Sunni tribes did not take part in the 1920 revolt because, among other reasons, the British increased their subsidies to the tribal chiefs. Joyce N. Wiley, *The Islamic Movement of Iraqi Shi'as* (Boulder, Colo., 1992), pp. 17, 27.

39. Al-'Alawi, *Al-Shi'a*, pp. 333–336. The Shi'i fundamentalist al-Mudarrisi declared that *qawmiyya* and the Westernizing trends had come to an end. Muhammad Taqi al-Mudarrisi, *'An al-'Iraq wa-l-haraka al-Islamiyya* (London, 1988), p. 107.

40. Muhammad Taqi al-Mudarrisi, *Al-'Iraq thawra tantasir* (Beirut, 1983), p. 23.

CHAPTER 8

1. Sami Shawkat, *Hadhihi ahdafuna* (Baghdad, 1939), pp. 34–35, 57, 102.

2. *Nidal al-ba'th fi sabil al-wahda al-hurriyya wa-l-ishtira kiyya*, vol. 1 (Beirut, 1963), p. 175.

3. Jalal al-Talabani, *Kurdistan wa-l-haraka al-qawmiyya al-Kurdiyya* (Beirut, 1971), pp. 308–309.

4. *Al-Ta'akhi*, 8 April 1973. Talabani rejected such "imaginary stories." Talabani, *Kurdistan*, p. 26. In his book on the Ba'th, Hani al-Fukayki noted that some Ba'this were trying hard to find books and other sources to "prove" the Arab origin of the Kurds. See Hani al-Fukayki, *Awkar al-hazima: tajribati fi hizb al-ba'th al-'Iraqi* (London, 1993), p. 76.

5. Michel 'Aflaq, *Nuqtat al-bidaya* (Beirut, 1974), pp. 107–108 (statements made on 10 June 1969); *Eleventh National Congress*, pp. 278–279.

6. *Al-Ta'akhi*, 10 November 1971. The paper replied to Talfah's claim that many Muslim military commanders, writers, and scientists had excelled in Arabic and served the Arab nation well but nevertheless "they are not Arab."

7. *Al-Thawra*, 23 February, 22 March 1979; *Los Angeles Times*, 20 April 1979; Radio Baghdad, 15 April, in DR, 17 April 1980.

8. Basile Nikitine, *Les Kurdes: Étude sociologique et historique* (Paris, 1956), p. 225; I'met cherif Vanly, "Kurdistan in Iraq," in Gerard Chaliand (ed.), *People without a Country* (London, 1980), p. 198.

9. *Al-Thawra*, 19 July, 9, 13 November 1968, 11 January 1969; *al-Jumhuriyya*, 31 July, 8 November 1968.

10. *Al-Thawra*, 13 November 1968, 11 January, 28 November 1969. On one occasion, the Kurds were even referred to by the term *umma* rather than *qawm*. *Al-Thawra*, 15 January 1973.

11. *Al-Ta'akhi*, 15 November 1972, quoting *al-Thawra*, 22 December 1969, and, similarly, *al-Thawra al-'Arabiyya*, no. 1, 1970. The originals were not available to me, but the quotations may be considered authentic both because they were not denied by the Ba'th and because other quotations cited by *al-Ta'akhi* were indeed found to have been correct.

12. *Hukm dhati* is not found in the two dictionaries from early in the twentieth century: Lewis Ma'luf, *Al-Munjid* (Jaffa, n.d.), and J. B. Bello, *Al-Fara'id al-durriyya* (Beirut, 1920).

13. 'Aflaq, *Nuqtat al-bidaya*, p. 105 (statement made on 10 June 1969); Fa'iq Batti, *Al-Sihafa al-yasariyya fi-l- 'Iraq, 1924–1958* (London, 1985), p. 121. The Iraqi Communist Party had inserted this clause into its platform at its second congress in September 1956.

14. *Al-Thawra*, 17 December 1969.

15. Muhammad Taqi al-Mudarrisi, *'An al-'Iraq wa-l-haraka al-Islamiyya* (London, 1988), p. 37. These words were said in the second half of the 1980s when there were attempts at rapprochement between the Shi'i and the Kurdish opposition.

16. *Al-Jumhuriyya*, 26 January 1970.

17. *Al-Thawra*, 12 March 1970; *al-Jumhuriyya*, 17 July 1970.

18. *Al-Ta'akhi*, 13 September 1971. The Ba'th view on the same point appeared in *al-Thawra*, 16 November 1972.

19. The Ba'th used the term *ittifaq* only rarely and then in a restrictive meaning such as *ittifaq waqf al-qital* (ceasefire agreement) or *ittifaq muwaqqat* (pro-

visional agreement). See *Dawr al-jaysh al-'Iraqi fi harb tishrin 1973* (Beirut, 1975), pp. 139, 147.

20. Sa'd Naji Jawad, *Al-'Iraq wa-l-mas'ala al-Kuridyya, 1958–1970* (London, 1990), p. 139, n. 33.

21. *Al-Jumhuriyya*, 12 March 1970, 16 March 1971.

22. *Al-Kifah* (Lebanon), 16 March 1971; *al-Thawra*, 20 October 1972; *al-Ta'akhi*, 15 November 1972.

23. Saddam Husayn, *Hawl kitabat al-ta'rikh* (Baghdad, 1976), p. 17.

24. Earlier, the terms "Kurdistan" and *Kurdistan al-'Iraqiyya* were used freely by non-Kurds. See Mahmud al-Durra, *Al-Qadiyya al-Kurdiyya*, 2d ed. (Beirut, 1966), pp. 17, 248. The Ba'th party used the term "Kurdistan" during attempts to work out a conciliation with the Kurds. See Husayn in *al-Jumhuriyya*, 31 January 1988.

25. *Al-Jumhuriyya*, 19–20 May 1971.

26. *Al-Thawra*, 30 July 1990.

27. Ibid., 12, 27 March 1974.

28. Relatively free elections for a Kurdish Assembly were held in May 1992 when the Kurdish region was not under the regime's control.

29. See Muhammad bin al-Mukarram bin Manzur, *Lisan al-'Arab* (Cairo, n.d.); Ma'luf, *Al-Munjid*; Ami Ayalon, "From Fitna to Thawra," *Studia Islamica* 67 (1987): 157–158.

30. *Al-Thawra*, 9 February 1976; *Regional Report No. 9*, p. 56.

31. Muhammad Amin Zaki, *Khulasat ta'rikh al-Kurd wa-Kurdistan: Ta'rikh al-duwal wa-l-imarat al-Kurdiyya fi-l-'ahd al-Islami* (Cairo, 1948), trans. Muhammad 'Ali 'Awni (London, 1986), p. xii.

32. Jawad, *Al-'Iraq*, p. 121, n. 56. Earlier, the splinter group headed by Ibrahim Ahmad and Jalal al-Talabani had attacked Barzani and President 'Abd al-Salam 'Arif for intentionally avoiding the term "Kurdistan" in the cease-fire agreement between them. Ibid., p. 100.

33. Talabani, *Kurdistan*, p. 30. Terms such as "chauvinist," "fascist," "racist," or "fanatic" were current at that time with both sides when referring to the other.

34. *Al-Thawra*, 30 October 1972. This might be compared with Israeli and Palestinian usage for disputed areas; e.g., "Palestine" versus "the occupied areas" or simply "the areas" or else "Judea and Samaria," the choice being determined by the speaker's ideology.

35. *Al-Ta'akhi*, 8 April 1973.

36. For quotations from *al-Kadir* and comments on them, see *al-Thawra*, 30 October 1972. For later use of this term, see *al-Kadir*, May 1974, no. 22. It was also used extensively by Talabani; see *Kurdistan*, pp. 326–327.

37. Talabani, *Kurdistan*, p. 331.

38. Jawad, *Al-'Iraq*, p. 67; *al-Thawra*, 30 October 1972, quoting *al-Ta'akhi*, 15 November 1972, and *al-Kadir*, May 1974.

39. *Al-Kadir* quoted in Jawad, *Al-'Iraq*, p. 67.

40. Talabani, *Kurdistan*, p. 137, quoting "goal no. 1" of the Ruzgari party, set up in 1935. Federation became the Kurds' declared goal after the Gulf War.

41. *Al-Kadir*, May 1974.

42. *Al-Ta'akhi*, 13 September 1971, 5 July, 6, 21 November, 7 December 1972, 11 March 1973; *al-Kadir*, May 1974, no. 22. Later, Saddam Husayn re-

acted to the Arabization issue by saying that there was no law forbidding Arabs to live in areas with a Kurdish majority. *Al-'Iraq*, 22 July 1978.

43. *Al-Ta'akhi*, 29 August 1968, as quoted by *al-Jumhuriyya*, 19, 20 May 1971. The term *al-'Iraq* had in fact existed in the Middle Ages, referring only to lower Mesopotamia, whose northern borders run through the towns of Tikrit (on the Tigris) and Hit (on the Euphrates). A. Miquel, "Irak," in *EI²*.

44. Talabani, *Kurdistan*, p. 323; Jawad, *Al-'Iraq*, pp. 82, 148; Uriel Dann, *Iraq under Qassem: A Political History, 1958–1963* (New York, 1969), p. 141.

45. Jawad, *Al-'Iraq*, p. 67; Talabani, *Kurdistan*, p. 19; *al-Ta'akhi*, 15 January, 15 November 1972.

46. Jawad, *Al-'Iraq*, p. 82, quoting a statement by Ibrahim Ahmad, one of the leaders of the Kurdish movements, to *Kha-bat* in the 1960s.

47. Ibid., p. 84.

48. Ibid., p. 67; Talabani, *Kurdistan*, p. 137.

49. *Al-Ta'akhi*, 21 November, 7 December 1972, 11 February 1973. The quotation is from 21 November.

CHAPTER 9

1. Salah al-Din-al-Sabbagh, *Fursan al-'Uruba fi-l-'Iraq* (Damascus, 1956), p. 29.

2. *Al-Jumhuriyya*, 22 July 1968.

3. *Al-Thawra*, 10 November 1968, 6 January, 26 February 1969.

4. *Al-Jamahir*, 20 April 1963; *al-Thawra*, 6 January 1969; *al-Jumhuriyya*, 18 June 1980, 21 June 1982; *Regional Report No. 9*, pp. 190, 279; *al-'Iraq*, 7 January 1989.

5. *Al-Jumhuriyya*, 16 November 1971. See also *al-Thawra al-'Arabiyya*, March 1975, p. 23; *Eleventh National Congress*, p. 181; As'ad AbuKhalil, "A New Arab Ideology?: The Rejuvenation of Arab Nationalism," *MEJ* 46 (1992): 27.

6. *Al-Jumhuriyya*, 11 August 1990.

7. *Al-Thawra*, 23 February, 22 March 1979; INA, 12 July, in SWB, 14 July 1982.

8. *Regional Report No. 9*, p. 37.

9. Muhammad bin al-Mukarram bin Manzur, *Lisan al-'Arab* (Cairo, n.d.); see also sura *al-Baqara*, vv. 96, 187, 189; sura *al-Anfal*, vv. 25, 74; sura *al-Anbiya'*, v. 36; and sura *al-Hajj*, v. 52.

10. *Al-Qadisiyya*, 11 April 1991; *al-Thawra*, 15 September 1991.

PART IV

1. *Baghdad Observer*, 1 December 1977; INA, 12 July, in DR, 14 July 1992. The image of the United States as a wolf is inspired by al-Sabbagh's depiction of Britain. The same image also appeared in the writing of another Iraqi who contended that U.S.-Iraqi relations were characterized by "the complex of creating an enemy" (*'uqdat sina'at al-'aduw*). Sa'd al-Bazzaz, *Harb talid ukhra: al-ta'rikh al-sirri li-harb al-khaij* (Amman, 1992), pp. 11, 155.

2. Hisham B. Sharabi, *Nationalism and Revolution in the Arab World: The Middle East and North Africa* (Princeton, 1966), p. 101. The sense of conspira-

cies being afoot was so strong that Zaki Arsuzi was said to have blamed a British conspiracy when he fell in the street. Al-Bazzaz, *Harb talid ukhra*, p. 157.

3. *Al-Jumhuriyya*, 6 May 1987. Husayn's biographer, Fuad Matar, said that Husayn had begun readying himself for war immediately after signing the 1975 agreement with Iran. Fuad Matar, *Saddam Hussein: The Man, the Cause, the Future* (London, 1981), p. 12.

CHAPTER 10

1. Saddam Husayn, *Al-Thawra wa-l-nazra al-jadida* (Baghdad, 1981), pp. 27, 52.

2. Richard Koebner and Helmut Dan Schmidt, *Imperialism: The Study and Significance of a Political Word, 1840–1960* (Cambridge, England, 1964), pp. xii–xxv, 301–325. Interestingly, one of the first persons to use *isti'mar* was A. T. Wilson, the British administrator high commissioner. In a proclamation in 1919, he asserted that Britain had not entered Iraq for reasons of *isti'mar* but in order to free it from its (Ottoman) yoke. 'Abd al-Razzaq al-Hasani, *Al-Thawra al-'Iraqiyya al-kubra* (Sidon, 1965), p. 22.

3. *Al-Thawra*, 9 November 1968. Koebner and Schmidt in *Imperialism* noted that *isti'mar* was the equivalent of imperialism (p. 320). However, a listing of foreign terms that had entered into Arabic by the 1960s did not mention *imbiryaliyya*. Charles Issawi, "European Loan-Words in Contemporary Arabic Writing: A Case Study in Modernization," *MES* 3 (1967): 110–133.

4. Muhammad Taqi al-Mudarrisi, *'An al-'Iraq wa-l-haraka al-Islamiyya* (London, 1988), pp. 17, 79–80, 158; *al-'Alam*, 1 August 1991.

5. *Al-Jumhuriyya*, 13 November 1986; *al-Qadisiyya*, 18 December 1990.

6. I was told of the origin of the name by Jews from Iraq.

7. *Al-'Iraq*, 16 February 1980; *Babil*, 24 August 1992.

8. The original quotation is from Salah al-Din al-Sabbagh, *Fursan al-'Uruba fi-l-'Iraq* (Damascus, 1956), pp. 29–30; the rest of the passages are from pp. 29, 34, 246. The simplified version appeared in *al-Qadisiyya*, 26 April 1990. The quotation from the Qur'an is taken from sura *al-Naml*, v. 34.

9. *Al-Zaman*, 12, 17, 23 May; 17, 24 June; 6, 12, 13 July 1958.

10. Michel 'Aflaq, *Ma'rakat al-masir al-wahid* (Beirut, 1963), p. 27. The remarks were made on 17 April 1955.

11. *Al-Thawra*, 31 January 1969, 30 July 1971; Husayn, *Al-Thawra wa-l-nazra*, p. 256.

12. *Al-Thawra*, 25 April 1969, 29 August, 13 September, 7 December 1971, 30 August 1972; *al-Jumhuriyya*, 17 October 1969.

13. *Al-Jumhuriyya*, 13 August 1970.

14. *Thawrat 17 tammuz, al-tajriba wa-l-afaq: al-taqrir al-siyasi al-sadir 'an al-mu'tamar al-qutri al-thamin li-hizb al-ba'th al-'Arabi al-Ishtiraki* (n.p., January 1974), pp. 190–191; *al-Thawra*, 5 October 1973, 8 April 1974; *al-Jumhuriyya*, 10 June 1975; Husayn, *Al-Thawra wa-l-nazra*, p. 267; Sabah Mahmud Muhammad, *Al-Fikr al-jiyubulitiki li-Saddam Husayn* (Baghdad, 1982), pp. 205–207 (statements made in 1975).

15. An Iraqi historian, Nizar 'Abd al-Latif al-Hadithi, perceived in the thirteenth-century Mongol conquest of Iraq the beginning of imperialism in the Arab region. *Al-Jumhuriyya*, 28 December 1987.

16. Sabbagh, *Fursan al-ʿuruba fi-l-ʿIraq*, pp. 29, 35; Hizb al-baʿth al-ʿArabi al-ishtiraki, al-qiyada al-qawmiyya, *Al-Minhaj al-thaqafi al-markazi*, vol. 2 (Baghdad, 1977), p. 92.

17. Hizb al-baʿth, *Al-Minhaj*, vol. 2, pp. 85–102.

18. *Al-Jumhuriyya*, 19 September 1988. See also an article on "cultural imperialism" in *al-Jumhuriyya*, 22 May 1989.

19. *Al-Thawra*, 26 January 1989.

20. Ibid., 25 February 1990; Radio Baghdad, 28 May, in DR, 29 May 1990. For the genesis of the crisis, see Ofra Bengio, "Iraq," in *MECS 1990*, pp. 387–397.

21. *Al-Qadisiyya*, 18 June, 1 November 1990, 15, 16 January 1991; *al-Thawra*, 18 July 1990. In his book on the 1991 Gulf War, al-Bazzaz mentioned that before the war, Iraqi writers had propagated the "conspiracy theory" as an explanation for U.S. policy toward Iraq. Saʿd al-Bazzaz, *Harb talid ukhra: al-taʾrikh al-sirri li-harb al-khalij* (Amman, 1992), p. 157.

22. *Al-Jumhuriyya*, 5 September 1992.

23. Koebner and Schmidt, *Imperialism*, p. 324.

24. *Al-Thawra*, 4 February 1969. It had appeared once before in ʿAflaq, *Maʿrakat al-masir*, in an article dating from 1956, p. 45. For examples of the use of the two forms at one and the same time, see *al-Thawra*, 2 April 1969; Fadil al-Barrak, *Al-Madaris al-Yahudiyya wa-l-Iraniyya fi-l-ʿIraq* (Baghdad, 1985), p. 167, "*Israʾil*," p. 183, *Israʾil*.

25. On *al-dakhala* and other tribal customs, see ʿAbdallah Fahd al-Nafisi, *Dawr al-Shiʿa fi tatawwur al-ʿIraq al-siyasi al-hadith*, 2d ed. (n.p., 1986), pp. 32–46. To an Arab to be called *dakhil* is deeply offensive because it has the connotation of strangeness and remaining outside the nation *umma*. A true Arab is *asil* (pure, genuine).

26. *Al-Thawra*, 10 November 1968, 5 January, 26 February, 2 June 1969, 8 March, 17 October 1990; *al-Jumhuriyya*, 19 July 1968, 14 May 1970, 18 October 1978; Hizb al-baʿth, *Al-Minhaj*, vol. 2, p. 93; *al-ʿIraq*, 11, 24 June 1981; *Thawrat 17 Tammuz*, p. 190.

27. *Al-Jamahir*, 21 April 1963; *Thawrat 17 Tammuz*, p. 211; *al-Thawra*, 1 June 1972, 28 January 1991; *al-ʿIraq*, 15 November 1990; *al-Qadisiyya*, 11 April 1991; al-Barrak, *Al-Madaris*, p. 227; Saʿd al-Bazzaz, *Al-Harb al-sirriyya: Khafaya al-dawr al-Israʾili fi harb al-khalij* (London, 1987), p. 89. The image of Israel as a cancerous growth appeared earlier in ʿAbd al-Rahman al-Bazzaz, *Safahat min al-ams al-qarib: thawrat al-ʿIraq . . .* (Beirut, 1960), p. 173.

28. *Al-Thawra*, 26 October 1971, 3 August 1972; *al-Qadisiyya*, 12 June 1990; Tariq ʿAziz, *Thawrat al-tariq al-jadid* (Baghdad, 1975), p. 88; al-Bazzaz, *Al-Harb al-sirriyya*, p. 89.

29. "Hal iktamal al-sinaryu al-Sahyuni fi-l-mintaqa," *Al-Thawra al-ʿArabiyya*, p. 43; *al-Thawra al-ʿArabiyya*, 1984, p. 43. See the chapter dealing with the Iraqi strategy vis-à-vis the Zionist-Persian challenge, ibid., p. 5. See also al-Bazzaz, *al-Harb al-sirriyya*, pp. 25, 77.

30. *Al-Thawra*, 1 July 1990; *al-Jumhuriyya*, 18 November 1991.

31. Michel ʿAflaq, *Fi sabil al-baʿth* (Beirut, 1974), p. 329; Fadil al-Barrak, *Dawr al-Jaysh al-ʿIraqi fi hukumat al-difaʿ al-watani wa-l-harb maʿ Baritaniya ʿam 1941: dirasa tahliliyya wa-naqdiyya wa-muqarina li-l-khalfiyyat al-ijtimaʿiyya wa-l-ʿaskariyya*, 2d ed. (Beirut, 1987), p. 11; Hizb al-Baʿth, *Al-Minhaj*, vol. 2, p. 92; *al-Qadisiyya*, 13 June 1990; *al-Thawra al-ʿArabiyya*, March 1983, pp. 51–52.

32. Al-Bazzaz, *Al-Harb al-sirriyya*, p. 25; *al-Jumhuriyya*, 14 May 1970; *al-*

Thawra, 1 June 1972, 17 April 1973, 17 October 1990; *Eleventh National Congress*, p. 31; 'Aflaq, *Fi sabil al-ba'th*, p. 223; al-Barrak, *Dawr al-Jaysh*, p. 30; "Mustaqbal Iran bayn hukm al-tafwid al-ilahi wa-l-jumhuriyya al-mustaqilla," *Al-Thawra al-'Arabiyya*, p. 52.

33. *Al-Jumhuriyya*, 18 May 1983, 12 November 1987.

34. Bazzaz was director of the Iraqi cultural center in London from 1980 until 1984 and later director-general of the Iraqi News Agency, director of the Iraqi radio and television, and editor of *al-Jumhuriyya*. He has been in exile since 1993. At the end of the Iraqi-Iranian war, Muhammad Jasim al-Hindawi published "Al-Thaqafat al-mudadda al-Isra'iliyya al-Iraniyya" (The conflicting Israeli-Iranian cultures) in *al-Jumhuriyya*, 18 August 1991.

35. Al-Bazzaz, *Al-Harb al-sirriyya*, pp. 59–60.

36. *Al-Qadisiyya*, 9 July 1986. The quotation is from al-Barrak, *Al-Madaris*, p. 183.

37. "Mustaqbal Iran," pp. 51–55; "Hal iktamal," pp. 42–43; *al-Jumhuriyya*, 12 August 1987; Al-Bazzaz, *Al-Harb al-sirriyya*, pp. 53–77.

38. *Al-Jumhuriyya*, 6 December 1987. *Al-Bunduqiyya* means "gun" but is also the name of Venice. The pun equates *The Merchant of Venice* with modern arms dealers.

39. *Al-Jumhuriyya*, 11 August 1983. On the arch, see Samir al-Khalil, *The Monument: Art, Vulgarity, and Responsibility in Iraq* (Berkeley, 1991), pp. 49–54.

40. *Al-Jumhuriyya*, 16 March 1971, 18 October, 3 November 1978; *al-'Iraq*, 1 April 1978, 26 March 1980, 24 June 1981; *al-Thawra*, 19 March, 1 June, 1973, 19 April 1976.

41. *Al-Jumhuriyya*, 7 February 1969; *al-Thawra*, 2 April, 2 June, 19 September 1969, 11 February 1990; *al-'Iraq*, 18 November 1985; Hizb al-Ba'th, *Al-Minhaj*, vol. 1, p. 130. See wa'd in Muhammad bin al-Mukarram bin Manzur, *Lisan al-'Arab* (Cairo, n.d.).

42. *Al-Jumhuriyya*, 20 August 1980; *al-'Iraq*, 7 January 1981. Husayn's only relatively moderate expression was recorded when he met the Jewish U.S. congressman Stephen Solarz; he said that *Israelis* (but not the state of Israel, as some papers wrongly cited him) were entitled "to conditions of security" (*hala amina*). *Al-Jumhuriyya*, 3 January 1983.

43. *Al-Qadisiyya*, 3 April 1990; *al-Thawra*, 28 January 1991. Already, in 1989, *al-Thawra* predicted that the "Zionist entity" would not manage to enter the twenty-first century (20, 26 March 1989).

44. The usual sixteenth-century name was Mamalik-i Iran or just Iran. See Roger Savory, "The Safavid State and Polity," *Iranian Studies* 7 (1974): 179–180. In 1934, the use of the name "Persia" was formally forbidden, as it was explained, it referred only to the province of Fars.

45. In the first decade of the Ba'th, "Persia" or "Persian" were used sporadically. See *al-Jumhuriyya*, 17 October 1969; *al-Thawra*, 27 December 1972; Hizb al-Ba'th, *Al-Minhaj*, vol. 1, p. 133.

46. "Mustaqbal Iran," pp. 54–55.

47. *Al-'Iraq* published a weekly column entitled "Iraqi National Security and Persian Ambitions [*atma'*]"; see, for example, 12 April 1980.

48. For Khalij Basra, see al-Sabbagh, *Fursan al-'Uruba fi-l-'Iraq*, p. 29. For *al-Khalij al-'Arabi*, see, e.g., *al-Thawra*, 3 February 1969, 27 December 1972; *al-Jumhuriyya*, 24 April 1970.

49. *Al-Jumhuriyya*, 24 April 1970; *al-Thawra*, 1 July, 22 August, 7 Decem-

ber 1971, 27 December 1972, 24 November, 17 December 1974; *al-ʿIraq*, 11 August 1977; Hizb al-baʿth, *Al-Minhaj*, vol. 1, pp. 133, 140.

50. "Mustaqbal Iran," p. 60, gave a full list of such changes. In 1935, Riza Shah initiated a campaign to purify the Persian language by discarding Arabic and other foreign words. Donald N. Wilber, *Riza Shah Pahlavi: The Resurrection and Reconstruction of Iran* (New York, 1975), p. 163.

51. *Al-Thawra*, 24, 25 April 1969.

52. Sharif al-Ras, *Katibat dabbabat raʾiʿa* (Baghdad, 1981), p. 10.

53. *Afaq ʿArabiyya*, July 1991. The declared aim of digging the canal was to carry away salty water and thereby make new lands arable. Others discerned a different target: to give Baghdad a better grip on the Shiʿi areas by eliminating potential areas of refuge. *The Economist*, 12 December 1992.

54. *Al-ʿIraq*, 12 April 1980; *al-Jumhuriyya*, 1 October 1980; *al-Thawra*, 20 December 1981; *al-Watan al-ʿArabi*, 2 April 1982. The expression "hatred stretching over generations" was coined by a Shiʿi, Saʿdun Hammadi, writing in *al-Watan al-ʿArabi*. Hammadi is typical of the "establishment Shiʿis" who seek to counteract any suspicion of sympathy for their Iranian coreligionists.

55. *Al-Jumhuriyya*, 8 August 1980. See, e.g., *al-Qadisiyya*, 14, 21, 28 March, 4 April 1989.

56. "Mustaqbal Iran," p. 65.

57. *Al-Jumhuriyya*, 21 June 1982. Parts of this speech were quoted in *Regional Report No. 9*, pp. 254–255.

58. *Al-Jumhuriyya*, 13 November 1982.

59. Ibid., 15 September 1968, 29 October 1980, 14 February 1988; *al-ʿIraq*, 16 October 1983. The Iraqi communists called the Baʿth regime "yellow." *Tullab al-ʿIraq* (a communist underground paper), July 1989.

60. *Al-Jumhuriyya*, 21 November 1982, 12 January 1983.

61. Ibid., 4 March 1987. *Al-Thawra al-ʿArabiyya* spoke of "barbarous Khomeinist raids" ("Mustaqbal Iran," p. 54).

62. *Al-ʿIraq*, 7 January 1989; INA, 11 February, in DR, 12 February 1992.

63. *Al-Jumhuriyya*, 29 April 1984; Radio Baghdad, 2 August, in DR, 4 August 1986.

64. This saying is also quoted in al-Sabbagh, *Fursan al-ʿUruba fi-l-ʿIraqi*, p. 243. *Al-Thawra al-ʿArabiyya* commented that an *aʿjami* could not be a friend of the Arabs ("Mustaqbal Iran," p. 66).

65. See the entry "aʿjami" in Ibn Manzur, *Lisan al-ʿArab*. In a similar vein, the Greeks called speakers of other languages barbarians, literally "stammerers"; in Russian, the Germans are called *nemtsy* (dumb); in Morocco, Spanish-speaking Jews called Jews who spoke Arabic or French *forasteros* (foreigeners).

66. This should be compared with the demonization of Saddam Husayn by the West. Luisa Martin Rojo, "Division and Rejection: From the Personification of the Gulf Conflict to the Demonization of Saddam Hussein," *Discourse and Society* 6 (1995): 49–80.

67. *Al-Qadisiyya*, 29 January 1987; Mahfuz Dawud Salman, *Intazirini bi-thiyab al-qital* (Baghdad, 1988), p. 252. On Abu Lahab, see W. Montgomery Watt, "Abu Lahab," in *EI²*.

68. "Mustaqbal Iran," p. 36.

69. *Regional Report No. 9*, p. 208; *al-Jumhuriyya*, 4 April 1981.

70. *Al-Thawra*, 20 December 1981.

71. Sura *Yusuf*, v. 2. The same expression is found in four other suras.

72. Husayn to *al-Mustaqbal*, 13 October 1979; the quotation is from *al-Jumhuriyya*, 12 August 1987. On the ideological conflict between Iran and Iraq, see Bruce Maddy-Weitzman, "Islam and Arabism: The Iran-Iraq War," *Washington Quarterly* 5 (1982): 181–189.

73. *Al-'Iraq*, 24 April 1980.

74. *Al-Watan al-'Arabi*, 9 March 1982.

75. Ibid., 2 April 1982.

76. The story appeared as part of a series of children's books entitled "Qadisiyyat Saddam," 1981.

77. INA, 17 July, in DR, 18 July 1991.

CHAPTER 11

1. *Al-Jumhuriyya*, 1 January 1980.

2. On Sami Shawkat and the revolt, see Majid Khadduri, *Independent Iraq: A Study of Iraqi Politics since 1932* (London, 1951), pp. 160–161.

3. Sami Shawkat, *Hadhihi ahdafuna* (Baghdad, 1939), pp. 3, 21, 36.

4. This doctrine is set in simplistic form in an essay entitled "Sina'at al-mawt" (The art of death), ibid., pp. 1–3, but it can also be recognized in other parts of Shawkat's book, e.g., ibid., p. 78. Compare Saddam Husayn in *al-Jumhuriyya*, 1 February 1979, 2 November 1987.

5. Sura *al-Anfal*, v. 62. The quotation is found in Salah al-Din al-Sabbagh, *Fursan al-'Uruba fi-l-'Iraq* (Damascus, 1956), p. 10. See also *al-Qadisiyya*, 5 April 1990.

6. Al-Sabbagh, *Fursan al-'Uruba fi-l-'Iraq*, p. 10.

7. *Al-Thawra*, 20 April 1973; *al-Jumhuriyya*, 15 April 1975.

8. *Al-Jumhuriyya*, 29 November 1978. Ironically, as late as 1988 a Kuwaiti paper praised "Saddam's military school" for turning out men with the right principles for achieving victory. Quoted in *al-Jumhuriyya*, 26 August 1988.

9. Ibid., 3 November 1987; *al-Thawra*, 24 April 1990.

10. Zuhayr Sadiq Rida Al-Khalidi, *Al-Qiyam 'ind Saddam Husayn* (Baghdad, 1989), pp. 239–240.

11. Amir Ahmad Iskandar, *Saddam Husayn munadilan wa-mufakkiran wa-insanan* (Paris, 1980), p. 23.

12. Such expressions are found in Saddam Husayn, *Al-Thawra wa-l-nazra al-jadida* (Baghdad, 1981), p. 93; *al-'Iraq*, 5 February 1978; *al-Jumhuriyya*, 3 January 1988, 21 May 1989.

13. *Al-Jumhuriyya*, 1 June 1970; *al-'Iraq*, 5 February 1978; *al-Thawra*, 4 September 1983; *al-Qadisiyya*, 4 March 1989; *Regional Report No. 9*, p. 173.

14. "Mutaba'at," *al-Thawra al-'Arabiyya*, 1985, pp. 69–74.

15. *Al-Jumhuriyya*, 1 December 1987, 9 January 1988.

16. *Al-'Iraq*, 17 September 1977.

17. *MECS 1979–1980*, p. 530, quoting *Military Balance* (London: International Institute for Strategic Studies, 1980–1981); Shlomo Gazit (ed.), *The Middle East Military Balance, 1988–1989* (Jerusalem, 1989), p. 178.

18. "Al-jaysh al-'aqa'idi al-tajriba al-Ba'thiyya fi-l-qutr al-'Iraqi," *al-Thawra al-'Arabiyya*, pp. 35–47.

19. 'Abd al-Razzaq, al-Hasani, *Ta'rikh al-wizarat al-'Iraqiyya* vol. 3 (Sidon, 1940), vol. 3, pp. 192–193.

20. *Al-Jumhuriyya*, 30 July 1979.

21. Ibid., 21 June, 22, 23 July 1980.

22. *Al-Jumhuriyya*, 16 February 1981.

23. Michel 'Aflaq, *Nuqtat al-bidaya* (Beirut, 1974), p. 88.

24. Ramadan later wrote a book about it: *Al-Jaysh al-sha'bi wa-l-tajriba al-namudhaj* (Baghdad, 1987).

25. *Al-Thawra*, 7 July 1969; "Al-Jaysh al-sha'bi bayn al-tajriba wa-l-namudhaj," *Al-Thawra al-'Arabiyya*, 1983, p. 82.

26. Women began training in 1978; sometimes mothers and daughters trained together. Ramadan, *Al-Jaysh*, pp. 37–39.

27. "Al-jaysh al-sha'bi bayn al-tajriba wa-l-namudhaj," *Al-Thawra al-'Arabiyya*, pp. 11–26.

28. INA, 15 July, in SWB, 16 July 1984.

29. *Al-Dustur* (London), 15 February, in DR, 18 February 1982.

30. INA, 3 February, in DR, 9 February 1982.

31. *Al-Thawra*, 22 October 1985. *Sha'bi* means both "of the people" and "popular."

32. Ramadan, *Al-Jaysh*, p. 13.

33. *Al-'Iraq*, 20 September 1977.

34. For somewhat contradictory reports see *al-'Iraq*, 14 December 1977; *Regional Report No. 9*, p. 169. Already in 1969, there is mention of a *futuwwa* law. *Al-Thawra*, 26 February 1969.

35. *Regional Report No. 9*, p. 169; *al-Qadisiyya*, 7 February 1985. According to Samir al-Khalil, the age of *futuwwa* members ranged between fifteen and twenty. *Republic of Fear: The Politics of Modern Iraq* (Berkeley, 1989), p. 88.

36. Shafiq 'Abd al-Razzaq al-Samarra'i, *Saddam Husayn nidaluh wa-fikruh al-siyasi* (n.p., 1982), pp. 62–63; *al-Qadisiyya*, 19 August 1989.

37. C. Cahen, "Futuwwa," in *EI²*.

38. *Al-Qadisiyya*, 3 June 1990; *Afaq 'Arabiyya*, July 1991.

39. *Al-Thawra*, 2 May 1978; *al-Qadisiyya*, 3 June, 21 July 1990.

40. *Al-Qadisiyya*, 21 July 1990.

41. Muhammad bin al-Mukarram bin Manzur, *Lisan al-'Arab* (Cairo, n.d.), says the word comes from *lahm* (flesh) and hints at the flesh of the many fallen.

42. *Al-Jumhuriyya*, 1 October 1980.

43. Radio Baghdad, 5 November, in DR, 8 November 1983.

44. *Newsweek*, 19 March 1984.

45. *Al-Jumhuriyya*, 17 July 1986.

46. Ibid., 1, 11, 29 March 1984, 17 January, 17 March 1985; *al-Thawra*, 24 February 1984. *Falasha* is colloquial Iraqi meaning "to cause to collapse," "to destroy." D. R. Woodhead and Wayne Beene, *A Dictionary of Iraqi Arabic* (Washington, 1967).

47. *Al-Thawra*, 2 February 1987.

48. *Sharaf* derives from a word connoting height, whether physical or social. Abou A. M. Zeid, "Honour and Shame among the Bedouins of Egypt," in J. G. Peristiany (ed.), *Honour and Shame* (London, 1965), p. 245. *Al-karim*, from the same root, is one of the "ninety-nine names of Allah." *Al-kariman* are the two things that give honor to a Muslim: *jihad* and the pilgrimage to Mecca.

49. Literally, *wajh* means face. Among the Shi'i tribes of Iraq, it means the permit given by a shaykh to someone from another tribe to pass through the former's tribal territory. 'Abdallah Fahd Al-Nafisi, *Dawr al-Shi'a fi tatawwur*

al-'Iraq al-siyasi al-hadith, 2d ed. (n.p., 1986), pp. 35–40. *Wajh abyad* (white face) means honor; *bayyad wajhah* means to show honor to someone.

50. For an interpretation of the sense of honor conveyed by the poem, see Asher Goren, *Ancient Arabic Poetry* (H) (Jerusalem, 1970), pp. 17–23.

51. See Zeid, "Honour and Shame," p. 258. For a comparative analysis of the European idea of honor and that of Bedouin society, see Frank Henderson Stewart, *Honor* (Chicago, 1994).

52. *Al-Jumhuriyya*, 7, 12, 23 February 1979, 1 January, 4 July 1980.

53. *Al-Jumhuriyya*, 21 April 1982.

54. *Al-Thawra*, 20 December 1981; *al-Jumhuriyya*, 30 July 1987. On one occasion, Husayn was referred to as *hami al-a'rad* (he who safeguards women's honor). *Al-Jumhuriyya*, 19 May 1981.

55. Radio Baghdad, 23 September, in DR, 24 September 1990; INA, 31 October, in DR, 1 November 1990.

56. Radio Baghdad, 23 August, 5 September, in DR, 23 August, 6 September 1990; *al-Jumhuriyya*, 1 October 1990; *al-Thawra*, 2 November 1990.

57. *Al-Thawra*, 12 November 1990.

58. R. Baghdad, 12 October, in DR, 12 October 1990. "Sweets with honor" was an expression used in the indoctrination of children.

59. *Al-Thawra*, 12 January 1986; *Risalat al-'Iraq*, January–February 1986. For a short period, the regime pushed the "policy of shame" to the point of permitting the killing of women who had been caught transgressing against the honor of the family. The law, which remained rabid only for two months, detailed the degree of kinship for which such "wiping out of shame" (*ghaslan li-l-'ar*) was allowed. *Al-Qadisiyya*, 1 April 1990. "Ghaslan li-l-'ar" was the title of a famous protest poem by the Iraqi poetess Nazik al-Mala'ika, written in 1949. Cf. al-Nafisi, *Dawr al-Shi'a*, p. 42; and Sana al-Khayyat, *Honour and Shame: Women in Modern Iraq* (London, 1990), pp. 34–36.

60. See Ibn Manzur, *Lisan al-'Arab. Shahid* is one of Allah's ninety-nine names.

61. Shawkat, *Hadhihi ahdafuna*, pp. 1–5.

62. Husayn, *Al-Thawra wa-l-nazra*, p. 52 (speech originally given on 19 February 1975).

63. *Al-Jumhuriyya*, 19 October 1980; *Regional Report No. 9*, p. 215 (statement made in October 1980).

64. *Al-Jumhuriyya*, 5 January, 4 September 1981, 8 December 1982.

65. Ibid., 4 February 1981.

66. Ibid., 23 March 1985.

67. *Al-Thawra*, 17 July 1990.

68. *Al-Jumhuriyya*, 4 May 1988.

69. See Amatzia Baram, *Culture, History, and Ideology in the Formation of Ba'thist Iraq, 1968–89* (Oxford, 1991), pp. 77–78; Samir al-Khalil, *The Monument: Art, Vulgarity, and Responsibility in Iraq* (Berkeley, 1991), pp. 23–24.

70. *Al-Jumhuriyya*, 26 January, 2 December 1982.

71. Radio Baghdad, 6 January, in DR, 7 January 1981.

72. *Al-'Iraq*, 1, 3 December 1983. Ironically, some Iranian influence can be discerned here. In Iran during the war, the families of casualties received congratulations rather than condolences. David Menashri, "Iran," *MECS 1981–1982*, pp. 543–544. Also on this subject, see Chagay Ram, *Islamic Symbolism: The Ideology of the Islamic Revolution in Iran as Reflected in Friday Communal Sermons, 1979–1989* (Ann Arbor, 1992), pp. 186–188.

PART V

1. On the use of myths in Arab society, see Emmanuel Sivan, *Arab Political Myths* (H) (Tel Aviv, 1988). On the myths in Khomeini's Iran, see Chagay Ram, *Islamic Symbolism: The Ideology of the Islamic Revolution in Iran as Reflected in Friday Communal Sermons, 1979–1989* (Ann Arbor, 1992).

CHAPTER 12

1. Quoted in Emmanuel Sivan, *Arab Political Myths* (H) (Tel Aviv, 1988), p. 49.

2. *Al-'Iraq*, 22 January 1989.

3. Saddam Husayn, *Al-Thawra wa-l-nazra al-jadida* (Baghdad, 1981), p. 50.

4. See, e.g., *al-Thawra*, 3, 16 May, 25 June 1978; *al-Jumhuriyya*, 28, 29, 30 December 1987.

5. The modern Hebrew dictionary by Even-Shushan also gives the Arabic *arkh* as the root of the Hebrew *ta'arikh* (meaning "date" alone). This is worth mentioning because Muhammad bin al-Mukarram bin Manzur, *Lisan al-'Arab* (Cairo, n.d.), says that the Arabs learned historiography from the *ahl al-Kitab* (the people of the book; i.e., Jews and Christians).

6. *Kitab muhit al-muhit* (Beirut, 1868); Jacob Lassner, "Concerning Time, Historiography, and Political Consciousness" (unpublished), p. 10; Edward William Lane, *An Arabic English Lexicon* (London, 1863–1893).

7. The tenth-century historian Mas'udi was the first to write history according to subjects rather than chronologically.

8. See Lassner, "Concerning Time," pp. 33–34; Morroe Berger, *The Arab World Today* (New York, 1964), p. 17; Sivan, *Arab Political Myths*, pp. 27–29. On history and the writing of history, see Bernard Lewis, *History Remembered, Recovered, Invented* (Princeton, 1975), pp. 3–41.

9. Saddam Husayn, *Hawl kitabat al-ta'rikh* (Baghdad, 1976), pp. 23, 165; *al-'Iraq*, 14 March 1978; *al-Jumhuriyya*, 29 November 1978, 16 May 1981; *al-Thawra*, 18 January 1991.

10. *Al-Jumhuriyya*, 15 May 1981; Husayn, *Hawl kitabat al-ta'rikh*, pp. 173–186; 'Abd al-'Aziz al-Duri, "Kitabat al-ta'rikh al-'Arabi," *al-Mustaqbal al-'Arabi* 163 (September 1992): 5. For a diametrically opposed view on historiography, see the Iraqi historian 'Ali al-Wardi, *Lamahat ijtima'iyya min ta'rikh al-'Iraq al-hadith* (Baghdad, 1969), pp. 5–6.

11. *Al-Jumhuriyya*, 25 March 1981.

12. Sami Shawkat, *Hadhihi ahdafuna* (Baghdad, 1939), pp. 11, 36.

13. *Al-Thawra*, 14 July 1978; *al-'Iraq*, 2 April 1980; *al-Jumhuriyya*, 4 July 1980. See also Amatzia Baram, *Culture, History, and Ideology in the Formation of Ba'thist Iraq, 1968–89* (Oxford, 1991), pp. 97–109.

14. *Al-Thawra* (international), 3 April 1990; *al-'Iraq*, 4, 22 November 1990; INA, 28 August, in DR, 29 August 1990; Radio Baghdad, 29 November, in DR, 30 November 1990; Radio Baghdad, 22 June—DR, 22 June 1992.

15. *Al-Thawra*, 1 July 1971; *al-Jumhuriyya*, 17, 29 November, 25 December 1978, 23 February 1979, 1 January, 19 October 1980; *al-'Iraq*, 14 March 1978.

16. *Al-Jumhuriyya*, 27 November 1982.

17. A *migwar* is a wooden club with nails on it and a ball of pitch at the end.

The word became symbolic of Iraqi resistance against the British and later emblematic of any war. *Al-Jumhuriyya*, 27 November 1982; *al-'Iraq*, 22 November 1990; *al-Thawra*, 18 January 1991; Radio Baghdad, 29 November, in DR, 30 November 1990; Paris Antenne 2 Television, 2 December, in DR, 3 December 1990.

18. Sabah Salman, *Saddam Husayn qa'id wa-ta'rikh* (Baghdad, 1986), pp. 49–51, 86–88, 251. A member of the Iraqi opposition contended later that it was Husayn's obsession with history and his desire to "enter" it that drove him to invade Kuwait. *Al-Hayat*, 17 August 1994.

19. Shawkat, *Hadhihi ahdafuna*, pp. 42–45.

20. Husayn, *Hawl kitabat al-ta'rikh*, pp. 7–9; Amir Ahmad Iskandar, *Saddam Husayn munadilan wa-mufakkiran wa-insanan* (Paris, 1980), p. 143; Husayn, *Al-Thawra wa-l-nazra*, p. 52; Reeva S. Simon, *Iraq between the Two World Wars: The Creation and Implementation of National Ideology* (New York, 1986), pp. 96–97.

21. Husayn, *Al-Thawra wa-l-nazra*, p. 48; *al-Thawra*, 30 May 1978. The words are reminiscent of the views of Sati' al-Husri, a nationalist and educator active in Iraq in the 1920s and 1930s. He held that instruction of history must fire the students' imagination; history was the pivot of nationalist education. Muhammad 'Abd al-Rahman Burj, *A'lam al-'Arab: Sati' al-Husri* (Cairo, 1969), pp. 161–162.

22. On the "Arabization" of ancient periods, its causes, and its manifestations, see Lewis, *History*, pp. 36–37; Baram, *Culture*, pp. 97–105. For an attempt to correlate the emergence of Islam with the overall theory of the eruption of "Semitic waves," see Nimrod Hurvitz, "Muhibb al-Din al-Khatib's Semitic Wave Theory and Pan-Arabism," *MES* 29 (1993): 118–135.

23. Shafiq 'Abd al-Razzaq al-Samarra'i, *Saddam Husayn nidaluh wa-fikruh al-siyasi* (n.p., 1982), p. 53.

24. Husayn, *Hawl kitabat al-ta'rikh*, pp. 23–24, 28; *al-Thawra* (international), 3 April 1990.

25. Husayn, *Hawl kitabat al-ta'rikh*, pp. 8–9. Before becoming president, Husayn told Majid Khadduri in an interview that he was inspired by al-Sabbagh's book, *Fursan al-'Uruba fi-l-'Iraq* and that he aspired to attain the heroic goals that Sabbagh had failed to realize. Majid Khadduri, *Socialist Iraq: A Study in Iraqi Politics since 1968* (Washington, 1978), p. 73.

26. Husayn, *Hawl kitabat al-ta'rikh*, p. 25; *al-Thawra*, 3 May 1978.

27. *Al-Thawra*, 30 May, 25 June 1978. The historian quoted here is Hashim Yahya al-Mallah. Husayn, *Hawl kitabat al-ta'rikh*, pp. 64, 235–237.

28. On the use of stamps, see Donald Malcolm Reid, "The Postage Stamp: A Window on Saddam Hussein's Iraq," *MEJ* 47 (1993): 77–89.

29. Similar salience was given to the 1920 uprising, which came to be called "The Great Iraqi Revolution." Fadil al-Barrak, *Hukumat al-difa' al-watani: al-badhra al-qawmiyya li-l-thawra al-'Arabiyya* (Baghdad, 1980), pp. 13–17; *al-Thawra*, 27 June 1989. Al-Barrak was reportedly executed by the Ba'th in 1992. *Al-Ahram*, 14 October, in DR, 14 October 1992.

30. See, e.g., "Al-'alaqa al-samimiyya bayn al-ba'th wa-thawrat mayis 'am 1941," *al-Thawra al-'Arabiyya*, 1984, pp. 5–9.

31. See, e.g., *al-Qadisiyya*, 11, 12 April 1990. On statues of these heroes, see Baram, *Culture*, p. 82. *Al-Qadisiyya* began publishing police diaries on 4 June 1990.

32. They were Fahmi Sa'id, Mahmud Salman, and Kamil Shabib. *Babil*, 3 May 1992.

33. *Al-Jumhuriyya*, 29 December 1987.

34. Lutfi Ja'far Faraj, *Al-Malik Ghazi wa-dawruh fi siyasat al-'Iraq fi al-majalayn al-dakhili wa-l-khariji, 1933–1939* (Baghdad, 1987). On Ghazi's part in proffering claims to Kuwait in his time, see ibid., pp. 218–228.

35. *Al-Qadisiyya*, 10 August 1989; *al-Jumhuriyya*, 5 February 1990. The book on Faysal I was 'Ala' Jasim Muhammad, *Al-Malik Faysal al-awwal: hayatuh wa-dawruh al-siyasi fi-l-thawra al-'Arabiyya wa-Surya wa-l-Iraq*; another book on Nuri al-Sa'id was Su'ad Ra'uf Shir Muhammad, *Nuri al-Sa'id wa dawruh fi al-siyasa al-'Iraqiyya hatta 'am 1945* (Baghdad, 1988).

36. *Al-Sharq al-Awsat*, 8 March 1989. The books were Ahmad Fawzi, *'Abd al-Karim Qasim wa-sa'atuh al-akhira* (Baghdad, 1988); and Muhammad Kazim 'Ali, *Al-'Iraq fi 'ahd 'Abd al-Karim Qasim. Al-Thawra*, 4 December 1989.

37. *Al-Thawra*, 18 December 1990.

38. *Al-Qadisiyya*, 9 July 1990. On the place of Saladin and of the wars against the crusaders in Arab historiography, see Sivan, *Arab Political Myths*, pp. 97–120.

39. *Al-Jumhuriyya*, 14 January 1980.

40. On the battle, see L. Veccia Vaglerii, "Al-Kadisiyya," in *EI*².

41. *Al-Jumhuriyya*, 5 April, 16, 29 September 1980. Immediately after the beginning of the war, *al-Jumhuriyya* started printing "Qadisiyyat Saddam" at the head of every page.

42. *Al-Jumhuriyya*, 24 June, 9 July, 20 September 1980.

43. Ibid., 30 March 1983, 29 June 1988.

44. *Al-Qadisiyya*, 6 January 1988. *Al-Qadisiyya* had begun publication immediately after the start of the war as a daily supplement to the military weekly *al-Yarmuk*. It became independent in 1985.

45. "Al-umma al-'Arabiyya bayn Qadisiyyatayn," *Al-Thawra al-'Arabiyya*, 36–44; *al-Jumhuriyya*, 22 October 1980, 26 February 1984; *al-'Iraq*, 21 July 1985.

46. *Al-Qadisiyya*, 17 February, 1 March 1988. Al-Khansa' was famous for composing lamentations after two of her brothers had been killed in tribal fighting. Asher Goren, *Ancient Arabic Poetry* (H) (Jerusalem, 1970), pp. 25, 76–77.

CHAPTER 13

1. Samir al-Khalil, *Republic of Fear: The Politics of Modern Iraq* (Berkeley, 1989), pp. 209–211.

2. *Nidal al-ba'th fi sabil al-wahda al-hurriyya wa-l-ishtirakiyya*, vol. 1 (Beirut, 1963), p. 176.

3. Michel 'Aflaq, *Fi sabil al-ba'th* (Beirut, 1963), pp. 52–58.

4. Ibid., (1974), pp. 161–167, 172, 186, 201, 205; Michel 'Aflaq, *Ma'rakat al-masir al-wahid* (Beirut, 1963), p. 13; *al-Thawra al-'Arabiyya*, no. 1, 1976, p. 15.

5. *Al-Thawra al-'Arabiyya*, no. 1, 1976, p. 15. 'Aflaq's approach elicited a great deal of scorn and mockery from the rivals of the Ba'th—for example, a story about a stork who, when questioned about its faith, drank *arak* (an alcoholic drink), ate pork, and spoiled the church bells with its droppings. Khalid Kishtainy, *Arab Political Humour* (London, 1985), p. 140.

6. *Al-Jumhuriyya*, 22 September 1968, 17 July 1970.

7. *Al-Thawra*, 13 September 1974. In May 1977, the government appointed 1,236 new men of religion in the Kurdish region alone. *Al-Thawra*, 3 May 1977.

8. The efficiently censored media carried a few items on men of religion condemning "criminal acts." *Al-Thawra*, 23 February 1977. Such protestations of loyalty are at times the only indication of untoward events.

9. Saddam Husayn, *Hawl kitabat al-ta'rikh* (Baghdad, 1976), pp. 28–37 (remark made on 11 August 1977); Amir Ahmad Iskandar, *Saddam Husayn munadilan wa-mufakkiran wa-insanan* (Paris, 1980), pp. 158, 321; *al-Jumhuriyya*, 17 October 1981, 9 December 1982.

10. The committee was made up of religious functionaries loyal to the Ba'th. By 1980, its men had spread out all over Iraq; one of their tasks was to deal with "reactionary, communal, and racist propaganda." *Al-Thawra*, 4 November 1981.

11. *Al-'Iraq*, 14 December 1977.

12. *Al-Thawra*, 6 June 1978.

13. Husayn was addressing a meeting of the local Baghdad party branch on 28 July 1979. The speech was included in Saddam Husayn, *Bi-l-fikr wa-l-mumarasa wa-l-namudhaj al-hayy yatahaqqaq al-iman* (Baghdad, n.d.), pp. 11–40.

14. *Al-Thawra*, 1 February 1983.

15. Ibid., 7 June 1990.

16. *Al-'Iraq*, 27 November 1985; *Hurras al-Watan*, August 1989, no. 8.

17. *Al-Jumhuriyya*, 28 March, 14 July 1982, 12 May 1987, 28 January 1988. See also As'ad AbuKhalil, "Al-Jabriyyah in the Political Discourse of Jamal 'Abd al-Nasir and Saddam Husayn: The Rationalization of Defeat," *Muslim World*, 84 (July 1994): 240–257.

18. Husayn had already opened his presidential inauguration speech with the *basmala*. *Wa 'y al-'Ummal*, 21 July 1979.

19. Al-Thawra, 10 October 1990. In 1993, Husayn initiated "the National Campaign of faith" for teaching the Qur'an to students of all grades, women, and even Ba'th party members. Ofra Bengio, "Iraq," in *MECS 1993*, pp. 391–393; *MECS 1994*, pp. 336–337.

20. E.g., a letter to Asad ending with these words. *Al-Thawra*, 14 January 1991.

21. *Al-Qadisiyya*, 1 November 1990; *al-'Iraq*, 22 November 1990.

22. M. Canard, "Da'wa," in *EI²*; Hizb al-ba'th al-'Arabi al-ishtiraki, al-qiyada al-qawmiyya, *Al-Minhaj al-thaqafi al-markazi*, vol. 2 (Baghdad, 1977), pp. 501–503; *al-Thawra*, 17, 22 September 1991.

23. *Al-Thawra*, 18 January 1992. Qur'an commentators say that Allah added the word "safety" so that Abraham would not freeze to death once the fire went out. Al-Shaikh 'Abd al-Jalil 'Isa, *Taysir al-tafsir* (n.p., 1958).

24. *Al-Jumhuriyya*, 1 October 1980; *Alif Ba'*, 15 December 1982; *al-'Iraq*, 27 October 1983.

25. See Chagay Ram, *Islamic Symbolism: The Ideology of the Islamic Revolution in Iran as Reflected in Friday Communal Sermons, 1979–1989* (Ann Arbor, 1992), pp. 154–222. The name Karbala' is sometimes interpreted as a combination of two words, *karb* (grief) and *bala'* (suffering). 'Abd al-Razzaq al-Hasani, *Al-'Iraq qadiman wa-hadithan* (Sidon, 1956), p. 125.

26. *Al-Jumhuriyya*, 12 December 1981.

27. On *jihad* in Islamic law, see Majid Khadduri, *War and Peace in the Law of Islam* (London, 1955), pp. 51–141.

28. *Al-Jumhuriyya*, 19 October, 10 November 1980, 14 October 1981, 13 June 1982, 31 May 1986.

29. Ibid., 12 July 1987.

30. Ibid., 18 July 1987; e.g., *Alif Ba'*, 30 August 1989.

31. *Al-Jumhuriyya*, 28 September 1988.

32. *Al-Thawra*, 30 July 1990.

33. On the *munafiqun*, see H. A. R. Gibb and J. H. Kramer, *Shorter Encyclopaedia of Islam* (Leiden, 1953).

34. *Al-Jumhuriyya*, 12 August 1990. This verse appears twice: in sura *al-Tawba*, v. 74, and sura *al-Tahrim*, v. 9.

35. *Al-Jumhuriyya*, 6 September 1990.

36. *Al-Qadisiyya*, 15, 16 October 1990; *al-Thawra*, 21 December 1990. The expression *hayya* is usually used in the *mu'adhdhin*'s call to prayer, *hayya 'ala al-sala*.

37. Already, the second wartime communiqué of the Revolutionary Command Council opened with the *basmala*.

38. The names of the corps (numbered 1 to 7) were al-Rashid; al-Yarmuk; al-Qadisiyya; Hattin; 'Ammuriyya (a Byzantine city in Anatolia conquered by the Muslims in 838); al-Hakam (an Ummayyad ruler); Dhi-Qar; and al-Faris (the Republican Guard named after one of Husayn's titles).

39. The media exulted, with headlines reading: "The Night of the Iraqi Missiles"; "Al-Husayn Revenges Our Martyrs"; and "The Husayn Missiles Continue to Bring Down the Criminals." *Al-Jumhuriyya*, 1, 3, 4, 5 March 1988.

40. 'Adil 'Abd al-Mahdi, "Al-'Iraq wa-l-mashru' al-Islami al-watani ba'd harb al-khalij," *Qira'at siyasiyya* (Summer 1992): 155–156.

41. *Al-Qadisiyya*, 8, 15, 16, 28 December 1989, 1, 6, 15 January 1990.

42. On the attack against the Kurds during the Iraqi-Iranian war and at its end, see Ofra Bengio, "The Iraqi Kurds: The Struggle for Autonomy in the Shadow of the Iran-Iraq Conflict" *Immigrants and Minorities* 9 (1990): 249–268; George Black, *Genocide in Iraq: The Anfal Campaign against the Kurds* (New York, 1993).

43. Iraq presumably used *Anfal* rather than *Badr* because Iran had already so code-named some of its own offensives against Iraq.

44. S. D. Goitein, "Muhammad," in Hava Lazarus-Yafeh (ed.), *Studies in the History of the Arabs and Islam* (H) (Tel Aviv, 1982), pp. 63–65.

45. Khayrallah Talfah, *Kayf al-sabil ila Allah* (Beirut, 1976), 2:245, 253.

46. *Al-'Iraq*, 19 March 1989. For eyewitness testimonies on the *anfal* atrocities, see Kanan Makiya, *Cruelty and Silence: War, Tyranny, Uprising, and the Arab World* (New York, 1993), chap. 5.

47. A short time before the attack, Halabja had been taken by Iranian units assisted by Kurdish opposition forces. The use of chemical weapons was thus meant as a "lesson" for both the "Iranian heretics" and the "Kurdish traitors."

48. *Al-Jumhuriyya*, 26 June 1988.

49. *Al-'Iraq*, 19 March 1989.

50. This had already been the code name for an earlier (unsuccessful) attempt, in May 1986, to recapture Faw. *Al-Jumhuriyya*, 11 May 1986.

51. The root " *'amara*" originally meant performing an (unspecified) act of worship. Goitein, "Muhammad," p. 71.

52. *Al-Jumhuriyya*, 4, 12 June 1988.

53. *Al-Thawra*, 30 March 1990.

54. Ibid., 13 December 1990.
55. The Hebrew Psalms have similar expressions: e.g., Psalms 48:2, 86:13.
56. On *takbir*, see A. J. Wensinck, "Takbir," in *EI¹*.
57. *Al-Jumhuriyya*, 12 June, 27 December 1986.
58. *Al-Thawra*, 18 December 1990.
59. *Al-Qadisiyya*, 30 December 1990, 7, 15 January, 4 February 1991.

CHAPTER 14

1. *Al-Thawra*, 25 June 1989; *Alif Ba'*, 28 June 1989. Much later, the Ba'th claimed that 'Aflaq had converted to Islam in 1980. *Al-Thawra*, 23 June 1995.
2. *Al-Thawra*, 9 August 1989.
3. *Al-Tadamun*, 22 October 1989. Husayn's words were entitled *Nass risalat al-ra'is. Risala* may mean a letter or missive. Since they were not addressed to any particular individual or a group, the use of *risala* here evokes the connotation of "message" or "mission" such as Muhammad's.
4. *Al-Thawra*, 20 June 1990. The term *hizb Allah* appears three times in the Qur'an, connoting those who believe in God and who are successful. The *hizb al-shaytan* (the people of the devil) mentioned twice are the losers and the vanquished.
5. On Abraha, see A. F. L. Beeston, "Abraha," in *EI²*.
6. S. A. Bonebakker, "Abu Righal," in *EI²*.
7. On these interpretations, see Muhammad bin al-Mukarram bin Manzur, *Lisan al-'Arab* (Cairo, n.d.), and Al-Shaikh 'Abd al-Jalil 'Isa, *Taysir al-tafsir* (n.p., 1958).
8. In the Bible, Lot's wife is turned into a pillar of salt; in the Qur'an she is stoned.
9. *Al-'Iraq*, 6 July 1985.
10. *Al-Jumhuriyya*, 14 February 1988.
11. *Al-Thawra*, 16 August 1985.
12. *Al-'Iraq*, 22 September 1985.
13. *Al-Jumhuriyya*, 28 March 1988.
14. Ibid., 10 April, 21 August 1988.
15. *Al-Qadisiyya*, 2 December 1989. For a novella by a Moroccan writer bearing the same name, see Leila Abouzeid, *Year of the Elephant*, trans. Barbara Parmenter (Austin, Tex., 1989).
16. *Al-Qadisiyya*, 4 June 1990.
17. *Al-Jumhuriyya*, 6 September 1990.
18. INA, 8 September, in DR, 10 September 1990.
19. *Al-Jumhuriyya*, 22 September 1990; *al-Qadisiyya*, 4 October 1990; *al-Thawra*, 9 October 1990.
20. *Al-Thawra*, 10 October 1990; *al-Qadisiyya*, 11 October 1990.
21. *Al-Qadisiyya*, 12 October 1990.
22. Ibid., 12 October 1990; *al-Thawra*, 12 October 1990; *al-'Iraq*, 19 November 1990.
23. *Al-Thawra*, 16 December 1990.
24. INA, 10 February, in DR, 11 February 1991.
25. *Al-Thawra*, 8 February 1991.
26. Ibid., 18 February 1991. Other such instances include a poem about the

encounter of the *hijara* missile with the stones of the Palestinian *intifada* and an article saying that the *hijara* had now taken revenge for Israel's bombing of the Iraqi atomic reactor. *Al-Thawra*, 23, 24 February 1991.

CONCLUSION

1. The connection between a political crisis and a crisis of language has been noted by Ibn Khaldun. see Timothy Mitchell, *Colonising Egypt* (Cambridge, England, 1988), pp. 151–152.

2. To illustrate, an article attacking the United States was headed: "Hate Them!" It said in part: "Hate! Remember your dead and hate. Hate is not shameful, hate has something sacred about it. . . . Hate, so that love can bloom. . . . Hate America for generations to come." *Babil*, 25 January 1992. For a similar outburst from an Israeli source after the Iraqi missile attacks against Tel Aviv, see Dan Caspi and Yehiel Limor, *The Mediators: The Mass Media in Israel, 1948–1990* (H) (Tel Aviv, 1992), p. 88.

3. Ernst Cassirer, *The Myth of the State* (New York, 1955), p. 355.

4. For the link between changes of symbols and social crises, see Dov Landau, *From Metaphor to Symbol* (H) (Ramat Gan, Israel, 1979), pp. 210–211.

5. INA, 14 May, in DR, 15 May 1992. Shortly before, the Ba'th party's leadership forum had changed its name from *al-qiyada al-qutriyya* to *qiyadat qutr al-'Iraq*. *Al-Thawra*, 12 April 1992.

6. *Al-Thawra*, 3 December 1992. For Husayn's tribal politics, see Ofra Bengio, "The Challenge to the Territorial Integrity of Iraq," *Survival* 37 (1995): 74–94.

7. A. Miquel, "'Irak," in *EI²*; 'Abd al-Razzaq al-Hasani, *Al-'Iraq qadiman wa-hadithan* (Sidon, 1956), pp. 6–7.

8. Among the first was Muhammad 'Abid al-Jabiri, *Al-Khitab al-'Arabi al-mu'asir* (Beirut, 1982). More recently, Saudi author Zaki Ahmad published an article called "Democracy in the Modern and Contemporary Islamic Discourse," *al-Mustaqbal al-'Arabi* 164 (October 1992).

9. *Babil*, 15 March 1992. See also the article on national (*qawmi*) language, ibid., 22 March 1992.

10. *Al-Hayat* (London), 12 May 1992. For changes in Kurdish political speech in the wake of the Gulf War, see an article by a Kurdish journalist in *al-Hayat*, 15 June 1992.

11. Al-Sayyid Yasin, "Al-tahlil al-thaqafi li-azmat al-khalij," *al-Mustaqbal al-'Arabi* 148 (June 1991): 30–47. See also his critique of Arab intellectuals in the context of the Arab-Israeli conflict: *Al-Shakhsiyya al-'Arabiyya bayn al-mafhum al-Isra'ili wa-l-mafhum al-'Arabi* (Cairo, 1974).

12. *Babil*, 26 August 1992.

Bibliography

DOCUMENTS AND OFFICIAL PUBLICATIONS

Dawr al-jaysh al-'Iraqi fi harb tishrin 1973, Beirut, 1975.
Hizb al-ba'th al-'Arabi al-ishtiraki, al-qiyada al-qawmiyya, *Asbab naksat hukm al-hizb fi-l-'Iraq*, n.p., n.d.
———, *Bayan al-qiyada al-qawmiyya 'an al-mu'tamar al-qawmi al-thamin*, n.p., n.d.
———, *Al-Minhaj al-thaqafi al-markazi*, 2 vols., Baghdad, 1977.
———, *Muqarrarat al-mu'tamar al-qawmi al-tasi'*, n.p., n.d.
———, *Al-Taqrir al-siyasi li-l-mu'tamar al-qawmi al-hadi 'ashar*, Baghdad, 1977.
Hizb al-ba'th al-'Arabi al-ishtiraki, al-qutr al-'Iraqi, *Al-taqrir al-markazi li-l-mu'tamar al-qutri al-tasi'*, June 1982, Baghdad, 1983.
Al-Jaysh al-'Iraqi al-dhikra al-sittun, 6 January 1921–1981, Baghdad, 1981.
Likayy yusan al-salam wa-tata'azzaz al-wahda al-wataniyya, Baghdad, 1973.
Nidal al-ba'th fi sabil al-wahda al-hurriyya wa-l-ishtirakiyya, 5 vols., Beirut, 1963–1965.
Al-Thawra al-'Arabiyya.
Thawrat 17 tammuz, al-tajriba wa-l-afaq: al-taqrir al-siyasi al-sadir 'an al-mu'tamar al-qutri al-thamin li-hizb al-ba'th al-'Arabi al-ishtiraki al-qutr al-'Iraqi, n.p., January 1974.
Al-Waqa'i' al-'Iraqiyya.

NEWSPAPERS, PERIODICALS, MAGAZINES, AND BROADCASTS

Afaq 'Arabiyya (periodical)
Al-'Ahd al-Jadid (daily, Baghdad)
Al-Ahram
Al-'Alam (weekly, London)
Alif Ba' (weekly, Baghdad)
Babil (daily, Baghdad)
Baghdad (Baghdad, London)
Baghdad Observer (daily, Baghdad)
British Broadcasting Corporation, Summary of World Broadcasting: The Middle East and Africa
Daily Report: Near East and South Asia
Al-Dustur (weekly, London)
The Economist
Al-Hayat (daily, Beirut, London)
Hurras al-Watan (weekly, Baghdad)
Al 'Iraq (daily, Baghdad)
Al-'Iraq al-Hurr (weekly, London)
Iraq Today
Al-Jamahir (daily, Baghdad)
Al-Jumhuriyya (daily, Baghdad)
Al-Kadir (Kurdish periodical)
al-kifah (daily, Beirut)
Majallat al-Basra (Basra)
Al-Mustaqbal al-'Arabi (monthly, Lebanon)
Newsweek
The New Yorker
Al-Qadisiyya (Baghdad)
Risalat al-'Iraq (monthly)
Al-Sharq al-Awsat (weekly, London)
Al-Ta'akhi (daily, Baghdad)
Al-Tadamun (weekly, London)
Tariq al-Sha'b (periodical)
Al-Tayyar al-Jadid (weekly, London)
Al-Thaqafa al-Jadida (Communist monthly)
Al-Thawra (daily, Baghdad)
Al-Thawra al-Husayniyya
Tullab al-'Iraq (Baghdad)
Al-Watan al-'Arabi (weekly, Paris)
Wa'y al-'ummal (weekly, Baghdad)
Al-Yarmuk (weekly, Baghdad)
Al-Zaman (daily, Baghdad)

BOOKS AND ARTICLES IN ARABIC

'Abd al-Mahdi, 'Adil, "Al-'Iraq wa-l-mashru' al-Islami al-watani ba'd harb al-khalij," *Qira'at siyasiyya* 2 (Summer 1992).

'Aflaq, Michel, *Fi sabil al-ba'th*, Beirut, 1959, 1963, 1974.

——, *Ma'rakat al-masir al-wahid*, Beirut, 1963.

——, *Nuqtat al-bidaya*, Beirut, 1974.

Ahmad, Zaki, "Al-Dimuqratiyya fi-l-khitab al-Islami al-hadith wa-l-mu'asir," *al-Mustaqbal al-'Arabi*, 164 (October 1992): 112–123.

Al-'Alawi, Hasan, *Al-Shi'a wa-l-dawla al-qawmiyya fi-l-'Iraq, 1914–1990*, 2d ed., n.p., 1990.

Al-Arsuzi, Zaki, *Al-Mu'allafat al-kamila*, 4 vols., Damascus, 1972.

Al-'Awf, Bashir, *Al-Inqilab al-Suri*, Damascus, 1949.

Al-'Azzawi, 'Abbas, *Ta'rikh al-'Iraq bayn ihtilalayn*, 8 vols., Baghdad, 1935, 1956.

'Aziz, Tariq, *Thawrat al-tariq al-jadid*, Baghdad, 1975.

Al-Badrawi, Zahran, *Fi 'ilm al-lugha al-ta'rikhi: dirasa tatbiqiyya 'ala 'Arabiyyat al-'usur al-wusta*, Cairo, 1988.

Al-Bakr, Ahmad Hasan, *Al-Thawra 'ala tariq al-taqaddum*, Baghdad, 1977.

Ballal, Mazin, *Al-Mas'ala al-Kurdiyya al-wahm wa-l-haqiqa*, Beirut, 1993.

Al-Barrak, Fadil, *Dawr al-jaysh al-'Iraqi fi hukumat al-difa' al-watani wa-l-harb ma' Baritaniya 'am 1941: dirasa tahliliyya wa-naqdiyya wa-muqarina li-l-khalfiyyat al-ijtima'iyya wa-l-'askariyya*, 2d ed., Beirut, 1987.

——, *Hukumat al-difa' al-watani: al-badhra al-qawmiyya li-l-thawra al-'Arabiyya*, Baghdad, 1980.

——, *Al-Madaris al-Yahudiyya wa-l-Iraniyya fi-l-'Iraq*, Baghdad, 1985.

——, *Mustafa al-Barzani: al-ustura wa-l-haqiqa*, Baghdad, 1989.

Al-Basha, Hasan, *Al-Alqab al-Islamiyya fi-l-ta'rikh wa-l-watha'iq wa-l-athar*, Cairo, 1957.

Batti, Fa'iq, *Al-Sihafa al-yasariyya fi-l-'Iraq, 1924–1958*, London, 1985.

Al-Bazzaz, 'Abd al-Rahman, *Muhadarat 'an al-'Iraq min al-ihtilal hatta al-istiqlal*, Cairo, 1960.

——, *Safahat min al-ams al-qarib: thawrat al-'Iraq . . . hal kanat hatmiyya*, Beirut, 1960.

Al-Bazzaz, Sa'd, *Al-Harb al-sirriyya: Khafaya al-dawr al-Isra'ili fi harb al-khalij*, London, 1987.

——, *Harb talid ukhra: al-ta'rikh al-sirri li-harb al-khalij*, Amman, 1992.

Burj, Muhammad 'Abd al-Rahman, *A'lam al-'Arab: Sati' al-Husri*, Cairo, 1969.

al-Duri, 'Abd al-'Aziz, *Al-Judhur al-ta'rikhiyya li-l-shu'ubiyya*, Beirut, n.d.

——, "Kitabat al-ta'rikh al-'Arabi," *al-Mustaqbal al-'Arabi* 163 (September, 1992): 4–14.

Al-Durra, Mahmud, *Al-Harb al-'Iraqiyya al-Baritaniyya 1941*, Beirut, 1969.

——, *Al-Qadiyya al-Kurdiyya*, 2d ed., Beirut, 1966.

Fahd, Mu'allafat al-rafiq, *Min watha'iq al-hizb al-shuyu'i al-'Iraqi*, Baghdad, 1973.

Faraj, Lutfi Ja'far, *Al-Malik Ghazi wa-dawruh fi siyasat al-'Iraq fi al-majalayn al-dakhili wa-l-khariji, 1933–1939*, Baghdad, 1987.

Fawzi, Ahmad, *'Abd al-Karim Qasim wa-sa'atuh al-akhira*, Baghdad, 1988.

Al-Fukayki, 'Abd al-Hadi, *Al-Shu'ubiyya wa-l-qawmiyya al-'Arabiyya*, Beirut, n.d.

Al-Fukayki, Hani, *Awkar al-hazima: tajribati fi hizb al-ba'th al-'Iraqi*, London, 1993.

Al-Hasani, ʿAbd al-Razzaq, *Al-ʿIraq qadiman wa-hadithan*, Sidon, 1956.
———, *Taʾrikh al-ʿIraq al-siyasi al-hadith*, 3 vols., Sidon, 1957.
———, *Taʾrikh al-wizarat al-ʿIraqiyya*, 4 vols., Sidon, 1940.
———, *Al-Thawra al-ʿIraqiyya al-kubra*, Sidon, 1965.
Haykal, Muhammad Hasanayn, *Harb al-Khalij*, Cairo, 1992.
Husayn, Saddam, *Al-ʿAmal al-ʿArabi al-mushtarak asasuh al-tadhiya*, Baghdad, 1982.
———, *Bi-l-fikr wa-l-mumarasa wa-l-namudhaj al-hayy yatahaqqaq al-iman*, Baghdad, n.d.
———, *Hawl kitabat al-taʾrikh*, Baghdad, 1976.
———, *Al-ʿIraq wa-l-siyasa al-dawliyya*, Baghdad, 1981.
———, *Khandaq wahid am khandaqan*, Baghdad, 1976.
———, *Al-Kiyan al-Sahyuni amam al-maʾziq al-taʾrikhi*, Baghdad, 1981.
———, *Al-Thawra wa-l-nazra al-jadida*, Baghdad, 1981.
———, *Al-Thawra wa-l-tarbiya al-wataniyya*, Baghdad, 1977.
Al-Husri, Abu Khaldun Satiʿ, *Abhath mukhtara fi-l-qawmiyya al-ʿArabiyya*, Cairo, 1964.
———, *Hawl al-qawmiyya al-ʿArabiyya*, Beirut, 1961.
———, *Mudhakkirati fi-l-ʿIraq 1921–1941*, Beirut, 1967.
Ibrahim, Farhad, *Al-Taʾifiyya wa-l-siyasa fi-l-ʿalam al-ʿArabi: namudhaj al-shiʿa fi-l-ʿIraq*, Cairo, 1996.
Iskandar, Amir Ahmad, *Saddam Husayn munadilan wa-mufakkiran wa-insanan*, Paris, 1980.
Ismaʿil, Yusuf, *Inqilab tisʿa wa-ʿishrin tishrin al-awwal*, Baghdad, 1936.
ʿIzz al-Din, Yusuf, *Al-Shiʿr al-ʿIraqi al-hadith: wa-athar al-tayyarat al-siyasiyya wa-l-ijtimaʿiyya fihi*, Cairo, 1965.
Al-Jabiri, Muhammad ʿAbid, *Al-ʿAql al-siyasi al-ʿArabi*, Beirut, 1991.
———, *Al-Khitab al-ʿArabi al-muʿasir*, Beirut, 1982.
Jalil, Jalili, *Intifadat al-Akrad 1880*, Beirut, 1979.
Jamil, Husayn, *Al-ʿIraq al-jadid*, Beirut, 1958.
Jawad, Saʿd Naji, *Al-ʿIraq wa-l-masʾala al-Kurdiyya, 1958–1970*, London, 1990.
Al-Jundi, Sami, *Al-Baʿth*, Beirut, 1969.
Al-Khalidi, Zuhayr Sadiq Rida, *Al-Qiyam ʿind Saddam Husayn*, Baghdad, 1989.
———, *Saddam Husayn kama ʿaraftuh*, Baghdad, 1987.
Kuroda, Vasumasa, and Suzuki Tatsuzu, "Tahlil muqarin: al-lughat wa-l-qiyam al-ʿarabiyya wa-l-ingliziyya wa-l-yabaniyya," *al-Mustaqbal al-ʿArabi* 163 (September 1992): 14–32.
Al-Minhaj wa-l-nizam al-dakhili li-l-hizb al-dimukrati al-Kurdistani, min Manshurat parti dimukrati, Kurdistan, 1960.
Al-Mudarrisi, Muhammad Taqi, *ʿAn al-ʿIraq wa-l-haraka al-Islamiyya*, London, 1988.
———, *Al-ʿIraq thawra tantasir*, Beirut, 1983.
Muhammad, Sabah Mahmud, *Al-Fikr al-jiyubulitiki li-Saddam Husayn*, Baghdad, 1982.
Muhammad, Suʿad Raʾuf Shir, *Nuri al-Saʿid wa dawruh fi al-siyasa al-ʿIraqiyya hatta ʿam 1945*, Baghdad, 1988.
Mustafa, ʿAbd al-Rahman, *Al-Batal Salah al-Din*, Baghdad, 1987.

Al-Nafisi, 'Abdallah Fahd, *Dawr al-Shi'a fi tatawwur al-'Iraq al-siyasi al-hadith*, 2d ed., n.p., 1986.

Ramadan, Taha Yasin, *Al-Jaysh al-sha'bi wa-l-tajriba al-namudhaj*, Baghdad, 1987.

Al-Ras, Sharif, *Katibat dabbabat ra'i'a*, Baghdad, 1981.

Al-Razzaz, Munif, *Tatawwur ma'na al-qawmiyya*, Beirut, 1960.

Al-Rikabi, Fu'ad, *Al-Hall al-awhad*, Cairo, 1963.

Al-Sabbagh, Salah al-Din, *Fursan al-'Uruba fi-l-'Iraq*, Damascus, 1956.

Al-Sadr, Muhammad Baqir, *Falsafatuna*, 2d ed., Beirut, 1969.

Salman, Mahfuz Dawud, *Intazirini bi-thiyab al-qital*, Baghdad, 1988.

Salman, Sabah, *Saddam Husayn qa'id wa-ta'rikh*, Baghdad, 1986.

Al-Samarra'i, Shafiq 'Abd al-Razzaq, *Saddam Husayn nidaluh wa-fikruh al-siyasi*, n.p., 1982.

Sharabi, Hisham, *Muqaddimat li-dirasat al-mujtama' al-'Arabi*, Acre, Israel, 1987.

Shawkat, Sami, *Hadhihi ahdafuna*, Baghdad, 1939.

Al-Ta'i, Ghazay Dir', *Al-Bahr al-akhdar*, Baghdad, 1988.

Al-Talabani, Jalal, *Kurdistan wa-l-haraka al-qawmiyya al-Kurdiyya*, Beirut, 1971.

Talfah, Khayrallah, *Kayf al-sabil ila Allah*, 5 vols., Beirut, 1976.

Al-Tamimi, Kazim Ni'ma, *Mudhakkirat Basri fi zaman al-harb*, Baghdad, 1988.

Thawrat arba' 'ashar tammuz fi 'amiha al-awwal, Baghdad, 1959.

Al-'Ubaydi, Hasan 'Azba, *Al-Markaz al-dusturi li-hizb al-ba'th al-'Arabi al-ishtiraki*, Baghdad, 1982.

Al-'Umari, Khayri, *Hikayat siyasiyya min ta'rikh al-'Iraq al-hadith*, Cairo, 1969.

Al-Wa'ili, Ibrahim, *Al-Shi'r al-siyasi al-'Iraqi fi al-qarn al-tasi' 'ashar*, Baghdad, 1961.

Al-Wardi, 'Ali, *Lamahat ijtima'iyya min ta'rikh al-'Iraq al-hadith*, Baghdad, 1969.

Al-Yafi, Muhammad 'Abd al-Fattah Abu al-Nasr, *Al-'Iraq bayn inqilabayn*, Beirut, 1938.

Yasin, al-Sayyid, *Al-Shakhsiyya al-'Arabiyya bayn al-mafhum al-Isra'ili wa-l-mafhum al-'Arabi*, Cairo, 1974.

———, "Al-tahlil al-thaqafi li-azmat al-khalij," *al-Mustaqbal al-'Arabi* 148 (June 1991): 30–47.

Zaki, Muhammad Amin, *Khulasat ta'rikh al-Kurd wa-Kurdistan: Ta'rikh al-duwal wa-l-imarat al-Kurdiyya fi-l-'ahd al-Islami*, Cairo, 1948; trans. Muhammad 'Ali 'Awni, London, 1986.

BOOKS AND ARTICLES IN OTHER LANGUAGES

Abouzeid, Leila, *Year of the Elephant*, trans. Barbara Parmenter, Austin, Tex., 1989.

AbuKhalil, As'ad, "Al-Jabriyyah in the Political Discourse of Jamal 'Abd al-Nasir and Saddam Husayn: The Rationalization of Defeat," *Muslim World* 84 (July 1994): 240–257.

——, "A New Arab Ideology?: The Rejuvenation of Arab Nationalism,"
    MEJ 46 (1992): 22–36.
Adams, Michael (ed.), *The Middle East: A Handbook*, London, 1971.
Arberry, A. J., *The Koran Interpreted*, London, 1955.
Ayalon, Ami, "Dimuqratiyya, Hurriyya, Jumhuriyya: The Modernization of
    the Arabic Political Vocabulary," *AAS* 23 (1989): 25–42.
——, "From Fitna to Thawra," *Studia Islamica* 67 (1987): 145–174.
——, *Language and Change in the Arab Middle East*, New York, 1987.
——, "Sihafa: The Arab Experiment in Journalism," *MES* 28 (1992):
    258–280.
Barakat, Halim, *The Arab World: Society, Culture, and State*, Berkeley, 1993.
Baram, Amatzia, *Culture, History, and Ideology in the Formation of Ba'thist
    Iraq, 1968–89*, Oxford, 1991.
——, "National [Wataniyya] Integration and Exclusiveness in Political
    Thought and Practice in Iraq under the Ba'th, 1968–1982" (H), Ph.D.
    dissertation, Hebrew University of Jerusalem, 1986.
——, "Saddam Hussein: A Political Profile," *Jerusalem Quarterly* 17
    (1980): 115–144.
Barthes, Roland, *Le degré zéro de l'écriture: suivi de, nouveaux essais cri-
    tiques*, Paris, 1972.
——, *Mythologies*, Paris, 1957.
Batatu, Hanna, *The Old Social Classes and the Revolutionary Movements of
    Iraq*, Princeton, 1978.
Beeston, A. F. L., "Abraha," in *EI²*.
——, *The Arabic Language Today*, London, 1970.
Bellefonds Y. Linant de, "Darura," in *EI²*.
Bengio, Ofra, "The Challenge to the Territorial Integrity of Iraq," *Survival* 37
    (1995): 74–94.
——, "Iraq," in *MECS 1993, 1994, 1995* (various publishers).
——, "The Iraqi Kurds: The Struggle for Autonomy in the Shadow of the
    Iran-Iraq Conflict," *Immigrants and Minorities* 9 (1990): 249–268.
——, *The Kurdish Revolt in Iraq* (H) (Tel Aviv, 1989).
Berger, Morroe, *The Arab World Today*, New York, 1964.
Black, George, *Genocide in Iraq: The Anfal Campaign against the Kurds*, New
    York, 1993.
Blanc, Haim, *Human Language* (H), Jerusalem, 1989.
Bonebakker, S. A., "Abu Righal," in *EI²*.
Cahen, C. "Futuwwa," in *EI²*.
Canard, M., "Da'wa," in *EI²*.
Carr, E. H., *What Is History?* London, 1964.
Carré, Olivier, *Le nationalisme Arabe*, Paris, 1993.
Caspi, Dan, and Yehiel Limor, *The Mediators: The Mass Media in Israel,
    1948–1990* (H), Tel Aviv, 1992.
Cassirer, Ernst, *Language and Myth*, New York, 1946.
——, *The Myth of the State*, New York, 1955.
Chaliand, Gerard (ed.), *People without a Country*, London, 1980.
Close, David, and Carl Bridge (eds.), *Revolution: A History of the Idea*,
    Totowa, N.J., 1985.
Coffman, James, "Does the Arabic Language Encourage Radical Islam?,"
    Middle East Quarterly 2 (1995): 51–57.

Dann, Uriel, *Iraq under Qassem: A Political History, 1958–1963*, New York, 1969.

Devlin, John F., *The Ba'th Party: A History from Its Origins to 1966*, Stanford, 1976.

Douglas, Allen, and Fedwa Malti-Douglas, *Arab Comic Strips*, Bloomington, 1994.

Ehrenkreutz, Andrew S., *Saladin*, New York, 1972.

Eppel, Michael, *The Palestine Conflict in the History of Modern Iraq: The Dynamics of Involvement, 1928–1948*, London, 1994.

Al-Gailani, G., "Iraq's Journalism and Political Conflict, 1956–1963," Ph.D. dissertation, University of Iowa, 1971.

Gardet, L., "Fitna," in *EI²*.

Gazit, Shlomo (ed.), *The Middle East Military Balance, 1988–1989*, Jerusalem, 1989.

Gitlin, Todd, *The Whole World Is Watching*, Berkeley, 1980.

Goren, Asher, *Ancient Arabic Poetry* (H), Jerusalem, 1970.

Guillaume, A., *The Life of Muhammad: A Translation of Ishaq's Sirat Rasul Allah*, London, 1955.

Hanna, Sami H., and George H. Gardner, *Arab Socialism: A Documentary Survey*, Leiden, 1969.

Hawkes, Terence, *Structuralism and Semiotics*, London, 1977.

Henderson, Simon, *Instant Empire: Saddam Hussein's Ambition for Iraq*, San Francisco, 1991.

Hurvitz, Nimrod, "Muhibb al-Din al-Khatib's Semitic Wave Theory and Pan-Arabism," *MES* 29 (1993): 118–135.

Issawi, Charles, "European Loan-Words in Contemporary Arabic Writing: A Case Study in Modernization," *MES* 3 (1967): 110–133.

Jayyusi, Salma Khadra (ed.), *Modern Arabic Peotry: An Anthology*, New York, 1987.

Karsh, Efraim, and Inari Rautsi, *Saddam Hussein: A Political Biography*, London, 1991.

Kedourie, Elie, *Democracy and Arab Political Culture*, Washington, 1992.

————, "The Kingdom of Iraq: A Retrospect," in *The Chatham House Version and Other Middle Eastern Studies*, London, 1970.

Kelidar, Abbas (ed.), *The Integration of Modern Iraq*, New York, 1979.

Khadduri, Majid, *Independent Iraq: A Study in Iraqi Politics since 1932*, London, 1951.

————, *The Islamic Conception of Justice*, Baltimore, 1989.

————, *Socialist Iraq: A Study in Iraqi Politics since 1968*, Washington, 1978.

————, *War and Peace in the Law of Islam*, London, 1955.

Al-Khalil, Samir, *The Monument: Art, Vulgarity, and Responsibility in Iraq*, Berkeley, 1991.

————, *Republic of Fear: The Politics of Modern Iraq*, Berkeley, 1989.

Al-Khayyat, Sana, *Honour and Shame: Women in Modern Iraq*, London, 1990.

Kienle, Eberhard, *Ba'th vs. Ba'th: The Conflict between Syria and Iraq, 1968–1989*, London, 1990.

Kishtainy, Khalid, *Arab Political Humour*, London, 1985.

Koebner, Richard, *Empire*, Cambridge, England, 1961.

Koebner, Richard, and Helmut Dan Schmidt, *Imperialism: The Study and Significance of a Political Word, 1840–1960*, Cambridge, England, 1964.

Kvastad, Nils B., "Semantics in the Methodology of the History of Ideas," *Journal of the History of Ideas* 38 (1977): 157–174.

Landau, Dov, *From Metaphor to Symbol* (H), Ramat Gan, Israel, 1979.

Lassner, Jacob, "Concerning Time, Historiography, and Political Consciousness" (unpublished).

Lazarus-Yafeh, Hava (ed.), *Studies in the History of the Arabs and Islam* (H), Tel Aviv, 1982.

Lewis, Bernard, *The Arabs in History*, London, 1950.

――――, *History Remembered, Recovered, Invented*, Princeton, 1975.

――――, *Islam in History: Ideas, Men, and Events in the Middle East*, New York, 1973.

――――, *The Middle East and the West*, London, 1963.

――――, *The Political Language of Islam*, Chicago, 1988.

Lewis, Bernard, and F. Rosenthal, "Hurriyya," in *EI²*.

Lewy, Guenter, *Religion and Revolution*, New York, 1974.

Litvak, Meir, "The Shiʿi ʿUlamaʾ of Najaf and Karbalaʾ, 1791–1904: A Socio-Political Analysis," Ph.D. dissertation, Harvard University, 1991.

Longrigg, Stephen H., *Four Centuries of Modern Iraq*, Oxford, 1925.

――――, *Iraq, 1900 to 1950*, London, 1953.

Macdonald, D. B., "Shuʿubiya," in *EI¹*.

Maddy-Weitzman, Bruce, "Islam and Arabism: The Iran-Iraq War," *Washington Quarterly* 5 (1982): 181–189.

Makiya, Kanan, *Cruelty and Silence: War, Tyranny, Uprising, and the Arab World*, New York, 1993.

Mallat, Chibli, *The Renewal of Islamic Law: Muhammad Baqer al-Sadr, Najaf, and the Shiʿi International*, Cambridge, England, 1993.

Marr, Phebe, *The Modern History of Iraq*, Boulder, Colo., 1985.

Matar, Fuad, *Saddam Hussein: The Man, the Cause, and the Future*, London, 1981.

Mazraani, Nathalie, "Functions of Arabic Political Discourse: The Case of Saddam Hussein's Speeches," *Zeitscrift für Arabische Linguistik* 30 (1995): 22–36.

Menashri, David, "Iran," in *MECS 1981–1982*, pp. 532–581.

Miquel, A., "Iklim," in *EI²*.

――――, "ʿIrak," in *EI²*.

Mitchell, Timothy, *Colonising Egypt*, Cambridge, England, 1988.

Mottahedeh, Roy P., "The Shuʿubiyya Controversy and the Social History of Early Islamic Iran," *IJMES* 7 (1976): 161–182.

Nakash, Yitzhak, *The Shiʿis of Iraq*, Princeton, 1994.

Nikitine, Basile, *Les Kurdes: Étude sociologique et historique*, Paris, 1956.

Ogden, C. K., and I. A. Richards, *The Meaning of Meanings: A Study of the Influence of Language upon Thought and the Science of Symbolism*, 10th ed., London, 1966.

Patai, Raphael, *The Arab Mind*, New York, 1976.

Peristiany, J. G. (ed.), *Honour and Shame*, London, 1965.

Rabinovich, Itamar, *Syria under the Baʿth, 1963–1966: The Army-Party Symbiosis*, Jerusalem, 1972.

Ram, Chagay, *Islamic Symbolism: The Ideology of the Islamic Revolution in Iran as Reflected in Friday Communal Sermons, 1979–1989*, Ann Arbor, 1992.

Reid, Donald Malcolm, "The Postage Stamp: A Window on Saddam Hussein's Iraq," *MEJ* 47 (1993): 77–89.

Rivlin, Y. *The Life of Muhammad* (H), Tel Aviv, 1936.

Rodinson, Maxime, *Marxisme et Monde Musulman*, Paris, 1972.

Rojo, Luisa Martin, "Division and Rejection: From the Personification of the Gulf Conflict to the Demonization of Saddam Hussein," *Discourse and Society* 6 (1995): 49–80.

Rubin, Barry, *Cauldron of Turmoil*, New York, 1992.

———, "Pan-Arab Nationalism: The Ideological Dream as Compelling Force," *Journal of Contemporary History* 26 (1991): 535–551.

Rugh, William A., *The Arab Press: News Media and Political Process in the Arab World*, Syracuse, N.Y., 1979.

Salamé, Ghassan (ed.), *The Foundation of the Arab State*, London, 1987.

Sasson, Eliyahu, *On the Road to Peace* (H), Tel Aviv, 1978.

Saussure, Ferdinand de, *Course in General Linguistics*, New York, 1966.

Savory, Roger, "The Safavid State and Polity," *Iranian Studies* 7 (1974): 179–180.

Sharabi, Hisham B., *Nationalism and Revolution in the Arab World: The Middle East and North Africa*, Princeton, 1966.

Shemesh, Haim, *Soviet-Iraqi Relations, 1968–1988: In the Shadow of the Iran-Iraq Conflict*, Boulder, Colo., 1992.

Simon, Reeva S., *Iraq between the Two World Wars: The Creation and Implementation of a Nationalist Ideology*, New York, 1986.

Sivan, Emmanuel, *Arab Political Myths* (H), Tel Aviv, 1988.

Sluglett, Marion Farouk, and Peter Sluglett, *Iraq since 1958: From Revolution to Dictatorship*, London, 1987.

Sobernheim, "Saladin," in *EI¹*.

Soeterik, Robert, *The Islamic Movement of Iraq, 1958–1980*, Amsterdam Middle East Research Associates, December 1991, Occasional Paper, no. 12.

Sorel, Georges, *Reflections on Violence*, New York, 1961.

Stewart, Frank Henderson, *Honor*, Chicago, 1994.

Struever, Nancy S., "The Study of Language and the Study of History," *Journal of Interdisciplinary History* 4 (1974): 401–415.

Tritton, A. S., "Ba'th," in *EI²*.

Tyan, E., "Bay'a," in *EI²*.

Vaglerii, L. Veccia, "Al-Kadisiyya," in *EI²*.

Vatikiotis, P. J. "Ishtirakiyya," in *EI²*.

———, (ed.), *Revolution in the Middle East, and Other Case Studies*, London, 1972.

Watt, W. Montgomery, "Abu Lahab," in *EI²*.

Weinreich, V., *Languages in Contact: Findings and Problems*, The Hague, 1963.

Wensinck, A. J., "Rasul," in *EI¹*.

———, "Takbir," in *EI¹*.

Wilber, Donald N., *Riza Shah Pahlavi: The Resurrection and Reconstruction of Iran*, New York, 1975.

Wiley, Joyce N., *The Islamic Movement of Iraqi Shi'as*, Boulder, Colo., 1992.

DICTIONARIES AND LEXICONS

Badawi, A. Z., *A Dictionary of Social Sciences, English, French, Arabic,*
    Beirut, 1978.
Bello, J. B., *Al-Fara'id al-durriyya* (Arabic-French), Beirut, 1920.
Al-Bustani, Butrus, *Kitab muhit al-muhit,* 2 vols., Beirut, 1870.
Diab biq, Muhammad, *Mu'jam al-alfaz al-haditha,* n.p., 1919.
Dozy, Reinhart Pieter Anne. *Supplement aux dictionnaires arabes,* 2 vols.,
    Leiden, 1881.
Even Shoshan, Abraham, *The New Dictionary* (H), 3 vols., Jerusalem, 1972.
Gibb, A. R., and J. H. Kramer, *Shorter Encyclopaedia of Islam,* Leiden, 1953.
Al-Hilali, 'Abd al-Razzaq, *Mu'jam al-'Iraq,* Baghdad, 1953.
Ibn Manzur, Muhammad bin al-Mukarram, *Lisan al-'Arab,* 6 vols., Cairo,
    n.d.
'Isa, al-Shaikh 'Abd al-Jalil, *Taysir al-tafsir,* n.p., 1958.
Lane, Edward William, *An Arabic English Lexicon,* 8 vols., London,
    1863–1893.
Ma'luf, Lewis, *Al-Munjid,* Jaffa, 1908.
Al-Mu'jam al-'askari al-muwahhad, Cairo, 1970.
Al-Najafi, Hasan, *Mu'jam al-mustalahat al-tijariyya wa-l-masrifiyya,*
    Baghdad, 1976.
Al-Sabiq, Jirawn, *Mu'jam al-lughat,* Beirut, 1971.
Wahba, Majdi, Kamil al-Muhandis, *Mu'jam al-mustalahat al-'arabiyya fi
    al-lugha wa-l-adab,* Beirut, 1984.
Wehr, Hans, *A Dictionary of Modern Written Arabic,* Wiesbaden, 1971.
Woodhead, D. R., and Wayne Beene, *A Dictionary of Iraqi Arabic,* Washing-
    ton, 1967.

Index